MW01621124

contemporary art in the **northwest**

For Robina —

Lois Allan

contemporary art

in the northwest

Lois Allan

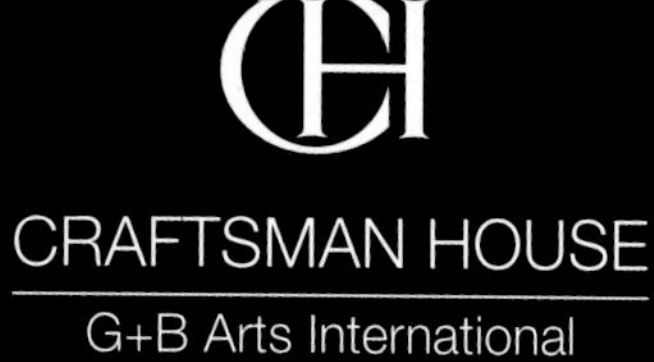

CRAFTSMAN HOUSE
G+B Arts International

Distributed in Australia by Craftsman House,
20 Barcoo Street, Roseville East, NSW 2069
in association with G+B Arts International:
Australia, Austria, Belgium, China, France, Germany,
Hong Kong, India, Japan, Luxembourg, Malaysia,
Netherlands, Russia, Singapore, Switzerland,
United Kingdom, United States of America

ISBN 976 6410 05 4

Design *Caroline de Fries*
Printer *Tien Wah Press Pte Ltd, Singapore*

pages 2–3: Norie Sato, *Book*, Etched glass, stainless mesh, wax and pigment, oil pastel, 68" x 45" x 2". Courtesy of the artist and Elizabeth Leach Gallery. Photograph: Tom Collicott.

contents

Acknowledgments

The interest and encouragement of many colleagues, friends, and family in bringing this book to fruition were an on-going stimulus for which I am most appreciative. Notably, the unstinting cooperation of the artists and their gallery representatives was both freely and quickly given; without it I might still be speaking to answering machines. Early on, as I struggled with difficult decisions concerning the selection of artist-subjects, I had the expert counsel of John Weber, Randy Gragg, Vicki Halper, Elizabeth Bryant, and Terri Hopkins. Terri Hopkins's reading of the manuscript when it was in its formative stages was most helpful at a critical time. I am indebted to Barbara Johns and Elizabeth Bryant who read later drafts of the introductory essay and made insightful comments, as did Rod Slemmons on the entries on photographers.

The personal support provided by my son and his wife, Tom and Catherine Allan, whose Bellevue home became the base for my Seattle activities, was indispensable. My husband, Wallace, and son Jon bore the considerable burden of computer crises, including the total breakdown of my old PC and the complications of replacing it. Through it all, my swim coach, Chris Perret, alleviated serious anxiety attacks with workouts that counterbalanced mental problems.

Finally, I am grateful for the beneficent presence of William Jamison whose gentle spirit will always inhabit Oregon's art endeavors.

Lois Allan

Preface

The forty-eight artists who are the subjects of this book were selected not only for the integrity and communicative strength of their art, but also as the strongest representatives of the range and diversity of contemporary art in the Northwest. They include senior artists and a few young, "emerging" artists; most, however, are in their highly productive, mid-career years. Some are active nationally, even internationally, and a few will be unknown to all but close followers of area artmaking. Without exception, the artists and their gallery representatives were cooperative in realizing this project, generous with their time and a pleasure to work with. I thank them all.

A geographic definition of the Pacific Northwest is elastic. It is commonly understood in the United States to be Oregon and Washington, although at a stretch it may include Alaska, Idaho, Montana, and when Canada is considered, British Columbia. For several reasons, I have limited it here to Oregon and Washington. These two states are a historical unit; lying at the end of the Oregon Trail they were opened to settlement at about the same time and have developed in tandem. Their similarities of geography, climate, and demographies also contribute to a shared identity. The two major cities, Seattle and Portland, are less than two hundred miles apart, linked by frequent air and train service and a heavily travelled freeway. They form a population nucleus. Seattle serves a metropolitan population of about three million (encompassing Bellevue, Tacoma, Bainbridge and Vashon Islands), about twice that of the Portland area. Both cities are notable for active art scenes including innovative public art programs, well attended museums, networks of galleries, and educational institutions.

The limited focus was desirable for another reason: It made possible a more comprehensive coverage. Even so, the selection of a mere forty-eight subjects was difficult, made after consultations with several curators and critics followed by careful consideration. My hope is that these artists and their work will kindle readers' curiosity, leading them from the book to the galleries, museums, and public places where the full range of Northwest art can be experienced.

Introduction

Approaching Seattle from the east by way of the long Evergreen Bridge that skims Lake Washington, drivers are treated to a view capable of calming the most harried commuters. Water and boats fill the foreground, house-studded hills interrupted by the wing-topped University of Washington stadium stretch along the middle ground, and in the far distance the Olympic mountain range blends into low-hanging clouds. From the west the approach is no less stunning. As the ferries cross Puget Sound toward the city, they become moving scenic viewpoints bringing the skyline ever nearer until it becomes a jumble of docks, old industrial buildings and new shining highrises.

North and south entries herald a different city. The I-5 freeway skirts industries, divides suburbs, neighborhoods, and the central city, and spawns webs of overpasses and arterial intersections. On this route nature quickly gives way to the city's architecture; the view is all verticals, cubes, and grids. Visually, Seattle is like no other city in the country. Culturally, politically, and economically, it is very much like other cities at the end of the twentieth century, coping with a steadily increasing and ethnically mixed population, with diminishing financial and natural resources, and with the far-reaching effects of changing technologies.

One hundred eighty miles to the south, just across the mighty Columbia River that divides Washington and Oregon, Portland also struggles to maintain its scenic allure and livability in the face of social and economic realities. As the major urban centers in a region where more than fifty per cent of the land is under Federal jurisdiction, Seattle and Portland are indicative of the breach between nature and human needs (some would say, greed) that marks the history of the Northwest. On one hand, there is a proud and passionate attachment to the region's natural splendor; on the other are the demands of a consumer society. It is this intermix of politically charged issues — cultural, environmental, and economic — and their impact on individual lives that form the matrix of contemporary art. Northwest art, most of which is created within the paradigm of international trends, differs from that of other regions only as it is more likely to draw on relationships between societal issues and aspects of the natural environment than on theory and art histories.

Because settlement of the region is relatively recent, the evolution from primordial wilderness to one perforated by cities, towns, farms, roads, and clear-cuts is both dramatic and abrupt. Perhaps the vigor and diversity of Northwest art can be attributed, at least in part, to the artists' openness to change and independence of spirit that causes them to choose to live in such a problematic, rapidly evolving place. Although many are recent arrivals and relate their work to the future more than to the past, they are, in fact, the inheritors of a unique historical legacy. In no other region is history so marked by the close relationship between the inhabitants — from the indigenous tribal peoples through all the subsequent waves of settlers — and nature. And in no other region is the history so brief.

It is, after all, less than two hundred years since Lewis and Clark found their way across the Oregon Territory, and little more than a hundred since Oregon and Washington were admitted to statehood. Yet, beginning with the Lewis and Clark Expedition, and soon followed by numerous others, an artist — or at least someone who could draw reasonably well — was among the exploration parties and produced visual records of animals, plants, people, and land formations encountered along the way. By the middle of the nineteenth century a few of these early artists, notably Alfred Bierstadt (1830–1902), were producing dramatic paintings of the western landscape that dazzled Easterners, fueling interest in all things western. Bierstadt's enormous panoramas, such as his 1869 painting of Mt. Hood (now in the collection of the Portland Art Museum), romanticized the area as an unspoiled Eden, an interpretation that had immediate effects in its appeal to prospective settlers and long-lasting effects in its aesthetic hold on western landscape art.

By a fortunate turn of fate the development of photography and the opening of the Oregon Territory occurred in the same era, making possible what has become an extraordinary visual history of a wilderness region giving way to the environmental and social changes that come with settlement. Although early photographers lugging their heavy, cumbersome photographic paraphenalia along the trails were either government documentarians or entrepreneurs, a few produced work of true artistry. Carleton E. Watkins (1829–1916), who was based in San Francisco, spent the summer and fall of 1867 photographing and making large albumen prints of Oregon and the Columbia River that now are considered as masterpieces of nineteenth century photography. Even though his pictures sometimes show evidence of human intrusions on the land, which are totally absent in Bierstadt's grandiose vistas, they did nothing to diminish the popular concept of the Northwest as a place of infinite natural abundance and beauty.

To be sure, it was abundance, not beauty, that kept the settlers coming. By 1900 the combined population of Washington and Oregon had reached one million, most of it in the Puget Sound area (at the time, Seattle and Tacoma competed for superiority) and Portland where shipping and railroad facilities served the fast growing timber and salmon industries. Portland already boasted an affluent, cultured group of citizens who, in 1892, had founded the Portland Art Association. In 1905, having acquired a building, the Association became the Portland Art Museum. The Seattle Art Museum, too, had its beginnings in the efforts of a few civic minded men who organized the Seattle Fine Arts Society in 1906. Even though the two cities were scarcely beyond the status of pioneering settlements, at the turn of the century they could and did provide a base for the development of the arts as well as the economy.

The geographic isolation of the region, which prevented easy access to larger established cities, such as San Francisco, about six hundred miles to the south, and Chicago, almost two thousand miles east, not to mention New York, was conducive to the promotion of art locally. Within the first two decades of the new century the University of Oregon, the Portland Art Museum School, the University of Washington, and the Cornish School in Seattle offered programs in the arts. Ambrose Patterson (1877–1966), director of the School of Painting and Design at the University of Washington in 1918, and Anna B. Crocker (1867–1961), director of the Portland Art Museum from 1909 to 1936, and Harry Wentz (1875–1965) on the faculty of the Museum School were artist-educators whose gifted teaching and wide knowledge of art were largely responsible for generating serious painting — and painters — in the Northwest.

At that time art meant painting and sculpture. Nevertheless, photography, without much notice, was in the process of establishing a presence that made itself felt well beyond local boundaries. Three Oregon photographers, Myra Albert Wiggins (1869–1956), Lily White (n.d., active 1892–1908), and Sarah Ladd (1857–1927), were among the one hundred five invited members of the elite Photo-Secession group, organized in 1902 to encourage pictorial photography by New York's renowned photographer and modern art advocate Alfred Stieglitz (1864–1946). In Seattle, Edward S. Curtis (1868–1952) already was well known for fashionable portraits and romantic scenic photographs. In 1899 he began the immense chronicle of North American Indians and tribal cultures that became his lifework. Imogen Cunningham (1883–1976), a young neophyte photographer and Curtis's darkroom technician, began her career in Seattle as a portrait photographer; at the same time she was experimenting with staged romantic scenes in the misty pictorial style. Though the pictures by these well known photographers may have been valued at the time as factual representations, in retrospect they represent cultural social biases, as well as a transference of nineteenth-century painterly aesthetics to the new medium.

Almost from its inception photography attracted women, for the probable reason that it could be practiced within the bounds of domesticity and Victorian, "lady-like" behavior. Julia Hoffman (1856–1934) was an upper class Portland matron who became an accomplished salon photographer using her family as subjects. She was also an amateur sculptor, metal worker, weaver, and most important, a patron of the arts. Her legacy, aside from photographs included in historical survey exhibitions, is the Oregon School of Arts and Crafts, which she founded in 1906 as the Portland Society of the Arts and Crafts. Her philanthropy and activism grew from an interest in the Arts and Crafts movement led by William Morris in England. Through her, his advocacy for replacing machined products with handcrafted objects (an art "made by the people, and for the people, as a happiness to the maker and the user") was well received in Oregon where pioneer self-sufficiency endured as an attitude long after its demise as a way of life. The classes and exhibitions offered by Julia Hoffman's fledgling society created a tradition of craft that figured prominently in Oregon history during the Great Depression of the 1930s.

The Work Projects Administration, which was created by the Roosevelt Administration in 1935 to provide employment for the multitudes on relief rolls, subsidized public works, including art, intended to benefit the community life of Americans. The importance of the contribution to American art that came about under the auspices of the Federal Art Program (the branch of the WPA for visual art) can hardly be overestimated. Among its most enduring successes is Timberline Lodge, a massive structure high on the slopes of Mt. Hood. Built by hundreds of WPA construction workers of native stone and timber felled on the site, it became a showcase for art and crafts. Margery Hoffman Smith, Assistant State Director for the FAP and also Julia Hoffman's daughter, supervised a large corps of designers and craftspeople who produced the lodge's furniture, rugs, woven draperies and bedspreads, massive carved newel posts, beam ends and doors, ornamental iron gates, latches and door handles. Murals, paintings, and etchings by prominent local artists were included in the interior design. (Although the building fell into disrepair in the war years, it has been repaired and refurbished with the guidance of patrons and artists who comprise the Friends of Timberline, founded for that purpose. It again houses guests plus a gallery where its construction and history are documented and examples of its crafts are displayed.)

Through WPA employment artists experienced a new-found identity and usefulness. Some, including Ambrose Patterson and Kenneth Callahan (1906–1986) — later to become the curator of the Seattle Art Museum — were commissioned to produce specific projects to decorate Federal buildings. Most were employed by the FAP, which was designed to pay artists to produce studio work as they saw fit, or to teach. Not surprisingly, most of the WPA art has been destroyed or lost and many artists are no longer known. Nevertheless, some gained lasting prominence and were of crucial importance in advancing Northwest art into the national mainstream.

Even though progressive ideas emanating from Europe already were being introduced by artists, notably Ambrose Patterson who had exhibited in Paris and the well travelled Mark Tobey (1890–1976) who first came to Seattle in 1923 to teach at the Cornish School, the prevailing styles were conservative. Innovation was not unknown, however. C.S. Price (1874–1950), in Oregon, departed from literal representation in favor of a painterly surface using color blocks to build form. Others, like Maude Kerns (1876–1965) at the University of Oregon, were beginning to emphasize color and form over representation, which, in Kerns's case, led to pure, geometric abstractions by 1941. With worsening economic conditions, however, art most often reflected hardship, drawing on grim reality in what were sometimes obvious but more often, covert political statements. Landscape, formerly a genre imbued with romantic idealism, now included subject matter related to working the land with machinery; urban landscapes were dominated by industrial and slum scenes; figure paintings glorified workers.

These characteristics, with a few variations, describe almost all American art of the period. Seattle's relatively large Asian population, as well as the fine collection of Asian art at the Seattle Art Museum (donated by Margaret MacTavish Fuller and her son, Dr. Richard E. Fuller, the first director of the Museum) stimulated interest in the philosophies as well as the art of the Far East and sowed the seeds of the mystical quality that became identified with Northwest art. It has been speculated that the rainy, gray climate contributed to muted palettes and that the proximity of unspoiled wilderness areas attracted rugged individualist artists, who were not much interested in "foreign" ideas. These are specious arguments, pleasant to discuss but impossible to prove. What is certain is that the WPA projects and the artists they supported fomented the vitality of art in Washington and Oregon in the period immediately preceding World War II.

A few of the WPA artists whose work has endured were native Northwesterners, notably Morris Graves, born in Fox Valley, Oregon, in 1910, Guy Anderson, born in Edmonds, Washington in 1906, and Kenneth Callahan, born in Spokane, Washington in 1905 (died in 1986), but most were from elsewhere, attracted by the projects or other employment. Ambrose Patterson, one of the early transplants, was an Australian who had lived in Paris. In 1918 he came to Seattle to teach at the University of Washington. Mark Tobey, a middle-Westerner and, like Patterson, a mature artist when he first arrived in Seattle in 1923 to teach at the Cornish School, moved about from Seattle to New York to England, then back to Seattle until 1960 when he settled in Switzerland. C.S. Price, parapetetic before moving to Portland at age forty-four, was born in Wyoming. Minor White (1908–1976), also a middle-Westerner, began his career in Portland as a creative photographer for the Oregon Art Project, the state arm of the WPA. All were attuned to modernism which they adapted to their individual visions.

Of the WPA teaching centers in Oregon and Washington, one, in particular, had consequential effects. Carl Morris (1911–1993), then an instructor at the Chicago Art Institute, was recruited in 1938 to set up a center in Spokane that would serve eastern Washington. A young New York artist, Hilda Grossman, arrived soon after to teach sculpture. Within a year she and Carl began their lifelong relationship in art and marriage. The center under Carl and Hilda (1911–1991) flourished, and provided a stimulating environment for eastern Washington's isolated art community. Guy Anderson (b. 1906) joined the staff and Clyfford Still (1904–1980), then a painting instructor at Washington State College in Pullman, was a frequent visitor. When Carl Morris was transferred to Seattle in 1940 to head the art center there, his friendship with Guy Anderson brought him and Hilda into the group that gravitated around Mark Tobey.

Although the Morrises moved to Portland the following year (Carl was commissioned by the FAP to create a mural for the Eugene, Oregon, post office), they maintained friendships with the Seattle group who became the nucleus of what soon would be widely known as the Northwest School. The bond among these artists was their interest in non-Western religions and in advanced art. Of the four "founders," Tobey was a Bahai; Graves, a student of Zen Buddhism and Hinduism; Callahan and Anderson did not profess belief but had an intellectual appreciation of Eastern religions and art. The references to nature, even when oblique and abstracted, the calligraphic markings, and a spritual dimension, all of which characterized their paintings, sprang from a philosophical base. Morris insisted, however, that his intellectual sources were entirely Western, and for that reason, he separated his art from that of the others.

There were other important artists who, either by inclination or circumstances, were not within the inner circle but were loosely associated with the regional developments. Three Japanese immigrants, Kamekichi Tokita (1897–1948), Kenjiro Nomura (1896–1956), and Paul Horiuchi (b. 1906), were primarily American Scene painters who exhibited with Callahan and others as the Group of Twelve. James Fitzgerald (1910–1973), a sculptor and painter, took over the Spokane Art Center in 1941 after Carl Morris's departure. Margaret Tomkins (b. 1916) came from Los Angeles in 1939 and after a year on the staff at the Spokane Art Center, settled in Seattle with Fitzgerald, whom she married.

In Oregon, C.S. Price was the acknowledged leader among early modernists. A younger artist, Louis Bunce (1907–1983), who trained in New York, returned to his native Oregon to head the WPA Art Center in Salem. In 1946 he joined Harry Wentz on the faculty of the Museum School. William Givler (b. 1908), a WPA easel painter, became dean of the Museum School in 1944. To the south, at the University of Oregon in Eugene, painter-professors David McCosh (1903–1981) and Maude Kerns (1876–1965) were laying a strong modernist foundation for their students and themselves.

In the years immediately preceding World War II, these were the artists whose innovations set the direction of post-war developments. All exhibited regularly in the Seattle and Portland museums' yearly regional shows, and many — Tobey, Graves, Callahan, Anderson, Tompkins, Price, Bunce, Morris — exhibited in the East and California. Also, these were the artists of an age to be deeply affected by the war. Tokita and Nomura were forced into internment camps. A young Japanese-American artist, George Tsutakawa (b. 1910), whose parents and other relatives were interned, enlisted in the U.S. Army. Tobey, who was too old for the draft, Callahan, Graves, and Anderson were pacifists. Graves, however, was the only one to be interned for refusing the draft. Nonetheless, artmaking continued and the pacifists were united in seeking an art of spiritual universality that would stand in opposition to war.

Although unified aims held them together during the time of crisis, for reasons personal as well as professional they went in separate directions at the war's end. Ironically, it was about that time that Graves, Tobey, Callahan, and Anderson became the defining artists of the Northwest School, a perception due largely to an article published in *Life* magazine in 1953 ("Mystic Painters of the Northwest," September 28, 1953). Their New York successes brought national attention to those mystical qualities that already were seen as emergent in the art of the Northwest. Art historian Martha Kingsbury writes, "By 1944 the quality of 'mysticism' was firmly attached to Graves's work — which was said to combine qualities of Occident and Orient — and was spoken of at length in the catalog for his Willard Exhibition, *Morris Graves: Exhibition of Recent Work.* This approach must have seemed useful and important, for by 1945 it was broadened to include other Seattle artists."[1]

Even though quite a few active and influential artists, some of whom were associated with the central four, were not included in the original "school," a tradition was established. Long since eclipsed, it is so ingrained in history that references to it, usually as a point of comparison, continue to be commonly used and understood.

The quiescent Portland art community sprang to life just after the war. Carl and Hilda Morris, who had settled permanently in Portland in 1941, brought with them from Seattle and New York an intellectual vigor that generated a circle of artists, poets, and philosophers who met regularly for discussion at the Morris home. Neither of the Morrises taught, yet the powerful abstract styles each developed during this period not only drew national attention but influenced an approach to nature that was new in the Northwest. Rather than actively engaging a sense of the transcendental as their Seattle colleagues did, Carl, in painting, and Hilda, in sculpture, drew on natural processes — light and movement, growth and degeneration — and conveyed them in dynamic forms that were both sensual and cerebral.

The Museum School, directed by William Givler, required additional faculty for the surge in enrollment spurred by the enactment of the GI Bill which provided education funds for returning veterans. Givler, a painter and printmaker, never departed from depicting representational, although expressionistic, Oregon scenes and landscape, yet he presided over the school's evolution from conservatism to the styles and practices associated with midcentury modernism. Louis Bunce (1907–1983) was a catalyst for much of the change. Having retained New York ties from his Art Students League years in New York, he, and through him, his students, kept abreast of changing trends on the national and international scene. His own paintings were abstractions from nature, organic forms suggesting their relationship to landscape. Most of all, he was totally dedicated to painting, "to the specialized art of laying color on canvas," according to Portland Art Museum curator Rachel Griffin.[2]

As Bunce brought heightened awareness of formal elements and painting technique to the Museum School, Michele Russo (b. 1909), who arrived in 1947, brought a background in history and social consciousness. A Yale-educated Easterner, he had been a labor organizer and political activist during the Depression. His early work was figurative and realist, falling into the social realist style, although he has always insisted that his politics and his art are quite separate. Like most artists who came to Portland at that time, including Bunce and the Morrises, he and his wife, the painter Sally Haley (b. 1908), relished the unhurried pace and the enveloping natural environment. Louis Bunce spoke for all when he quipped, "Here you can't get away from nature. It flows up the streets."[3] Indeed, nature has never ceased to be a driving force in Northwest art, but with the advent of the post-World War II period, formalism and social themes altered and varied its expression.

The conclusion of World War II marks a sea change in American social history. A largely rural and small town culture, two wars, and the Depression shape the history of the first half of the century, and World War II itself was the crucible for the second. At its conclusion victory and pent-up demand for houses, automobiles and all other consumer goods generated an optimistmic, booming economy; the politics and fears of the Nuclear Age and Cold War were not yet omnipresent. Technologies that had been advanced by combat needs were soon applied to civilian uses, and as a result, "progress" in transportation, communication, and chemistry revolutionized the middle-class way of life. "Bringing you a better world through chemistry," a popular advertising slogan, meant myriad plastics, synthetic fibers, and pharmaceuticals. But it was the ease of air travel, the advent of communications technology, and television that soon blurred regional distinctions. Northwest demography was altered when many servicemen returning from the Pacific theater of war elected to remain near their ports of entry along the west coast. Northwest universities and colleges filled with veterans making use of the GI Bill's funds for education. The Hanford Nuclear Reservation transformed desert acreage in eastern Washington into a center for advanced technology, attracting scientists and technicians to an area formerly inhabited mainly by jackrabbits and reptiles. Throughout Washington and Oregon, opportunity knocked and artists, as well as aspiring artists, were among the eager respondents.

The heavy demand for art education had a ripple effect. New faculty members had to be recruited for art departments at the universities and colleges so that more and more artists could be trained. Commercial galleries, heretofore unneeded, began to appear in answer to the increasing supply and to stimulate demand. With a growing number of Northwest artists included in New York and travelling exhibitions, critical writing and press coverage led to higher visibility. The new ideas informing art in New York and those energizing art in the Northwest converged in an expanding field of variations on the basic theme of abstraction.

In retrospect, the decade of the 1950s has assumed significant historical interest. A major exhibition at the Tacoma Art Museum in the spring of 1995, "Jet Dreams: The Fifties in the Northwest," and its catalog (published by the Tacoma Art Museum in association with the University of Washington Press, 1995) provided a comprehensive evaluation of architecture, crafts, and art as the influences of modernism swept through their practice. Curator Barbara Johns noted (*Introduction*, catalog) that modernism was directly related to "the optimistic belief in social and economic progress and [about] abstraction as its visual expression." The European international style deriving from the Bauhaus credo (that form follows function) became popular because it tapped into that belief. In the Northwest the style was especially evident in the architecture of unadorned, earth-hugging residences designed to blend into the natural environment of their sites. In art and crafts the same tendency was expressed in a preference for natural materials, simplified, organic forms, and muted colors. There were exceptions, however, and Maude Kerns was one.

Among Oregon's native artists Maude Kerns (1876–1965) was an anomaly. While her contemporaries based their modernist adaptations on some aspect of nature, she discarded any such reference and devoted herself exclusively to geometric abstractions. Head of the art education department at the University of Oregon from 1921 until 1947, she had an academician's deep interest in art history, and her early painting styles range from pre-Raphaelite to Fauvist. During her frequent trips to Europe she was profoundly influenced by the work of such artists as Wassily Kandinsky and Nicolas Delaunay, and in her own paintings introduced their non-objective style to an unappreciative Oregon public. By the 1950s she had exhibited in Paris and at the Museum of Non-Objective Art in New York (later to become the Guggenheim Museum), and had had, in 1947, a one-person show at the Seattle Art Museum. Only recently, however, has her work assumed aesthetic as well as historical importance in her home state.

Although Carl and Hilda Morris were unquestionably the standard-bearers in Portland's art community, the Museum School faculty, mainly Bunce, Givler, Russo, and Jack McLarty (b. 1918), were its nucleus. McLarty, a figurative painter, was moved more by events and human activities than by pure nature. He produced series on specific themes, including some, such as the devastating Vanport flood of 1948, the Rose Festival, and the city at night, that offer a sense of Portland life at that time.

Reed College harbored two teachers who had a lasting impact on art in Portland. Lloyd Reynolds (1902–1978), a professor in the Literature, Language, and Art Division, was a charismatic teacher of calligraphy, so much so that his influence continues to be seen in abstract paintings and prints by artists who were his students. Reed lacked an art department in the 1950s but from 1956 to 1959, retained as artist-in-residence, James McGarrell (b. 1930), whose strong figurative work and equally strong personality strengthened the liaison with the Museum School. (A joint degree program existed in which Reed students studied technique at the Museum School and Museum School students studied liberal arts at Reed.)

Portland State College (later, Portland State University) also had a small but active art faculty, notably Robert Colescott (b. 1925). However, none of the three Portland colleges came close to the size and influence of the University of Washington. Under the leadership of Walter Isaacs (1886–1964), dean of the School of Painting, Sculpture and Design, programs in ceramics, printmaking, weaving, and metalworking were initiated. By offering options beyond painting and sculpture, the School not only strengthened each of the disciplines but also generated an atmosphere conducive to experimentation in advancing and combining the materials and technical possibilities of all. Dale Chihuly, an illustrious, later alumnus, began his studies (in 1960) in interior design, added weaving, and when he incorporated glass into weaving designs, found the medium that became his passion, with which he revolutionized studio glass art.

Historian Barbara Johns ("Jet Dreams," *Introduction*) emphasizes the importance of design in artworks of the postwar period and credits it to the close working relationship between the schools of art and architecture and to curricula in industrial design, interior design, and graphic design. The sculptures and fountains by George Tsutakawa, who taught in both art and architecture, are exemplary results, demonstrating the austere, modular forms of contemporaneous modern architecture and a Japanese proclivity for natural materials.

Photographic art gained momentum from workshops conducted by Minor White (1908–1976) at the Museum School in Portland each summer from 1959 through 1967. White's residence in Oregon ended with an exhibition at the Portland Art Museum, his first, and his induction into the army in 1942. Although he settled in New York after the war, his ties to Portland continued. His students worked and exhibited in his absence as the Interim Workshop, so named because they met and engaged in critiques with him via mailed prints. The "straight photography" (sharply focused and unmanipulated images) practiced and advocated by White continues to characterize much contemporary Northwest photography as is evident in the work included in this book by Terry Toedtemeier, Diane Kornberg, and Glenn Rudolph.

As art production in Washington and Oregon increased and strengthened, the dearth of exhibition opportunities became acute. While the Seattle and Portland art museums, the Henry Gallery at the University of Washington and other institutional galleries periodically presented exhibitions by Northwest artists (also, a few cooperative galleries and short-lived private galleries provided limited public viewing), it was not until 1950 that a commercial gallery in Seattle, established by Zoe Dusanne, offered Northwest artists professional representation. In 1961 Arlene Schnitzer opened the Fountain Gallery in Portland, bringing about similar leadership and advocacy in Portland. The commitment and energy of these two women stimulated patronage and collecting of Northwest art that heretofore had been almost non-existent.

Gradually, an increasing number of privately owned galleries germinated a modest but important market for regional art. At the same time new, non-commercial work that was not considered suitable for galleries and museums was on the rise. Much of this art was politically oriented in reaction to a culture in crisis; it was the tumultuous period of the Vietnam War, the rise of the women's movement and the "sexual revolution," the popularization of drug use, and the beginning of environmental activism. Many artists turned to unconventional, non-art materials and means — performance, video, site-specific impermanent works — to challenge the status quo, including that of museums.

In order to exhibit and advance their work, some began to cooperate in establishing what soon were known as "alternative spaces." While these spaces began as high energy and low budget operations, a few flourished thanks to another phenomenon of the times: In 1965, the Congress, in enacting President Lyndon Johnson's Great Society legislation, authorized the National Endowment for the Arts as a unit of the National Foundation for the Arts and Humanities. Not since the termination of the WPA had the federal government dedicated funding to the arts, and even though most support went to well established, mainline arts institutions, the NEA encountered the opposition of conservative legislators, as had the WPA, from its inception. Nevertheless, during the 1970s, it became a lifeline for many experimental group and individual endeavors, among them the Portland Center for the Visual Arts and in Seattle, and/or.

The Portland Center for the Visual Arts, founded in 1972 by three local artists was one of the earliest alternative spaces to apply for and receive NEA grants, and was so successful the NEA promoted it nationally as a role model. PCVA's purpose, as conceived by Mel Katz, Michele Russo, and Jay Backstrand, was to invigorate the local art scene by showing first-rate national and international contemporary art. Renowned artists, Andy Warhol, Frank Stella, Roy Lichtenstein, Alice Aycock Donald Judd, Sol LeWitt among them, not only exhibited but also came to talk. Performance and cross-media works by Rachel Rosenthal, Philip Glass, and John Cage packed the hall, which in fact was a big, loft-like space on the third floor above a downtown restaurant.

Although Northwest art was not PCVA's priority, a major exhibition in 1976 was organized by Lucy Lippard. Lippard, who came from New York and travelled around Oregon and Washington to visit artists' studios (and wrote about the experience for *Art in America*, July/August, 1976), chose to relate her show to qualities still resonating with Northwest School traditions. The title, "In Touch: Nature, Ritual and Sensuous Art from the Northwest," spanned thirty-five artists whose disparate work demonstrated the lengths to which the theme can be stretched. Judy Cooke's uncompromising abstract paintings were there. Dennis Evans, whose interest in metaphysics was much more in keeping with the theme, contribued a box holding sculptural music instruments and drawings of "scores," things he used in his ritualistic performances.

It was a heady period, lasting almost fifteen years, but the momentum could not be sustained. NEA and other public and private funding diminished; administrative problems increased; volunteers became exhausted and friction developed, and ultimately, the financial and personnel burdens became overwhelming. In 1987 a PCVA merger with the Portland Art Museum was agreed upon whereby the Museum would continue similar programs and assign a curator to the specific area. John Weber, a conceptual artist who had headed Northwest Artists Workshop (an alternative space dedicated to experimental projects by area artists), took over the PCVA function which now, though reduced, continues as Art/On the Edge, an annual series of cross-media performances plus occasional gallery exhibitions by out-of-the-area progressive artists. Weber left in 1993 (to take a curatorial position at the San Francisco Museum of Modern Art) but the program, in particular the performance art series under the direction of multi-media artist Kristy Edmunds, has been influential in developing artists and venues for performance art in Portland.

Seattle's near equivalent for PCVA was and/or, and a little later, its spin-off, the Center on Contemporary Art. Both organizations were the outgrowth of artists' and other art professionals' conversations which, in founder Anne Focke's words, centered "on how best to provide a place for experimental art to be and to happen." and/or, organized in 1974, became a cauldron of ideas, a library and a gathering place, as well as an exhibition space. The name chosen by the organizers, "and/or", indicated the lack of restraints, ideological, aesthetic, and logistical. Another lack, that of funding, might have daunted a less creative group, and though and/or remained essentially a bootstrap operation, means were found, often by sharing expenses with another organization, such as PCVA, to bring artists and exhibitions from New York and other distant locations for appearances in both cities. Equally important, regional non-traditional art—video, book art, performance, and cross-media—was given public visibility at and/or well before it was accepted elsewhere.

With time and growth, funding through the NEA, plus the Washington Arts Commission and private foundations eased the financial burden. Nonetheless, by 1981 a "critical mass" of ideas and efforts caused a revaluation and consequently, an evolution of and/or's identity. Whether to become larger and more formally organized or to break up according to more specialized focuses was the question that was resolved by the dissolution of and/or (in 1981) and the start-up of the Center on Contemporary Art (for visual art), the 911 Media Arts Center (for video and other media) somewhat later, and Soundwork (for composer oriented contemporary music). Anne Focke, the primary organizer and driving force behind and/or, kept an assistance program that she had initiated and with it, established Artists Trust which continues to assist and advocate for artists in Washington. Focke, it should be mentioned, has made an art-form of advocacy and administration. In 1988 she organized a national conference in Seattle to address problems that are both practical and philosophical focusing on the basic question of how artists and art can survive in today's political and economic environment. As a result, spin-off groups and networking endeavors such as Arts Wire, a computer online service developed by Focke, have come about. Although her activities now reach far beyond Seattle, her creative energy has been of seminal importance in advancing contemporary art in the Northwest.

The Center on Contemporary Art (COCA, as it continues to be known) like its parent, and/or, was organized by artist members and operated under their auspices. As planned, it had no fixed space and no fixed policies; exhibitions were selected and scheduled by a program committee who made their decisions solely on the soundness of proposals. Their choice for the opening exhibition, however, tested the founders' limits of feasibility. James Turrell, whose large scale projects using directed natural light were attracting major critical interest, agreed to construct aperture works in Seattle. Months of preparation by COCA members went into searching for a space, which was found in an old building on Pioneer Square, then to renovating and making it usable before Turrell's arrival to calculate and create the apertures that would move light through the rooms. The highly successful exhibition, which was on view for six months, set a precedent that was difficult to follow. After several years of utilizing temporary spaces and except for a curator, relying on volunteer labor, COCA was installed in a downtown storefront. Although its curatorial focus has evolved over the years with changes in membership, it continues as a venue for non-traditional work, much of which now is related to the sub-culture that has emerged from Seattle's innovations in rock music.

Since 1988 the Henry Art Gallery at the University of Washington has to some extent assumed COCA's function. Under the direction of Richard Andrews (a founding member of COCA, also the director of Washington's Percent for Art program, and from 1984 to 1988 the Director of Visual Arts at the NEA in Washington, D.C.,) and curator Chris Bruce the gallery maintains a schedule of one-person and thematic exhibitions by leading national and Northwest artists plus the annual University of Washington M.F.A. exhibition. By virtue of its affiliation with the University, however, it is removed from the kind of free-wheeling experimentation and camaraderie that characterized and/or and the early period of COCA.

The most important institutional support is vested in the Seattle Art Museum. Since 1933 it has supported regional art, first with monthly one-person exhibitions for local artists and until 1975, with Northwest annuals that covered Washington, Oregon, Idaho, Montana, British Columbia, and Alaska. Yearly competitive exhibitions of the Northwest Printmakers, the Northwest Watercolor Society, and the Seattle Photographic Society also tracked regional developments. With an eye to the future, the Museum's founder and first director (from 1933 to 1976), Dr. Richard E. Fuller, acquired works, often from the exhibitions and purchased from his personal funds, thus establishing an acquisition tradition that continues to expand SAM's holdings in Northwest art.

The exhibition policy that remains in place today was initiated by Bruce Guenther who was Curator of Modern Art from 1979 until 1987 and introduced the first of the salient Northwest Document series in 1983. Today, under the direction of curators Patterson Sims, Vicki Halper, and Rod Slemmons, three or four exhibitions per year are scheduled. By the end of 1994 eighty-six artists had been exhibited through the series, thirty-three in one-person shows and the others in thematic presentations. In addition to the Northwest Documents gallery the Museum devotes another gallery to regional art from the permanent collection. Among the major museums in the United States, the Seattle Art Museum is unusual, and possibly unique, in its commitment to the art of its region.

The Portland Art Museum, with less space and fewer resources, mounts a biennial survey plus infrequent one-person exhibitions. In the early 1980s a series patterned after Northwest Documents was initiated under the heading Northwest Viewpoints. When the PCVA function was folded into the Museum's, gallery space and staff time became overextended and the series was dropped. Occasional one-person exhibitions, such as the Carl Morris retrospective in 1993 and a mid-career survey of the work of Lucinda Parker scheduled for fall, 1995, must be fitted into the general scheduling priorities. Since the purchase of the neighboring Masonic Building in 1991 and the arrival of a new director, John Buchanan, in 1994, the Portland Art Museum is beginning a period of expansion which opens possibilities for more active support of contemporary Northwest art in the future.

Currently, there are few other non-commercial venues for regional art in Oregon. The kind of spirited shows with strong curatorial points of view that once were the province of alternative spaces are most closely approximated by the Art Gym at Marylhurst College. The Coos Museum in Coos Bay and the Schneider Gallery on the campus of Southern Oregon State College in Ashland are of considerable interest in their locales but seldom reach beyond.

In Washington, however, several outposts are significant. Eastern Washington is well served by the Washington State University Museum of Art in Pullman. Located about three hundred miles east of Seattle, the WSU gallery has a separate constituency led by an active community of artists in the immediate area, including Gaylen Hansen and Robert Helm. The gallery also draws energy from western Idaho, in particular the University of Idaho at Moscow and the colony of artists in Hope that has grown under the influence of the late Ed Kienholz and his wife, Nancy Reddin Kienholz.

Several small Washington museums give high priority to contemporary regional art. The Whatcom Museum in Bellingham and the Cheney Cowles in Spokane combine history and art. The Tacoma Art Museum places high priority on regional art, exemplified by the travelling exhibition, "Jet Dreams: The Fifties in the Northwest," which was organized by TAM curator-historian Barbara Johns. The Bellevue Art Museum, located in the huge Bellevue shopping mall, is dedicated to contemporary regional art and to complementary education and outreach projects. A recent exhibition featuring drawings and small works by Joseph Beuys (1921–1986) was accompanied by an installation and performance by Dennis Evans who, like Beuys, links art to shamanism. Curator Diane Douglas extends the exhibitions' scope through the production of interactive videos and CD-ROMs as well as catalogs.

The craft tradition continues to flourish in the Northwest, supported by galleries and educational institutions. The Oregon School of Arts and Crafts, with BFA and certificate programs in ceramics, wood, metal, fiber, and book art is a place of cross fertilization of ideas, techniques, and materials. The School's Hoffman Gallery is a showcase for national as well as regional art that demonstrates contemporary eclecticism.

The ceramics program at the University of Washington began in the 1920s and has been a force in the development of ceramic art ever since. In recent years, the faculty, especially Howard Kottler (1930–1989), Robert Sperry, and Patti Warashina, have been influential in expanding the use of clay to include sculpture that challenges the expressive limits of both the material and techniques.

No one in the Northwest, or anywhere else, for that matter, epitomizes the glorification — and resurrection — of craft more than glass artist Dale Chihuly. In ebullient defiance of postmodern critics who abhor "lack of content," Chihuly's blown glass sculptures assert the viability of sheer visual pleasure. In addition to his creative output, his efforts and influence have caused studio glass to become a recognized medium of individual expression and Seattle to become an international center for glass art. In 1971, Chihuly and patrons Anne Gould Hauberg and John Hauberg founded the Pilchuck School near Stanwood, an hour's drive north of Seattle, as a residential workshop where faculty, visiting artists, and students work and learn collaboratively. Pilchuck has become renowned as a setting for experimentation and innovation in all aspects of glass techniques. Chihuly's Seattle workshop also attracts glass artists from Europe and this country to work in the hot shop under his direction while also pursuing their own projects.

Contemporary print art, like that of glass, stems from a long, craft-based tradition strong in the Northwest since the founding of the Northwest Printmakers by teachers and students at the University of Washington in 1928. After more than a quarter of a century the organization disbanded, and in 1981, the Northwest Print Council was formed in Portland with much the same function. While both the Northwest Printmakers and the Northwest Print Council have been instrumental in increasing a strong print production in the region, the impetus in Portland's emergence as a national center for print art is due to a distinguished and formidable artist-teacher-collector-curator-advocate named Gordon Gilkey.

Gilkey (b. 1912) earned the University of Oregon's first M.F.A. with an emphasis on printmaking in 1937, and from that time to the present he has been absorbed in all aspects of print art. In 1978, after his retirement from the faculty of Oregon State University in Corvallis, he gave his vast collection of fine art prints to the Portland Art Museum on the condition that the Museum would establish a center for the study, exhibition, and conservation of prints as well as studio facilities. Since its completion in the fall of 1993, the Gordon and Vivian Gilkey Center for the Graphic Arts provides access (on request) for professionals, students, and the interested public to its collections of historical, modern, and contemporary works on paper, including photography. Exhibitions, lectures, and a comprehensive studio program in conjunction with the Pacific Northwest College of Art[4] flesh out a resource that is unique on the West Coast. Gordon Gilkey, still active as the curator of prints and drawings, continues to add to the collection, to produce his own monotypes and computer designed prints, and to teach at PNCA as Artist-in-Residence.

In 1942, with the impetus of the Minor White show, the Portland Art Museum initiated a collection of photography that has become an important resource of historical photographs related to Oregon. Curator Terry Toedtemeier, a photographic artist and a fifth generation Oregonian, has a personal affinity for collecting in this area. His sense of the relationship of visual images to history is evident in exhibitions he has curated, in particular, "The Vision at the End of the Trail: A History of Oregon Photography," in 1992.

The Seattle Art Museum began its collection of photographs much more recently. Since 1981 curator Rod Slemmons has amassed a significant collection centered on American photography with supplemental European material. Both Slemmons and Terry Toedtemeier are actively engaged in the Northwest photographic art community; their contributions to the preservation of regional history and to the advocacy of current work are crucial in the expanding presence of photography in Northwest art.

The 1980s, more than any previous period not affected by war, were marked by social changes. The populations of Seattle and of Portland and their surrounding areas increased markedly, not only with New Yorkers and Los Angelenos looking for a more pleasant and less expensive way of life but also by Southeast Asian and Hispanic immigrants. Boeing and Microsoft in Seattle, Tektronix and other high tech companies in Portland provided jobs for trained workers but lay-offs in other industries, especially timber and fishing, worsened the economy and accentuated the problems of homelessness, drug abuse, and street crime. Issues of the body, especially abortion and AIDS became as much political causes as health problems. Ecological issues polarized supporters of timber, fishing, and agriculture industries on one side and environmentalists on the other.

Nonetheless, the number of galleries burgeoned and so did the number of artists; by 1987 both Seattle and Portland were enlivened by monthly evening gallery openings, called First Thursdays, that immediately attracted lively crowds. These public receptions are immensely popular, and while there is debate over their significance to the art market or to serious consideration of the art being shown, there is no doubt that they have engendered a new young audience for art and earned the respect of city officials as a stimulus to economic development. The Pearl district in Portland, a rundown neighborhood of warehouses and small industries on the fringe of the retail center, underwent a quick transformation when artists' studios located in the old buildings were followed by galleries, cafes, and other compatible businesses. Possibilities for future development have not been lost on city leaders nor on developers of up-scale lofts and condominiums.

State, county, and city percent-for-art programs in Washington and Oregon also are evidence of the strong link between art and civic life. These programs, which have been in existence since the early 1970s amplify a historical tradition in Portland and Seattle that is nearly as old as the cities themselves. A larger than life-size bronze elk standing in the middle of downtown Portland's Main Street (between 3rd and 4th) has been there, parting traffic, since 1900 when its location was in keeping with traffic needs: the horses could drink from the troughs at the monument's base. The city grew up around *The Elk* (by Roland Perry, n.d.) which has become one of its emblems. Seattle's early sculptures, also in the tradition of monuments, were the result of commissions for the Alaska-Yukon-Pacific Exposition in 1909. The most germane of these, a bust of Chief Seattle (by James Wehn, n.d.), is a prominent fixture in Pioneer Square.

Despite meager funding by any government entity — local, state, or federal — until recent years, both Seattle and Portland are fortunate in having had art supporters and patrons who fostered public art through private commissions. In fact, King County (Seattle is its county seat) in 1967 was the first in the nation to create a publicly funded arts commission. Both cities' large collections, consisting of paintings and other indoor works as well as sculptures, fountains, and murals, were instrumental in creating support for the statutes requiring one percent (in some cases, one-half of one percent) of construction budgets for public buildings to be dedicated to art. Nevertheless, it was the federal government which took the lead in 1962 by setting aside one-half of one percent of renovation and construction budgets for federal buildings specifically for art. Since 1966 the NEA also has provided partial funding for selected public art projects. All these influences culminated between 1973 and 1980 in Seattle and Portland, as well as in their respective counties and states, in percent-for-art programs that have become valuable, not only as nationally respected additions to the cities' forward-looking identities, but also as an area of opportunity for artists. Almost all artists are involved occasionally in public projects, and a few, like Buster Simpson who has produced major ecological works in both cities, have made public art their sole activity.

Still another effect of the increased attention paid to public art has been a revaluation of its function within the communities it serves. Defining the meaning of public life, which has occupied philosophers since Aristotle, now is brought to bear on the meaning of public art. It is not by chance that heroic statuary produced by single artists has given way to non-traditional, non-art forms addressing issues of public concern and designed by committee, i.e., by teams selected by advisory panels. Individuality and "authorship" continue to be important in many projects, although the combination of changing values and exigencies of funding leads increasingly to a multi-lateral process. Artists, architects, construction engineers, administrators, and government officials collaborate in defining as well as producing the public art of today. Two large projects in the Northwest, Portland's Westside Light Rail and "In Public: Seattle 1991", encapsulate the evolution of its meaning and production.

Because federal money, which funds about three-quarters of the Westside light rail system's $944 million projected cost, cannot be designated for specific art projects, officials from Tri-Met (the regional transportation agency) with the help of advisers from the Metropolitan Arts Commission decided to include artists on the over-all design team. In 1992 five artists (Tad Savinar and Bill Will of Portland, Norie Sato of Seattle, Mierle Laderman Ukeles of New York, and Richard Turner of Orange, California) were selected. They have worked in tandem with architects, engineers, administrators, as well as the art advisory panel to integrate art in both the function and the aesthetic character of the stations along the eighteen mile system. Adding to the Advisory Committee's mandate "to connect riders with their environment, their history and with the technology that moves them," the artist team also aimed to implement concepts that will retain viability well into the future.

Although the system will not be completed until late 1997, each station has been designed to reflect its immediate natural or social environment. The Civic Stadium Station, for example, is near the location of the original east-west trail and the cluster of small frame buildings that marked Portland's beginnings as a city. Drawing on the idea of a clearing in the forest, the artists designed a large plaza as a potential forum for speakers and listeners. The plaza will contain three cast-bronze podiums in the shapes of a stump, a soapbox, and a pedestal, plus built-in seating. Symbolizing the importance of free speech, the architecture and installation provide a setting for public oratory and for perusing text pertaining to history of the place which will be inscribed on plaza structures.

Departing radically from a utilitarian policy, "In Public: Seattle 1991" pioneered new territory in public art. A deliberate attempt was made by the Seattle Arts Commission to counter the limitations and disadvantages of the team approach (SAC had initiated the use of design teams during the 1970s) by offering individual artists the opportunity to create projects anywhere in Seattle. With a budget of $847,000, which came from a percent-for-art program applied to the construction of the new Seattle Art Museum, plus grants and gifts, twenty-four projects were undertaken, of which eighteen were completed. The participating artists, eight of whom were local and the others, national and international, were asked "to encourage their works to address, intervene in, and engage the public life of the city."[5]

By these criteria "In Public" fulfilled its purpose. Los Angeles installation artist Daniel Martinez displayed seventy-nine banners in the retail core of downtown Seattle, each addressing disparities between the "haves" and "have-nots" with a question that ended with a period rather than a question mark. All the banners, like "Did you attend Private School. Was it Ivy League." more than fulfilled their aim to undermine the complacency of affluent shoppers. Merchants objected and public response was immediate and divided, spilling into the press and talk shows. A uniformly well-received project was the work of Edgar Heap of Birds, of the Cheyenne and Arapaho Nation in Oklahoma, who installed large porcelain panels next to the bust of Chief Seattle in Pioneer Square with texts in both English and Lusootseed that spoke to and about Native Americans, some of whom now are among the homeless inhabitants of the neighborhood.

Except for the single permanent sculpture (Jonathan Borofsky's huge mechanical *Hammering Man* standing on the corner next to the Seattle Art Museum entrance), very little physical evidence of "In Public" remains. Much was ephemeral — public service announcements on television, newspaper ads, rack cards — and none (except for the Pier 62/63 project which was heavily altered) was intended to be on view longer than six months. The tangible remains consist primarily of printed documentation, in particular the catalog published in 1992 by the Seattle Arts Commission. In addition to its descriptions and photographs of the individual projects, the book is a valuable compendium of essays covering administrative and logistical problems as well as conceptual and philosophical considerations. "In Public," the writers emphasize, was an experiment. Its intent was to move the role of public art from one of urban enhancement to one of social and political intervention. Seattle's large collection of art as objects in public places, long a source of civic pride and national prominence, was radically altered by art as action, art that engages mentally rather than aesthetically, art that subverts its own canons as it infiltrates "real" life. Quite possibly, the most important result of the experiment has been in the discourse that it advanced concerning the relationship of public art, and by extension, of all art, to a rapidly changing, increasingly complex, post-industrial society. Is the role of art to mirror society or to engage in the *Sturm und Drang*? Should public art continue in its traditional mode of celebrating the city and its history or attempt to change it? Considerable public — and some critical — debate turned on whether or not the "In Public" projects were art at all.

A more pragmatic question generated by the discourse is that of area specificity. Eleanor Heartney, in her catalog essay (*Art and Its Audience: A Public Experiment*), noted that the unfinished projects were by non-Northwest artists and wondered if outside artists working from a mental as well as a physical distance can compete with local artists in speaking to a community's specific concerns. In a larger sense her rumination leads to the inevitable question, what is different, or special, which is to say, regional, in Northwest art? Are the concerns, or the manner in which they are addressed, different from those that can be seen in the art of other regions?

Not since the time of the Northwest School has an ideological and stylistic identity been ascribed to the art of the Pacific Northwest. More recently, Chicago Imagist and Bay Area Figurative have been characterized as styles particular to their regions, but in this time of instantaneous dissemination of ideas and information, distinctions among regions are negligible. New York City remains the center of activity and by reason of its concentration of marketing, critical and theoretical writing, and patronage, the center of authority. Artists who chose to work outside that center are *per se*, "regionalists," a term that is gradually shifting from judgmental to geographic in its meaning, although a pejorative edge has not yet been eliminated. Nonetheless, as living and working in New York become increasingly expensive and difficult, and its art community becomes more inbred, many artists opt for livability and escape from market pressures. A few, like Gaylen Hansen and Robert Helm, achieve national success even though — or perhaps because — they have utilized the solitude of their remote locations in eastern Washington to create highly individualistic work that is far removed in style as well as miles from New York influences. As astute observers have pointed out, when eastern power brokers look elsewhere it is for a signifcant break from the trends within the international style of which they are arbiters, not for similarities, which they will judge as derivative.

When contemporary Northwest art is considered within the

context of its particular historical development and its natural and social environment rather than in the context of comparison, which is what Eleanor Heartney's question implies, success can be measured by other criteria. How well does it address concerns of its region? Does it vitalize civic life? Does it represent the archetypical human condition in terms relevant to a population that is closely allied with a rural past and an Information Age future?

The art that is surveyed in this book manifests the diversity of concerns and the individual ways in which they are addressed. Politics, race, and social inequities are no less potent issues in Oregon and Washington than elsewhere and they dominate the work of Mike Taylor, Marita Dingus, Cris Bruch, Robert Herdlein, and Cecilia Conception Alvarez. The effects of communications technology absorb Paul Berger and Norie Sato. Continued interest in formalist issues of materials and composition occupy Judy Cooke and Mel Katz. The dominance of idea over form, a strong trend throughout the country, is especially evident in the work of the young artists.

Still, certain Northwest characteristics observed in earlier art continue to be seen. Respect for craft is one. Painting as the preferred medium by far is another. By all counts, however, nature as subject, theme, and influence is the dominant distinguishing mark of Northwest art, past and present. While Terry Toedtemeier reveals the landscape as the creation of awesome geologic forces, most focus on the interaction of humans and the land. For Native American artists Rick Bartow and James Lavadour nature has a metaphysical dimension that permeates their responses to it. Gaylen Hansen, Sherry Markovitz, and Malia Jensen draw on the psychology of anthropomorphism. Like Carl Morris's sweeping abstract paintings, which were inspired by the minutia as well as the cosmology of nature, Lucinda Parker's powerful paintings are representations of felt rather than observed nature.

Of all the themes related to nature none is more relevant in such a geographically beautiful area as the Northwest than that of environmental loss. Buster Simpson's public, ecological projects forcefully draw attention to the intertwining of cause and effect in natural processes as they are altered by human intervention. Dennis Cunningham and Michael Brophy couch their concerns in metaphoric imagery of great personal as well as regional resonance, Cunningham through fishing and Brophy through forests.

In its inclusiveness contemporary art in the Northwest is no different from that of other regions, including New York. To some its lack of a reigning dogma may imply a lack of quality — an "anything goes" mentality. Yet the culture itself is increasingly pluralistic. The optimism that prevailed in the post-World War II period now is eroded by job dislocations and economic insecurity, by political cynicism, and the sense that the future has ceased to be bright with promise. No longer subscribing to the "melting-pot" idea, ethnic groups heretofore marginalized as "minority" insist on their cultural identities and demand a political voice. Native Americans, African Americans, Asian Americans, and Hispanic Americans are intent on utilizing the arts as well as politics to revise the Euro-American version of Northwest history.

Art that accomodates so many differences but also draws on continuity, that opposes but also celebrates, and that encompasses all manner of expression, from the activist art of "In Public" to Terry Toedtemeier's quiet acknowledgment of nature's omnipotence to Dale Chihuly's gloriously indulgent glass, attests to the Northwest's cultural energy and to the growing importance of this region within the totality of American art.

1. *Art of the Pacific Northwest From the 1930s to the Present*, essay by Martha Kingsbury. (catalog published by the Smithsonian Institution, 1974) p. 58
2. Ibid, p. 14
3. Quoted by Rachel Griffin in the introductory essay for the catalog *Paintings and Sculptures of the Pacific Northwest: Oregon, Washington, and British Columbia* (published by the Portland Art Museum, 1959). Also quoted in several other sources.
4. In 1981, the Museum Art School underwent a name change to the Pacific Northwest College of Art
5. Catalog, *In Public: Seattle 1991*, edited by Diane Shamish (published by the Seattle Arts Commission, 1992) p. 10

Cecilia Concepcion **Alvarez**

Cecilia Concepcion Alvarez is the daughter of a Cuban father and a Mexican mother. She was reared in the border town Tijuana, Mexico, educated in California schools, and now lives in Seattle. It is hardly surprising that her art is concerned with cross-cultural politics, shaped by her personal experience and cultural heritage. Although she does not consider herself a political activist, she consistently opposes the cultural, racial, and gender biases that devalue those of minority ethnic and cultural groups. Her statement for the brochure accompanying the quincentenary exhibition *1492/1992* at the Seattle Art Museum is to the point: "In my work I speak of the continuing efforts of the dominant culture to convert all to homogeneity via consumerism, religion, and colonial democracy."

Alvarez's opposition to that homogeneity is seen in the style of her work as well as in its subjects. She is largely self-taught, having been discouraged as a young student by the gender bias of a male Mexican art teacher. Turning to Mexican art history books, she soon assimilated the figurative stylization and vivid palette of the Mexican aesthetic established by the great muralists Diego Riviera, David Alfaro Siqueiros, and Jose Clemente Orozco, and found in it a powerful referent to cultural pride. The monumental female figure of *La Tierra Santa* (The Sacred Earth) is in that tradition, commanding the picture plane in a flat, frontal presentation. Like a reincarnation of a pre-Columbian goddess, she is a modern-day guardian of indigenous people, animals, and plants standing in resolute opposition to the forces of destruction.

Alvarez frequently uses the female figure, as in *La Tierra Santa*, as a symbol of creativity and nurturance. A similar figure shown in the process of giving birth was interpreted by some as pornographic when it was shown in Spokane in 1992. The resulting press coverage caused a heated public debate, unintentionally illustrating the presumptive moralistic authority that Alvarez assails. In the same year two works, both denunciations of imperialistic exploitation in Latin America, were created for *1492/1991*, and although politically provocative, caused no moral outrage. The titles, as much as the art, address the history of European colonialism from the point of view of its victims: *Codex Chicon Alvarez/Cuando El Oportunista Es Rey En El Barrio las Calles Estan Pavimentadas Con Oro y Sangre/Codex Chicon Alvarez/When the Opportunist is King in the Neighborhood, the Streets Are Paved With Gold and Blood) and Resistencia a La Continuacion de la Limpieza de Sangre/En Memoria a los Arawaks y Tainos (Resistance to the Continuation of the Clearing of the Blood/In Memory of the Tainos and Arawak).*

Every detail in the altar-like construction *En Memoria* and the *Codex*, which is a two-dimensional mixed-media work, contributes to a horrific representation of greed and oppression. Elemental forces of destruction and rebirth are represented at the base of *En Memoria* by the copper phalangeal disk symbolizing fire plus a female nude (replicating the pose in Leonardo's classic "canon of proportions" drawing) as the potentiality — and vulnerability — of humans. The altar's plexiglass niche enshrines the false gods of money and power and supports at its apex a gold cross intertwined with a dollar sign. Suspended between the niche and the base, bundles of thirteen small gold figures refer to the Columbian method of execution by suspending victims over a fire in rows of thirteen, the number chosen to "honor" the Redeemer and the twelve apostles.

In using the continuing cycles of colonization as the subject of *Codex Chicon Alvarez*, the artist draws on analogous Aztec codices that recorded cycles of drought and famine. Referring to the naive belief that the streets in the United States "are paved with gold," Alvarez depicts gold skulls as symbols of those sacrificed for the profit of others. The blue suited profiteers wear blinders, oblivious to the effects of their avarice. Assassins in the uniforms of Mexico's various invaders fire at the innocent while images of old women and one of Alvarez's painting, *La Tierra Santa*, suggest the loss of history and culture. Through the use of a bird's-eye perspective making the entire scene uniformly visible, Alvarez follows the muralist tradition of telling a story boldly and simply.

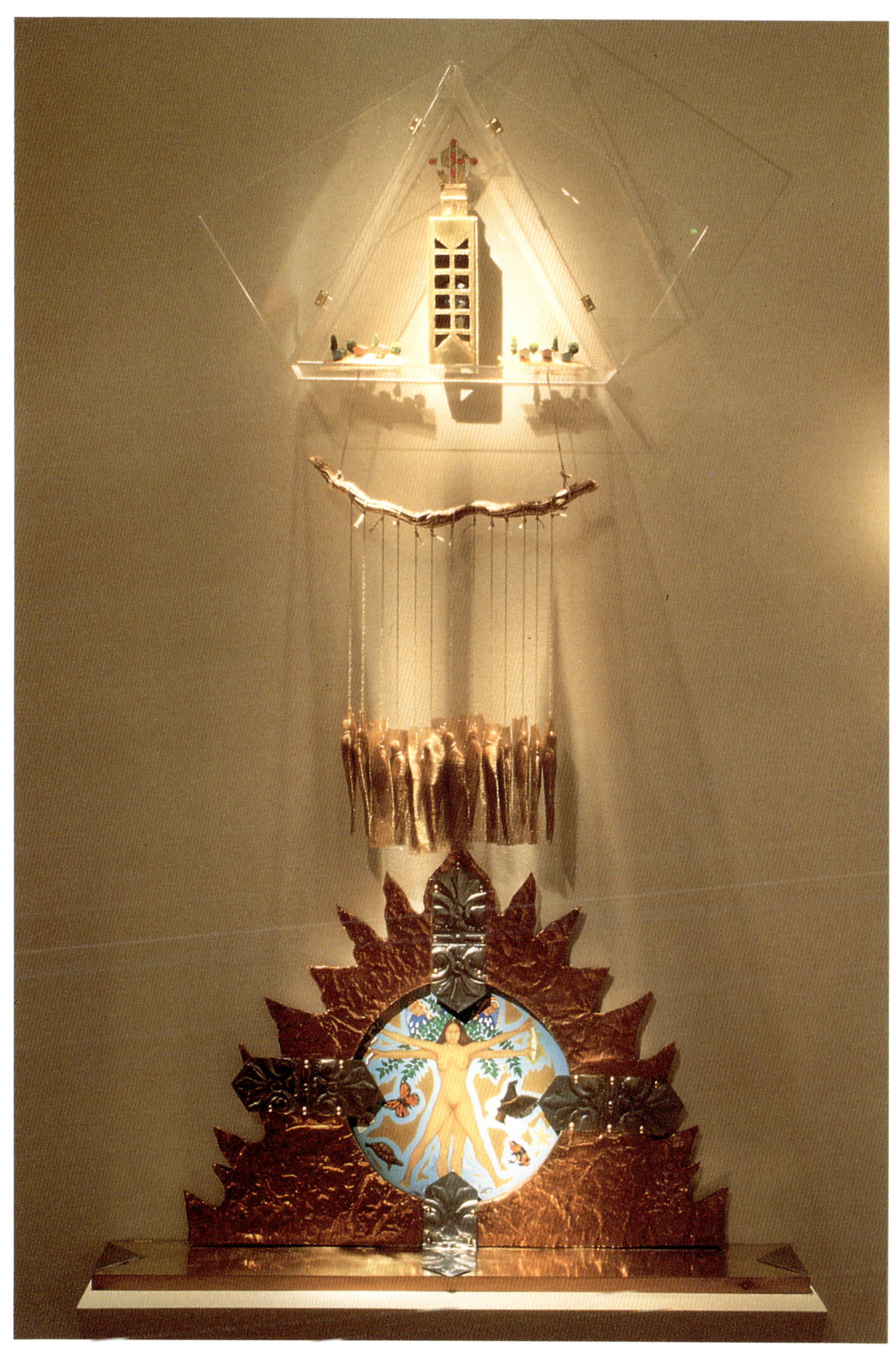

Cecilia Concepion Alvarez **En Memoria**
Mixed media, 7'h x 48"w x 6"d. Courtesy of the artist. Photograph: Susan Dirk.

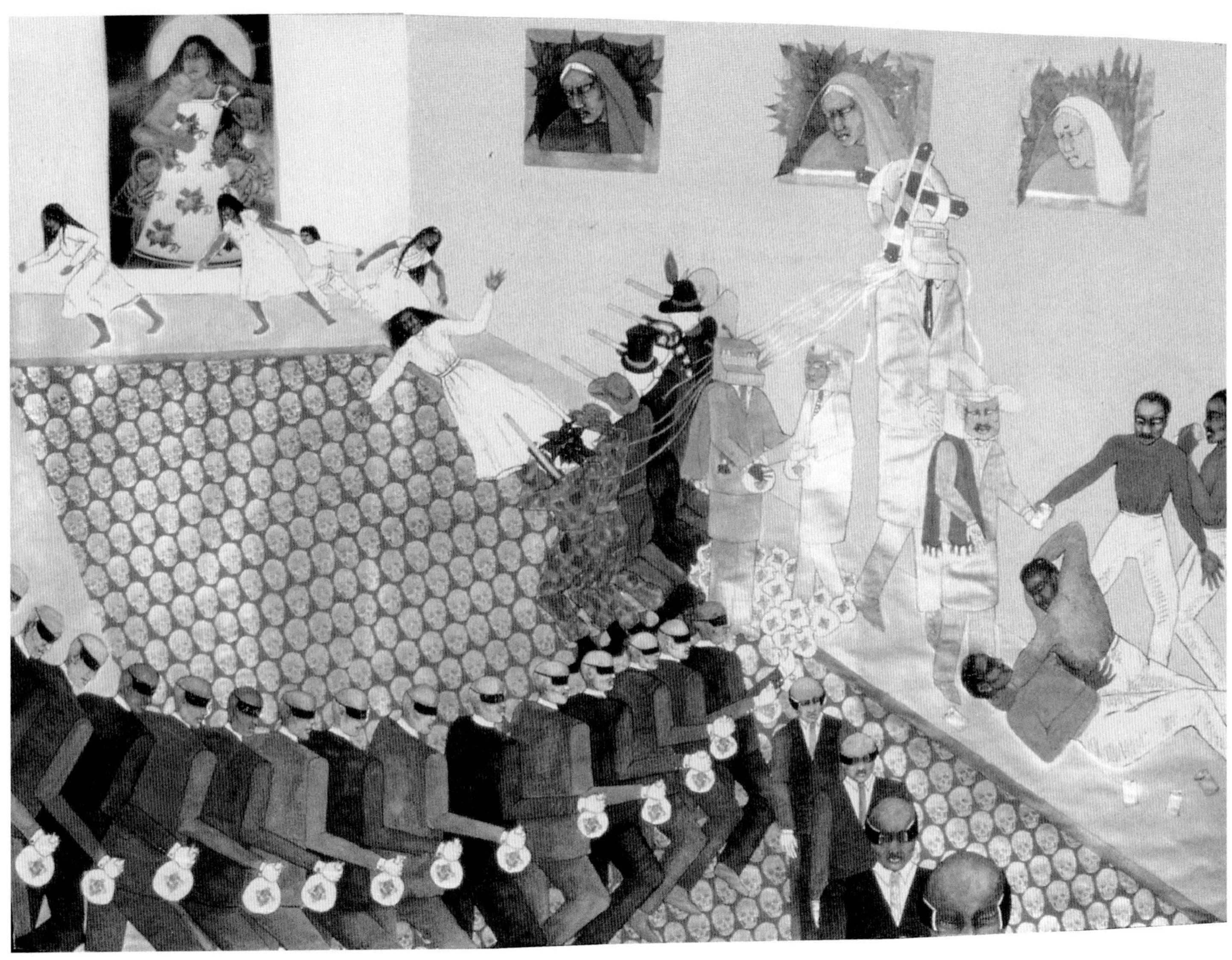

Cecilia Concepion Alvarez **Codex**
1992, Acrylic on paper, 22" x 33". Seattle Art Museum permanent collection. Photograph: Kathi Drummond.

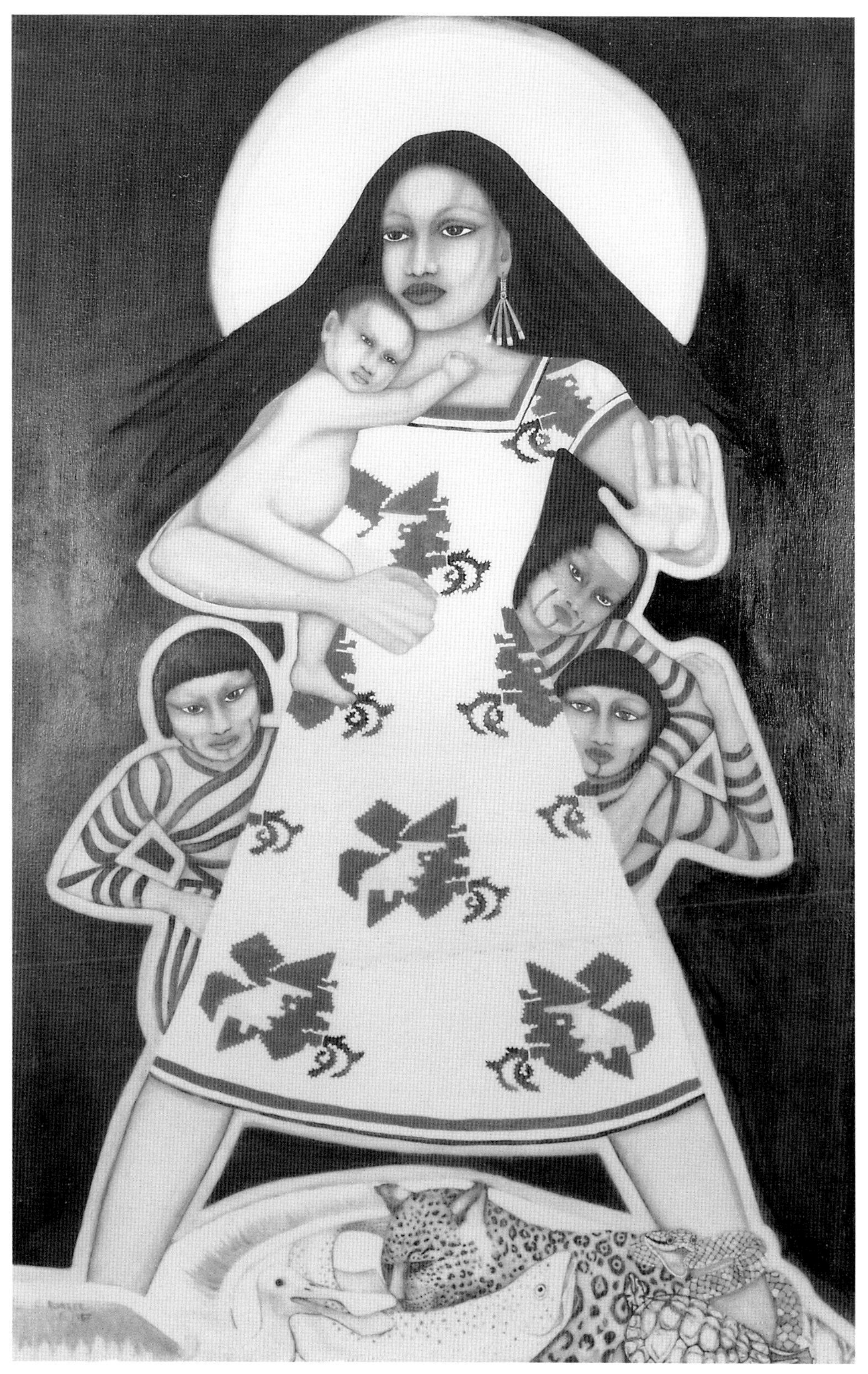

Cecilia Concepion Alvarez **La Tierra Santa**
1985, Oil on canvas, 5' x 4½'. Courtesy of the artist. Photograph: Kathi Drummond.

Guy **Anderson**

Guy Anderson's identification with the "Northwest School" and more important, his unwavering dedication to a cogent artistic vision have made him a seminal figure in the history of Northwest painting. The representation of cosmic wholeness that has absorbed him from the beginning of his career continues to permeate his work well into the ninth decade of his life. The late paintings' chthonic connotations are indicated in his own statement of purpose: "Whether the condition of the world in its light and dark hours changes greatly for the enlightenment of man, he still is a night swimmer among its mysteries. For many years when asked what I most hope to achieve in paintings, my response has not changed: I hope to use the human figure symbolically."[1]

As one of the four progenitors of the famed "Northwest School" of the 1940s, Anderson's public identity was set early. The shared humanist and modernist principles that united these philosophically inclined artists — Mark Tobey, Morris Graves, Kenneth Callahan, along with Anderson — led them, each in his own way, to search for a universal language of form that would draw on pan-cultural imagery and experimentation in painting styles. Their interest in the transcendental spirituality common to all religions, which, they believed, is also experienced in nature, directed their pictorial pursuits toward distillations of representation in various degrees of abstraction. Anderson was particularly attracted to the shifting planes of Cubism and the disjunctive images of Surrealism. Unlike his New York counterparts whose similar goals and adaptations of European modernism resulted in Abstract Expressionism, he never abandoned recognizable, albeit abstracted, references to nature, especially to the human figure. As his mature style developed, he settled on a vocabulary of reductive, symbolic imagery within a flat, linearly structured picture plane. Typically, his emblematic images — the human figure, variations on circles, spheres, and other elemental shapes — are formed in muted, earth colors applied with sweeping brushstrokes.

Anderson's roots in the Northwest are abiding and deep, the foundation of his art as well as his personal life. He was born in 1906 in the coastal town of Edmonds, Washington, and has lived most of his adult life in LaConner, a village about fifty miles up the coast from Edmonds. His only formal training was obtained in Seattle in private study with Eustace Ziegler, a Yale-trained painter of Alaska and the Northwest. He had, however, the advantages of a natural intellectual curiosity and a dynamic family environment, as well as the inculcation of the land, sea, and gray skies framing his daily experience. In 1926, Anderson was awarded a Tiffany Foundation Resident Scholarship which took him for the first time away from his native state and gave him the opportunity to work and visit museums in New York. Upon returning to Edmonds a year later he set up a studio and began to exhibit in Seattle, and, in 1929, in New York.

Anderson's association with the group of progressive artists in Seattle was at its closest in the atmosphere of World War II. In addition to their exchange of philosophical ideas and sharing of artistic activities, all were pacifists who searched for an art of opposition to war. This cohesiveness contributed to their identification as the "Northwest School" that was the basis for the influential article in *Life* magazine ("Mystic Painters of the Northwest," September 23, 1953). Anderson, Kenneth Callahan, Morris Graves, and Mark Tobey were featured as leaders of the group, and their work was described as strongly influenced by a combination of Asian philosophies and the mist-shrouded landscape. Ironically, the group dispersed soon after and Anderson moved to LaConner in 1954 where he has lived and worked ever since in near solitude, choosing contemplation and the beauty of the Skagit Valley over the clamor of the art world.

In the work of the past several decades Anderson has dealt extensively with the relationship of humans to the universe. Drawing with a loaded, wide brush, he develops a rhythm and tension within the composition as a parallel to the same elements in the cosmos. His preference for a subdued, near monochromatic palette endures, although it it is often spiked with a strong contrasting color. With age, his painterly manifestations of human one-ness have become more distilled, and their many references — to Greek classicism, Haida totemic designs, static Egyptian composition, Hindu mandela configurations, and yin-yang interconnections — more encompassing.

1. Cited in *50 Northwest Artists* by Bruce Guenther (San Francisco: Chronicle Books, 1983), p.17, and in *Still Working: Underknown Artists of Age in America*, catalog, ed. by Stuart Shedletsky (Parsons School of Design, New York, in association with University of Washington Press, Seattle and London, 1994), p. 20.

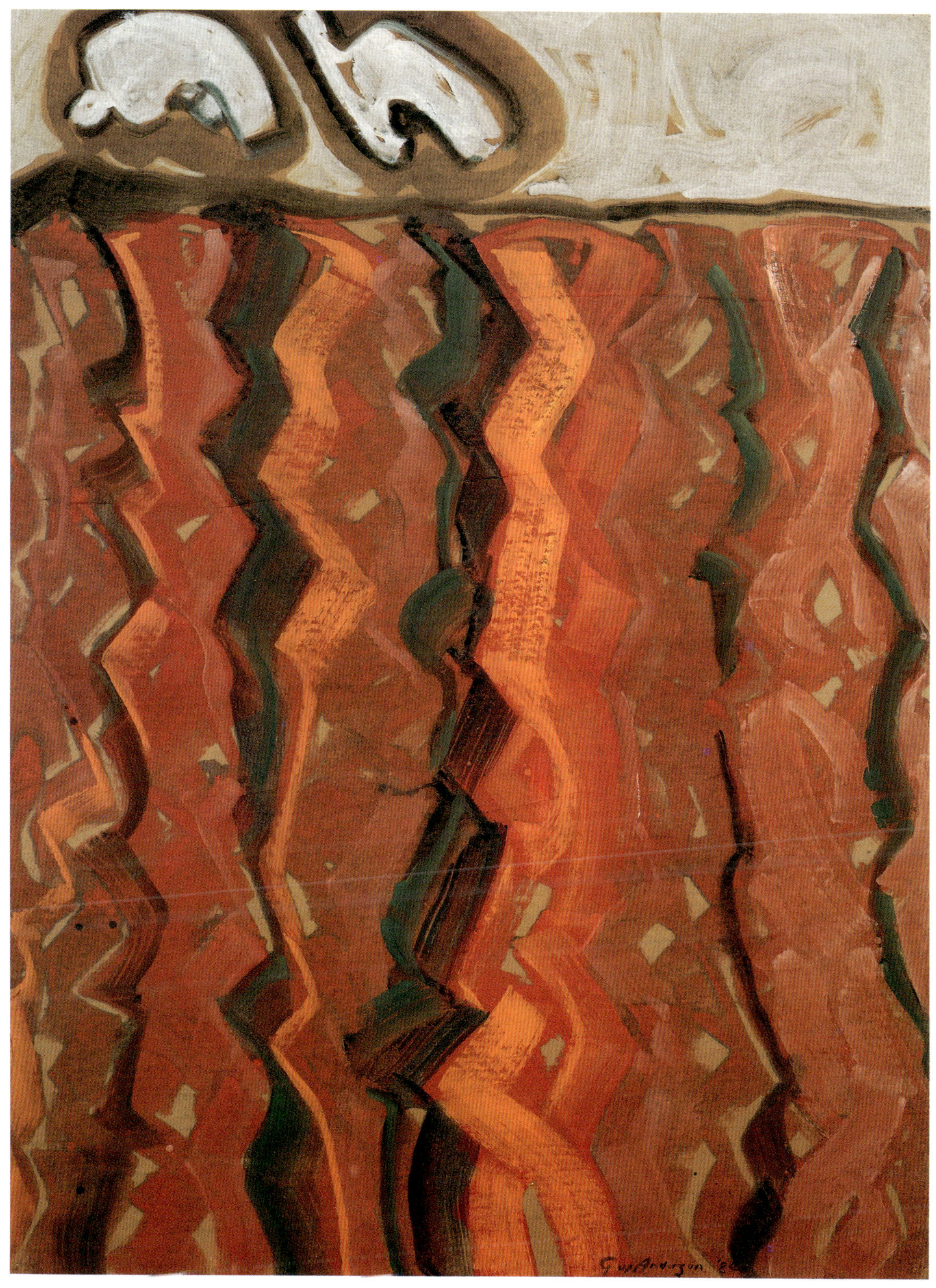

Guy Anderson **Red Sea**
1984, Oil on paper, 96" x 72". Courtesy of the artist and Francine Seders Gallery. Photograph: Spike Mafford.

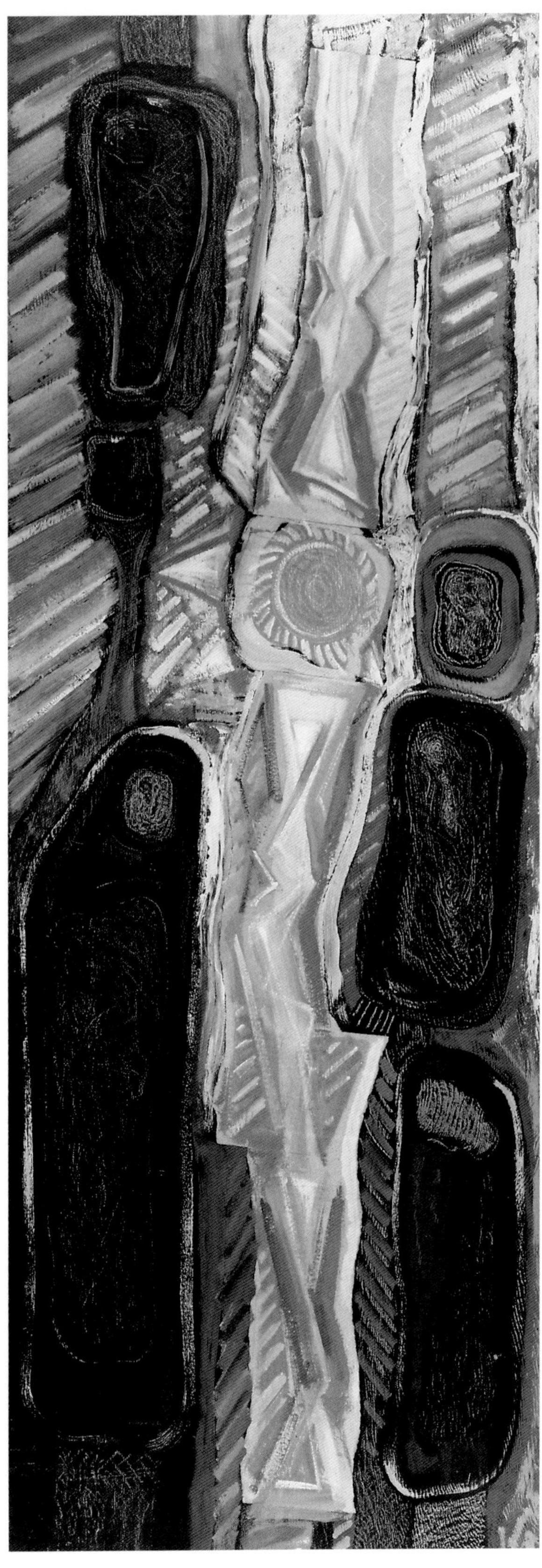

Guy Anderson **Ultima Thule under Sunlight**
1959, Oil on wood, 83" x 29½".
Courtesy of the artist and Francine Seders Gallery.
Photograph: Chris Eden.

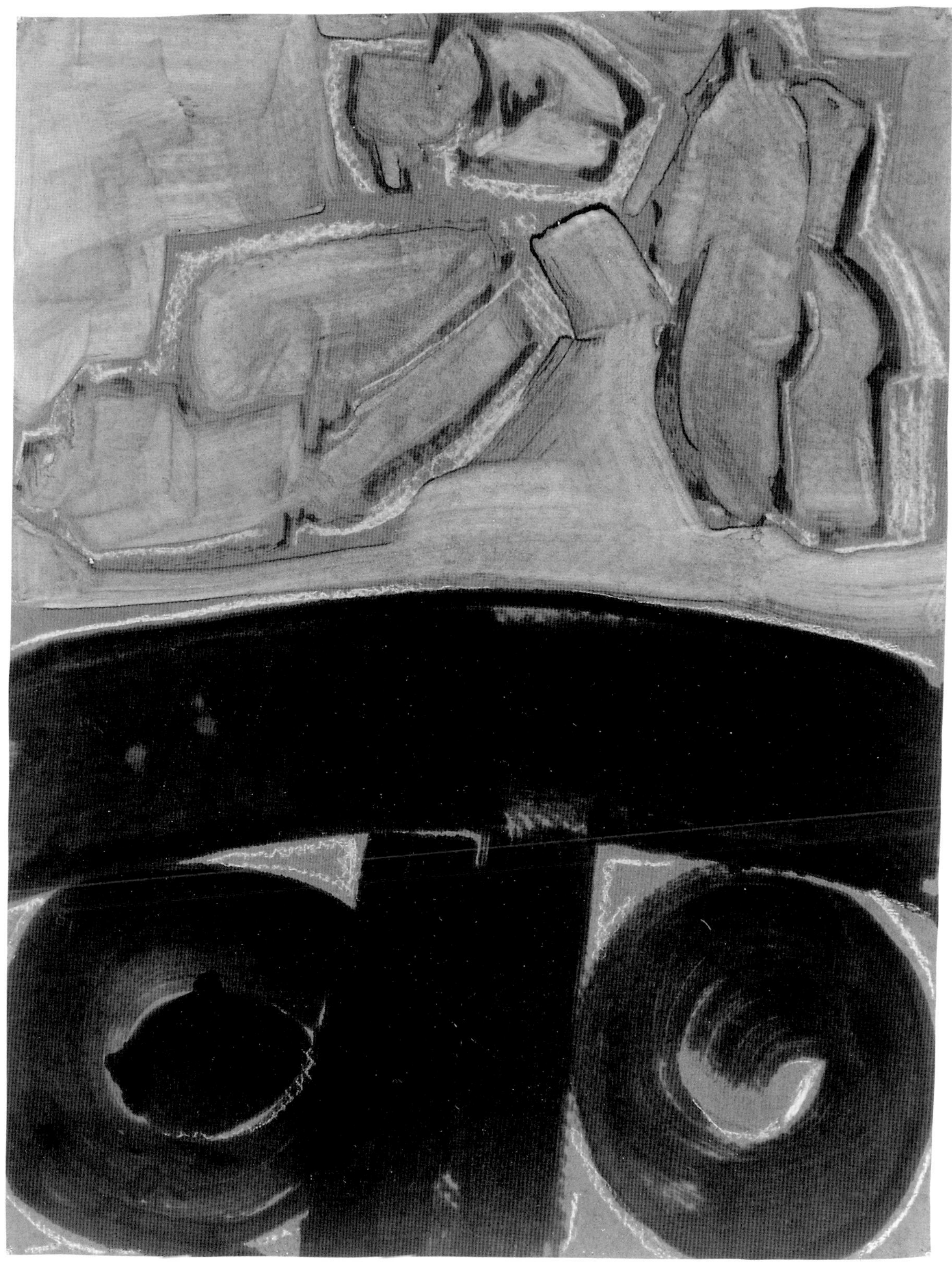

Guy Anderson **The Heavy Decision**
1986, Oil on paper, 60 x 46¼". Courtesy of the artist and Francine Seders Gallery. Photograph: Chris Eden.

Rick **Bartow**

Rick Bartow's pastel and graphite drawings, with their haunting images and electric colors, are a distinctive fusion of Native American motifs and mainstream aesthetics. Part Yurok, he draws deeply on images from Native American mythology as well as archetypal and personal symbols, encapsulating them in a maelstrom of colors and pulsating lines. The result is an art that is passionately personal yet broadly communicative through its range of affective associations, from psychological to cultural to spiritual to visually sensual. Bartow's own soul-searing struggles with personal problems, his search for cultural and individual identity, and his openly acknowledged need for human and spiritual bonds are the wellspring of a vision that is compelling in its directness and honesty.

Frequent subjects in the drawings are animals, especially birds, and humans who assume each other's personae. In some the human face is merely covered by an animal or bird mask; in others there is an amalgamation of attributes of both in a single figure. The 1991 monoprint, *Crazy Crow*, which depicts a crow's head on a male torso, typifies Bartow's concern with the transformational aspects of life and ultimately, death. Through the dynamic mix of freely expressionistic drawing and coloration, he conveys the range of emotions that are implicit in the process.

Bartow speaks freely of the transformations in his own life that propel his art. He was born in 1946 near Newport, Oregon, where he still lives. His father, who was the source of his Yurok heritage, died when he was five, a loss that fueled his adult search for roots within the Native American culture. The most significant factor in his personal as well as artistic development, however, was his service in the Vietnam War. He returned from Vietnam wounded, not physically but psychologically, and soon was enmeshed in divorce, depression, and alcoholism. In desperation he joined Alcoholics Anonymous and also, turned to drawing as a therapeutic outlet. Talented as a child, he had studied art at Western Oregon State College, graduating in 1969 just before being drafted and sent to Vietnam. The heavily black graphite drawings of this difficult, post-war period were a personal catalyst. Their evident honesty and powerful drawing style soon attracted the attention of artist friends and professionals who provided encouragement and support, enabling him, as he says, "to go public."

At the present time, with a new wife, a child, a discovery of spirituality in sweat lodge membership, and ever-expanding recognition, his drawings, while still representing mystical transitions, continue to evolve. Color has become crucial in large complex drawings such as *Wolf and Deer*. Layering, mixing, and actually mashing the pastel pigment into the paper, he creates an alluring surface that belies the ominous images. In fact, the potency of this — and of all Bartow's drawings — rests on a strikingly dramatic contradiction: content that combines life-affirming beauty with intimations of violence and death.

Although the pastel and graphite drawings are the core of Bartow's art, his paintings, prints, and most conspicuously, masks and sculptures flesh out a prolific body of work. Recent sculptures, in particular, have an animistic spirit comparable to that of African carvings. Using traditional crooked knives and adzes, he produces a rough shaping to pieces of weathered wood, then adds scraps of metal, feathers, corn husks, shells, or other found materials to create fetishistic apparitions of humans and animals. Like the two-dimensional work, these constructed figures are a combination of ethnic and modern assemblage traditions, reminiscent of Picasso's early experimentation in shamanistic artworks.

Since the 1970s when Rick Bartow began his personal catharsis through art, he has attained a remarkable level of creativity, culminating in 1994 with solo gallery shows in Portland, Seattle, Vancouver, Tokyo, and Frankfurt. The life transitions he once feared, he now welcomes as an unending source of creative discovery and growth.

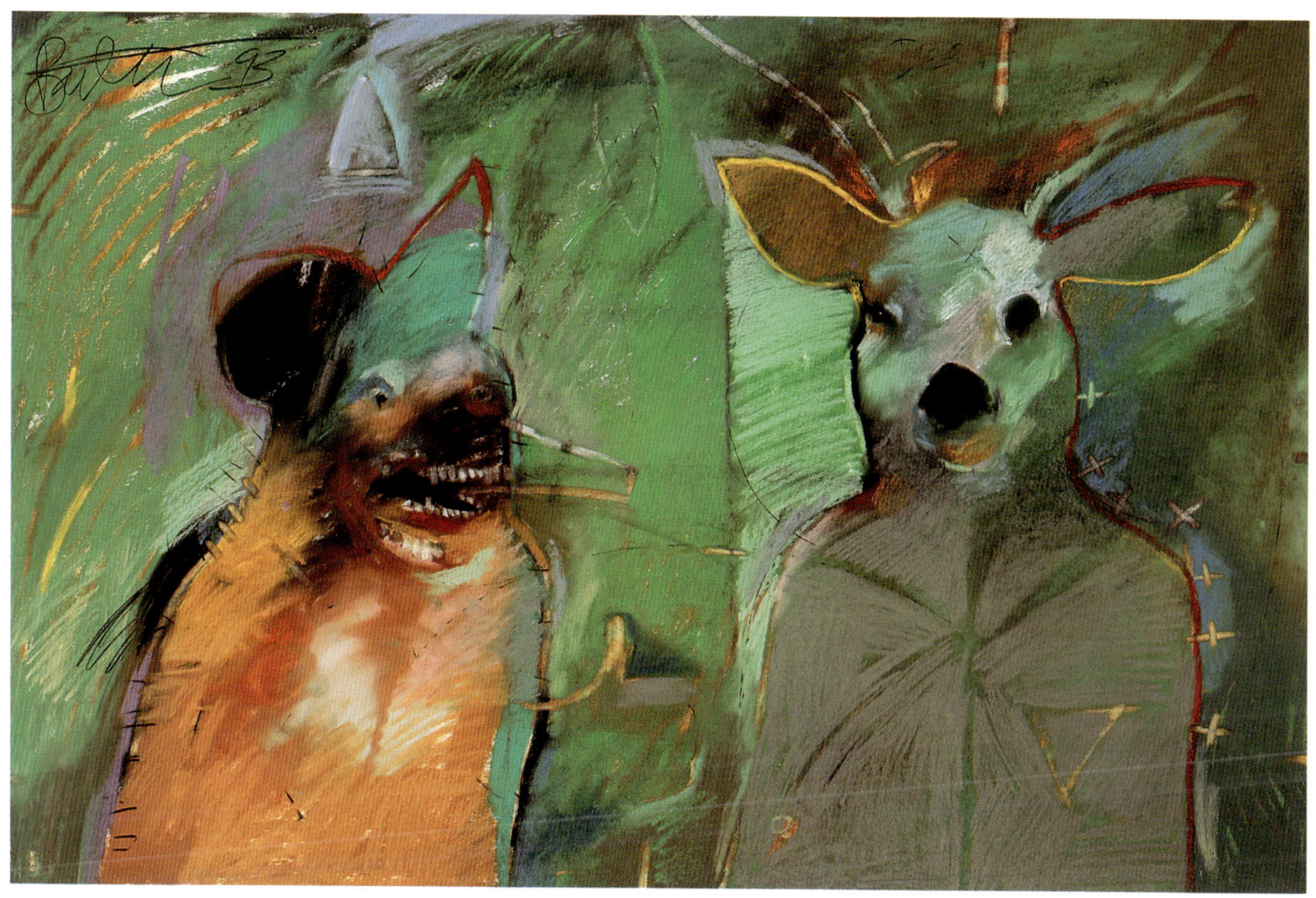

Rick Bartow **Wolf and Deer**
1993, Pastel, charcoal, graphite on paper, 26" x 40". Private collection. Courtesy of Jamison/Thomas Gallery. Photograph: Rebekah Johnson.

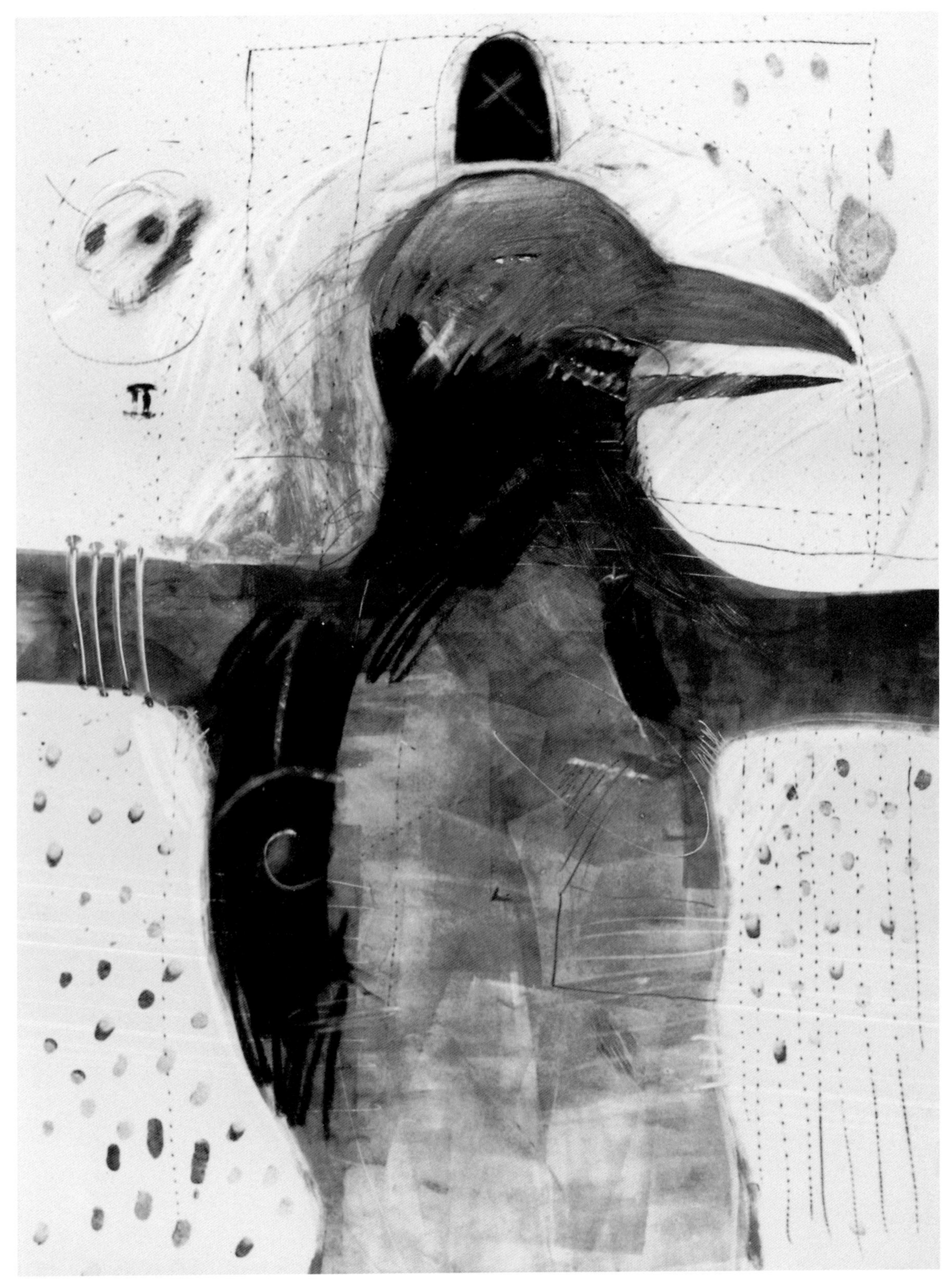

Rick Bartow **Crazy Crow**
1991, Monoprint/mixed media, 44" x 30". Private collection. Courtesy of Jamison/Thomas Gallery.

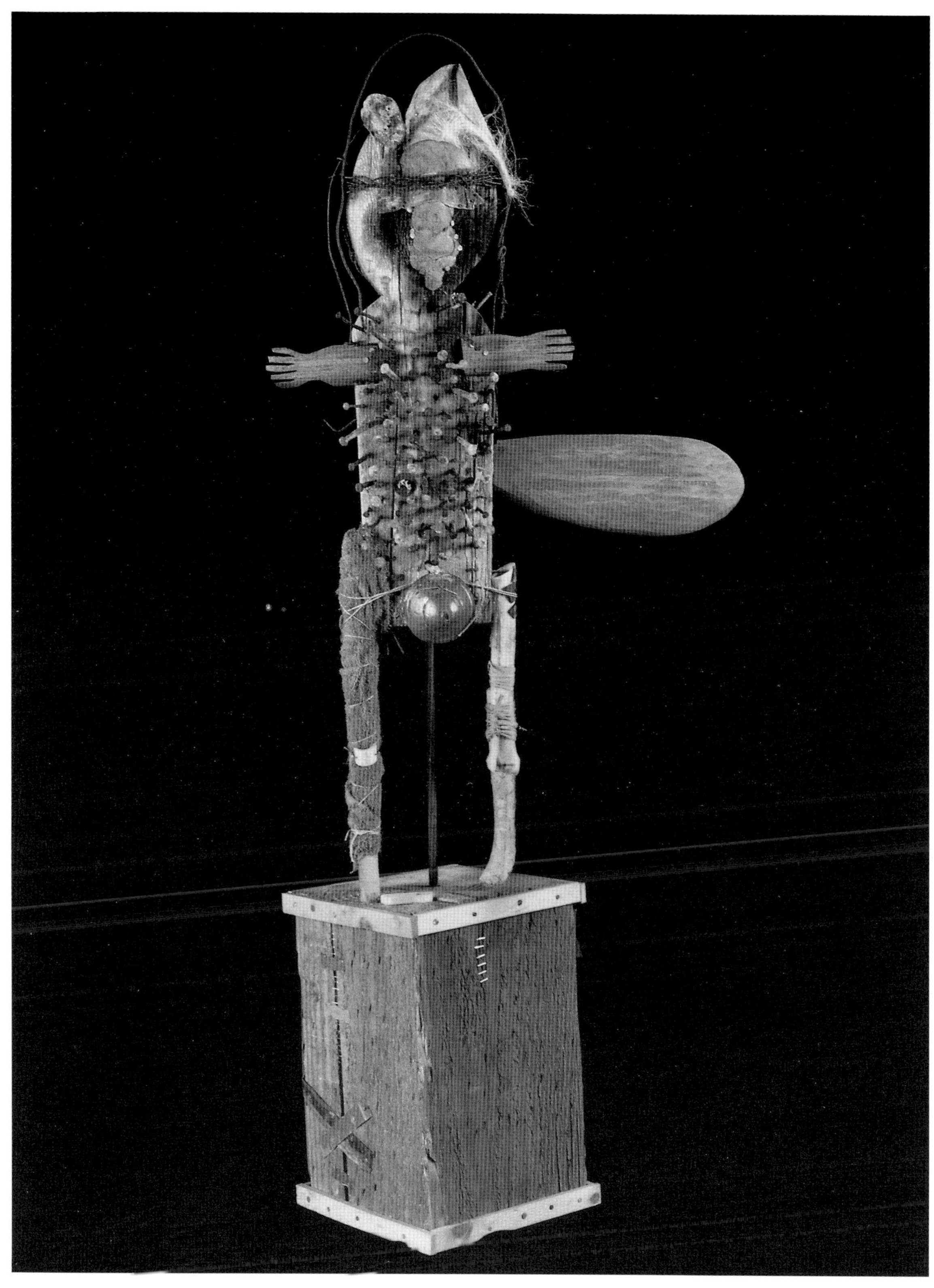

Rick Bartow **Prayer Figure**
1993, Mixed media, 43" x 18½" x 8¼". Private collection. Courtesy of Jamison/Thomas Gallery. Photograph: Rebekah Johnson.

Paul **Berger**

Paul Berger, whose first medium was photography, is one of the vanguard who are propelling digitized imagery from the status of a design tool to a genuine new artform. The applications of advanced computer technology — scanners, graphics software, color printers, digital cameras — are his "paintbox," the source of his richly layered montages that frequently confound usual modes of perception and interpretation. For all the work's opaque and technological references, however, Berger's underlying concern is the quintessential one of art: how to mediate experience through images. Rather than the experience itself, his focus is on the means of mediation, the hands, minds, and machines that devise the codes of transmittal and consequently, form their authority. His inquiry is not limited to pictorial images but encompasses the codes, including language, the symbols and systems, as well as their presentation in their capacity to generate illusions of direct experience. If his work seems uncommonly dense the reason lies as much in the electronic age of incessant information as it does in Berger's art. He utilizes the same electronic techniques in exposing the biases built into coded images.

Since the early 1970s, while still a graduate student at the Visual Studies Workshop in Rochester, New York, Berger has been interested in sequences, not as narratives *per se* but in the relationships of the photographs, or their reproductions, to each other and to any accompanying text. He asks, in other words, how does an articulated sequence trigger a body of meaning in viewers' minds?

It was this conceptual process that culminated in a work of seminal importance in 1981. First exhibited as a series of photographs, video stills, and computer print-outs, *Seattle Subtext* was reconfigured as a book using a graphic, columnar format similar to that of *Time* magazine. Under such headings as "Economy and Business," "Display," and "Nation," Berger delivers a stunning array of information so layered and intricately interconnected that "readers" are likely to be beguiled by the sheer glut of shifting images, cryptic text, and computer language that fills each page. The text and images, photographed from a video monitor and processed through the computer, are combined with the codes that produce them to call attention to the systems hidden within the presentation of information, and consequently, the human decisions that go into its selection, editing, and appearance.

While still working directly with the camera in the late 1970s Berger produced a series of memorable works titled *Mathematics*. Each black-and-white print depicts overlapping images of fragments of mathematical notations chalked on blackboards — swooping curves and arcs, circles and lines in graceful choreographies. Berger's interest lay in much more than their arresting beauty, however. The blackboard tracings, including erasures, of the specialized language of mathematics represent to him "the site of notation" where the trajectories of hand and mind intersect.

As computer technology advanced into color and digitized image capabilities, Berger exploited its applications as both tool and subject. Combining scanned video images with those generated wholly by computer software, he now produces electronic collages that achieve a sensuality of color and surface comparable to that of traditional printmaking techniques. Among the earlier color works, which are astonishing in their revelation of the medium's beauty, was a series titled *Cards* that was exhibited in a mid-career survey at the Seattle Art Museum in 1990. Grouped under an overarching theme, as in *Seattle Subtext*, the "deck of cards" implies a familiar thinking mode, but *Cards* simultaneously disrupts the convention of art as metaphor, replacing it with disjunctive visualization patterns characteristic of commercial television.

Paul Berger's primary interests, exemplified in *Cards* and continuing in *World Information Series*, are the new modes of information transmission and the authority they generate and perpetuate. In an interview with Rod Slemmons, the curator of Berger's 1990 exhibition at the Seattle Art Museum, Berger made a comment that best summarizes his aims: "I think that much of our common experience is fantastically complex and multi-faceted, but because it is so embedded in use value (we just want to know who won the game), we do not reflect on it. When we don't reflect on systems of presentation, we are vulnerable to great manipulation by others, or ourselves."[1]

1. *Paul Berger: The Machine in the Window*, catalog, p. 46.

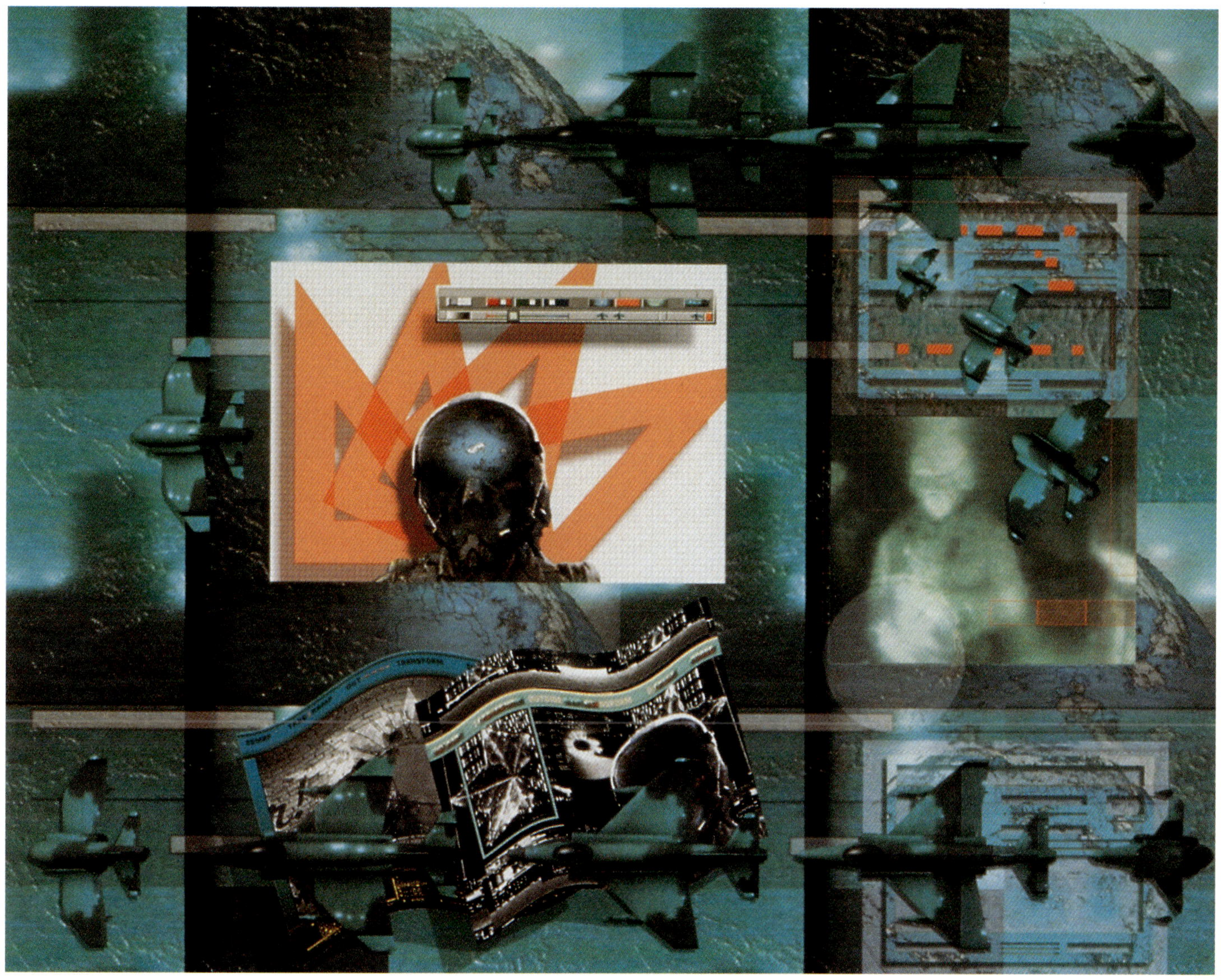

Paul Berger World Info Series **Face-02**
1993, Iris print, 22" x 30", Edition of 25. Courtesy of the artist and Fuel Gallery, Seattle.

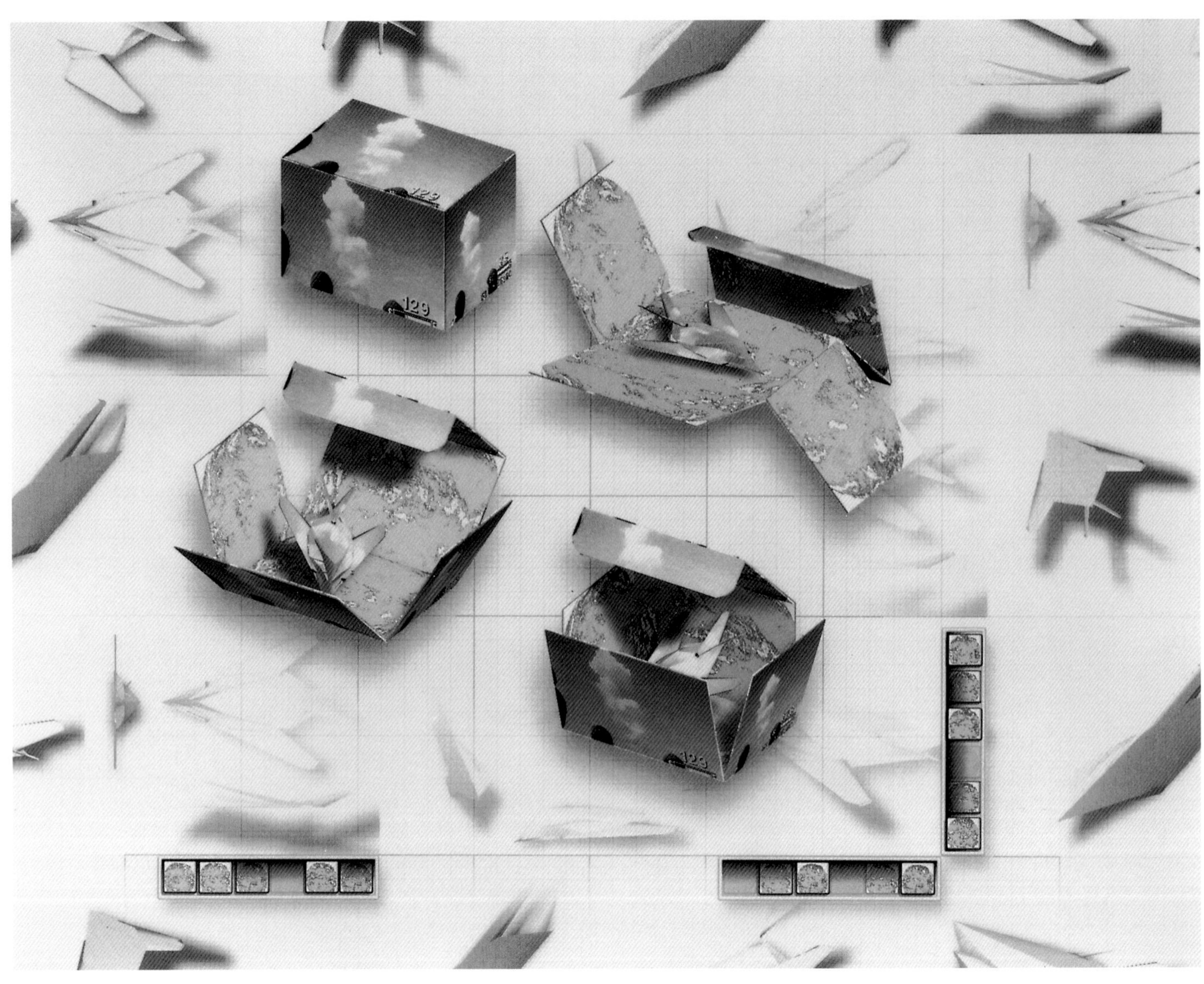

Paul Berger **Face-08**
1993, Iris inkjet print, 22" x 30", Edition of 25. Courtesy of the artist and Fuel Gallery, Seattle.

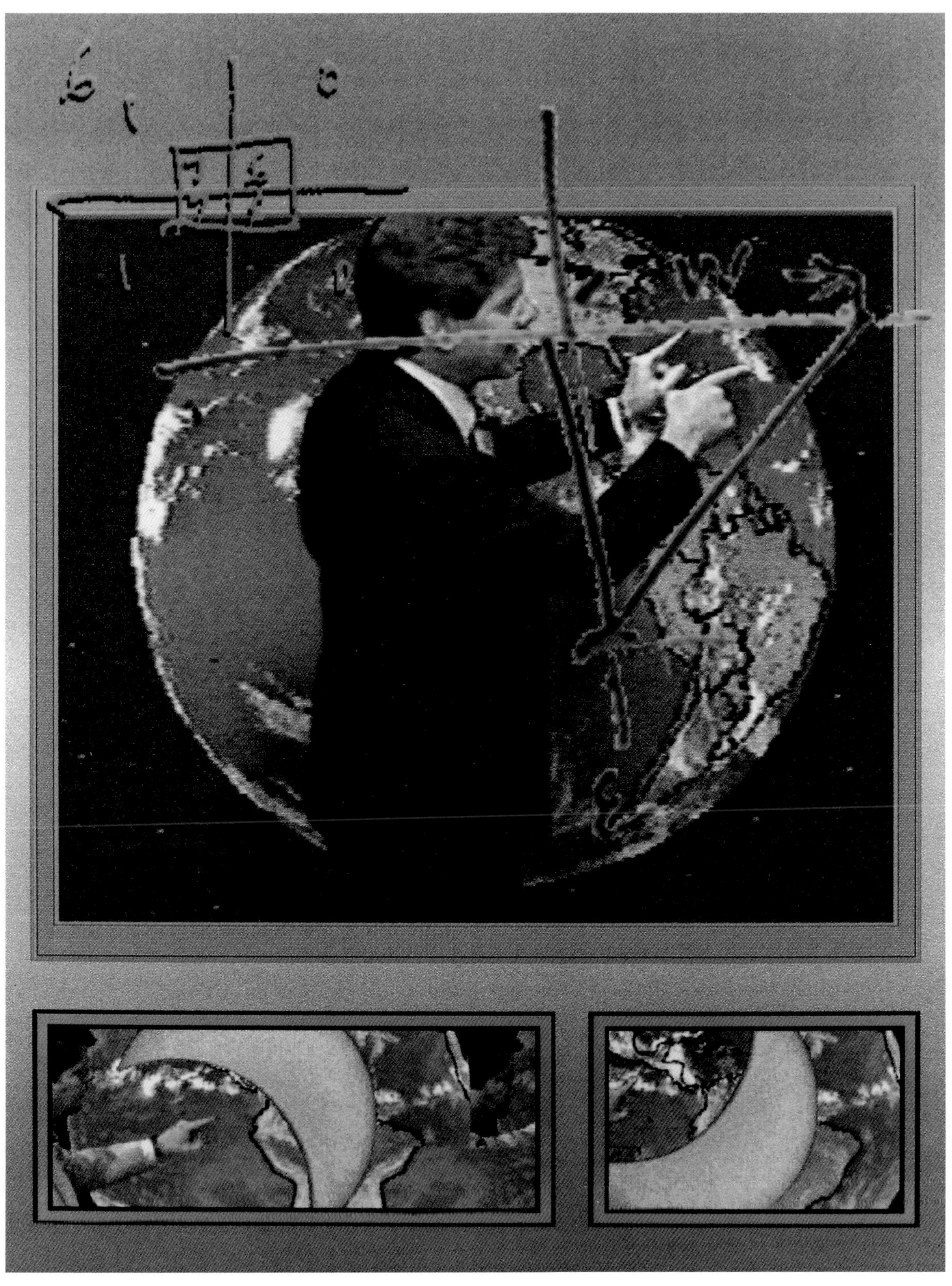

Paul Berger **World 2AA**
1989, Inkjet print, 30" x 24", Edition of 25. Courtesy of the artist and Fuel Gallery, Seattle.

Christine **Bourdette**

Christine Bourdette's sculptural "artifacts" — indeterminate vessels, vehicles, and humanoids — owe their existence not to some remote archeological site but to the originality of their creator. Elegant but quirky constructions carry associations almost pre-conscious in nature. Her "less-is-more" aesthetic and the importance she places on materials stem from Minimalism, which was the prevailing influence on artists of her generation. Philosophically, however, she belongs within a long humanist tradition that has ebbed and surged throughout the history of European and American art. Timeless issues at the heart of that tradition — mortality, transitions, pursuit of knowledge — are no less important to Bourdette than to *quattrocento* artists. In her work, however, nothing is explicit, much less didactic; significations are veiled in the histories of her materials, in the mystery of the interiors of the forms, and in their peculiar physicality.

A multi-dimensional installation of late 1993, *Capacity*, demonstrated Bourdette's primary concerns, both formal and conceptual. Created specifically for the architecturally unusual gallery at the Oregon School of Arts and Crafts, it played on several dualities: growth and degeneration, interior structure and surface appearance, movement and stasis. A perceptual duality stemming from the gallery's architecture underscored the work's content. Because visitors enter the gallery by descending a wide staircase leading directly into the exhibition area, their perspectives are in flux. Capitalizing on the moving viewpoint, Bourdette installed a "canopy" consisting of wire mesh squares hung from the ceiling, each with an egg (nature's prime example of the duality of interior and exterior) placed upon it. Seen from above, the white eggs were volumetric counterpoints to the geometry of the mesh grids, but from the level of the floor they were obscured from view and the canopy was then experienced in relationship to the forms below it. Several stark, talismanic structures, such as a rickety tripod holding a bowl of water, were spaced around the floor area, intimating a past human presence. Their placement and human-size scale contributed to an interactive relationship, both physical and mental, with visitors moving through the installation.

Along with a predilection for the anthropological, Bourdette has a strong interest in the formal and psychological effects of space and scale. Her desire to explore ideas relating to basic structure was the impetus that led her from painting, her major at Lewis and Clark College in Portland, to three dimensional constructions. In recent years she has included two-dimensional work in her output, creating drawings and prints that also are concerned with volume, space, and scale.

A group of rough-hewn, primitive figures called *Squatting Melissas*, exhibited in 1987, and the standing figure, *Calling Home*, of 1988, are precursors of Bourdette's visually austere works of the past few years. The three forms, *Punch*, *Tattler*, and *Comma*, 1992, though non-representational, lean toward each other as if in conversation, as the titles suggest. As volumetric as the earlier figures, their open structural elements expose the opposition of surfaces and interiors.

A similar contradiction pervades *Comparing Apples and Oranges*, a wood, wall-mounted object resembling a balance scale. It is one of a series based on tools, many of them measuring devices. Though spare and visually elegant, it, too, conveys a reference to human purpose. As a metaphoric scale it seems to weigh the "apples" of the object itself against the "oranges" of its associative imagery.

In 1994 a public art commission inspired a return to the human figure. Asked to produce an inviting outdoor visiting area at a county jail, Bourdette designed concrete benches with adjoining life-size topiary human figures as leafy companions for the benches' occupants. The topiaries, as they go through the seasonal changes, suggest the on-going changes in life with the passage of time. They also extend Bourdette's rigorous explorations of materials, form, and structure as they pertain to human experience.

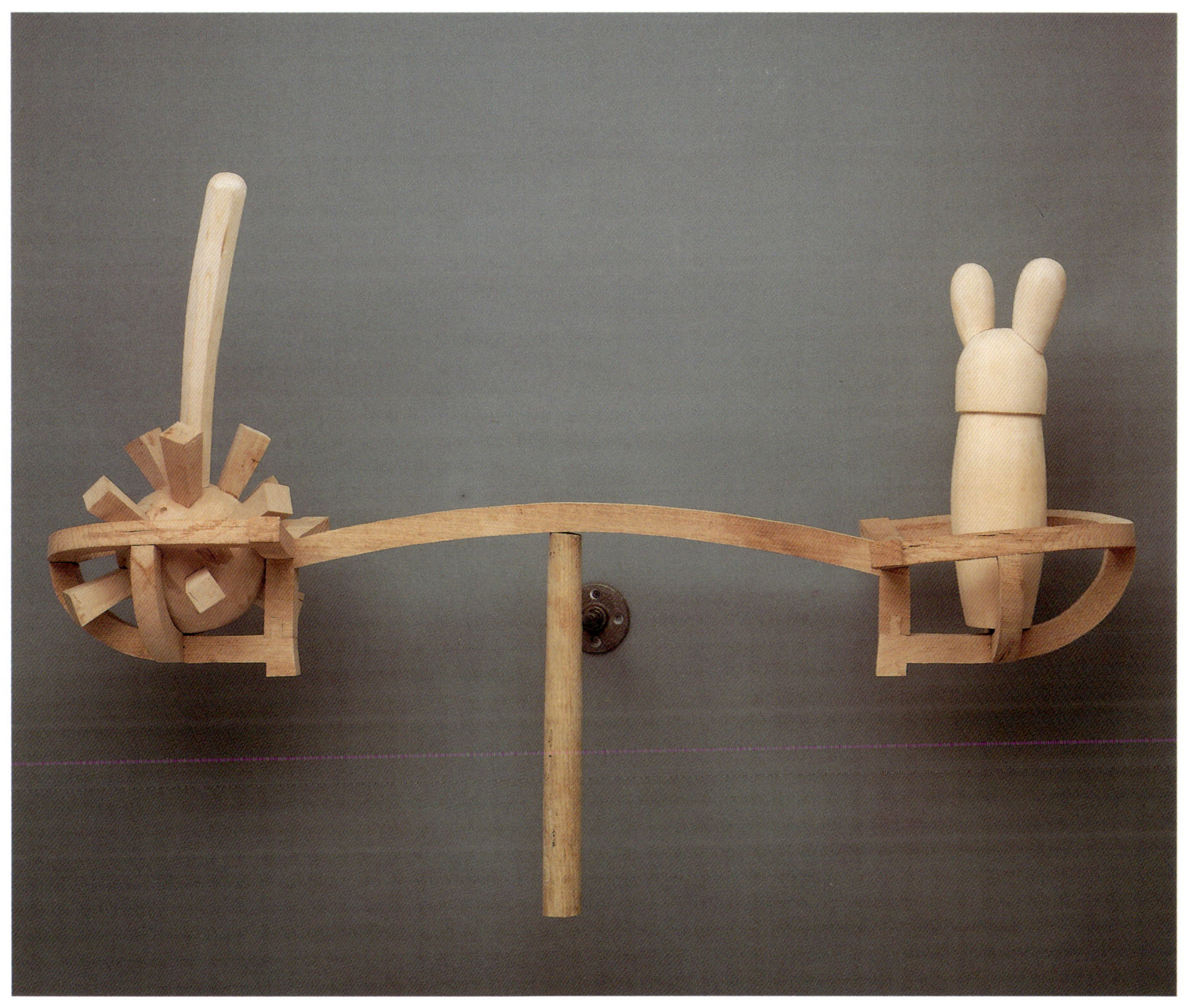

Christine Bourdette **Comparing Apples and Oranges**
1994, Wood, 28" x 42" x 14". Private collection. Courtesy of Jamison/Thomas Gallery. Photograph: Harold Wood.

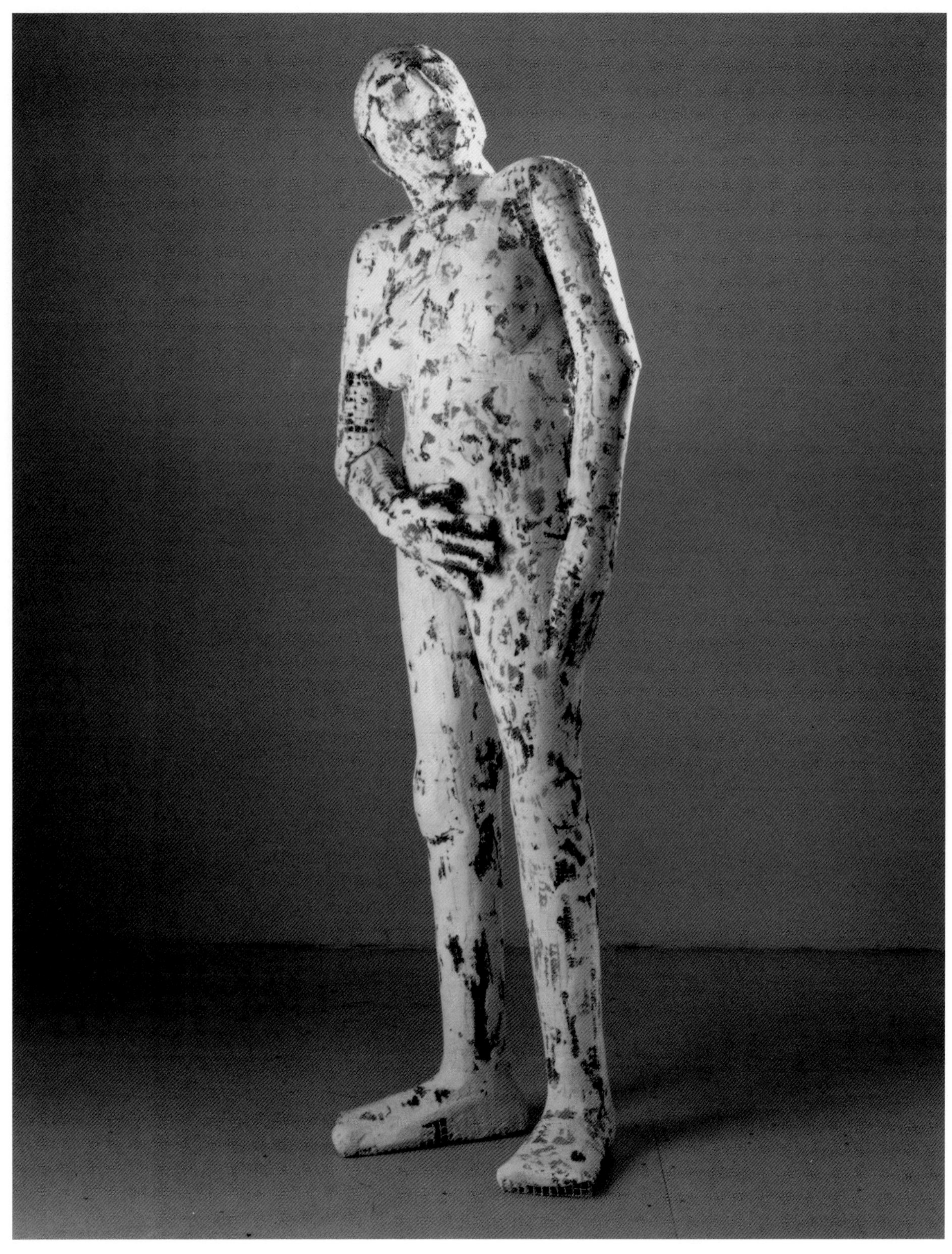

Christine Bourdette **Calling Home**
1988, Mixed media, 70" x 24" x 13". Private collection. Courtesy of Jamison/Thomas Gallery. Photograph: David Browne.

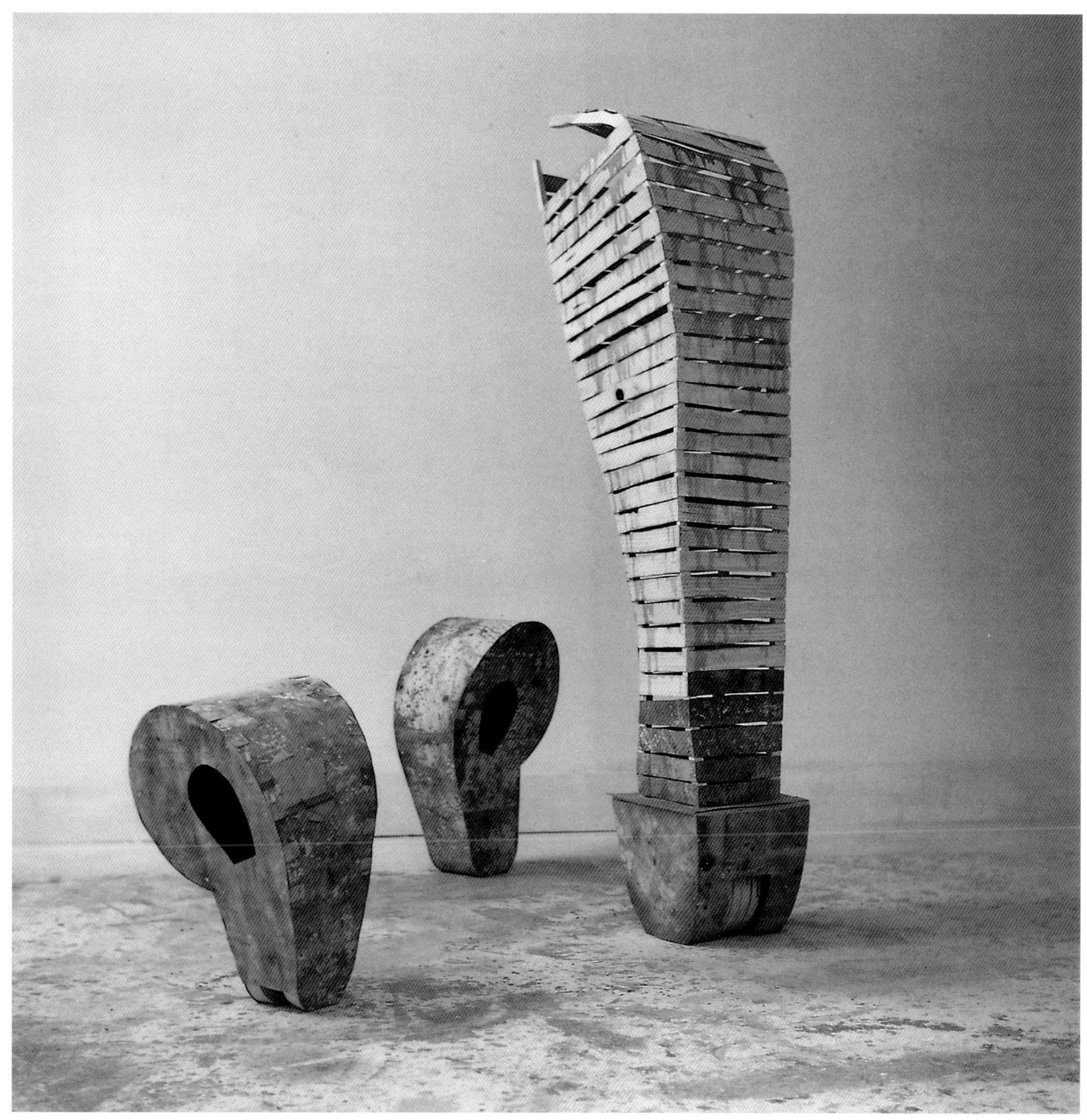

Christine Bourdette **Punch** 1992, 20" x 11" x 13", Found sheet metal. **Comma** 1992, 22" x 10" x 13", Found sheet metal. **Tattler** 1992, 62" x 18" x 22", Found sheet metal and wood. Private collection. Courtesy of Jamison/Thomas Gallery. Photograph: Christine Bourdette.

Michael **Brophy**

Michael Brophy's artistic terrain is a zone of conflict where the need for conservation of the wilderness collides head on with economic reality. Neither a politically inclined environmental activist, nor an apologist for the timber industry, and certainly not a nostalgic romanticist, Brophy might best be described as a fabulist. He paints forests and deserts as a theater of the absurd where humans seem to be searching for their roles in a scenario they do not understand. The same terrain in which Alfred Bierstadt saw the hand of God, Brophy sees, a century later, the hand of man, a hand that grips a chain saw, but also scatters flowers, or holds a paintbrush.

Obviously, it is not his aim to spell out a scenario. Instead, he creates quixotic *mise-en-scènes* in which viewers can play out their own scenarios *vis-à-vis* the land that sustains their psychic, as well as material well-being. Employing a drawing style and palette reminiscent of cartoons (a style acquired in copying comic strips as a child), he creates provocative but enigmatic settings: a logger approaching a tree, chain saw in hand though he gazes out at a clear-cut hillside in the distance; a man enveloped in flames rolling across a wide expanse of parched, cracked desert floor; a tiny artist perched in a tall fir tree drawing the stumps below; a man sitting on a grassy hilltop amid a column of flowers falling from the sky as he contemplates a slender stump.

If there is an autobiographical factor here, it is because Brophy is a native Oregonian at a time when the environmental and human cost of destroying natural resources is confronted daily. Born in 1960, he trained at the Pacific Northwest College of Art, and with the exception of a year-long residency at the Studio Arts Centers International in Florence, Italy, he is a lifelong resident of Portland. By choice as well as birth, he is a regional artist, one who roots his art in his own place and uses its exteriority to probe a personal interiority. Almost without exception the figures in his paintings are men. In hard hats and plaid shirts they are timber workers; in T-shirts and slacks they are observers, which is to say, artists. When he is asked, as he is frequently, if his work is politically motivated he answers, "This is what's out there. Look around."

Brophy's European experience of 1983–84, although lasting only a year, was deeply affecting, and continues to influence his work. From the early Italian painters he learned that graphically direct styles, what he calls "a hard look," can convey vulnerability without sentimentality. It was a Hans Beckmann exhibition in Germany, however, that forced him to think seriously about what he wanted his art to do. For several years afterward, while he was sorting out his ideas, the work was marked by Beckmannesque interlocking forms and colors compressed in shallow space. Now, having opened up his compositions spatially with well defined separations between figure and ground, he retains from the Beckmann influence a preference for graphic structure and, more important, for the ambiguities of open-ended, non-directed content.

Portentous content notwithstanding, Brophy occasionally permits his love of painting to take precedence, and indulges in lyrical forest scenes that celebrate nature and landscape painting. He delights in closely observed details — the bark of trees, the delicate mixed pastels of a summer sky — and in the forest's density, which he dramatizes by using shafts of light to pierce the dark foliage and to lead the eye through the composition. And yet, these lush paintings stop short of being total paeans to nature's beauty; invariably there is a sense of lurking disaster. It may be quite obvious, as in a fire beginning in the brush, or oblique in a single, sawed-off tree, or merely alluded to by the title, as in *Park*, in which a cathedral-like setting of trees becomes a human-designed facsimile of a forest. Much more typical of Brophy, however, is the ironic wit of *Swarm* in which a phalanx of self-guided chain saws, like a cloud of angry wasps, may descend at any moment on the verdant hills below.

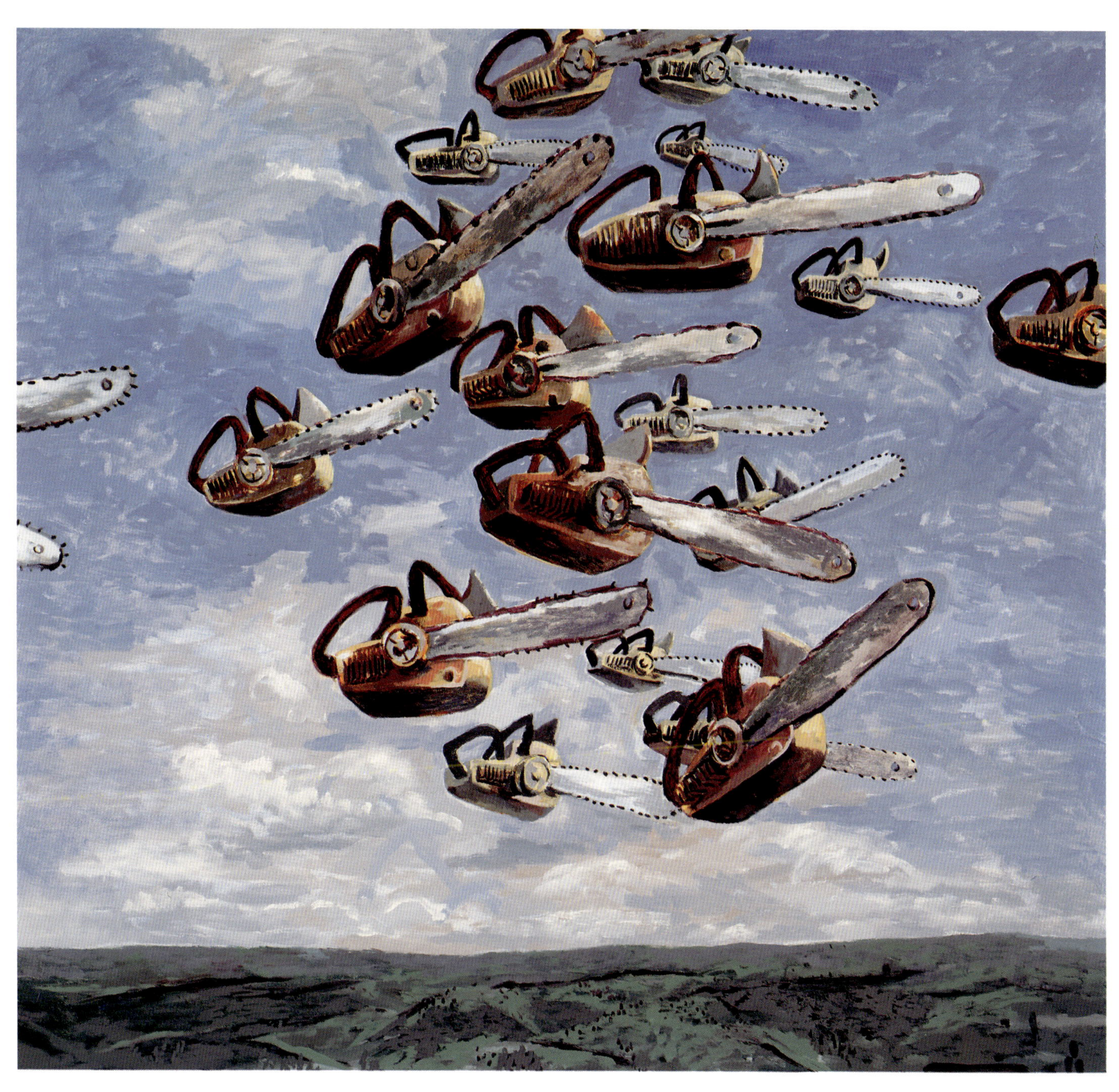

Michael Brophy **Swarm**

1994, Oil on canvas, 65" x 70". Collection of the artist, Courtesy of Laura Russo Gallery, Photograph, Bill Bachhuber.

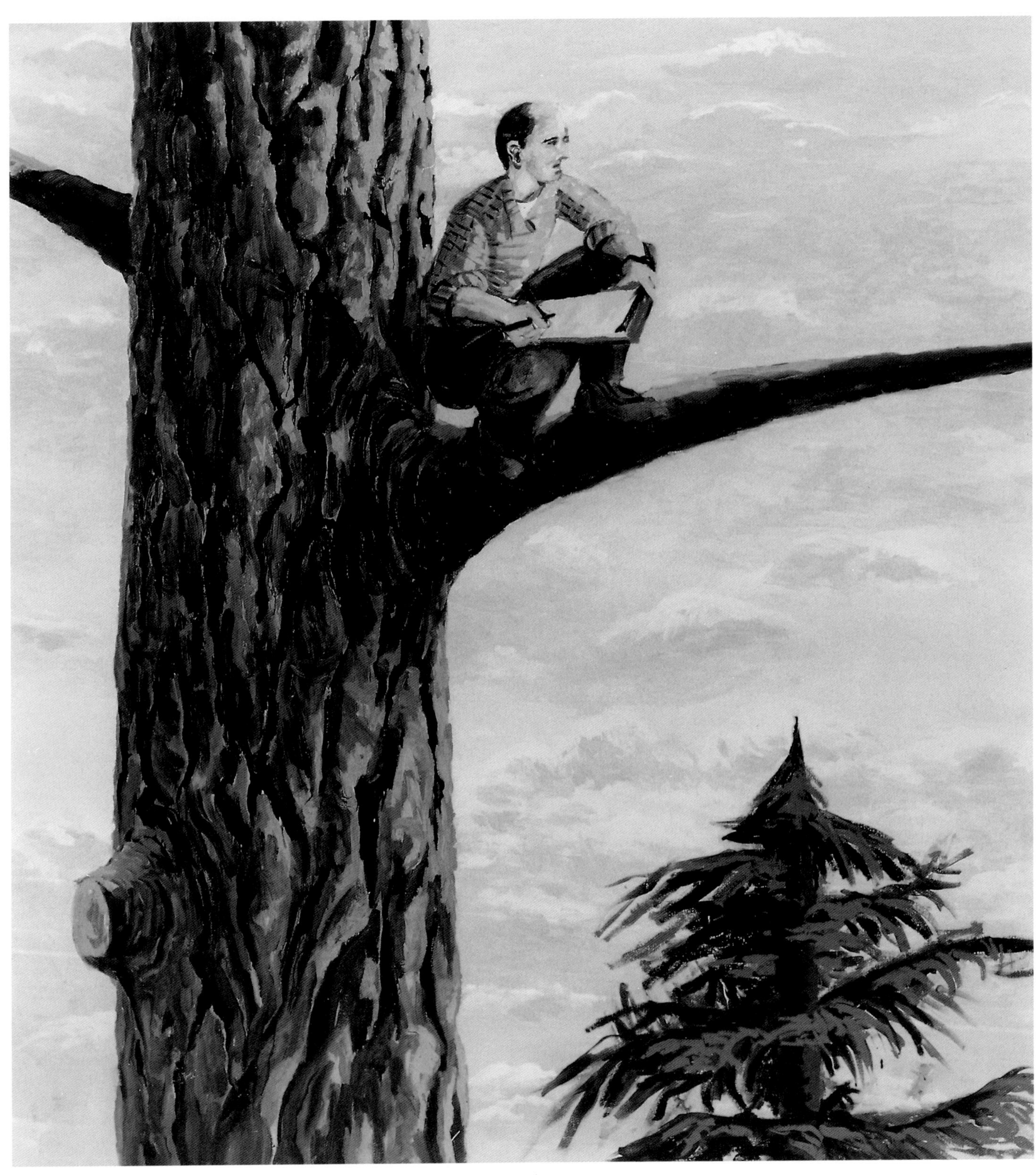

Michael Brophy **Perch**
1992, Oil on canvas, 70" x 65". Collection of the artist. Courtesy of Laura Russo Gallery. Photograph: David Browne.

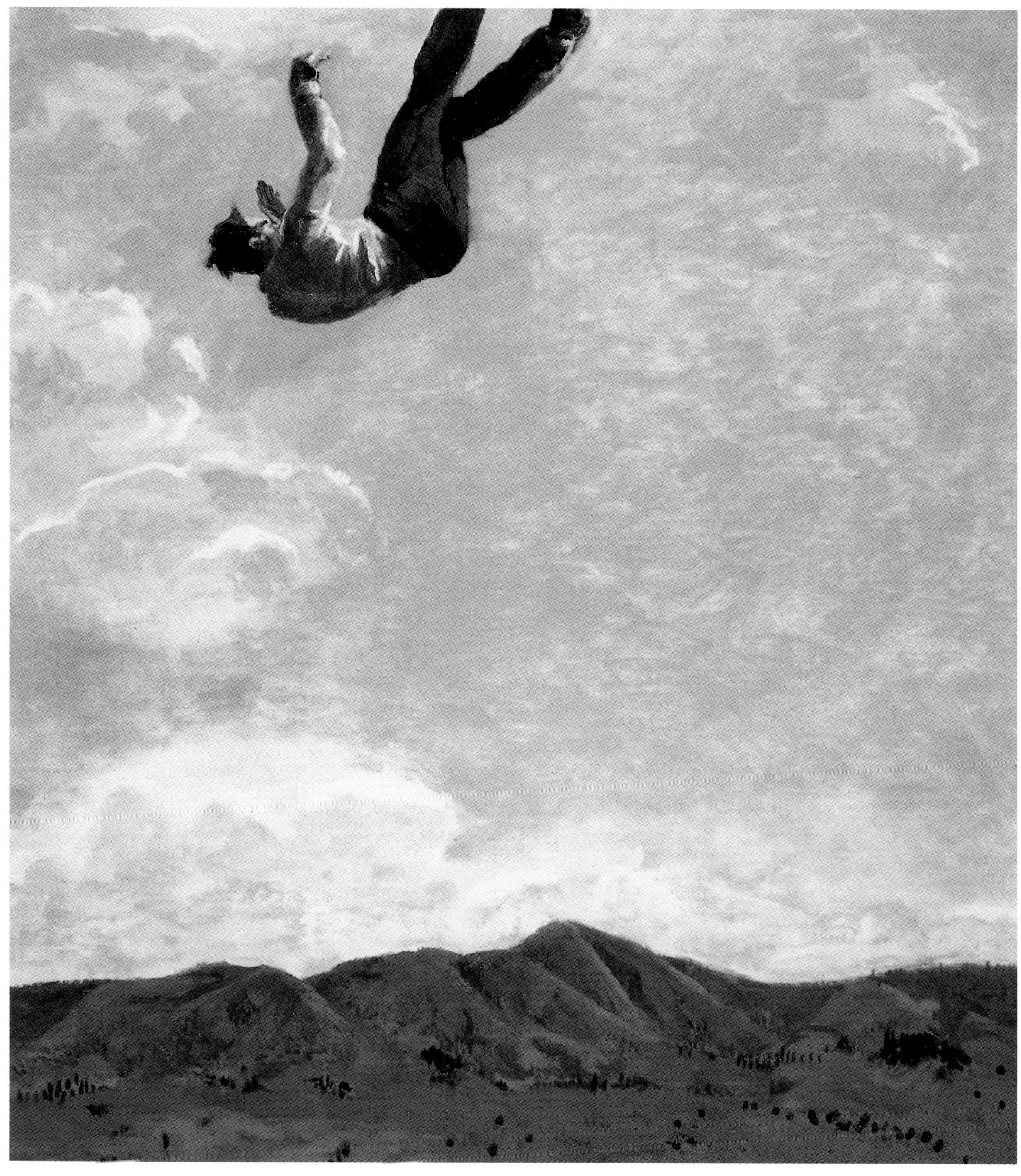

Michael Brophy **Fall**
1993, Oil on canvas, 60" x 54". Collection of Microsoft Corp., Redmond, Washington. Courtesy of Laura Russo Gallery. Photograph: David Browne.

Beliz **Brother**

Beliz Brother's art encompasses movement, sound, materials, and spatial architecture, all as structural elements in the realization of her ideas and projects. Her work is both performative and experiential, most often in the form of site-specific impermanent works, including highly innovative set and lighting designs. Ideas and subjects, though sometimes inspired by specific events such as the bombing of Sarajevo, are concerned, in their underlying essence, with the psychology of perception. How the perceptual process is influenced by the design of a given space, by the materials and lighting that define it, and by the time element as performers and viewers experience it are the subliminal factors that are central to her work. Outwardly, she is, by her own account, a teller of stories. Her stories, however, are both layered and open-ended, a rich mix of sensory and associative stimuli.

During the winter of 1990–91 and the increasing momentum of the Gulf War, Brother was in the process of creating an installation at Seattle's Center on Contemporary Art. Intended as a reflection on mortality and transformation, the war brought an aura of a requiem to the project. Titled *Count*, its thematic focus was on death that is imposed impersonally and randomly, as in war. As the only light in the gallery came from rows of low hanging blue lights, the atmosphere was eerily muted. The lights, electronically activated to sway slightly, formed blue pools on the floor that seemed to deepen the space, thus impeding passage, both physically and psychologically. The installation's crypt-like elements came to a climax in the placement of a simple white wall and seat constructed of stacked, eroded salt blocks opposite a metallic, fluttering expanse of 40,000 suspended tags for military body bags. Every ten minutes the entire wall of tags moved, causing the tags to knock against the aluminum wall emulating the sound of marching boots. Each tag had been dipped in shoe dye and shellac, adding the odor of polished boots to the already heightened sensory and emotional associations.

A specific incident prompted *Adagio 22* of 1992, which was a very direct, public, and stirring response to the tragedy of the Bosnian war. It was based on a newspaper account of the deaths in Sarajevo of twenty-two people, victims of a bomb as they stood in line at a bakery waiting to buy bread. After the bombing a Sarajevan cellist, Vedran Smailovic, played Tomaso Albinoni's elegaic *Adagio in G Minor* at the bakery site every day for twenty-two days. In Seattle Brother commemorated his action as well as the victims' deaths by enlisting the collaboration of twenty-two cellists, one of whom performed the *Adagio* each day in a public place. She obtained the use of a corner window in a downtown record store and installed in it a wall of stacked, well used bread pans. Some contained loaves of bread, some were empty, and some spilled out white powder, partially covering an empty cello case. On the last day of the performances all twenty-two cellists gathered to play the *Adagio* in an empty lot adjacent to the installation. As a result of the work's impact in Seattle, it received international attention and was performed in Washington, D.C., during the inaugural events that ushered in the Clinton administration.

Not all Brother's projects are so somber. When she was commissioned to create the visual elements for Seattle's performance series, Summer Nights on the Pier, she adopted a thematic reference to the long defunct Luna Park that had once provided entertainment for West Seattle. During the run of the series, visitors approach the pier through *Lunasphere*, a brightly lit, circular wood construction, a lighthearted reference to the architecture of an amusement park. In sculptural terms the construction defines space not by mass but by line and light, providing multiple sight lines from both outside and inside.

Brother's large scale, collaborative projects include lighting designs for dance in which light and choreography are so integrated that light and dancers perform and interact as partners. Recently, she has taken on a very large scale collaborative project of approximately three years duration. A fellowship awarded by the Lila Wallace-Reader's Digest International Artists Program in 1993 led to a six months residence in Indonesia. Travelling among the islands, she studied and participated in ceremonies and traditions pertaining to indigenous architecture and agricultural practices. The second part of the project, in Seattle, consists of working with Seattle's Southeast Asian community to create gardens that will incorporate sculptural and architectural elements. The purpose is threefold: to enhance community identity, to provide food that is culturally familiar, and to link people, nature, and cultural tradition in an experiential artwork.

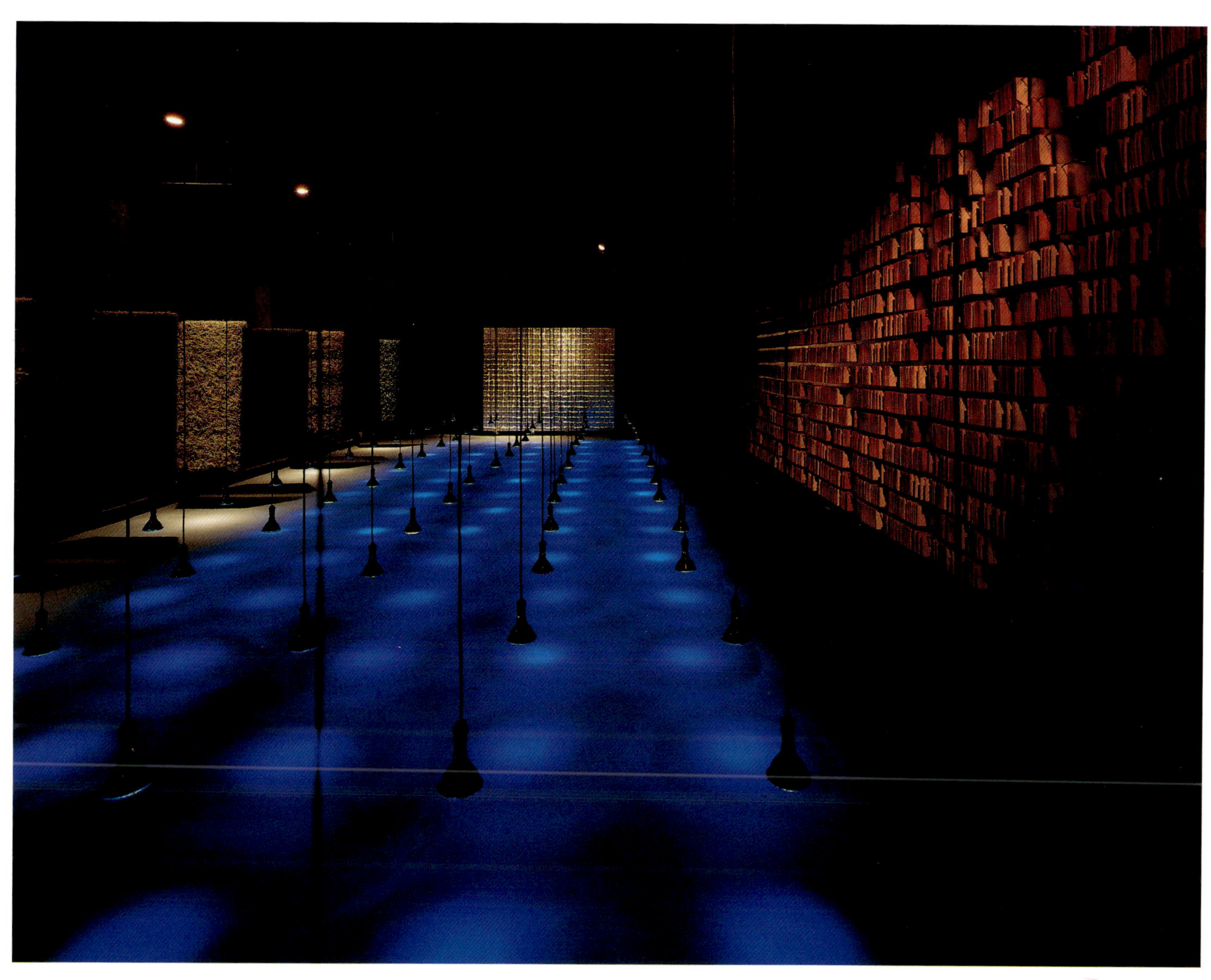

Beliz Brother **Count**
1990–91, Installation, Seattle Center on Contemporary Art. Courtesy of the artist and Fuel Gallery. Photograph: John Staments.

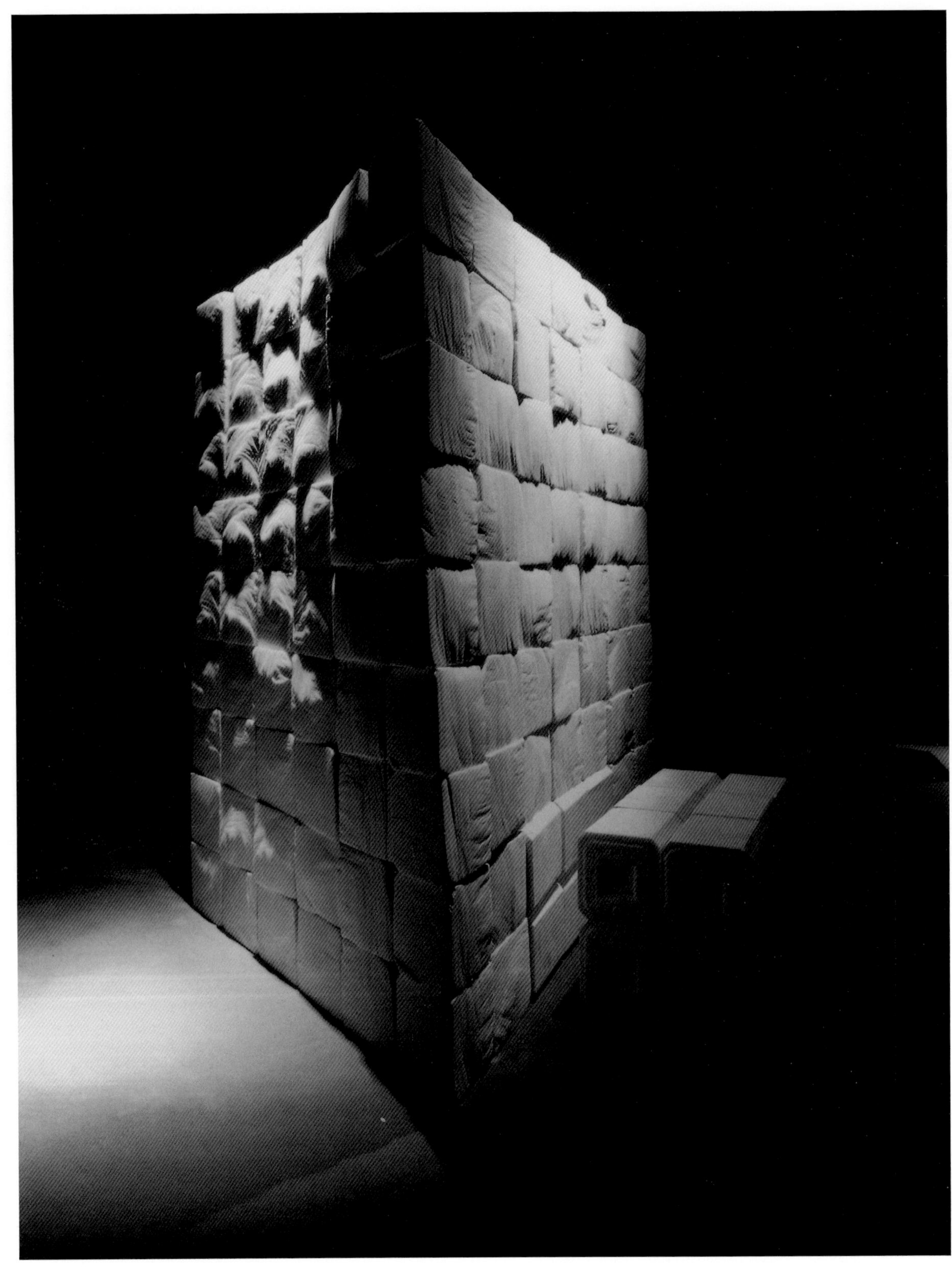

Beliz Brother **'Salt Block Wall'** from **Count**
1990–91, Installation, Seattle Center on Contemporary Art. Courtesy of the artist and Fuel Gallery. Photograph: John Staments.

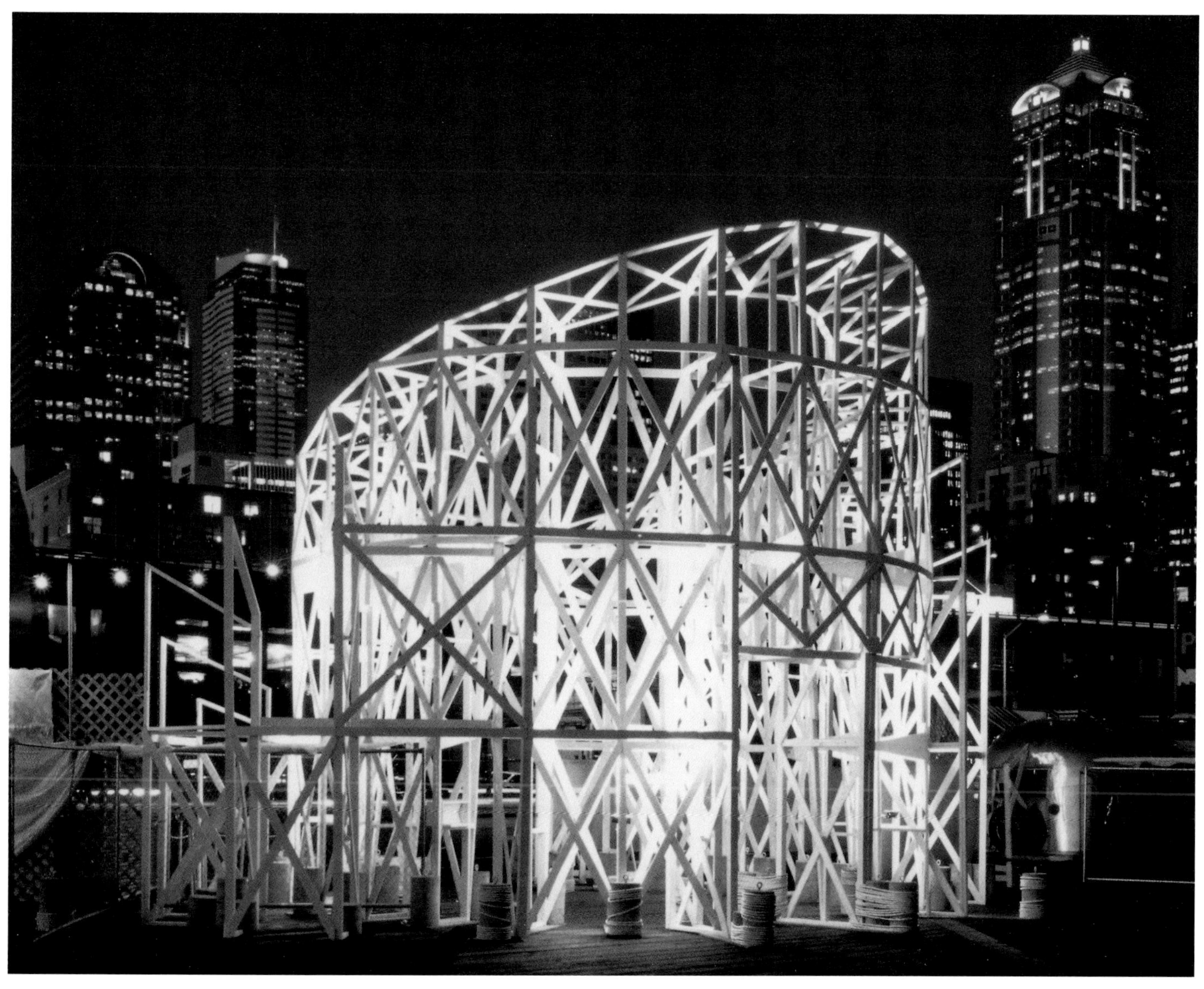

Beliz Brother **Lunasphere**
1991, Wood, 30' diameter x 20' height. Courtesy of the artist and Fuel Gallery. Photograph: John Staments.

Cris **Bruch**

Cris Bruch's art is like life itself — a mix of humor, anger, sorrow, routine work, creative play, and unanswered questions. Each project is inspired by a personal situation or question and is realized in a form appropriate to the concept, including street performance, installations, sculpture, drawings, and public works. His acute sensitivity to social inequalities, which he sees daily in the neighborhood at his studio doorstep in Seattle's Pioneer Square district, results in artworks and actions that bring him directly in contact with the homeless and derelict habituées of the district. He has gardened and cooked on the streets; spent many hours making rubbings from street textures; he has gathered and cleaned discarded liquor bottles, and with all these activities conversations with passersby frame the work's content. His studio work is less socio-political, more inner directed and concerned with artmaking as a process for self discovery.

Bruch moved to Seattle from Madison, Wisconsin, in 1986 and brought with him early versions of the "shopping cart" series, which he had produced during his M.F.A. residency at the University of Wisconsin. Continuing the series upon his arrival, he attracted immediate attention, both in the neighborhood and in the art press with *Roller Roaster,* which appeared on the streets around Pioneer Square in 1986 looking very much like a homeless person's cart. Encumbered with dozens of pans and cooking utensils, its primary feature is a grill on which Bruch roasted onions for trade and as gifts to neighborhood denizens as part of his "Vegetable Currency Project." *Home ala Cart,* a personal pop-up camper for the "dwelling impaired," complete with two lawn chairs, a grill, and port-a-potty, came with a wryly satirical instruction booklet that listed free materials, tips for prospective users, and also described the camper's advantages: "the economy minded homeless will appreciate the cost cutting aspect of the personal pop-up as much as its comfort and efficiency."

Bruch took over an abandoned, closed-off overpass for *Crusade,* his contribution to the city-wide public art projects produced for "In Public: Seattle 1991." The overpass, which once provided access to a factory on the waterfront, now stops in mid-air with access to it blocked by a fence. Bruch's project began with an "interactive performance" as he worked his way through officialdom to obtain a city permit which was necessary to allow the artwork to be placed on the truncated bridge and to provide pedestrian access. Next, he installed a mirror across its open end in order to compel visitors to observe themselves and the route by which they came rather than the impressive view of water and distant mountains beyond the mirror wall. The bridge could be entered only by squeezing through a narrow gate, walking across a field of scattered clothes, then passing two towers of more discarded clothing. Playing on the theory that the external enemy required by ideological crusaders is in truth a projection of their own fears and inadequacies, the work acted as a metaphor for shedding encumbrances, both material and psychic, in the pursuit of psychological wholeness.

While searching for a metaphoric representation of the tension between the poles of freedom and confinement, or of liberty and restraint, Bruch began working with enameled steel banding, bending, coiling, and fastening it into airy sculptural forms that embrace volume without creating mass. Ultimately, he produced an array of connected spheres, globes, and towers that, when exhibited as an installation, took over the gallery space like a living, undefinable organism ready to spring on the unwary visitor. *Don't Feed It* was the work's apt title. The banding's resemblance to line drawings in space was reinforced by the web of shadows the sculptures cast on the floor and walls. Also, by maximizing the sense of entrapment, the shadows contributed to a powerfully visceral experience.

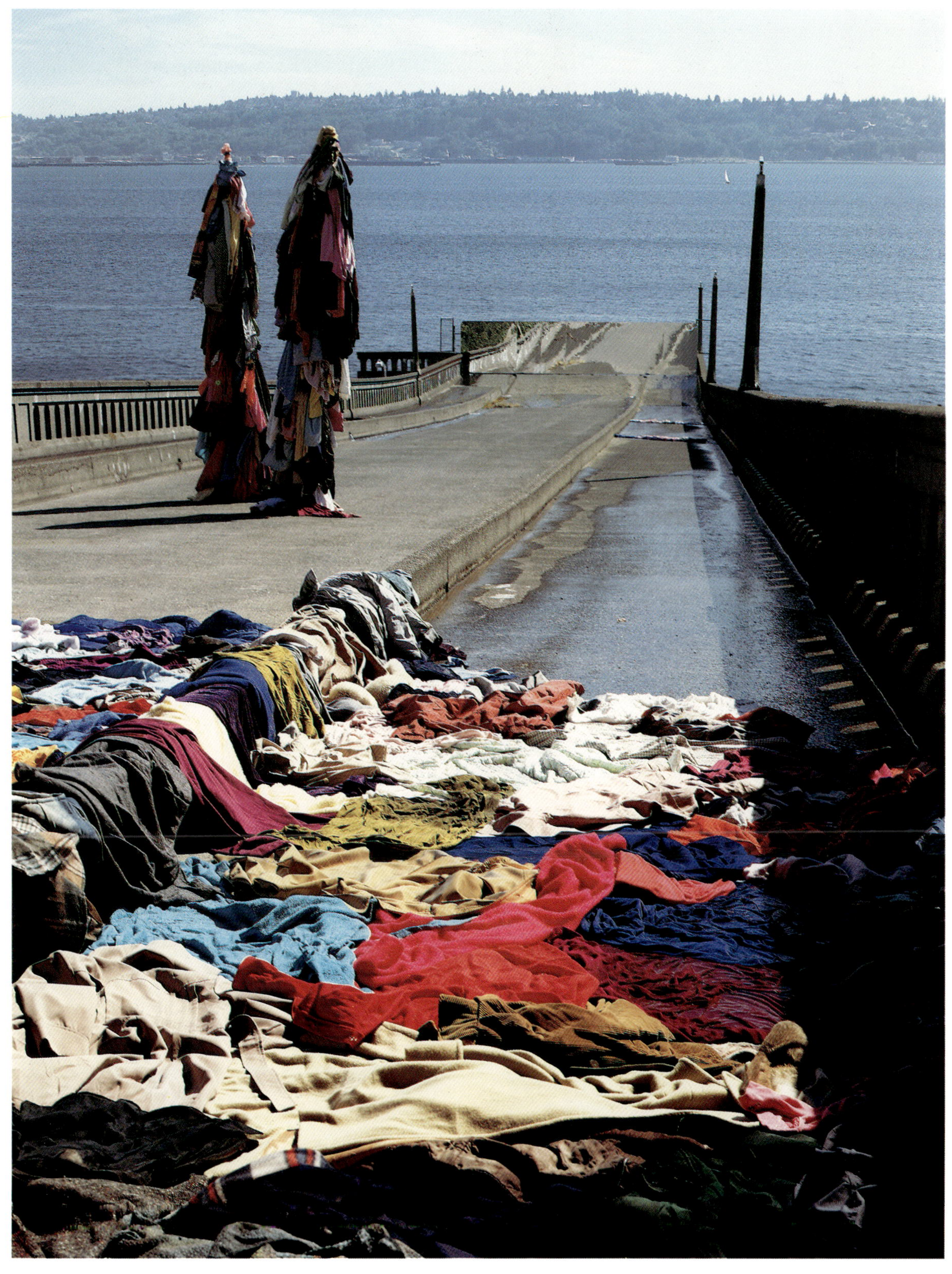

Cris Bruch **Crusade**
1991, Temporary public installation at abandoned bridge, Seattle, WA. Courtesy of the artist and Fuel Gallery. Photograph: Ken Wagner.

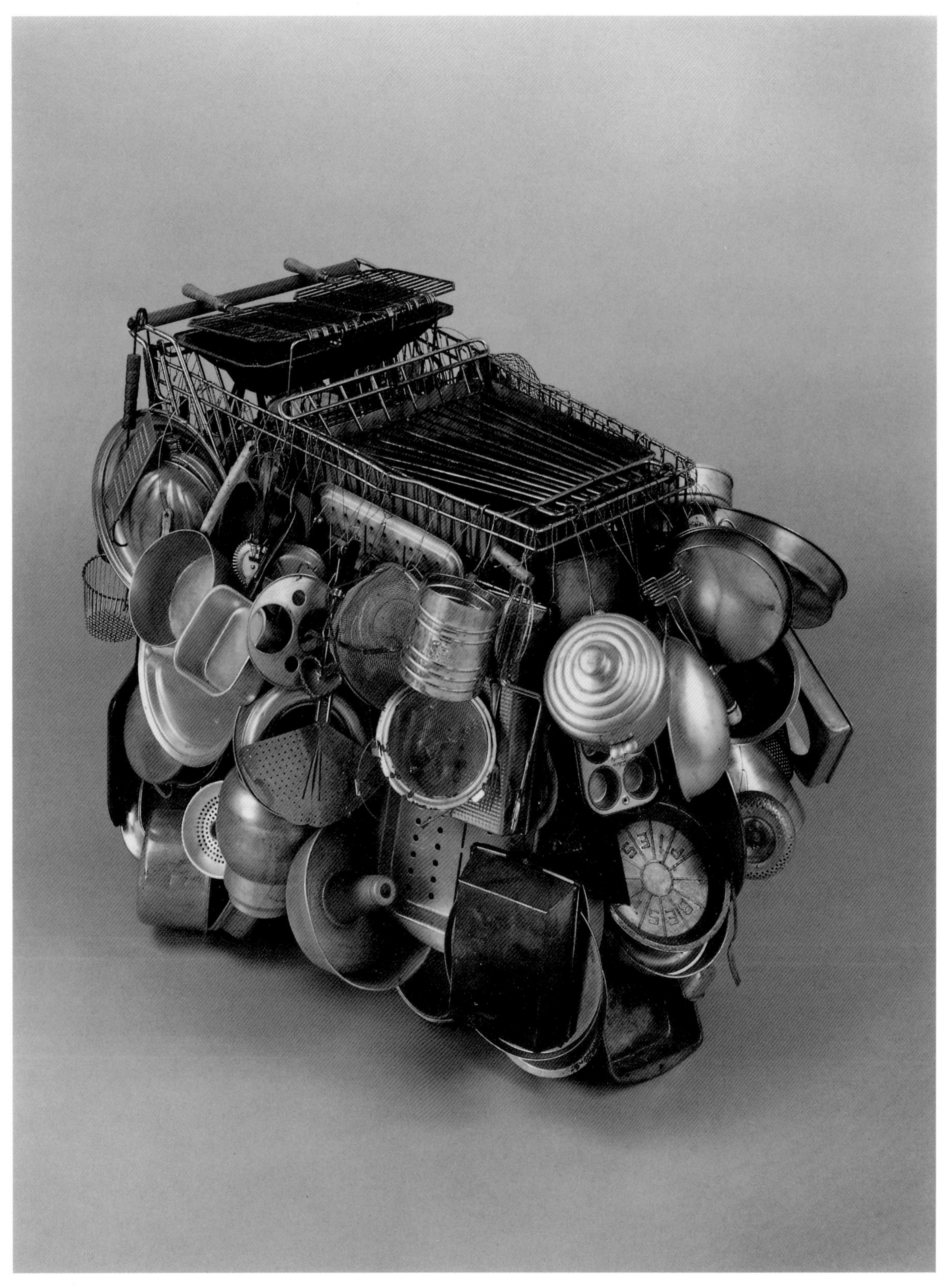

Cris Bruch **Roller Roaster**
1987, Modified shopping cart, 39" x 60" x 36". Courtesy of the artist and Fuel Gallery. Photograph: Alan Abrams.

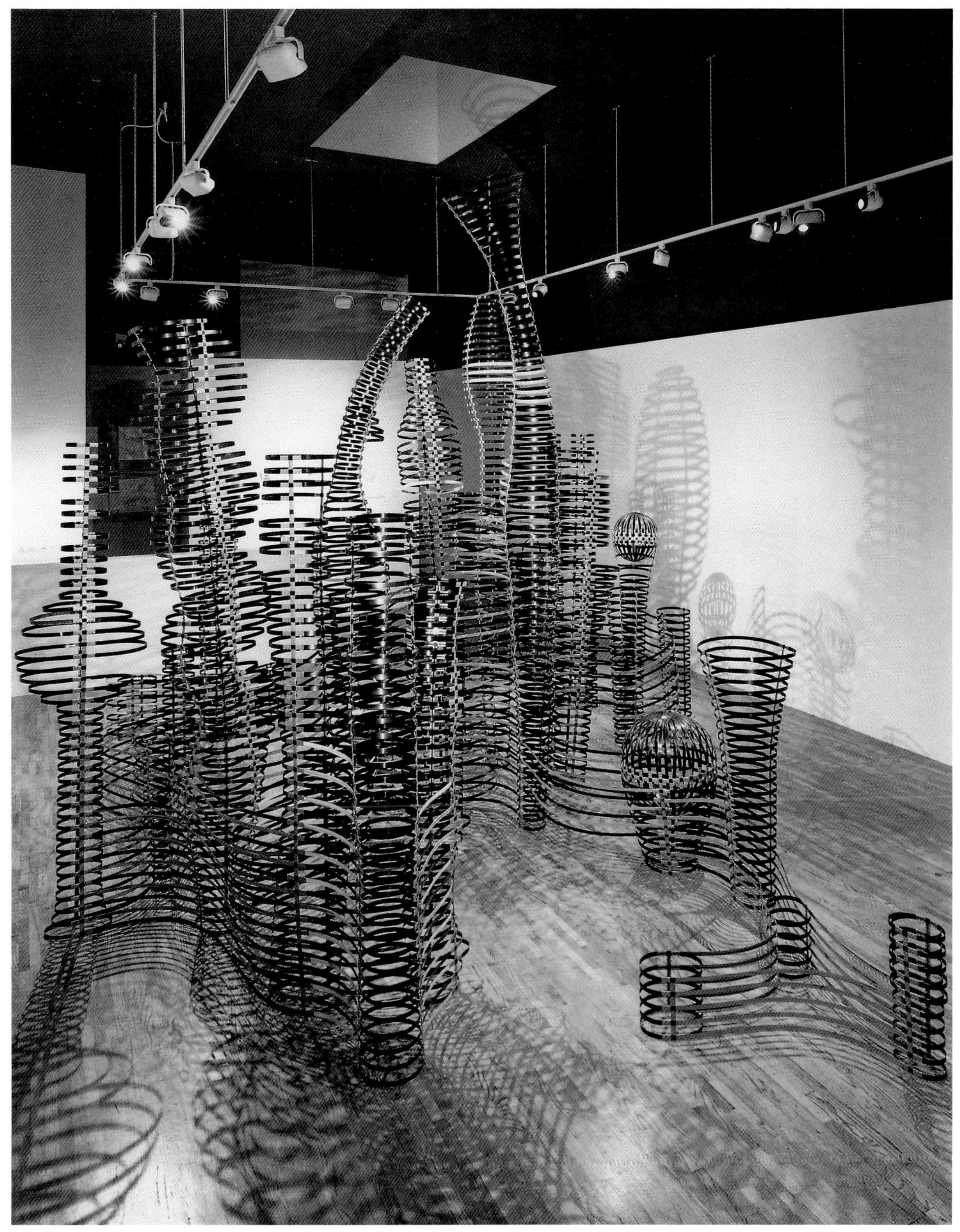

Cris Bruch **Don't Feed It**
1993, Steel, enamel, 11'6" x 12' x 18'. Courtesy of the artist and Fuel Gallery. Photograph: Spike Mafford.

George **Chacona**

George Chacona's richly montaged works focus on the two primal life forces, sex and death, through impious references to the belief systems, in particular religion and science, that encumber them with moralistic and analytical gravity. Through a process of transferring altered photographs onto a material that is thematically related, he creates a mix of references; in one series, ghostly images, bleached colors, and cryptic texts float on slabs of marble; in another, enlarged details of televised images fuse — and confuse — the characteristics of the medium in their effects on the impact of an actual event.

Chacona's preoccupation with themes relating to death began in the 1960s with paintings of Chopin on his deathbed. While he has continued to focus at times on specific individuals whose deaths hold political reverberations (Lee Harvey Oswald, Che Guevara, and Rudolph Hess), he draws deeply on anonymous deaths in antiquity, placing their funereal associations in present-day contexts. Modern industrial techniques applied to a material that has certain cultural associations, like marble, contribute to a fusion of shifting allusions. Contemporary techniques and materials, including audio tape, were used in the series *Detained*, which deals with Lee Harvey Oswald's televised moment of death. Enlarged video and reverse-process photography in repeated close-up images of Oswald's face as the bullets hit him underscore the gulf between the actuality of sudden death and that death as a spectacle created by television.

Chacona's long series of works on marble slabs began with visits to the Capuchin catacombs in Palermo, Sicily, and Pompeii. Mummified bodies in the catacombs and models of Mt. Vesuvius victims cast from cavities in the solidified ash were photographed and later, in his Seattle studio, transformed into halftone silk-screens, then transferred onto irregular shaped slabs by a photo-etching process. Pigment rubbed into the pits and depressions caused by the marble's reaction to acid further removed the overlapping images from a literal photographic reading. Nonetheless, the photographic implication of veracity accentuates the unsettling impact Chacona wrings from the attraction-repulsion syndrome concerning all manner of departures from this life.

Subjects taken from more recent horrific happenings — a caged rabies victim, an Armenian elementary school wall bearing pictures of students and lying in ruins after the devastating 1988 earthquake — have in common with the victims of Mt. Vesuvius a fate that flouts human control or judgment. In his explorations of the deaths of well-known historical figures, Chacona continues to reject moral judgement; instead he searches for evidence of the humanity that exists in all, even the most reprehensible evildoers. The subject of *Like a Ghost* is the Nazi war criminal, Rudolph Hess, in old age and pictured in profile against a brick wall of Spandau prison where he was confined as the sole inmate for many years until his death in 1987. Chacona's image, derived from an altered photograph of Hess, is a deathly white head above a black cloak that dissipates in a gray fog which in turn blends into the deteriorating marble slab on which it is imprinted. The colors are murky except for a vibrant green in the leaves of a vine reaching across the wall, a sign of life to which Hess, already bereft of his own life, is oblivious.

As one of the great mysteries of human existence, sex is tantamount to death, and Chacona plumbs its projections onto the loftiest of human endeavors. His religious upbringing (he was born in 1948 into a Greek Orthodox family) provided an early starting point for his insistent questioning of doctrinal, which is to say, male, control of female sexuality. He skewers pretensions of gender neutrality in science as well as in art. *Naked Singularity (Lilith)* does both with a screened image of Eve taken from Franz Stuck's painting and overlaid with revealing scientific terminology: "naked singularities" and "cosmic censorship." The beautiful Eve is paired with a tiny male figure ejaculating from a huge erect penis. Lilith, the mythological first wife of Adam who was banished because she refused his sexual demands, symbolizes, in Chacona's artistic lexicon, the exclusion of woman's voice from the development of Western culture.

While more direct as an image, *In Through the Out Door* also resonates with allusions to subconscious linkings of sex and death. In a seemingly spontaneous pose the prepubescent child looks out innocently (or is it enticingly?) from the "black hole" that is the entrance to death chambers.

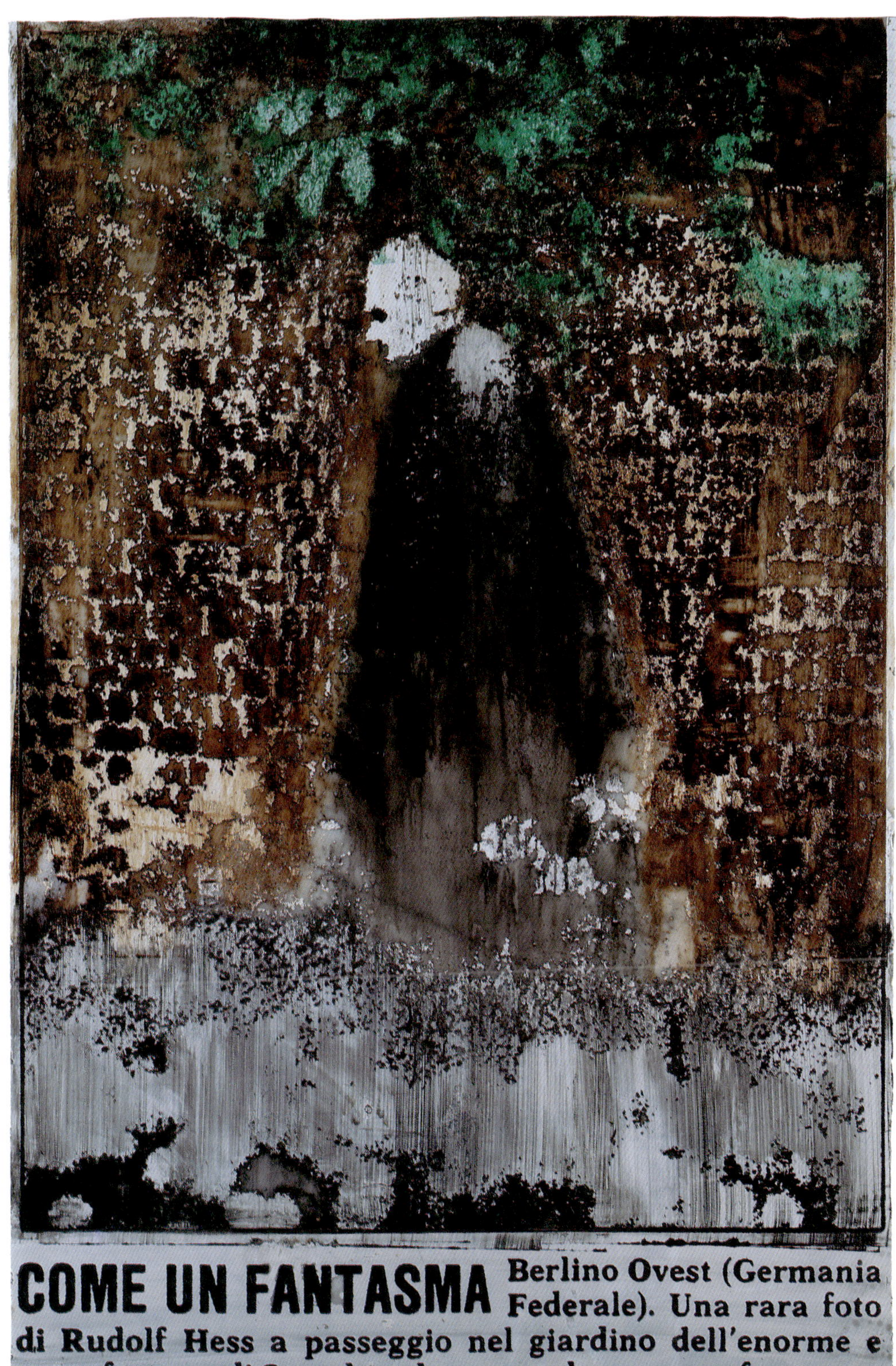

George Chacona Like a Ghost
1991, Oil etched marble, 98" x 60". Courtesy of the artist and Elizabeth Leach Gallery. Photograph: Spike Mafford.

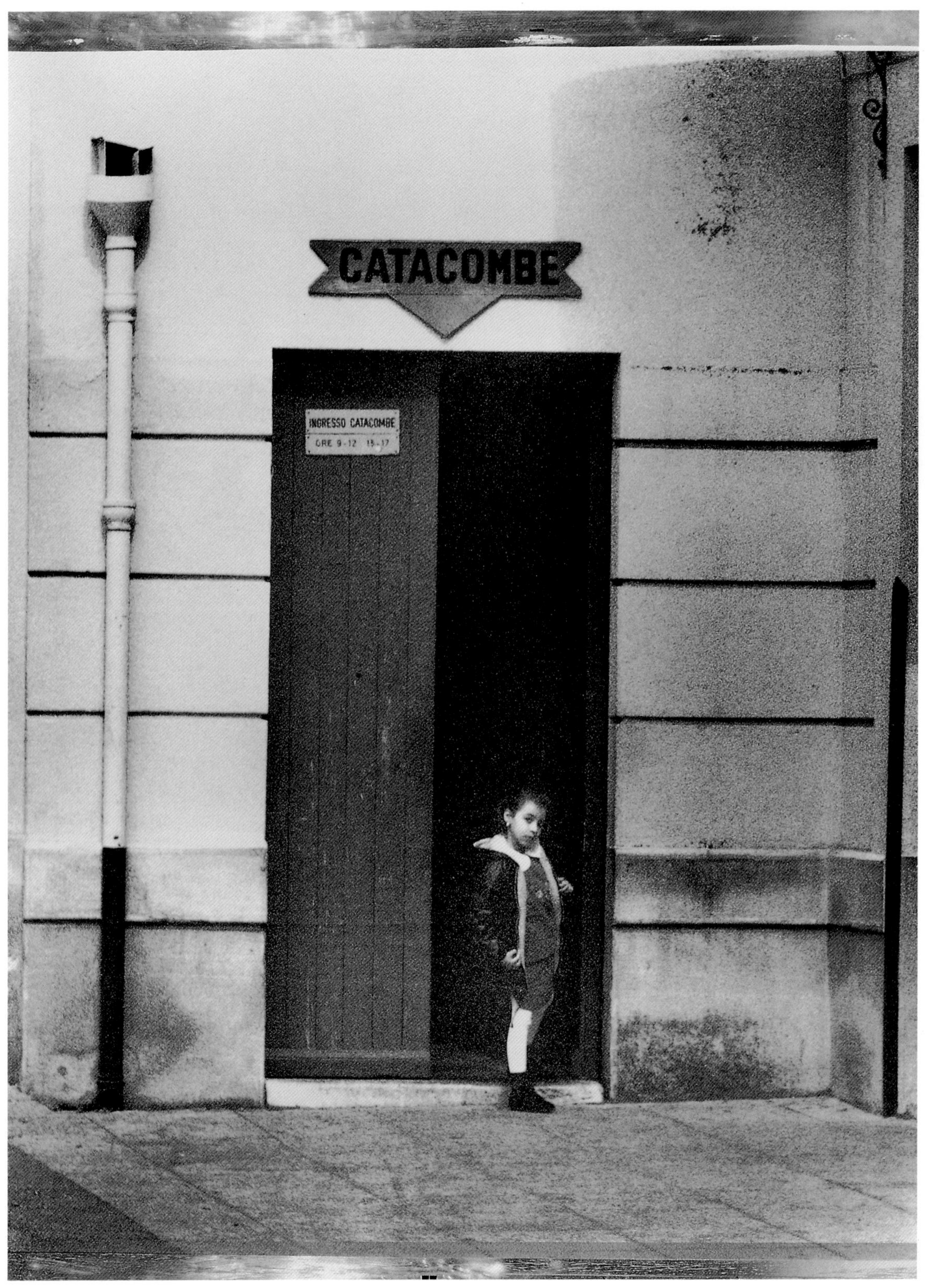

George Chacona **In Through the Out Door**
1992, Lacquer on copper, 48" x 60". Courtesy of the artist and Elizabeth Leach Gallery. Photograph: Spike Mafford.

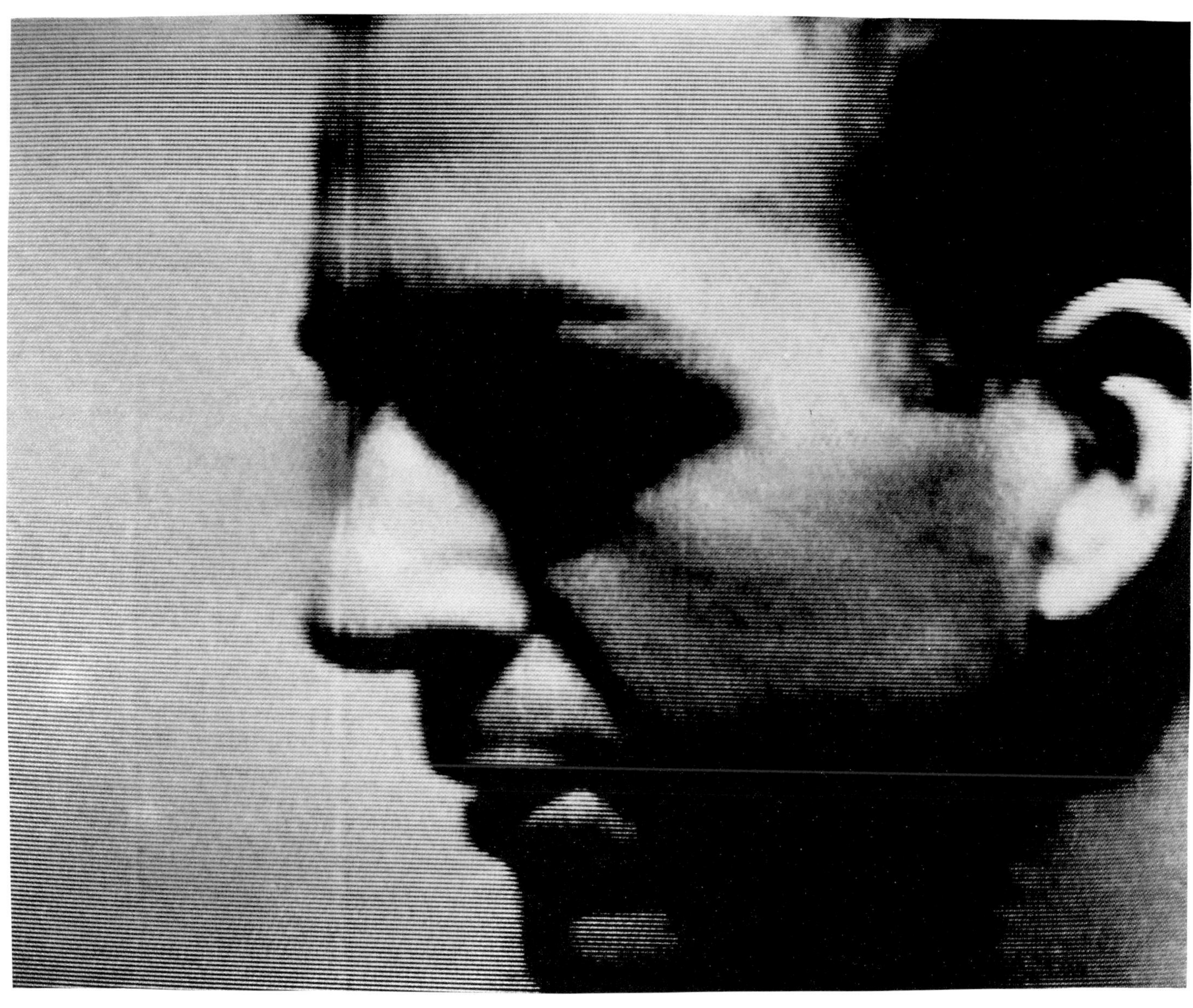

George Chacona **Detained**
1993, B&W Photo, 16" x 20". Courtesy of the artist and Elizabeth Leach Gallery.

Dale **Chihuly**

Dale Chihuly almost single-handedly revolutionized studio glassmaking, spearheading its transformation from craft to a vital sculptural art. In the process of expanding both the medium's technical and expressive abilities, he has become immensely successful, with frequent exhibitions and installations in major museums and galleries of Europe and the United States, plus many corporate, private, and public art commissions. Possessed of a strong and engaging personality, he has propelled Seattle, where he lives and works, into glass world prominence, second only to Venice as an international center for glass art.

In addition to his own prolific output Chihuly has fostered the work of many other glass artists who have passed through the ranks of teams working in his hot shop or who have trained at Pilchuck Glass School just north of Seattle, which he co-founded in 1971. Nevertheless, it is his distinctive, opulent style, developed in large multi-part, blown glass forms, that is the basis of his reputation. The various, on-going series that he creates, while distinct in their appearance, have in common experimental techniques and conceptually, a subversion of the notion of functionality. Among the most astonishing works are the exaggerated vase forms of the *Venetians* series which have been described as "exquisite vulgarities." Flamboyantly embellished with floral motifs, little angels, and looping, undulating glass "ribbons" all in a dazzling assortment of colors, they are a playful tribute to earlier Venetian art glass. At the same time, they are also a wittily satirical response to the criticism that glass is too seductively beautiful — and commercial — to be considered as a material for "serious" art.

Although each piece within a series is complete in itself, many frequently are grouped in presentations that spill out in pyrotechnical arrays. The care taken by Chihuly, who holds a degree in interior design, in designing and lighting such presentations is also crucial to his site-specific installations in which the architecture of the site and the luminous art must be integrated.

Chihuly was born in Tacoma, Washington, in 1941, where he lived until entering the University of Washington in Seattle. After graduation he went to the University of Wisconsin to study with Harvey Littleton but after only a year went on, in 1967, to the Rhode Island School of Design as a teaching assistant and to finish his graduate degree. While living in Rhode Island during the 1970s, Chihuly began a collaboration with sculptor James Carpenter that resulted in sculptures incorporating steel, neon, and other industrial materials with glass. Strongly influenced by Minimalism which was the avant-garde of the period, their sculptures were austere, non-referential, and often process-based, unlikely predecessors for the blown glass, vessel-based work Chihuly turned to after a year of work and study in Italy.

A 1968 Fulbright Fellowship enabled Chihuly to work at the Venini Fabrica on the island of Murano near Venice. The experience, along with providing access to the techniques of superb glassblowers, introduced him to the traditional European team method of working in which a master supervises a cadre of assistants. While teamwork and collaboration had an immediate, personal appeal to the gregarious Chihuly, they became essential after he lost an eye in an automobile accident in 1976.

After years of returning periodically to Seattle and Tacoma for personal reasons, Chihuly moved to Seattle in 1982. He now oversees teams of glassblowers who produce his designs in a renovated industrial building on the Lake Union waterfront. In addition to containing work and residential facilities, the building, called The Boathouse, is also a hub of educational and social activities, all of which feed Chihuly's creative energy.

Eager to respond to new challenges, Chihuly designed a set for the Seattle Opera Company's 1992 production of *Pélleas et Mélisande.* To suggest a forest, he created and installed closely placed, irregularly shaped cylinders, thirty feet high, which were made of transparent, synthetic materials approximating the shimmering translucence of glass. His next innovation, in 1994, was the creation of the largest yet constellation of blown glass elements, comprising a cobalt blue "chandelier" twenty feet long and weighing about two tons, that hangs from the apex of the Tacoma Union Station's glass dome. A public art commission, it heralds the future Chihuly Center for Glass, a museum with glass blowing facilities that will honor the artist in his home city.

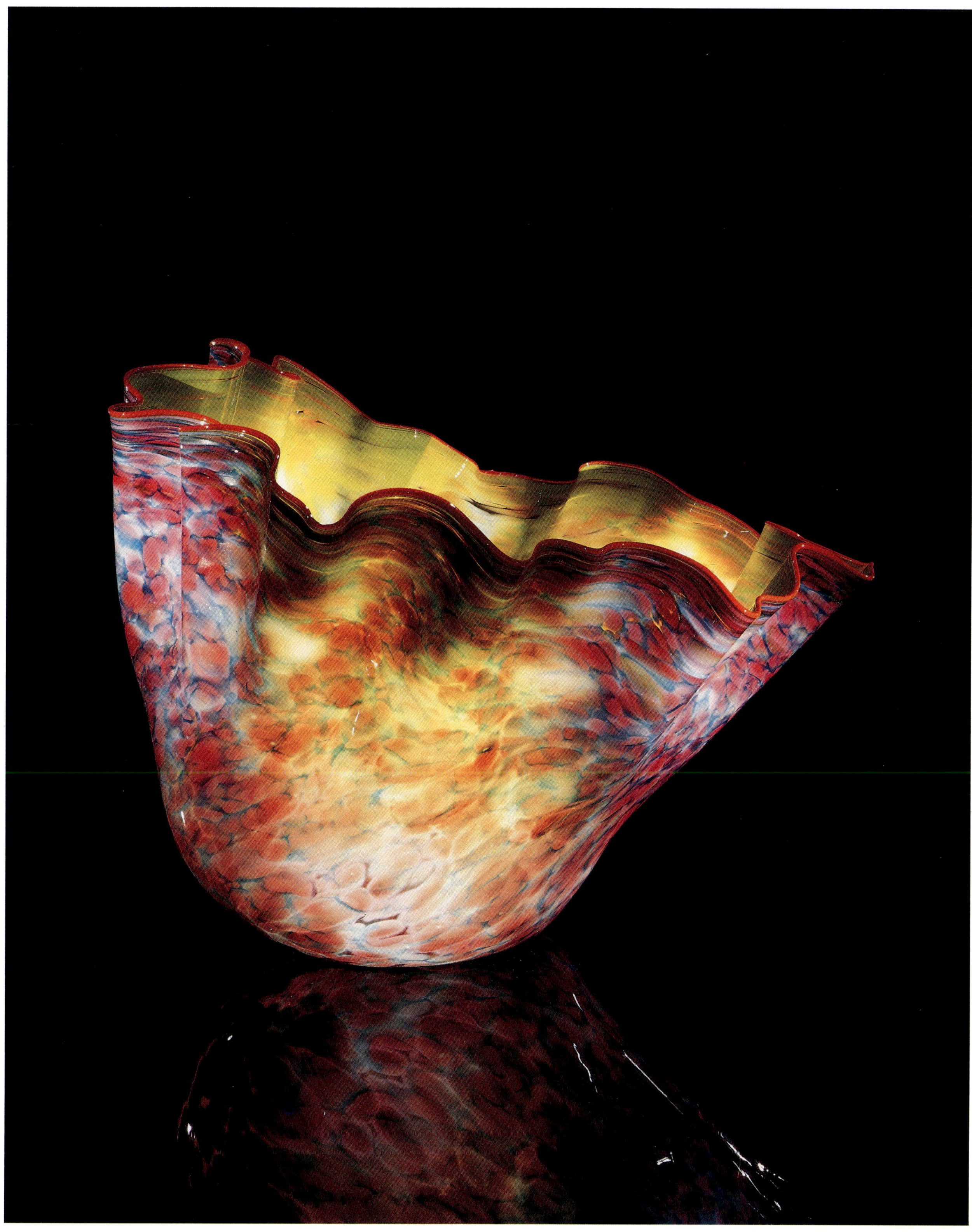

Dale Chihuly Chartreuse Macchia with Red Lip Wrap
1993, Glass, 22" x 28" x 28". Private collection. Courtesy of the artist. Photograph: Claire Garoutte.

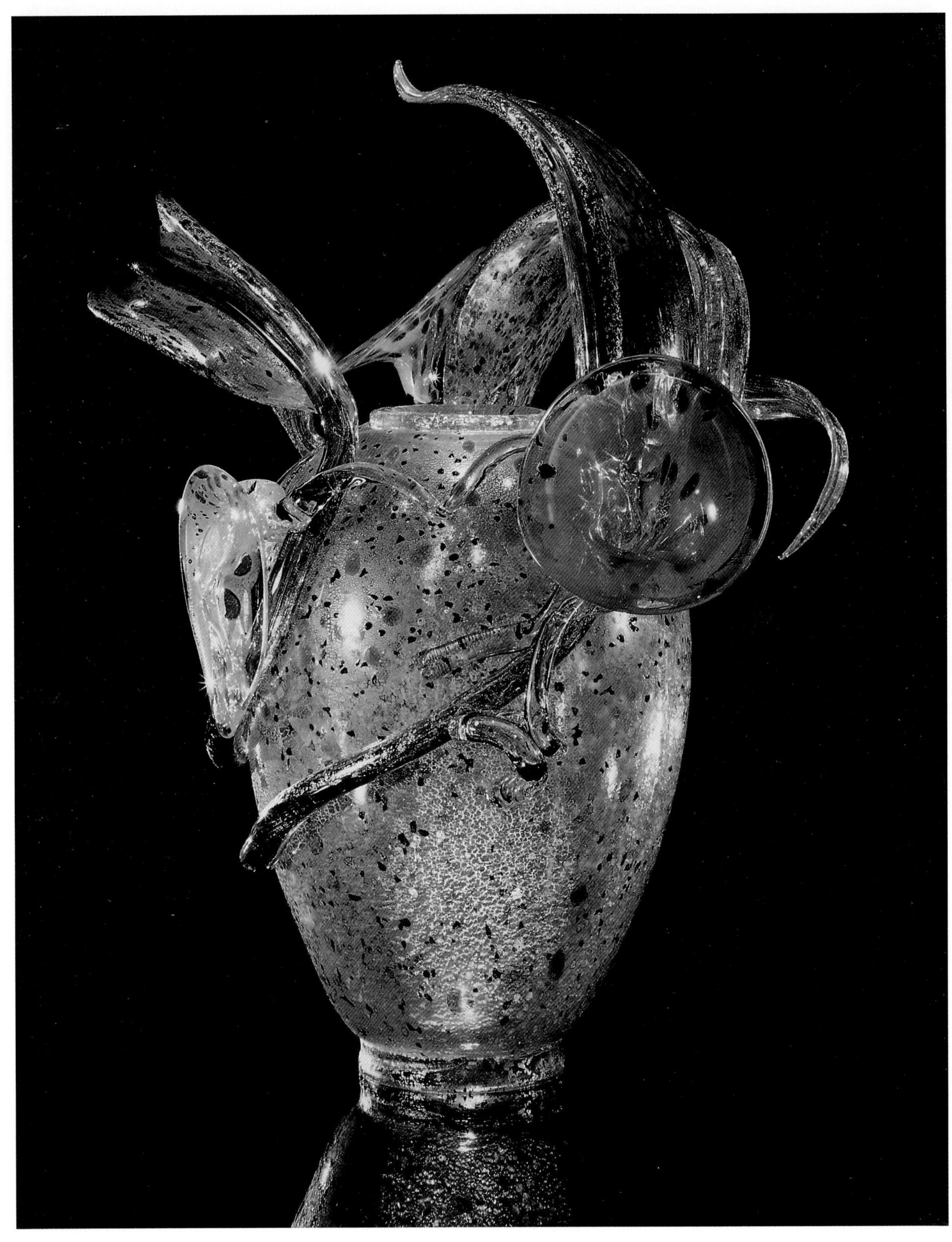

Dale Chihuly **Gold over Clear Venetian with Gold Leaves**
1991, 26" x 20" x 15". Private collection. Courtesy of the artist. Photograph: Eduardo Calderoń.

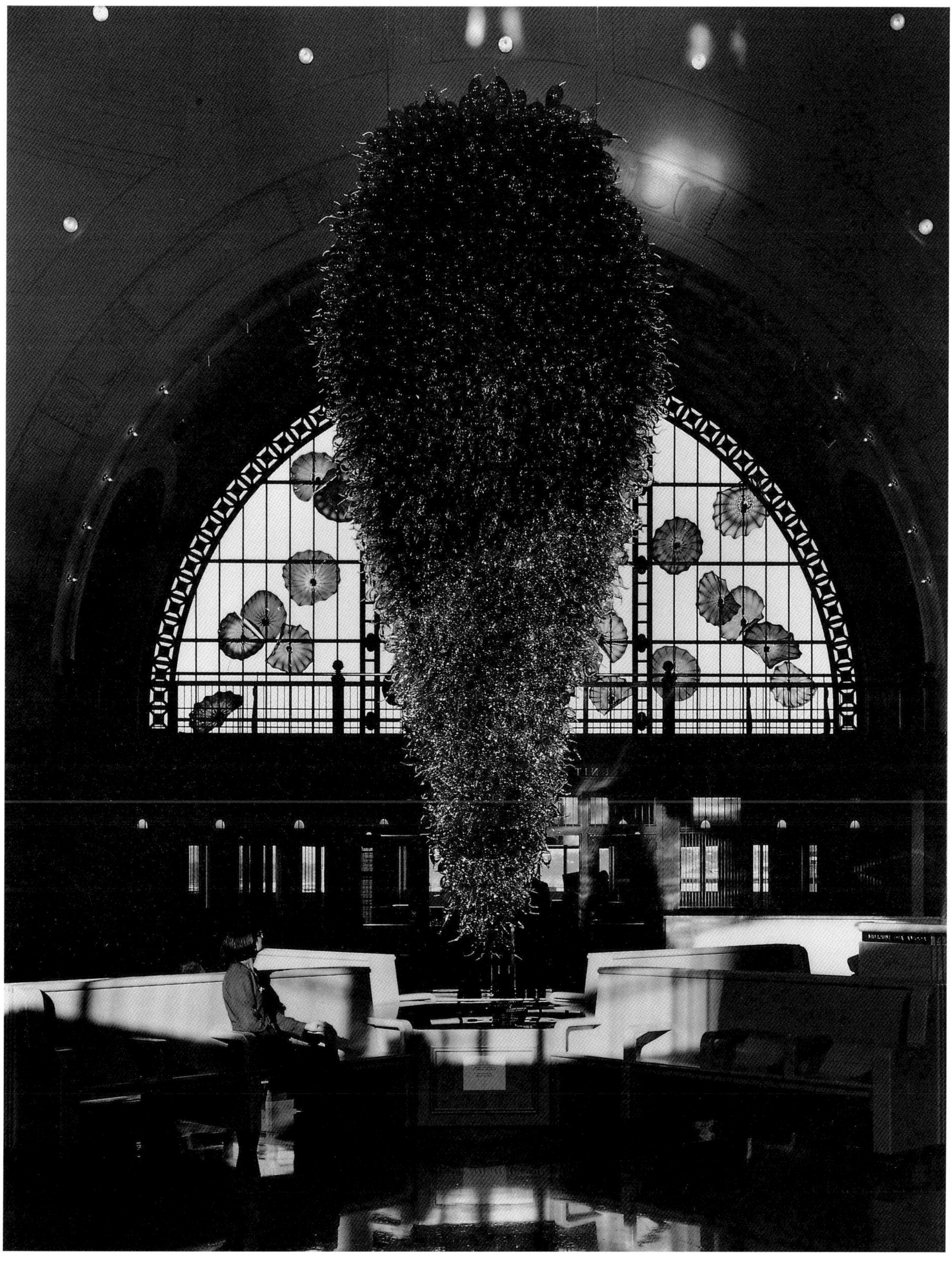

Dale Chihuly **Cobalt Blue Chandelier**
1994, Installed at Union Station, Tacoma WA, 20' x 9' x 3'. Courtesy of the artist. Photograph: Russell Johnson.

Judy **Cooke**

Judy Cooke's distinctive abstract paintings are, in essence, about the phenomena of seeing and sensing. They also have much to do with the process of painting. She is not totally averse to references outside the physicality of the paintings and in fact, by incorporating a simple shape may trigger associative connections. Nevertheless, her materials — she paints on copper, rubber, and wood as well as canvas — her choice of colors, surfaces, size and shape of supports, are all employed for the purpose of triggering a felt experience that can be likened to music, direct but indescribable. When she uses a long, narrow format, its primary purposes are to explore the import of an extending line and the linear format's relationship to the wall. If the format suggests a horizon line and thereby, a landscape, the thought comes from our habits of perception. If she employs a shape within the composition, it is to develop a strong relationship of figure to a densely painted and scraped ground. Like icons, the shapes, while derived from recognizable objects and symbols, are formulaic and act as similes.

The earliest of Cooke's paintings, dating from about 1970, were executed on huge, unstretched tarps tacked to the wall. The physicality of the work stimulated her interest in scale as well as a sensitivity to edges and to architectural relationships. Because of the tarps' humble origins — they were made from several sailors' hammocks combined and stitched together — they seemed less formidable than stretched canvas, and therefore, conducive to experimentation. As she observed, she had the freedom to "put things on and take things off." A combination of collage, charcoal drawing, and painting, the tarp-pieces, which were exhibited successfully at both the Portland and Seattle Art Museums, set the course for issues of physicality and scale that continue to drive her work.

Before taking up painting, Cooke was an intaglio printmaker, and she compares her painting method to that of working a plate — a long and physically active process of layering and subtracting, wiping and biting and reworking until the desired effect is achieved. Her experience in printmaking influences the paintings in other ways as well: She relies on drawing as a way to produce form; she carefully composes and limits colors, favoring black as both a structural and tonal element to produce a narrowed, more pronounced focus.

Although she was born in Michigan (in 1940), educated in New England, and has lived in Portland since 1969, Judy Cooke finds her artistic affinities in Europe where she travels frequently, filling sketchbooks and acquiring ideas for future work. She is intrigued, in particular, by the visual evidence of long cultural histories and a sense of the past fully inhabiting the present. A simulation of this phenomenon pervades much of her work and is clearly felt in a group of paintings employing the image of a cross, an ancient religious symbol also carrying contemporary secular meanings. History and the wear and tear of time are suggested again by the paintings' rough, abraded surfaces marked with glints and scratches of the many underlying layers of paint. Travellers may be reminded of the dim, sooty and smudged walls in medieval churches in southern Europe where a small cross painted on the wall is evidence of crusaders having passed through on their holy journeys.

The Warning (Angel) and *Erasure of Language*, both of 1994, are indicative of a few but striking shifts in Cooke's current approach to her work. Drawing is prominent in images that are strong but elusive; the shapes of the panels and the structural divisions in the dry, blotched and weathered surfaces (inspired by the paint on nineteenth century houses in New England that she had admired while a student) are their foils. Structurally, the paintings are the results of many layers of oil and wax carefully scraped and sanded to create and reveal the traces of their processing. The suggestion of a societal process, that of developing (or is it losing?) written language, seeps through the layers of *Erasure of Language*.

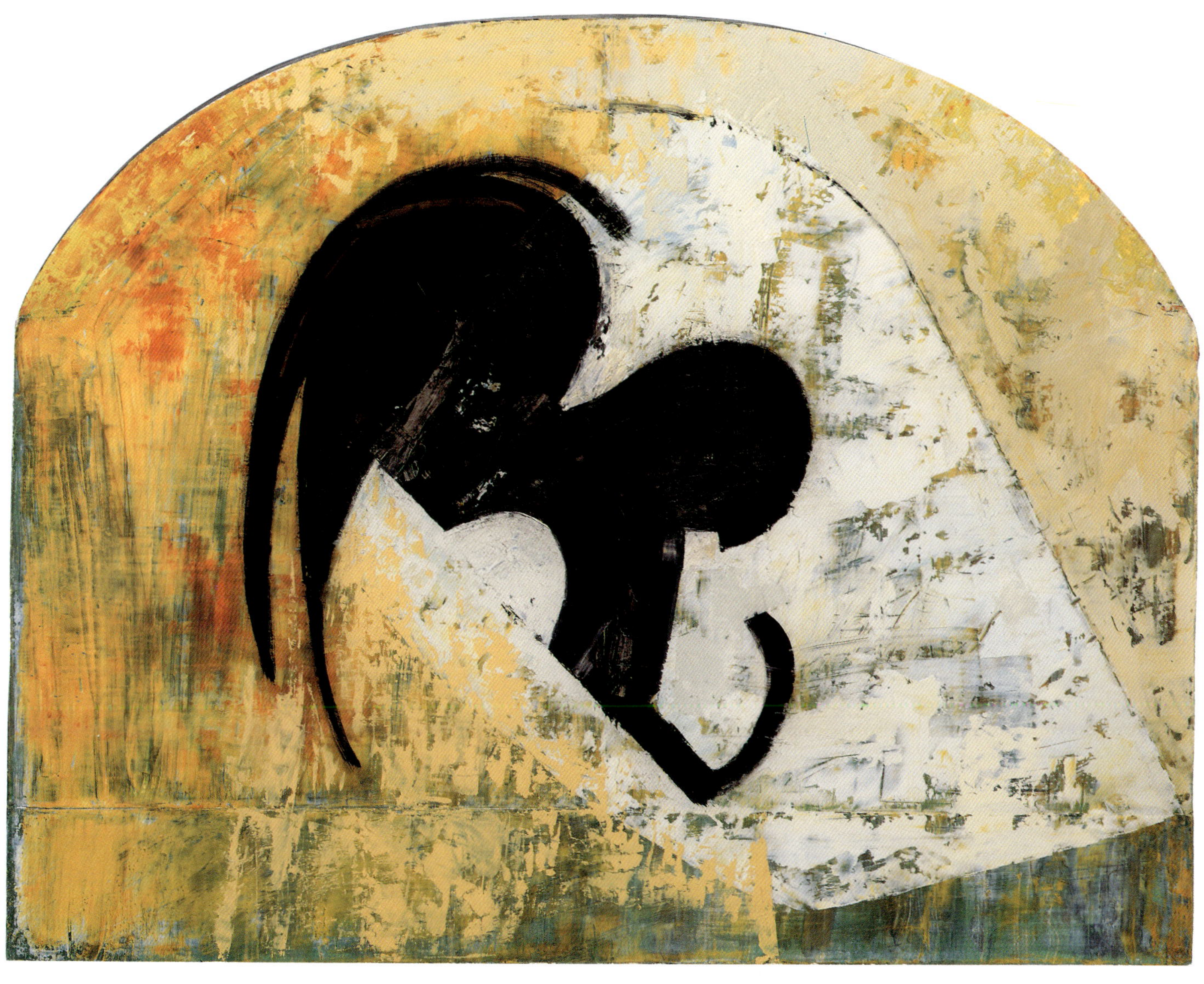

Judy Cooke **The Warning (Angel)**
1994, Alkyd, wax and oil on wood, 18" x 24" x 2". Collection of Al Miller and Beth Parmenter. Courtesy of the artist and Elizabeth Leach Gallery.
Photograph: Jim Lommasson.

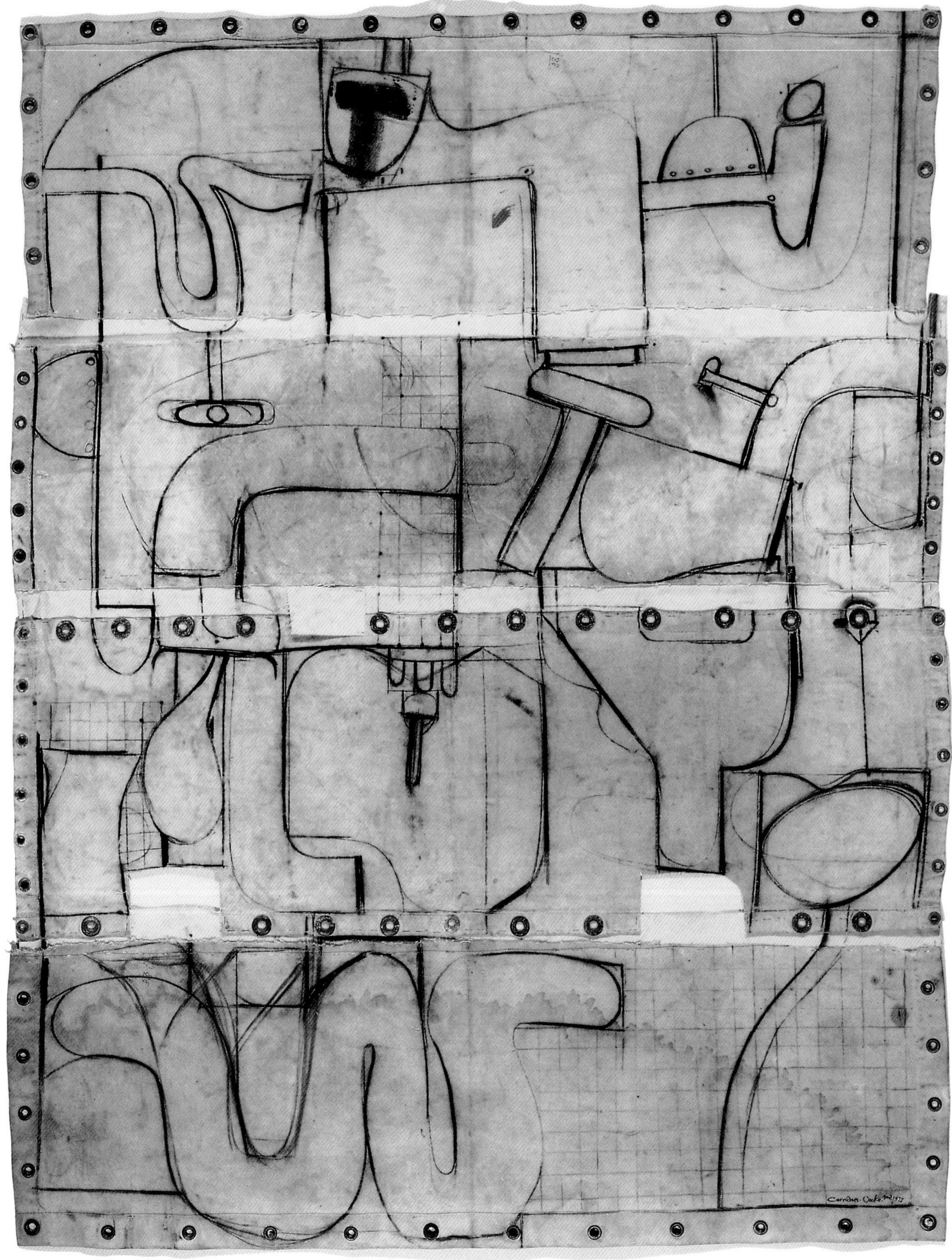

Judy Cooke **Corridor**
1973, Canvas tarp, charcoal, 72" x 64". Courtesy of the artist and Elizabeth Leach Gallery. Photograph: Jim Lommasson.

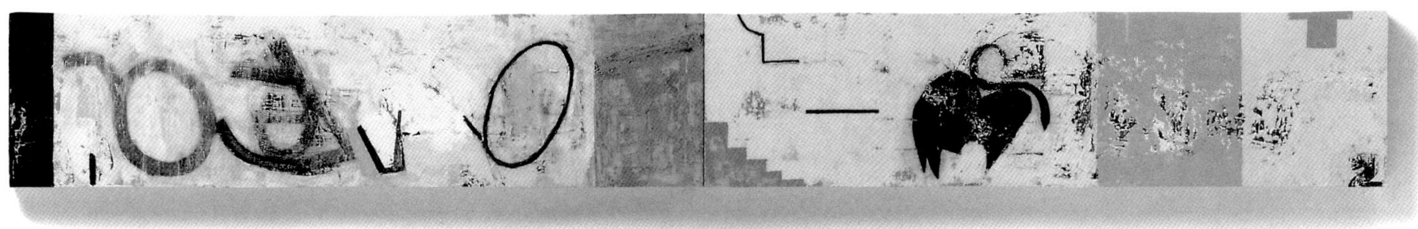

Judy Cooke **Erasure of Language**

1994, Alkyd, wax, oil on wood. Courtesy of the artist and Elizabeth Leach Gallery. Photograph: Jim Lommasson.

Dennis **Cunningham**

Dennis Cunningham is in every respect a regional, specifically Oregon, artist. A ceramist, a painter, and a sculptor, he is best known for distinctive black and white linocut prints that are based on what is probably the most celebrated of Oregon pastimes, fishing. Since 1980, when he decided to devote a considerable period of time to one medium and one basic subject, he has produced a body of prints that address social, moral, and environmental issues by focusing on fish and the activity of fishing, using them as symbols and metaphors. It is a subject that occupies him personally, as he is a serious fisherman; socially, in its centrality to Oregon's economic base in both commercial and sport fishing; and politically, as it affects the natural environment.

In the tradition of the fifteenth century master, Albrecht Dürer, Cunningham's virtuosic skill produces prints that are pictorially accessible and at the same time are firmly grounded in both philosophical convictions and rigorous principles of artmaking. He has developed a style uniquely his own in which composite images — pictures within pictures — as well as symbols and pictographs lead the viewer, step by step, through the picture's content. In *Big Fish Eats Little Fish* this visual syntax addresses drift-net fishing and the unscrupulous fishermen who practice it. We see a map showing the North American west coast and the Pacific Ocean; it is overlaid with directional signs emanating from a disembodied human head to indicate locations of the crime. This is the main subject which is the context for panels that relate to it. The spherical panel, crowded with images of fish and a fisherman holding a large knife, pays tribute to Pieter Breughel the Elder who used a similar device in 1556.

Dennis Cunningham was born in 1949 in Medford, Oregon, where his initiation into the mysteries of fishing came early, but hardly earlier than his discovery of art. By age ten he was working his way through "learn-to-draw" kits and at eighteen was ready to enter the Pacific Northwest College of Art. During that period he was also pursuing a career in music, playing harmonica and singing with a rock 'n' roll group, and as a result took eight years to earn a BFA. Since that time he has devoted his considerable energy to artmaking.

As the decade of the 1990s began, Cunningham, still working with the fish theme, returned to the use of color. In a gallery exhibition of late 1993 he introduced a series of brilliant-hued pastel drawings that are evidence not so much of a departure but of an evolution in the on-going "fishworks." The new drawings retain the angular, flat forms of the prints and more important, the multiple perspectives, pictographs, and pictures within pictures that are his hallmark. The addition of color, however, makes possible subtle tonal gradations and a dimensionality that are missing in the relief prints. Also, metaphysical implications in the imagery, which have been introduced in the new work, are heightened by the ethereal, golden light created by the seamless blending of the pastels.

The decision to use color, according to the artist, came in response to an urge to improvise and to give the work "an emotional charge." The limitations that he had imposed upon himself in 1980 had begun to chafe, and he was willing to forego the austere vigor of black ink for the more varied, expansive associations that color makes possible.

Although he admits to a moralistic substratum in his work, Cunningham describes himself as first and foremost a storyteller. Two experiences, one positive, the other negative, in a recent trip to Germany inspired the "stories" seen in the new works: He was fascinated by medieval German altarpieces and paintings but repelled by the country's pollution and apparent lack of concern for the environment. In drawings such as *Streamside* he brings the angels, devils, and skeletons (who once enjoyed fishing) of medieval allegories into a very contemporary setting of environmental devastation.

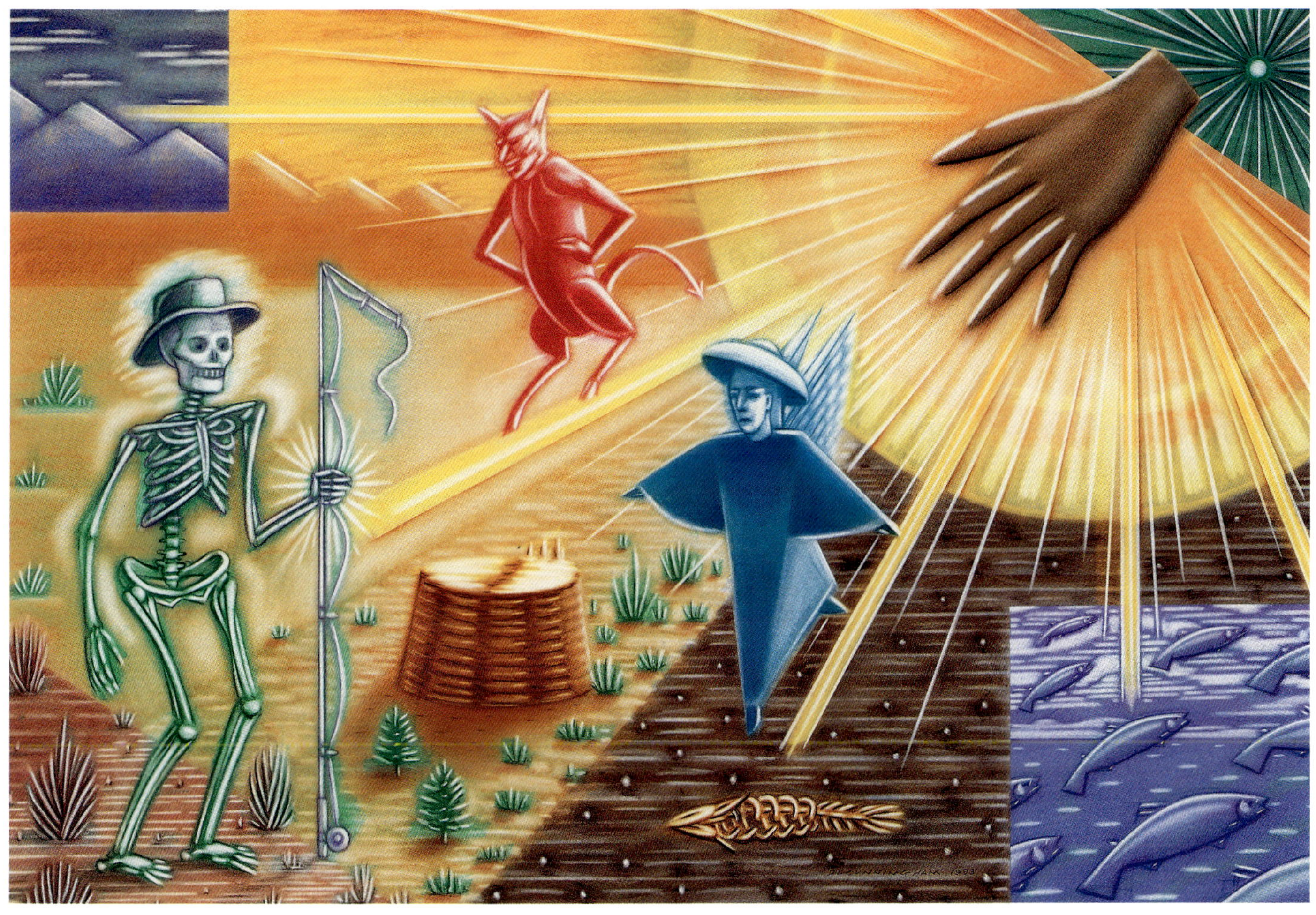

Dennis Cunningham **Streamside**
1993, Pastel on paper, 40" x 60". Private collection. Courtesy of the artist and Jamison/Thomas Gallery. Photograph: Bill Bachhuber.

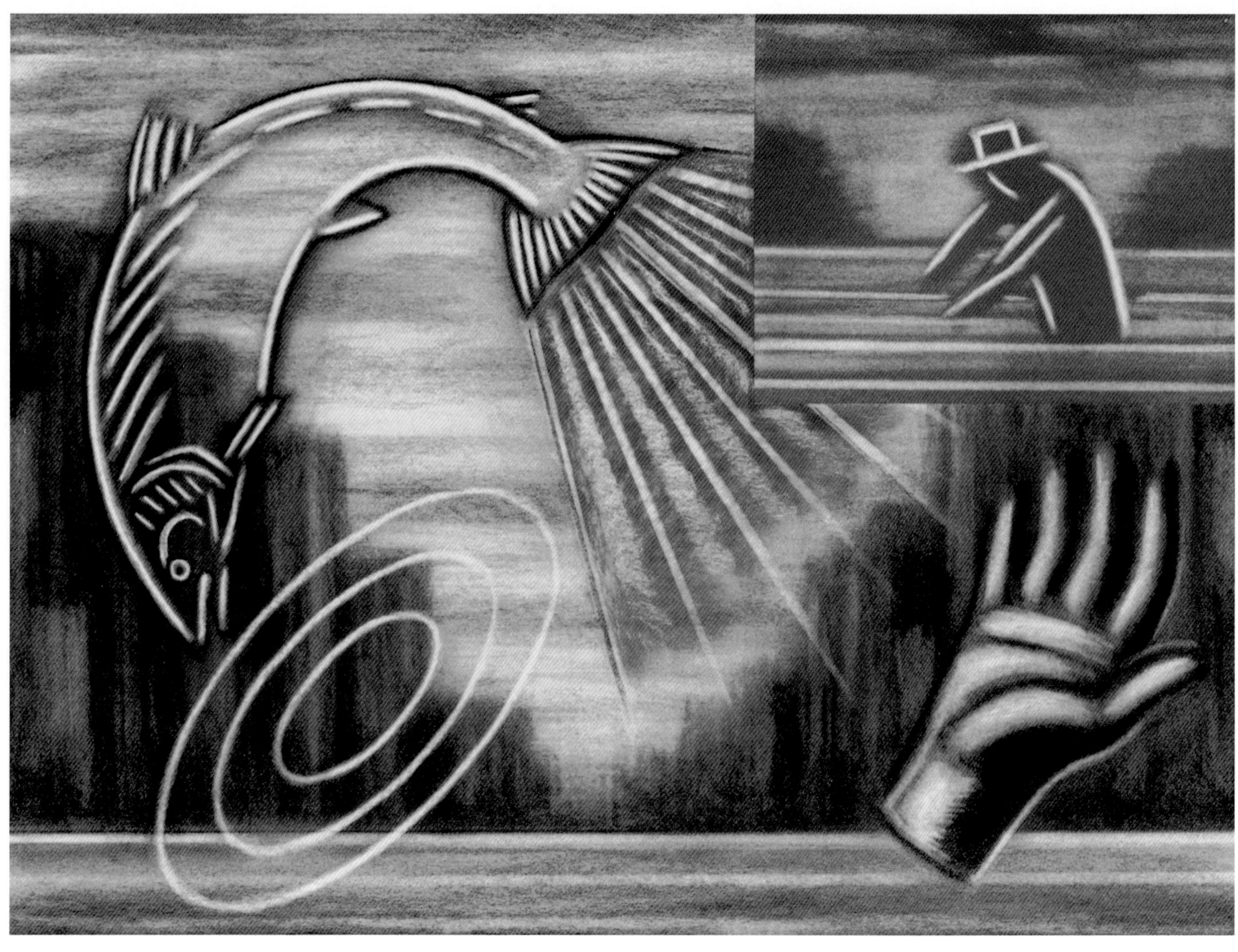

Dennis Cunningham **Target**
1993, Colored chalk on BFK Rives paper, 22" x 30". Private collection. Courtesy of the artist and Jamison/Thomas Gallery. Photograph: Rebekah Johnson.

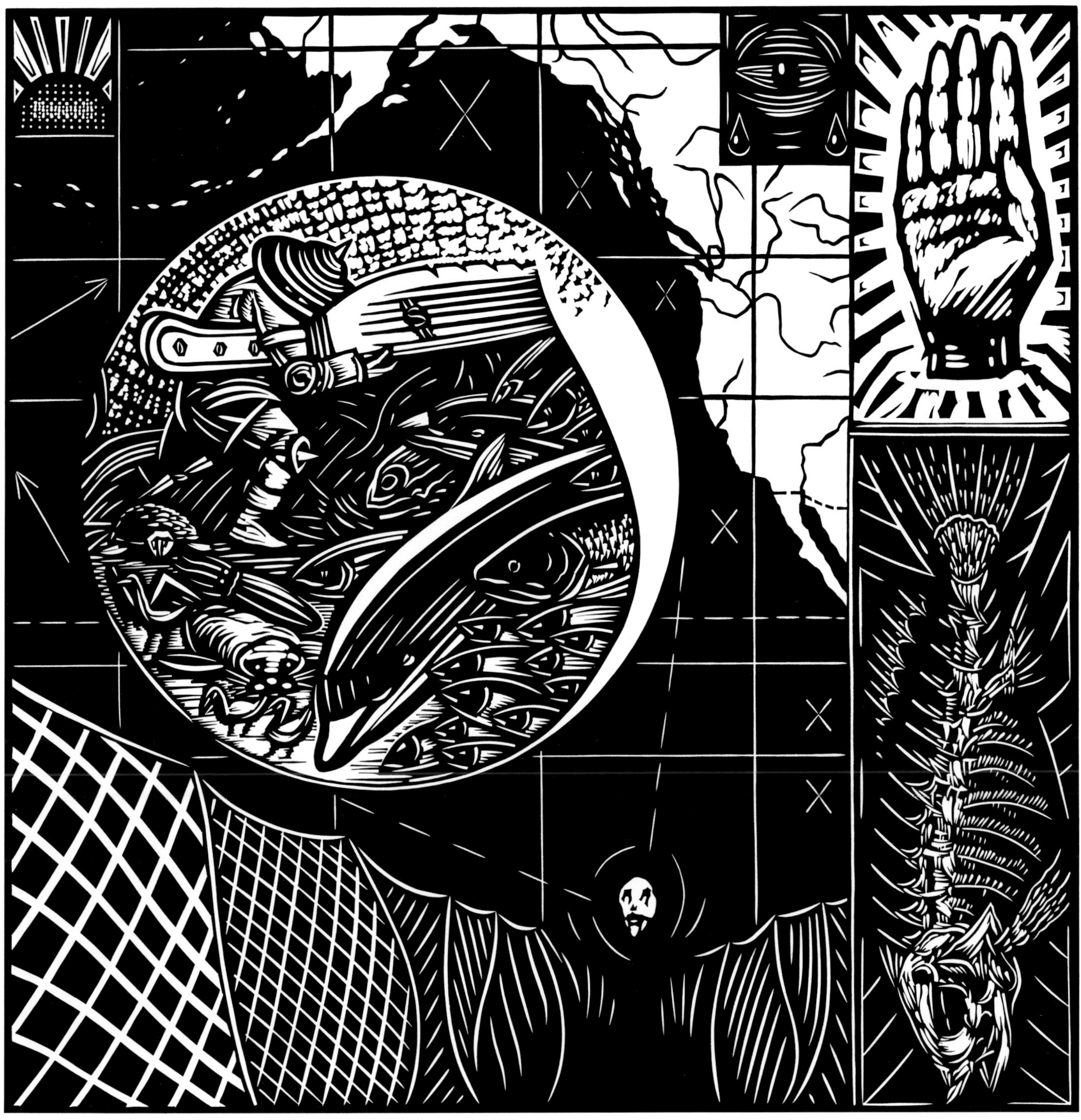

Dennis Cunningham **Big Fish Eats Little Fish**
1992, Linocut print, Edition of 25 on Arches 88 paper. Courtesy of the artist and Jamison/Thomas Gallery.

Fernanda **D'Agostino**

Fernanda D'Agostino is a maker and a thinker, a conceptually motivated artist who produces a variety of sculptural forms, from small carvings to impermanent installations and public art projects. Her psychically charged environments, which integrate space, architecture, and objects, combine an aesthetic of formal austerity and densely layered content. The installations and the objects within them may be enigmatic but they are haunting, just as the concerns they explore — memory, fate, family relationships, loss and mourning — are also deeply affecting but difficult to understand. Like visual emulations of ancient myths, her artworks communicate through symbolic individuals, events, stories, and objects. D'Agostino often derives subjects from her own life and family history, then interweaves them with references to history and myth.

Fate, a major work of 1994, and a collaboration with Kristy Edmunds (who shares D'Agostino's interest in exploring familial histories) dealt with the effects of life-changing decisions, whether made by choice or forced by circumstances, as they shape lives through several generations. Decisions within D'Agostino's own family constellation that have culminated in her daughter's birth provided the common thread linking components of *Fate*. D'Agostino's paternal grandparents were Italian immigrants; her mother belongs to an old New England Anglo family; her husband's Jewish grandfather survived Kristallnacht and with his family fled Europe. She is a native of Trenton, New Jersey, has lived in Montana (where she earned the M.F.A. at the University of Montana) and came to Portland in 1985 to spend a year as an artist-in-residence at the Oregon School of Arts and Crafts. During the year, she met the Portland man who became her husband. Her decision to marry and to remain in Portland was the last in forming her child's particular identity and heritage. As an indication of the chance circumstances that shape the history and decide the existence of each human being, D'Agostino sculpted three life-size hands in the positions used in the child's game, "paper, scissors, rock," and positioned them jutting from the wall near the entrance to the installation. Below the hands a floor-mounted video by Edmunds followed a young child wandering among adults and playthings. D'Agostino's objects alluding to personal histories — "photo albums" encrusted in wax, a beaker of water next to a container of dry seeds, and a large flat "clock" with hands moving over a background of faint handwriting — led viewers to a corner where a white stand-up desk and a white, wax coated suitcase stood on a slightly raised platform. The desk held the grandfather's diary describing his family's experience of Kristallnacht; the pages, readable within coats of white wax, were mute testimony to a capricious fate, far-reaching in its effects.

While gallery installations comprise most of D'Agostino's work, a project of 1993 featured a growing field of corn on the Marylhurst College campus near Portland. Titled *Abundance and Scarcity*, the half-acre cornfield encirled a small screened "granary" containing metaphoric objects relating to the factors that determine or prevent growth and productivity. As the corn grew and became higher and denser it altered the appearance, the function and concept of the campus; it also gradually obscured the little building, shielding the visitors who made their way to it through the corn rows. At the end of the growing season about a ton of corn was harvested and distributed among sixty needy families. By November, when the piece officially ended, the dry, rattling stalks provided the final, metaphoric connotation.

In 1991 construction in her studio forced D'Agostino to limit the size and range of her work for a few months. During this period she created a group of small, carved basswood sculptures based on sources in biblical and Greco-Roman mythology. Unpainted and ghostly, the austere, compact carvings seem to fetishize the chthonic underpinnings of Western culture's belief systems. As if to emphasize the mental distance that myths invoke, *Walking on Water*, one of this group, has the effect of one-point perspective in three-dimensions through the use of an inclined plane that supports a boat at the lower wide end and a tiny human figure at the upper, "vanishing point" end.

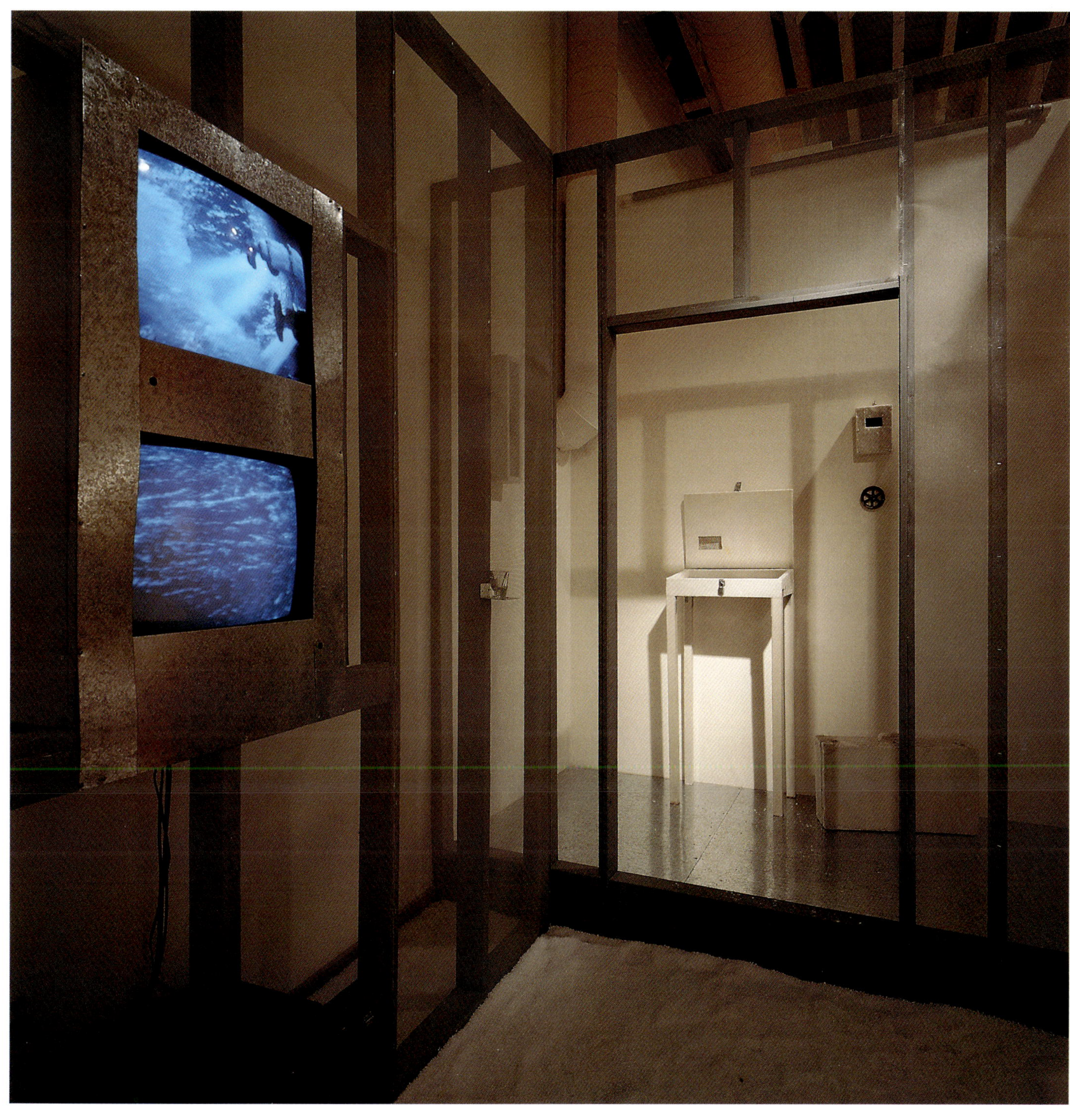

Fernanda D'Agostino with Kristy Edmunds **Fate**
1994, Installation at Elizabeth Leach Gallery. Photograph: Brian Foulkes.

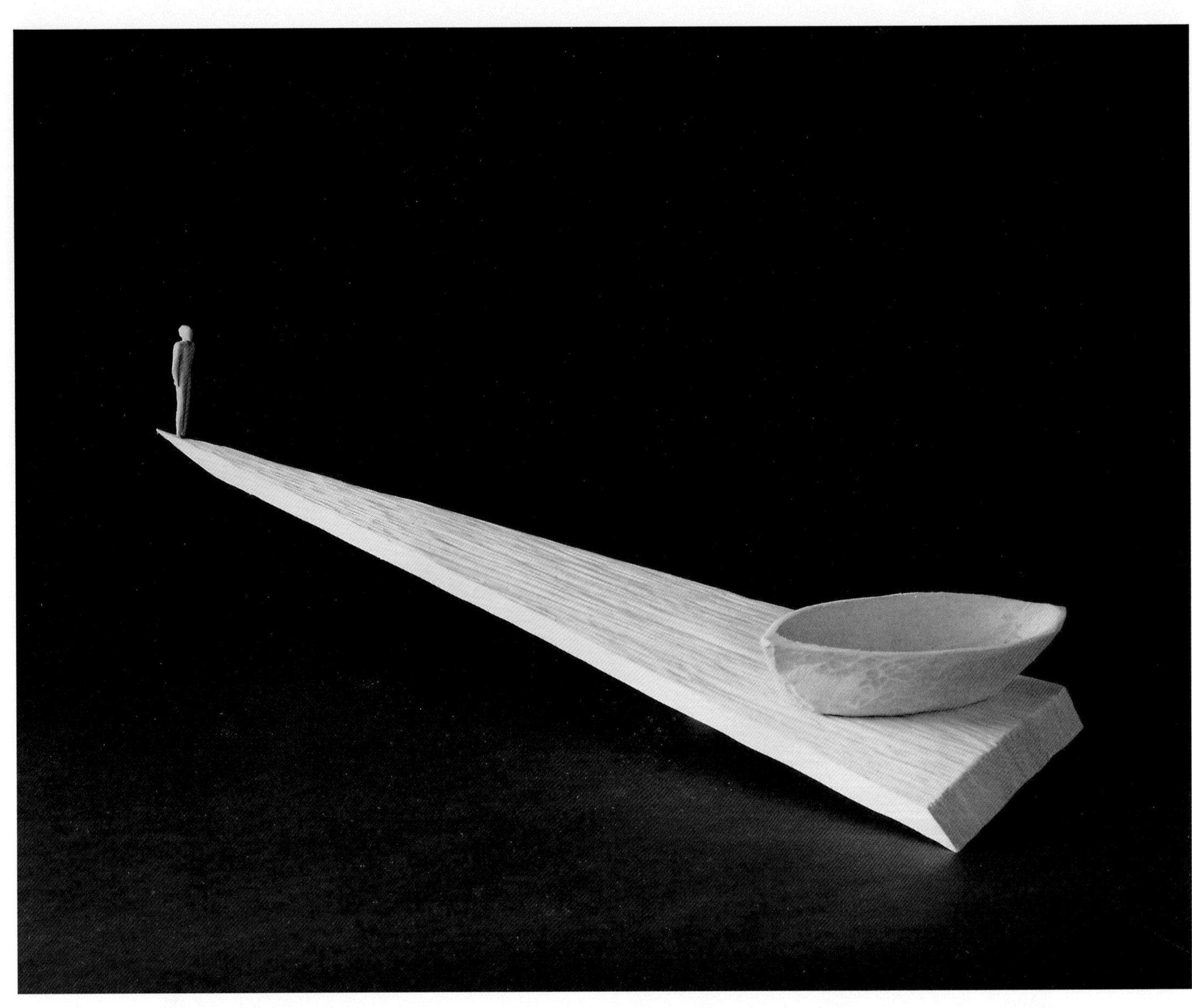

Fernanda D'Agostino **Walking on Water**
1992, Wood, 10" x 6" x 32". Courtesy of the artist and Elizabeth Leach Gallery. Photograph: Brian Foulkes.

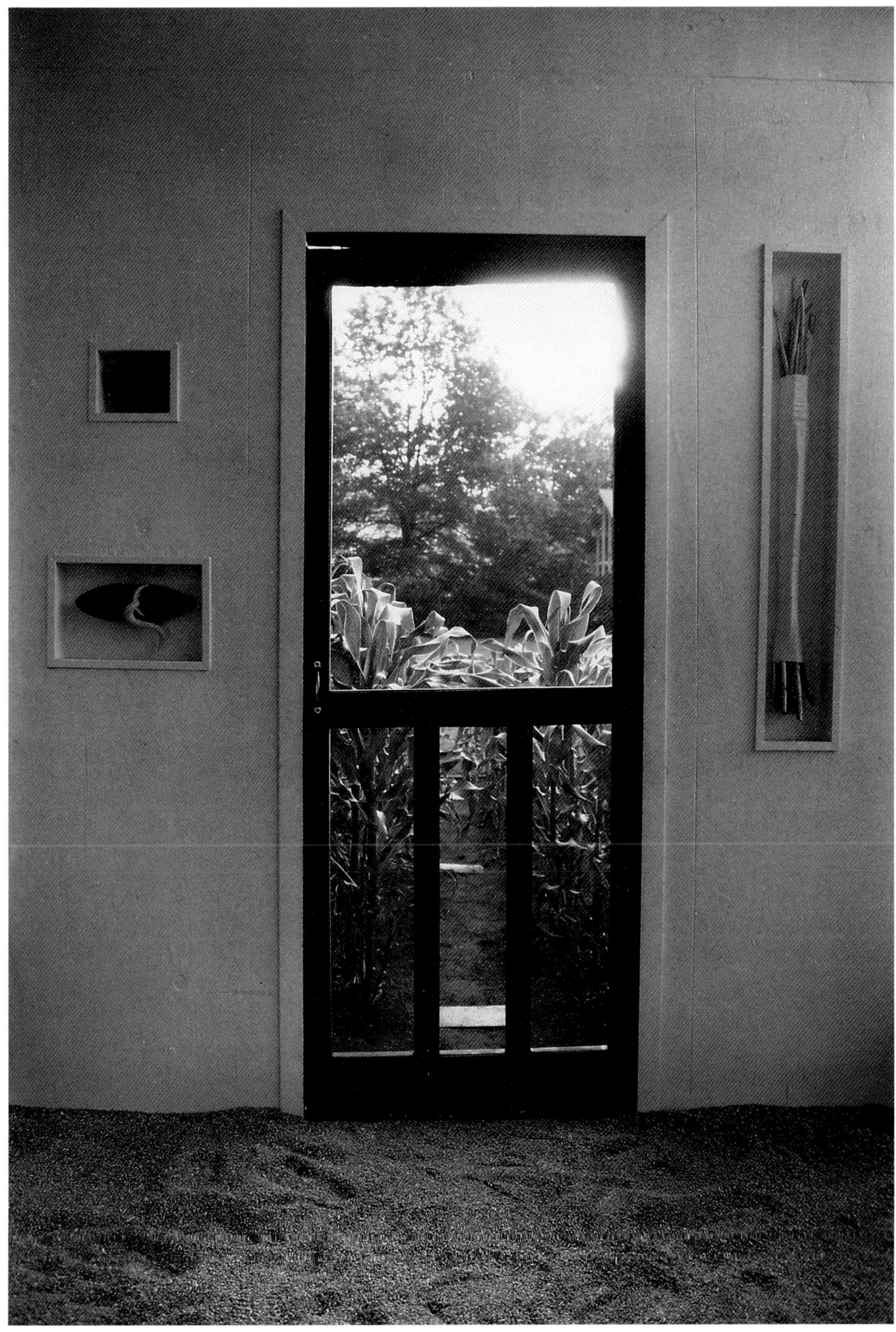

Fernanda D'Agostino **Abundance and Scarcity**
1993, Site specific installation at Marylhurst College. Photograph: Brian Foulkes.

Marita **Dingus**

Marita Dingus casts a sorcerer's spell over a pile of rubbish and causes it to turn into an assembly of bewitching messengers from an African spirit world. The detritus of Seattle consumerism — plastic milk jugs, straws, rags, buttons, string, pieces of film and audio tape, to name but a few of her materials — come together in "power figures" that speak not only of supernatural authority but also of First World material excesses and Third World poverty. Her work is raw and wildly expressionistic, based equally on African stylistic traditions, a Euro-American assemblage tradition, and feminist anti-formalism. Colorful and accessible, it constitutes a forceful statement on the social problems that most concern Dingus, i.e., the degradation of the environment and of Blacks, especially women. In describing the goals of her art she states, "By transforming junk into art I am showing people {how} to see beyond the single meaning in things and people."

Although she holds degrees in art (B.F.A., 1980, Tyler School of Art, Temple University, and M.A.,1984, and M.F.A., 1985, San Jose State University) with an emphasis on painting, Dingus was so profoundly affected by the hardships and poverty she saw while on work-visits in Morocco and Nigeria that she gave up painting, as it seemed to her to be a decadent artform, and began to develop an expression more directly related to life as she saw and felt it. Brushes and canvas were exchanged for a glue gun and sewing machine; her "palette" now holds an array of scraps instead of paints, and "re-cycling" is her watchword. The use of discarded objects and used materials is crucial to the work for symbolic, political, and aesthetic reasons: While she celebrates the animism of African belief — that ancestor spirits inhabit all things — Dingus underscores the immeasurable human as well as material wastefulness of an affluent, technological society. Her sculptures, like the haunting *Basket Head Mask*, are down-to-earth but magical in their transformative qualities.

Although her work is exhibited in mainstream galleries and museums, Dingus also places it in communities of which it speaks, both in Seattle and Africa (she has exhibited in Accra, Ghana), where consumption and recycling in their usual connotations are not of great interest. In a statement for the *Artist Trust Newsletter* (Spring, 1994) she noted that ecology and recycling are not "big issues in the African-American community. People with low incomes or no jobs still like to buy new items, cars or clothes, in order to boost their self esteem when they have none." Children, however, easily accept the idea that we, like the ancestors, are "recycled" material, and Dingus, in working with them, stresses African cultural values that can be transmitted through art.

The fetishistic figures that are the core of Dingus's work, much like the materials they are made of, carry associations of play, history, and use. Many are doll-size, evocations of rag dolls that comforted poor children in the time of slavery. With specifically personalized faces, which are photographic cut-outs, they may also suggest voodoo practices. Some, like a group of life-size plastic "spirit" figures, are inspired by nkondi (power figures in the Kongo culture of Zaire) noted for calm faces as well as bodies pierced by all kinds of small "offerings" nailed on by supplicants of the figures' healing powers.

In the early 1990s Dingus moved from a focus on single objects to installations in order to extend signification and to achieve a coherent relationship among the sculptures and their environmental space. In June of 1994 she transformed the Francine Seders Gallery in Seattle into a lively ethnic festival titled "Boundless Spirits," In addition to a profusion of figures — standing in groups, massed on walls, or attached to hanging streamers — there were masks, baskets, and more; all familiar objects, most carrying references to equally familiar societal issues, including AIDS, child abuse, rape, alienation, and pollution. Not all were ominous, however. *Two Hundred Women of African Descent* conveyed the collective strength of women in triumph over adversity. The tiny female torsos, covering an entire wall, were cut from black fabric and trimmed with scraps of colored material, beads, and ribbons. Some had sharp plastic or metal fragments between their legs, a clear reference to sexual exploitation. Nonetheless, through the formal beauty of the massed figures and their shadows against the white wall, Dingus celebrated the endurance and dignity of Black women everywhere.

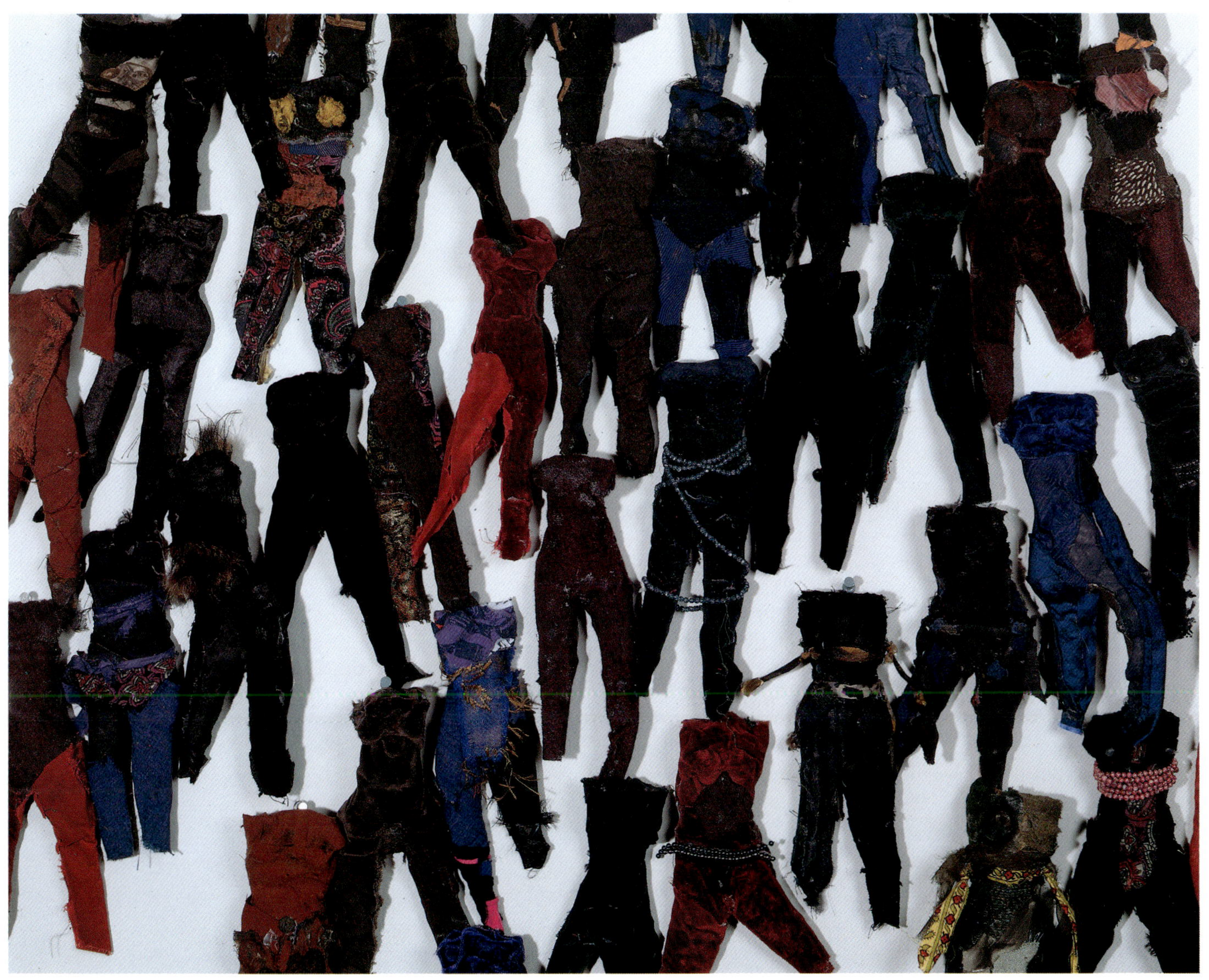

Marita Dingus **Two Hundred Women of African Descent** (detail)
1994, Mixed media, Each figure 7"h. Courtesy of the artist and Francine Seders Gallery. Photograph: Spike Mafford.

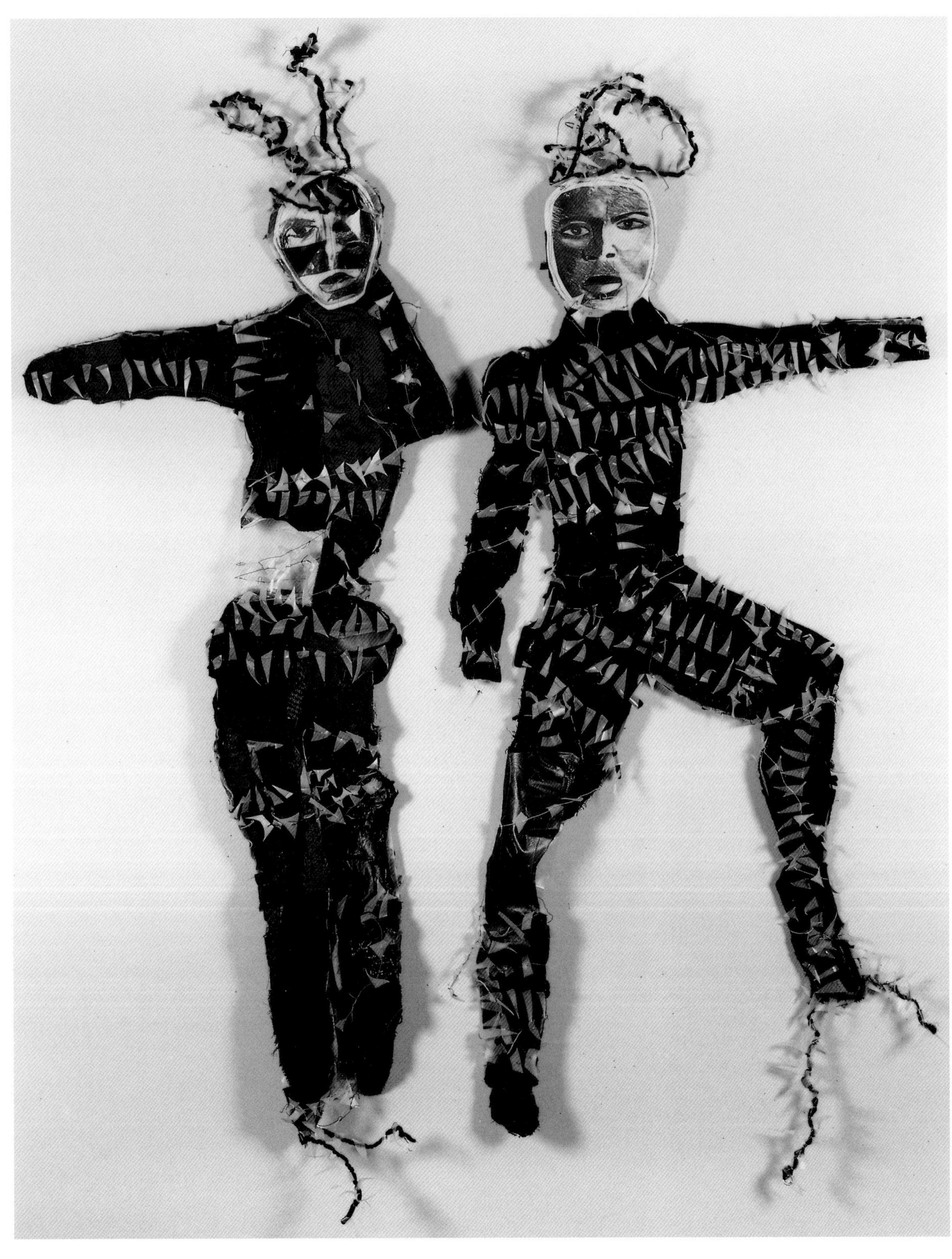

Marita Dingus **Figures, Blue**
1994, Mixed media, Figure 1: 74" x 28"; Figure 2: 74" x 31". Courtesy of the artist and Francine Seders Gallery. Photograph: Spike Mafford.

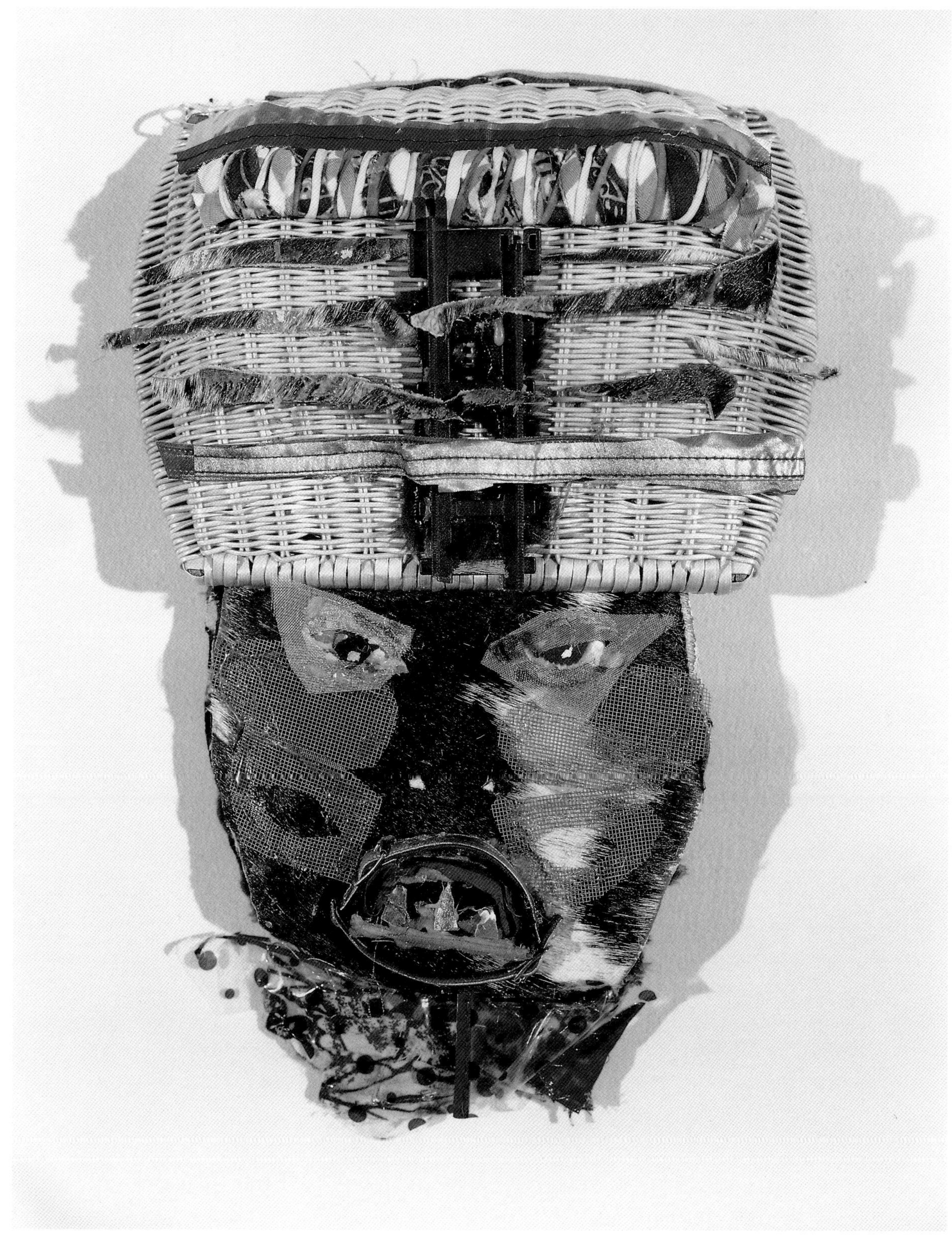

Marita Dingus **Basket Head Mask**
1988, Mixed media, 15" x 11" x 7". Courtesy of the artist and Francine Seders Gallery. Photograph: Chris Eden.

Kristy **Edmunds**

Kristy Edmunds is a multi-media artist whose synergistic collaborations with other artists in the performing as well as visual arts have produced some of the most unusual and exciting work seen in Portland. Theatrical productions, outdoor ephemeral works, video, film, dance, music, and gallery installations frame themes as old as their presentations are new. Among them, death, family relationships, and social injustices have been explored in recent provocative interdisciplinary projects. While she also continues to work in established formats such as performance and object making, she sees her art primarily as an activity rather than an "oeuvre," one that is directly connected to community life.

Edmunds was identified primarily with film and video art until her first large-scale, interdisciplinary production, titled *Partitio,* in 1992. Basing the work on her experience of her great-grandmother's last days in a nursing home, she created a poetic, spirited exposition of societal attitudes toward old age. Thirty performing and visual artists as well as non-professional elderly people participated, contributing to vignettes and impressions of an old woman's confused state of mind as she lay in her bed under the uncaring ministrations of a robotic nursing home staff.

The following year, as the recipient of Portland's first public art commission for a temporary work, Edmunds placed a series of ice walls in a rundown park that was undergoing renovation. Each of the five hundred blocks of ice required for the walls, which were built in a maze-like configuration, contained an object, "a gift," for the passersby, workers, and homeless people who habitually used the park. Although the piece was to be realized over a period of days as the ice melted and released the objects (lottery tickets, coins, food and clothing items, condoms, HIV pamphlets, a basketball), it had an unexpected conclusion. Within an hour following the performance marking its dedication, the ice blocks were destroyed by a large crowd who set upon them with whatever tools they could improvise in order to retrieve the objects. Far from being disturbed by the ruckus, Edmunds viewed it as an extension of the performative significance of the work.

Kristy Edmunds' background is as inclusive as her art. She was born in Chelan, Washington, in 1965, and by the time she entered college at Montana State University, she was already an experienced performer playing guitar and singing with a rock band, often using material that she had written. After trying and discarding visual arts as her undergraduate major, she graduated with a degree in film and production, then earned a master's degree at Western Washington University in theater with an emphasis on playwriting and directing.

Since moving to Portland in 1990 to become the Portland Art Museum's first curator of performance art, she has assumed several roles beyond her own creative work and curatorial position. As a mentor, teacher, and facilitator in artist-in-residence programs she has helped young people realize their ideas in films and videos that have attracted the attention of critics and the public alike. *Lost Angels: Life on the Streets,* a twenty minute video, was made under Edmunds' tutelage by Portland youths living on the streets. Because of its insight into the personal circumstances of homeless adolescents it has been widely distributed in school, professional, and public settings.

A collaborative installation with Fernanda D'Agostino, a contributor to *Partitio,* led Edmunds in 1994 to object making and a gallery exhibition. Titled *Fate,* the work drew on personal subjects from the family history of both artists relating to choices made by one person that have had decisive impacts, not only on that individual's life but on others as well. In addition to videos relating to childhood and old age she created a series of wall mounted glass squares imbedded with copper wire symbolizing qualities of conductivity, fragility and strength in life. These and a row of child-size, white T-shirts with patches "sutured" over the heart area were mute testimony to affective, unpredictable events in the formation of a life history.

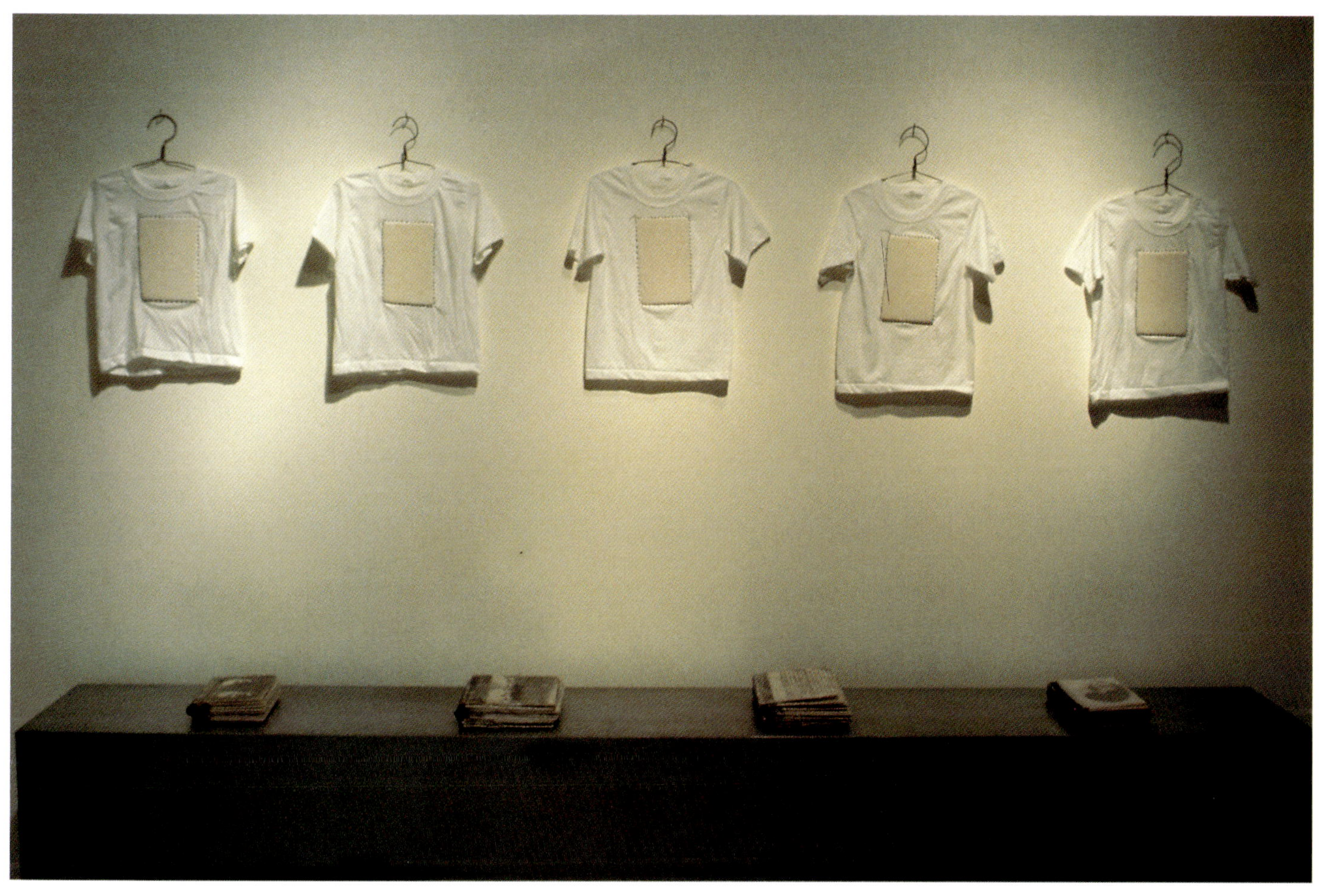

Kristy Edmunds **Fate**
1994, Padded T-shirt components of installation at Elizabeth Leach Gallery. Courtesy of the artist and Elizabeth Leach Gallery. Photograph: Brian Foulkes.

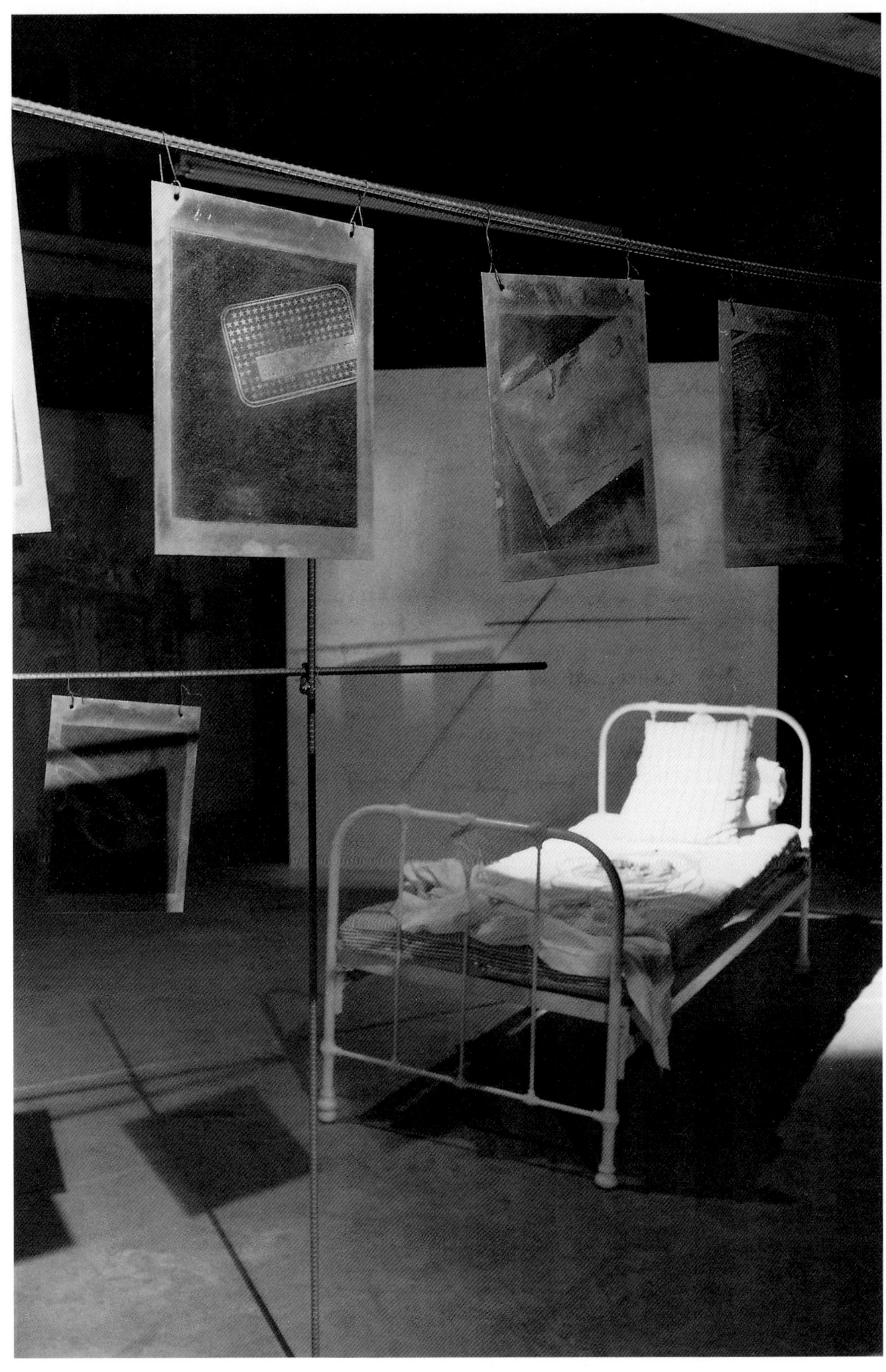

Kristy Edmunds **Partitio**
1992, Interdisciplinary production. Courtesy of the artist. Photograph: David Potter.

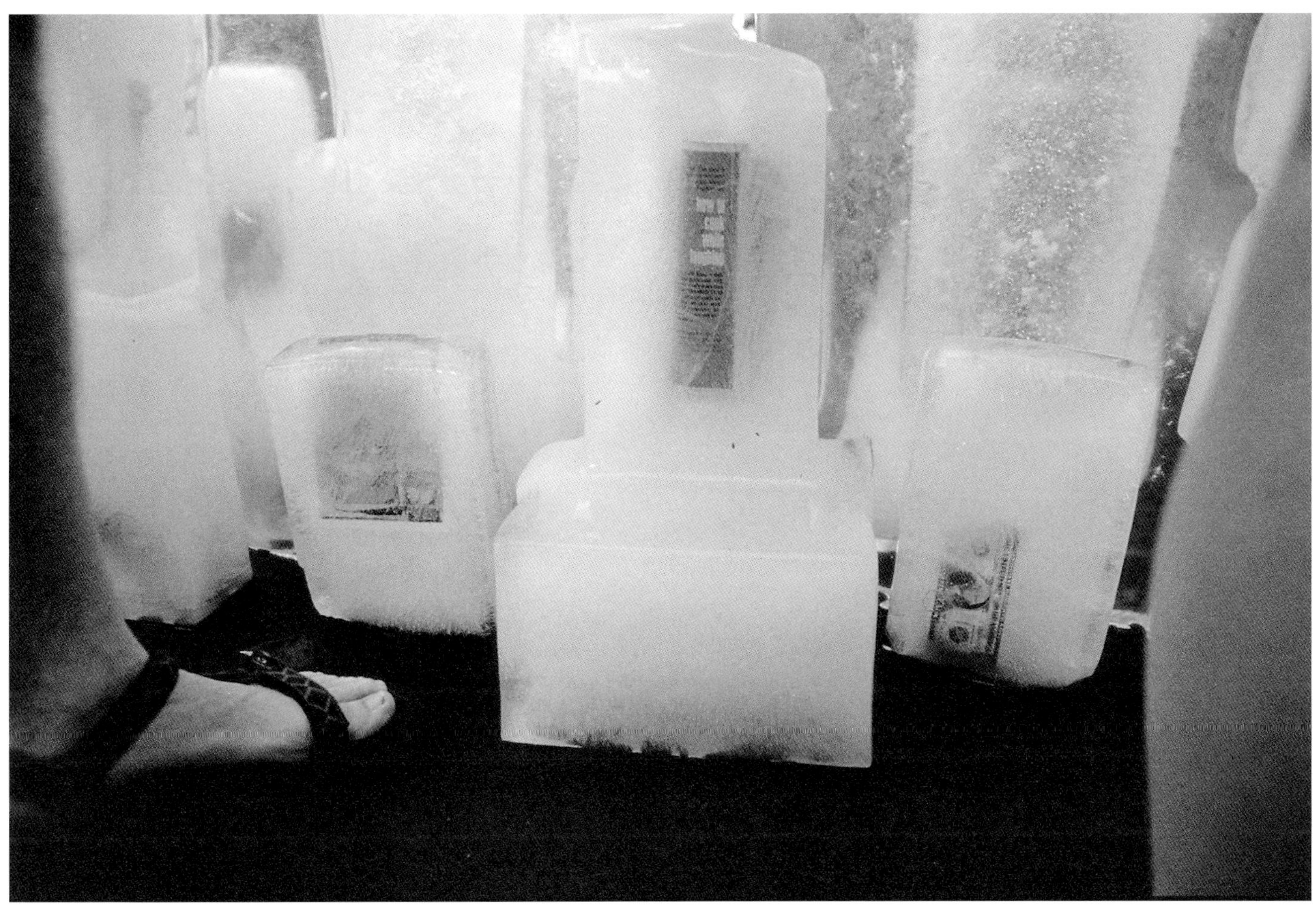

Kristy Edmunds **Perusal** (detail)
1993, Installation and performance, North Park Blocks, Portland. Courtesy of the artist. Photograph: Susan Seubert.

Dennis **Evans**

Dennis Evans's imposing artworks transport viewers into a world of exotica where the numinous past haunts the secular present. Throughout his body of work, beginning in the mid-1970s, Evans has explored the foundations of human thought, drawing on the myths, religions, philosophies, sciences and pseudo-sciences that have shaped human belief systems. Utilizing their codes — language, numbers, symbols, rituals — and the objects, especially books, that encode them, he creates visually and conceptually complex, mixed-media wall constructions and installations that are simultaneously resplendent and abstruse.

Evans's fascination with epistemology has its roots in personal, early experience. Born into a rural Catholic family in eastern Washington in 1946, a time when Latin was still the language of the mass, his schooling was administered by Jesuits who saw no contradiction between intellectual curiosity and religious practice. As an adult he pursues a continuing inquiry into all belief systems; how they are coded and transmitted has become the basis of his art. The panoply of secrets, mystical revelations, and other derivations of occult lore that are so prominent in Evans's work do not displace the rational systems of science and mathematics that have evolved through later ages; instead, they underscore the intermingling of the two.

In 1989 Evans created a major installation titled "tHE gaRden for remeMbered dEsireS" that conflated signifiers of myth, ritual, and destiny in artist-made artifacts within a dimly lit room reminiscent of a crypt. Basing the work on the now arcane symbols of the Tarot, he placed ten stations along the garnet colored walls and in the center of the gallery, each station corresponding to a Tarot card, not as illustration but as a point of reference, or clue, to possible associations and interpretations. While the work could be experienced solely for its visual complexity, rather like a walk-in spread of Tarot cards, familiarity with Tarot references was a boon. Evans, as Hermes, the messenger whose name is highlighted in the title, had dealt cards seeming to divine the sterility leading to the death of a culture devoid of metaphysical belief. That sense of loss, which was imparted by allegorical texts as well as a powerfully visceral impact, transcended the Tarot specificity.

Evans's love of arcane references is matched by his obvious delight in materials and meticulous craftsmanship. As he holds undergraduate degrees in chemistry and ceramics plus the M.F.A. in design, he is well versed in a range of materials that are equally useful in content and structure. The wall constructions, which are the core of his work, begin with wood or metal panels as a base for etched and drilled glass plates, collaged layers of text, rich color, encaustic, and always, actual books. Representing *logos*, their presence, even in unreadable states of mutilation, speaks of the ultimate authority of the word.

Parodying the idea of text as cosmic reason, Evans in 1992 began his *magnum opus*, "Liber Mundi/Liber Vitae, 'The Book of the World/The Book of Life, Containing the Seven Books of Revealed and Concealed Wisdom.'" Comprising seven sections, each to be exhibited as it is finished, it will stand as a collective in which the artist as "high priest" delivers his personal compendium of all knowledge, which he divides under seven headings:

1. *The 72 ( ) of God*
2. *The Theory of Religion*
3. *The Critique of Pure Writing*
4. *The Science of Secrets*
5. *The Periodic Table*
6. *The Four Forces of the Universe*
7. *The Mystery of the Nine Muses*

The Critique of Pure Writing, one of three sections completed by 1994, extends Evans's philosophical meanderings into the realm of poststructuralist theory. It includes twenty-six wall mounted, mixed-media and encaustic pieces, one for each letter of the alphabet. Words, images, and objects relate to a text that sets forth a definition for a word beginning with the subject letter. Beneath the definition, a short, Evans-composed "description" of the book's contents becomes artful obscurantism. The blithe intermixing of signifiers, beginning with the title's suggestion of Kant's *Critique of Pure Reason*, signals Evans's tongue-in-cheek deconstruction of all methods of systematizing knowledge. In his work the systems contain deeper mysteries than the body of knowledge they presume to reveal.

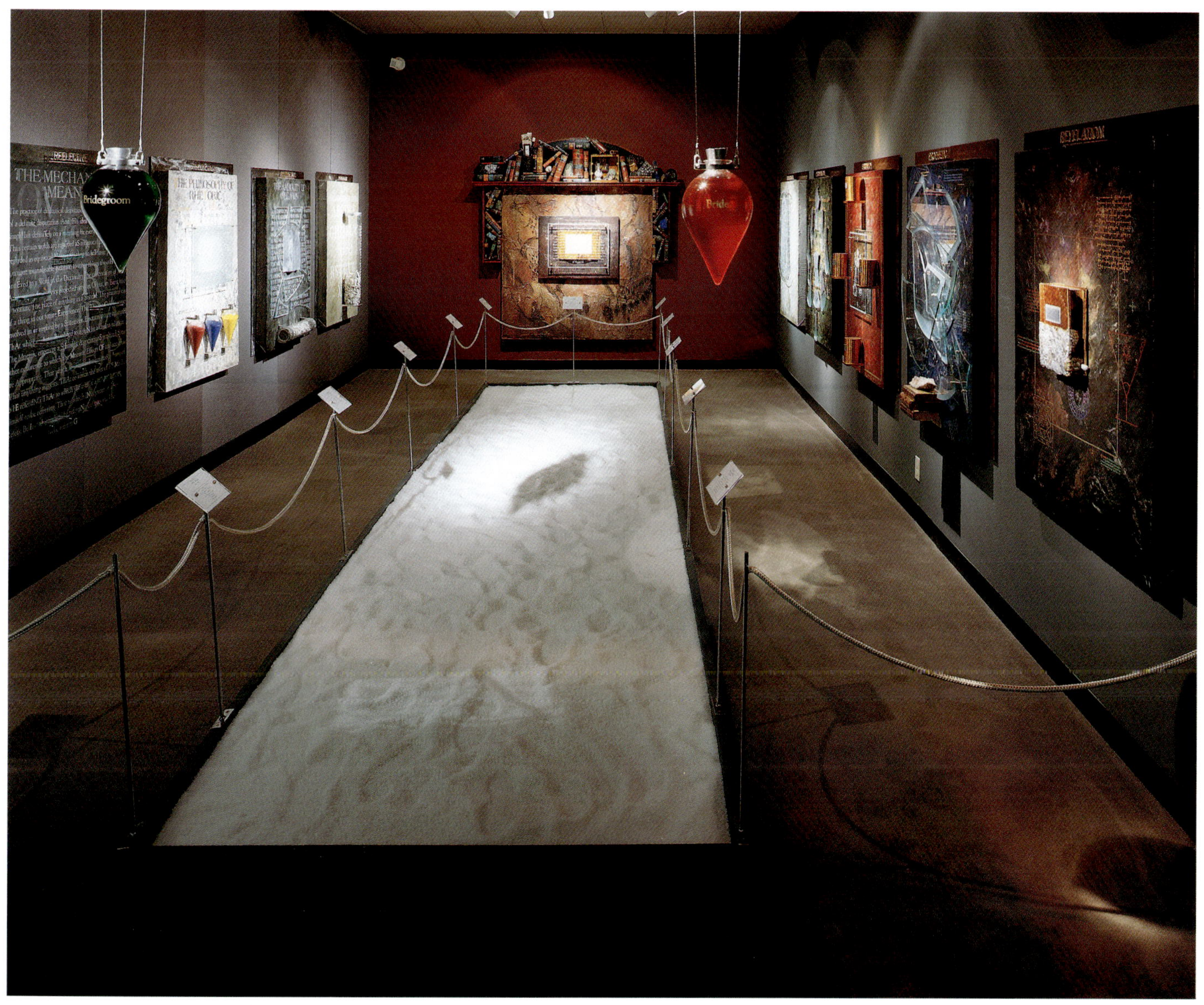

Dennis Evans **The Philosopher's Wedding**
1994, Multi media environmental installation, scale variable. Courtesy of the artist and Linda Farris Gallery. Photograph: Spike Mafford

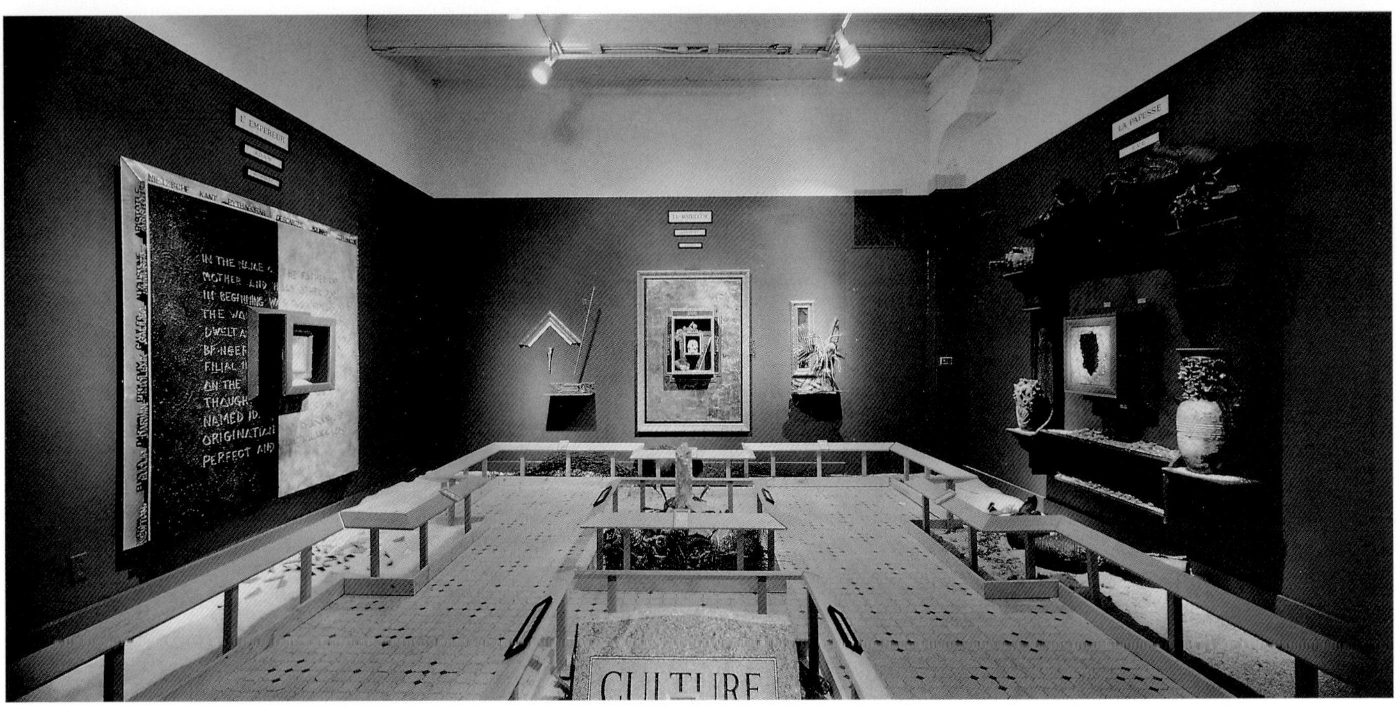

Dennis Evans **tHe gaRden for remeMbered dEsireS**
1989, Multi media environmental installation, size variable. Courtesy of the artist and Linda Farris Gallery. Photograph: John Stamets.

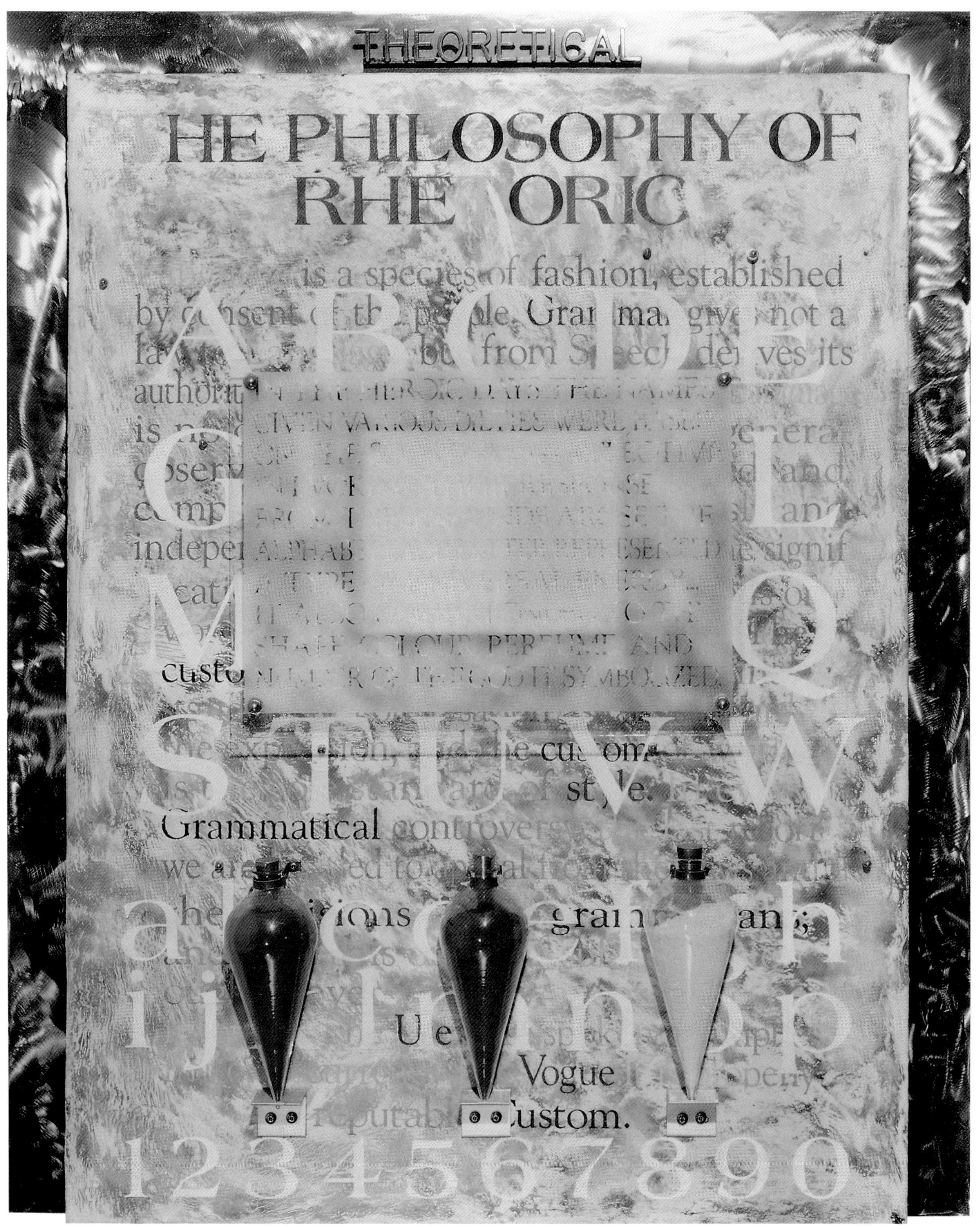

Dennis Evans **The Philosophy of Rhetoric**
1994, Encaustic and mixed media on canvas, 42" x 51" x 6". Collection of Richard and Diane Forman. Courtesy of the artist, Laura Russo Gallery and Linda Farris Gallery. Photograph: Spike Mafford.

Claudia **Fitch**

Claudia Fitch's installations and sculptures, though wide-ranging in subject and appearance, have in common an antic sense of the absurd. As eccentric as props for a Dada stage set, their incongruities, distortions, and omissions blithely thwart visual expectations. Banal subjects — shrubbery, houseplants, furniture, even hairstyles — assume bizarre proportions, becoming manifestations of a surreal subtext. Through their improbable configurations, materials, and spatial arrangements, as much as their imagery, they act as mediators between the physical world of appearances and a subconscious world of aspirations, motives, and desires.

Fitch's eccentric forms, both abstract and representational, are freighted with a latent anthropomorphism, as they are often made up of elements that relate to parts of the body or to a figural stance even when the figure itself is absent. It is not surprising that her art, which is such a potent blend of concept and physicality, has often been compared with that of Louise Bourgeois, and it is an influence she readily acknowledges. However, she credits various other sources as well, including a childhood fascination with Seattle's department store window displays which inspired fantasies of playing with the mannequins and their accoutrements, mentally arranging and re-arranging them to suit her private scenarios. Childhood fantasies have evolved into her adult fascination with displacement and re-inventions of "reality." Like a visionary window dresser, she turns a given, limited space into a radicalized version of a commonplace situation.

What could be more ordinary than a planter box crammed with fake houseplants? So much a part of office decor that it is a visual nonentity, it becomes, in Fitch's hands, a verdant theater of human foibles in which luxuriant artificial plants nearly engulf the ornate, equally artificial topiaries rising from their midst like camouflaged sentinels. Titled *Folly* (in addition to its vernacular meaning the word is an architecture term denoting an ornamental structure), the work was inspired by illustrations of Victorian amusement parks where mechanical wonders, purely decorative objects, and exotic plants were equally entertaining. In a psychological reading, *Folly* is a droll commentary on the strange guises that sublimation assumes.

Fitch's references, although manifestly in history, urban culture, and art, are invariably processed through her quite original perception of the relationship between material reality and one's inner experience of it. Reared and educated in Seattle (she holds a B.F.A. in painting, 1975, from the University of Washington), she lived in New York from 1979 until 1988 where her responses to claustrophobic architecture and "pocket" gardens were realized in "cityscape" tableaux. Since a residency in Rome, where she was impressed by the formal gardens of Italian villas with their topiaries and architectural ornamentation, she has placed many works within that thematic context. A series of "Topiary Studies," welded steel and steel mesh structures covered with plastic greenery and flocking, refer visually to a particular cultural and artistic tradition and conceptually to the artificiality and pretensions inherent in such aberrations of nature.

Now living again in Seattle where architecture and nature are wont to intermingle in close proximity, Fitch's spatial arrangements, as evidenced in *Folly*, reflect density and hidden relationships. While continuing with the garden theme, she is exploring fashion, as it also bears connotations of the tension between public display and private emotions and is produced for the same reasons of ostentation, concealment, and control. Hair fashion is the starting point for *Wig*, a wall-mounted, steel cage-like sculpure that is based on a bouffant 1950s style hairdo with a crowning "pouf" consisting of sharp claws curving inward toward the absent head. At once a sculpture and a picture drawn with steel lines, *Wig* is an illusionistic fusion of three and two-dimensionality, an illusion carried further by the sculpture's shadows as they project a silhouette onto the wall.

Figurine #2 is an even more complicated play on the two-dimensional construct, suggesting both silhouette and an exploded, flattened volumetric form. Like *Wig*, it is analogous to body parts but further removed from personal references. Constructed of steel and Styrofoam and covered with spray-on flocking, it might be taken for a cartoon figure in search of anatomical identity. More to the point, it is characteristic of Fitch's remarkable metamorphoses of the mundane into perceptually tantalizing works of art.

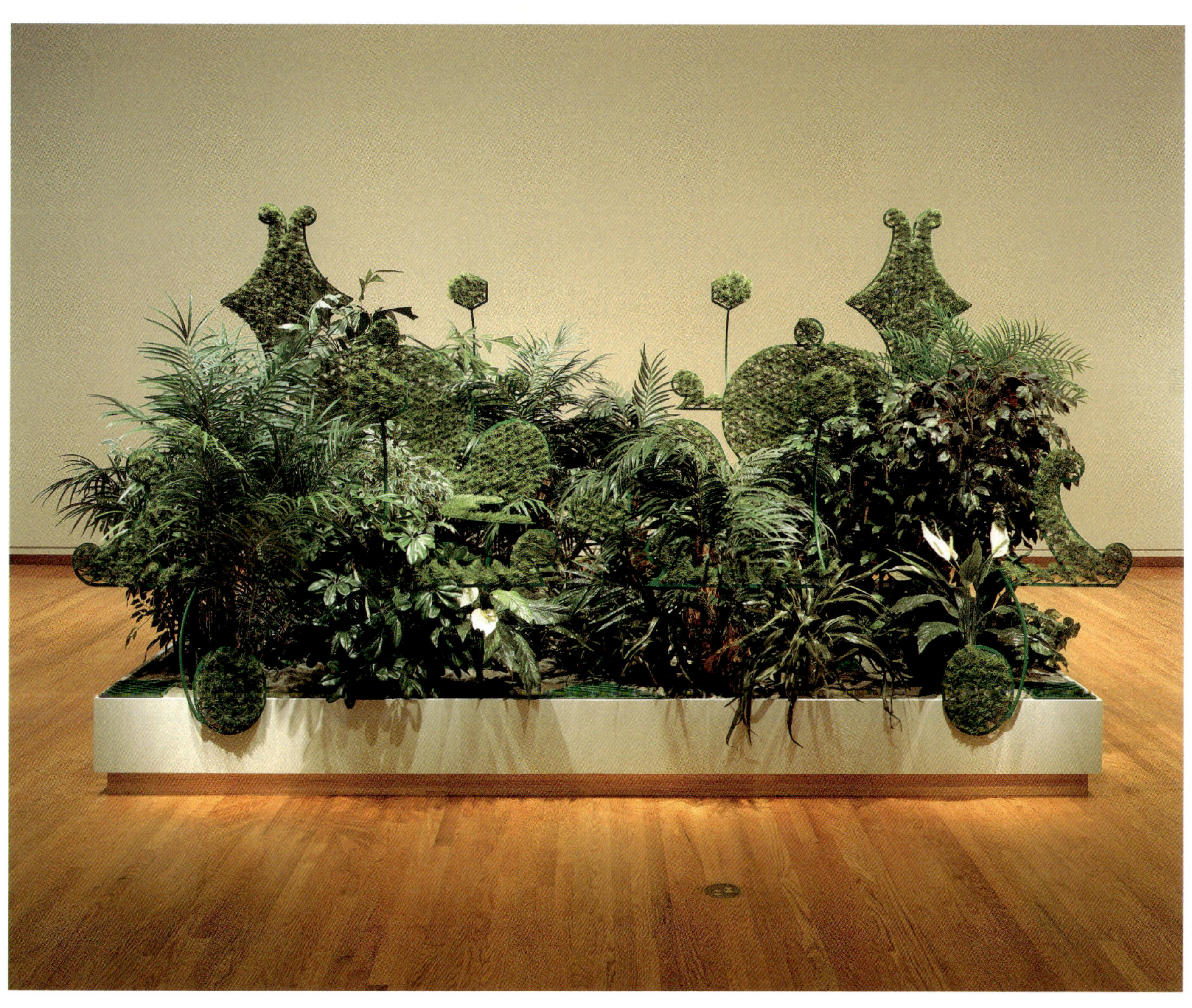

Claudia Fitch **Folly**
1994, Fabric, plastic, steel, paint, sand, 88" x 144" x 96". Courtesy of the artist and Fuel Gallery, Seattle. Photograph: Susan Dirk.

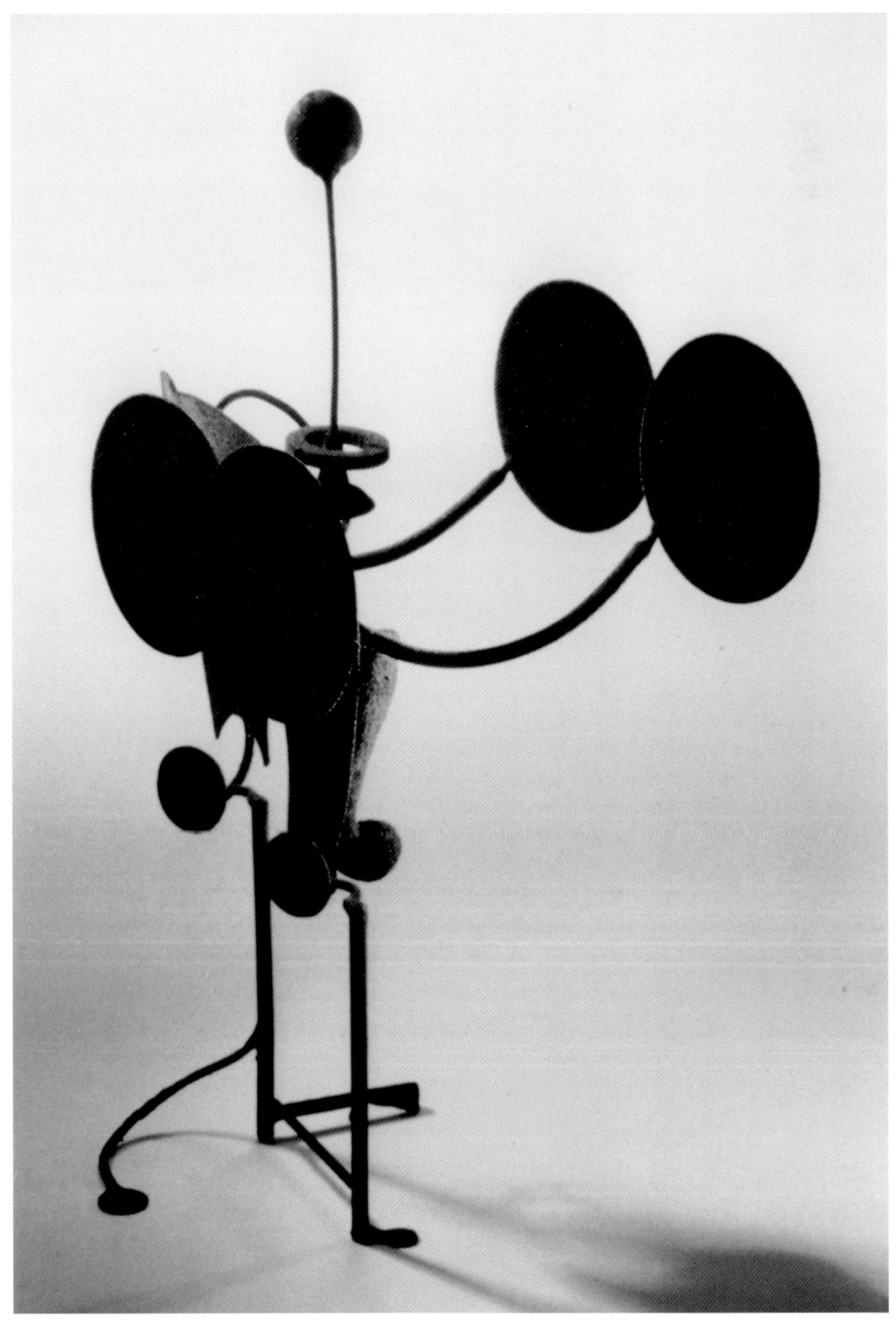

Claudia Fitch **Figurine #2**
1993, Steel, flocking, 20" x 10" x 11". Courtesy of the artist and Adam Baumgold Fine Art, New York. Photograph: Ken Wagner.

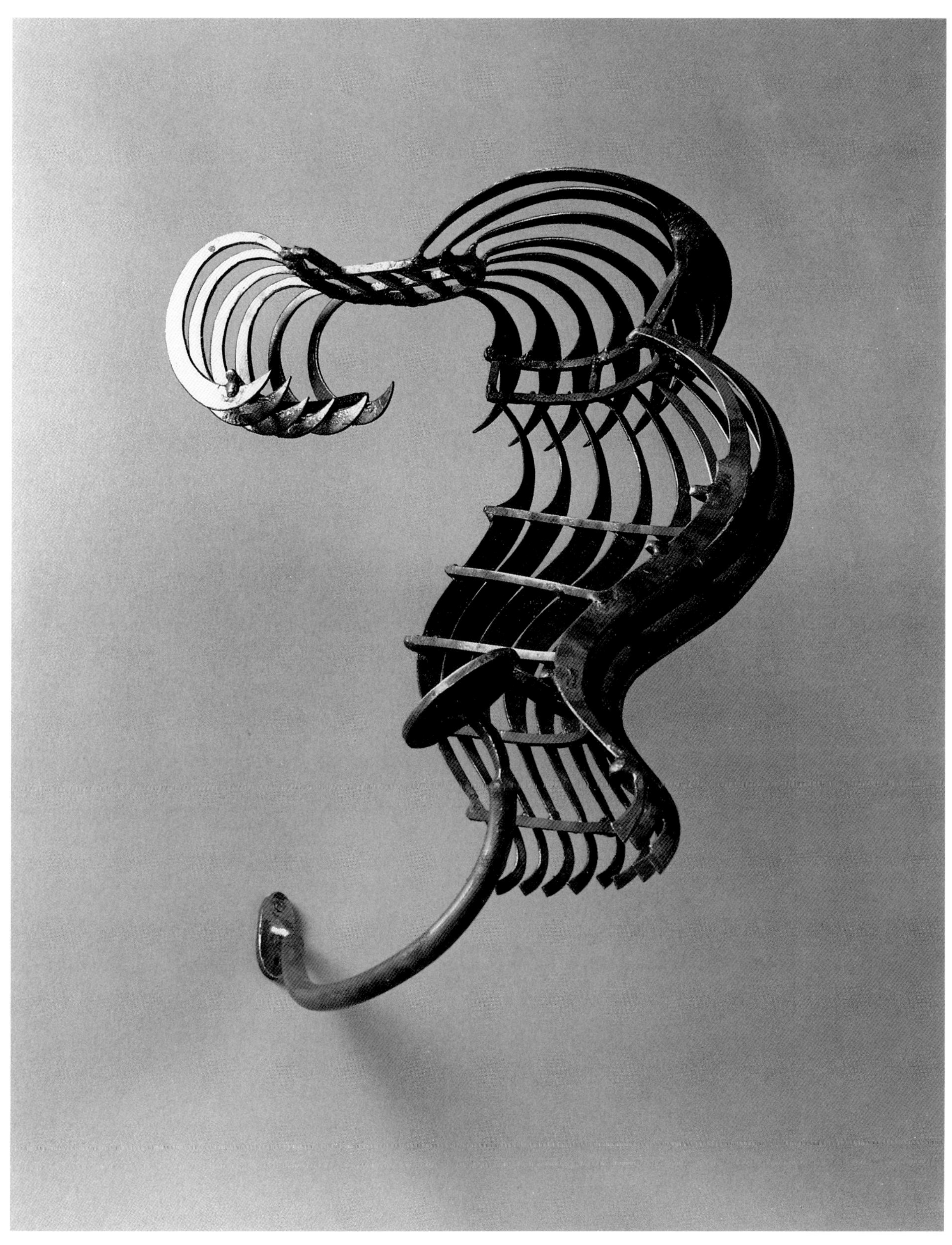

Claudia Fitch **Wig**
1990, Steel, 16" x 11" x 18". Seattle Art Museum permanent collection. Photograph: Lynn Hamrick.

Gregory **Grenon**

Gregory Grenon's stated aim, which he has achieved with notable success, is to "make paintings bold enough to be seen from across the room — or across the street." His expressionistic, figurative paintings are so bold, both in their subject matter and style, that they never fail to demand — and get — an immediate, visceral response; they may be rejected but they cannot be ignored. Arguably the strongest figurative painter in the Northwest, Grenon's forte is agonizingly subjective pictures of women. Most are of the face alone, up close and frontal, and it is not a pretty sight. Each face is, however, a gauge of the subject's state of mind, a psychic map of her personal journey through the ups and downs, mostly downs, of life. Grenon focuses on a particular strata of society, that of young, urban, worldly-wise women. Through the use of arbitrary, often lurid colors and simplified, aggressive drawing to heighten the level of emotive content, he approaches the artistic realm inhabited by those German Expressionists denounced by Hitler as "degenerate." He stops short of joining them, however, because he is neither a political activist nor a social critic. His territory is the intimate, interior lives of women, especially those whose conflicting id and ego never quite find equilibrium. Their sidelong glances, feline eyes, and self-absorbed expressions indicate a pronounced inner ambivalence.

The product of a harsh urban environment in Detroit where he was born in 1948, Grenon is well acquainted with the milieu he depicts. His early artistic endeavors were cultivated within a free-wheeling, inner city group of artist friends known as the Cass Corridor. Their "anything goes" approach to art and life was tempered for Grenon by the disciplined training he received a little later as a lithography printer. These experiences proved to be the the foundation of his aesthetic and his technique. The three years he worked at Landfall Press in Chicago gave him a proficiency at mixing colors that marks him today as a superb colorist.

Possibly as an outgrowth of the Cass Corridor influence, Grenon began painting on glass and plexiglass about 1973 using discarded windows and doors as frames. Already accustomed to the reverse procedure of printmaking, he easily visualized a finished composition as he applied colors in reverse order behind the glass. The frame's characteristics often dictate the direction of the painting and act as an extension of the imagery. Both border and enclosure, its decorated surface is a foil for the smooth reflective glass. Grenon works very fast, starting with a black oil stick to lay out a rough drawing, followed by a quick application of colors that form the mottled skin tones, vivid make-up, brushy hair styles, and trendy clothes of his subjects. His highly charged coloration continually moves between description and dramatic expressiveness.

In 1976, dissatisfied with his experience of living in three large cities, Detroit, Chicago, and New York, Grenon visited Portland and immediately decided that it offered the tranquility he sought. Soon after re-locating he obtained gallery representation and quickly became successful. He is now represented in Portland, Seattle, New Orleans, Chicago, and New York and is included frequently in exhibitions throughout the United States and in Europe.

Although modest-size portrait-heads are Grennon's hallmark, he has consistently, if less frequently, produced full figures, clothed and unclothed, and some male images. The heads are notable, however, not only in number, but because they are so trenchantly depicted. The raw energy that emanates from these works challenges viewers to assess — or re-assess — an image of women as primal narcissists beneath their worldly facades. Although he courts charges of misogyny in his pursuit of psychic reality, he creates from a profound inner need and like his subjects, is impervious to opinions and trends, especially those that move the art world.

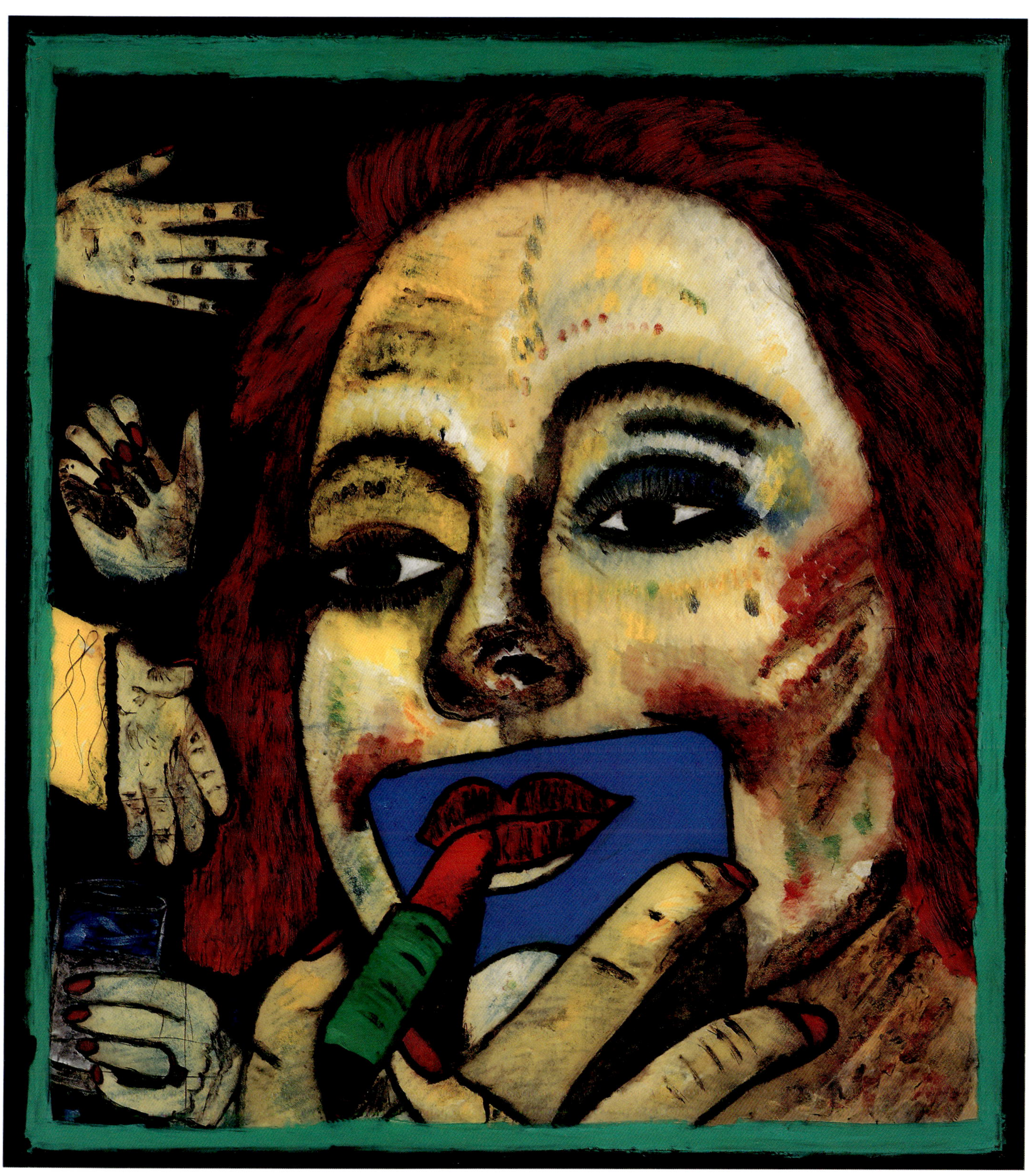

Gregory Grenon **We Are Not Here To Kill You**
1994, Oil on plexiglas, 81" x 73". Courtesy of the artist and Jamison/Thomas Gallery. Photograph: Bill Bachhuber.

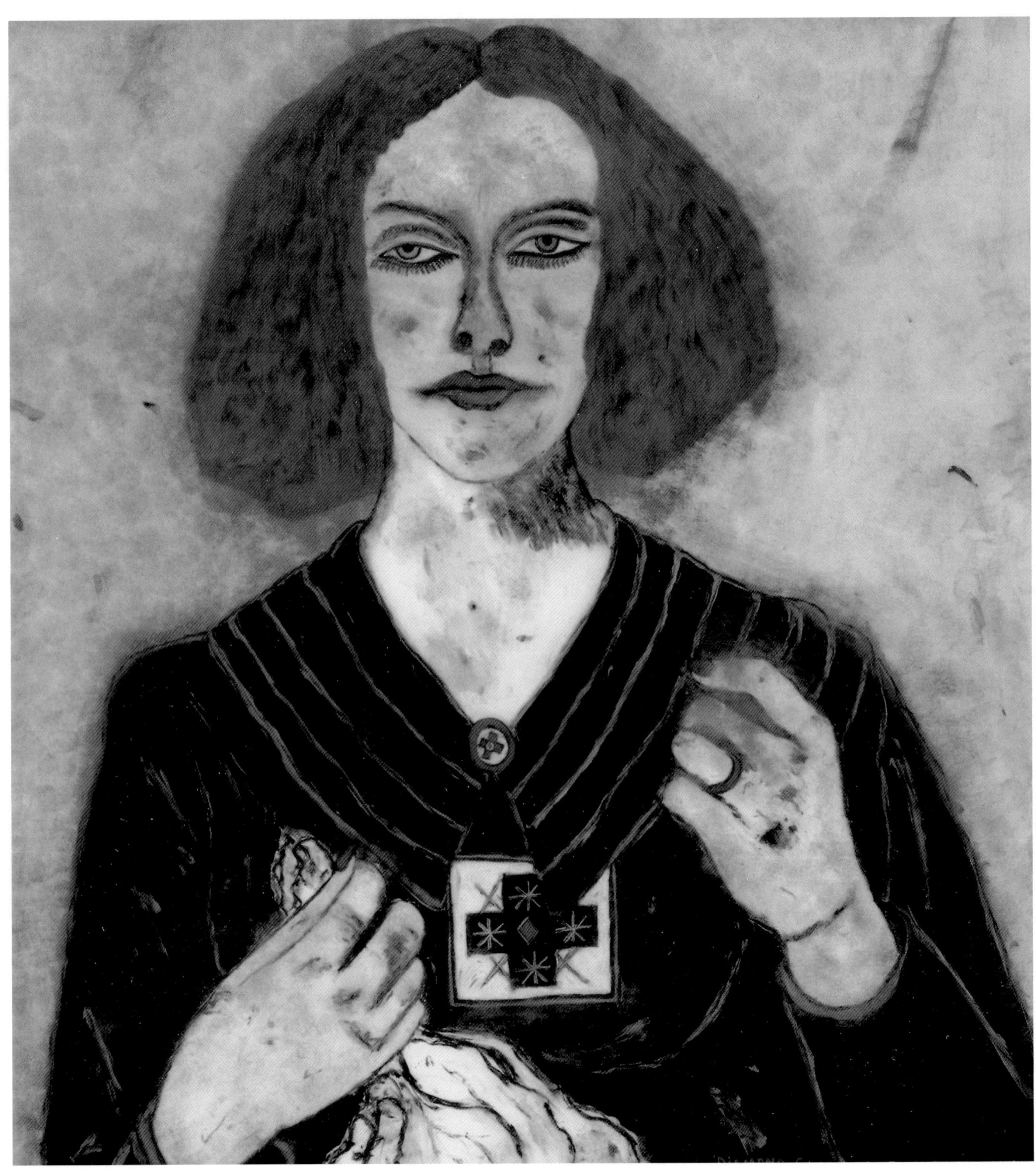

Gregory Grenon **Diamond Girls are Bad Girls**
1991, Oil on plexiglas, 82" x 73½". Private collection. Courtesy of Jamison/Thomas Gallery.

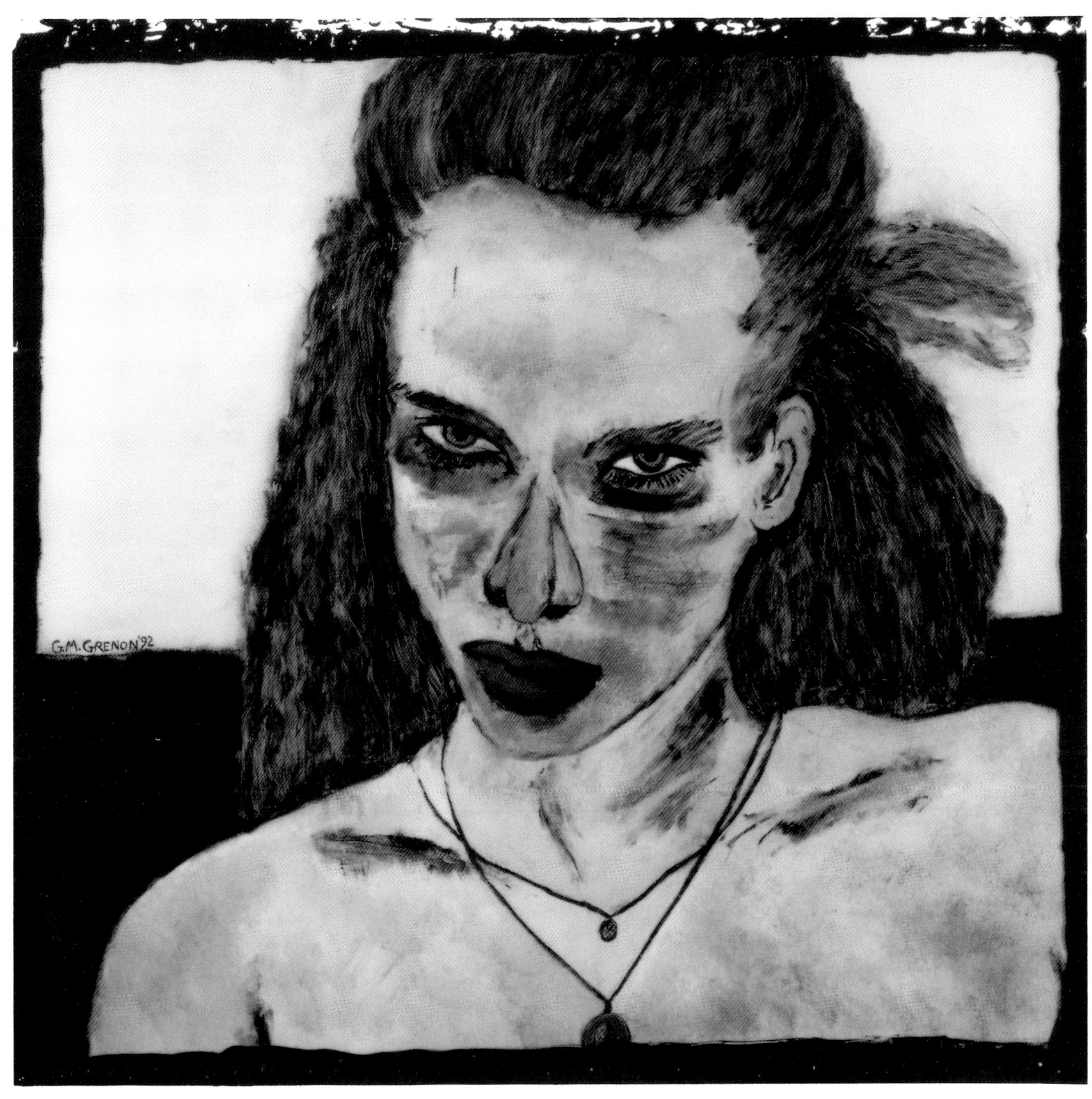

Gregory Grenon **Shock Me**
1992. Oil on plexiglas, 52" x 58" x 8¾". Courtesy of the artist and Jamison/Thomas Gallery. Photograph: Bill Bachhuber.

Sally **Haley**

Sally Haley has created a large body of work remarkable for its evidence of the development over more than a half century of a personal, independent vision. Since her arrival in Portland in 1947 she has worked consistently toward the perfection of a formalized still life painting style that brings a fresh perspective to the genre. Blending what seem to be contradictory traditions — fourteenth-century Italian art, seventeenth-century Dutch still life, and twentieth-century abstraction — she achieves an unusual marriage of representation and abstraction. Precisely and sensuously depicted, her images of everyday objects, mostly from kitchen and garden, epitomize her formal development, which has been in large part an exploration of historical problems having to do with the resolution of relationships between figure and ground and between flatness and dimensional illusion. When Haley paints a cut casaba melon, isolating it against a background of horizontal bands of black and brown, it is not only from her assimilation of Euro-American art history; it comes also from many years of thoughtful attention, philosophical and analytical, to her immediate surroundings.

The evolution of these unusual paintings began with her reaction to the classically academic preparation she received at Yale University where she graduated with a B.F.A. in 1931. Rejecting the conservatism then dominating art education, she turned her attention to modernism and found in it a particular affinity for the surrealist, architectural settings painted by Giorgio de Chirico. His treatment of pictorial space and scale was important to Haley who had already started to experiment with juxtaposing interior and exterior spaces. She was drawn, also, to the clarity and theatricality of his spare compositions, a quality she admired as well in Italian paintings by fourteenth century painters, in particular Simone Martini. Martini's acute observation, his architecture, and his earthy reality were absorbed into Haley's developing style.

During the 1950s her work was grounded on surrealist tenets. Rectangles and rhomboids of contrasting colors were utilized to indicate empty interior spaces and were angled in such a way that perspective is skewed. In a few paintings of this period representational images appear, harbingers of still lifes to come. One of these, depicting shrouded figures and architecture viewed from disorienting perspectives, was included in an international survey in 1954 at the Walker Art Center in Minneapolis, Minnesota, organized by H. H. Arnason.

As she turned her attention to the placement of objects in space Haley began to reduce pictorial depth, and by the 1970s the mass of the object-image was the only indication of volume. Backgrounds became flat fields of soft, tonally related colors. A fruit or other object was sometimes placed on or near a draped white napkin. The undulating folds of the napkin anchor the objects without disrupting the flat, uninflected background.

Haley shares with proto-Renaissance painters the egg tempera medium as well as an aesthetic viewpoint. It is a technique she learned at Yale and has practiced ever since. Although it is too restrictive for use in the large paintings which she executes in acrylics, she relishes the coupling of drawing and painting, the lustrous colors and creamy surfaces that tempera makes possible. Her small tempera panels, enclosed in deluxe frames of her own making, are vibrant portraits of modest still life subjects, as closely observed as if they were members of her family, which, in a sense, they are.

Haley, who was born in Bridgeport, Connecticut, in 1908, was a mature artist when she and her husband, fellow painter Michele Russo, moved from Connecticut to Portland soon after World War II. She established a studio in her home for practical family reasons, but over the years has found this arrangement to be both satisfying and productive. A very private person, she views her art not as something separate but as an integral part of her daily life. The objects she observes and paints with such acuity move easily back and forth between her kitchen and studio, valued equally in both settings.

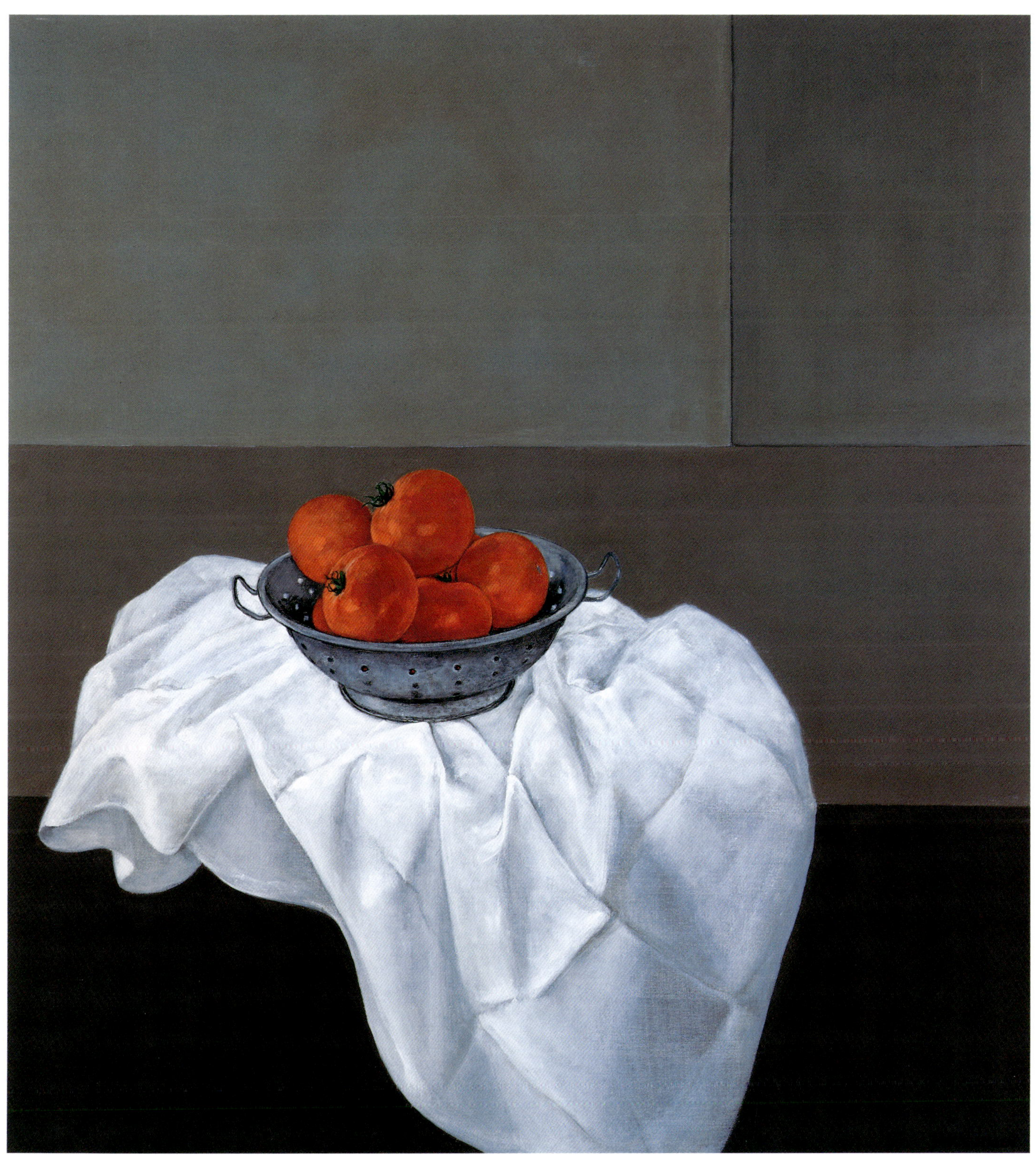

Sally Haley Untitled (tomatoes)
1991, Acrylic on canvas, 44" x 41". Private collection. Courtesy of the artist and Laura Russo Gallery. Photograph: David Browne.

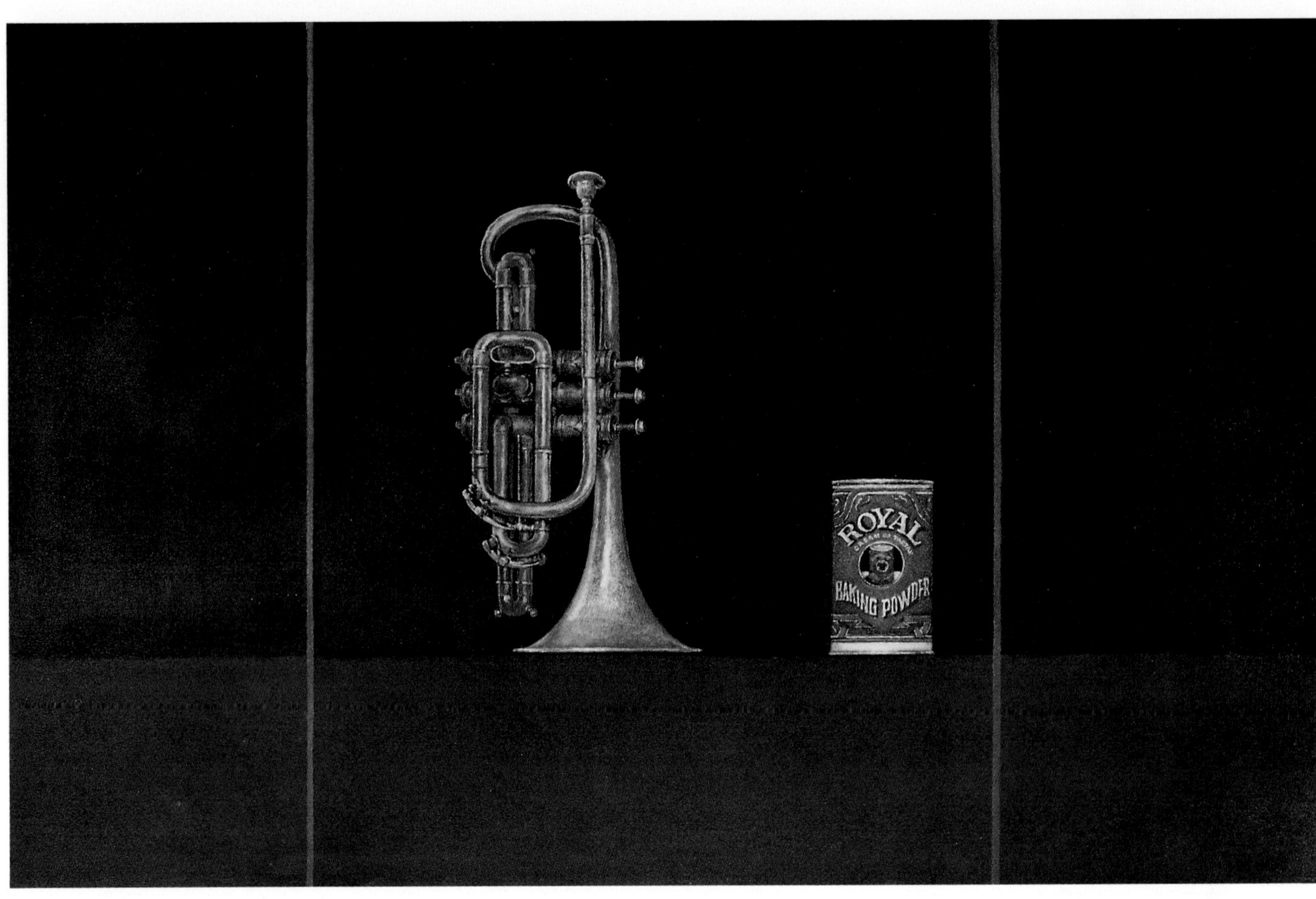

Sally Haley **Untitled**
1972, Acrylic on canvas, 31" x 48". Private collection. Courtesy of the artist and Laura Russo Gallery.

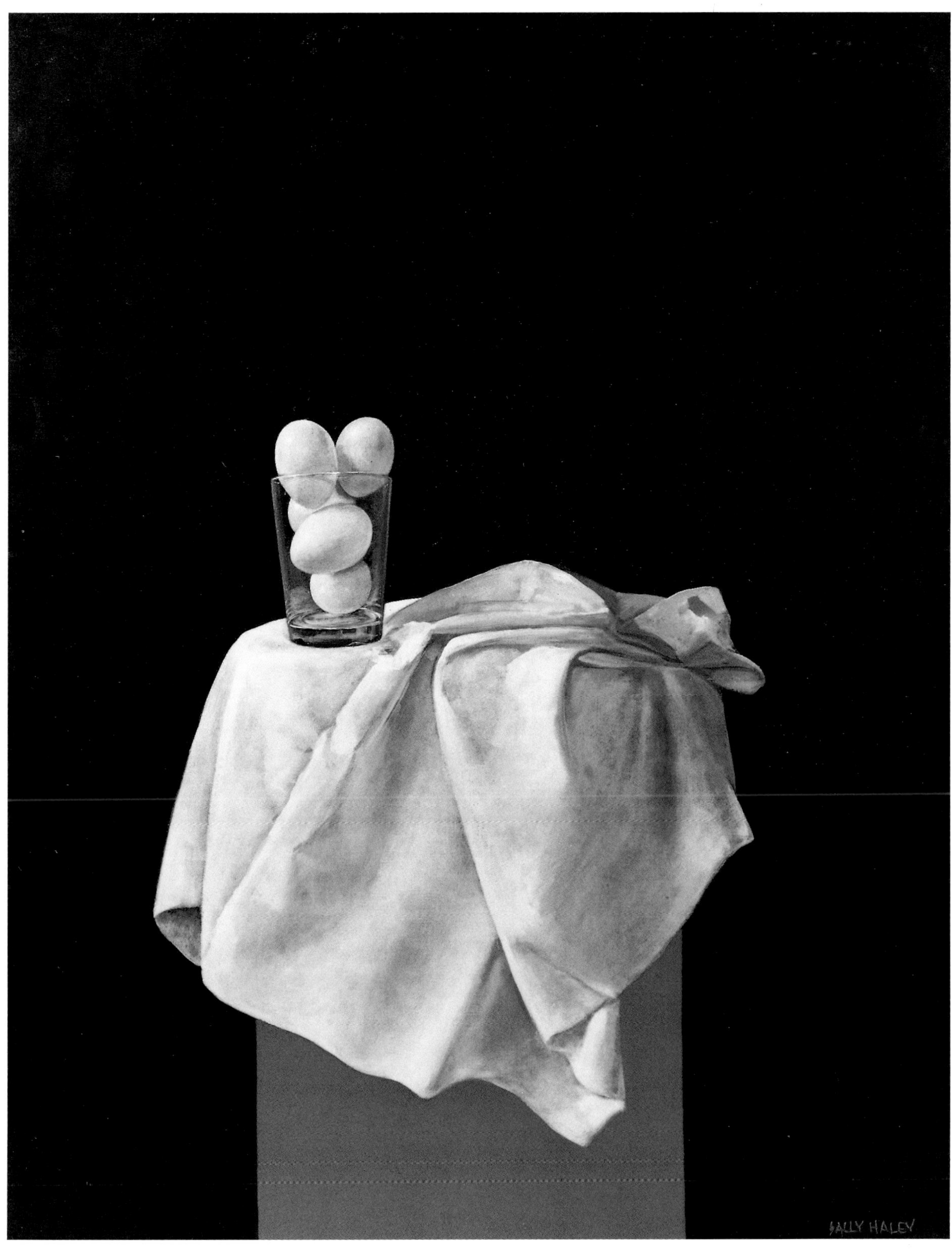

Sally Haley **Untitled (eggs, drape)**
1989, Acrylic on canvas, 46" x 36". Private collection. Courtesy of the artist and Laura Russo Gallery. Photograph: David Browne.

Gaylen **Hansen**

Gaylen Hansen paints tall tales in the way laconic cowboys are wont to tell them, with just enough truth to make the impossible seem plausible. A native Westerner, he has lived since 1957 in the High Palouse of southeastern Washington, a wide-open plateau that might easily accomodate the mythic proportions and exploits of the animals, including a few humans, and plants who populate his fabulations. Insects, birds, dogs, and fish grow bigger than humans in his world, and threaten to turn the tables on human claims to natural superiority. Surreally entrancing, his large oil paintings on unstretched canvases are a unique blend of narration and dynamic visual effects, both drawing directly on his experience of the time and place in which he lives.

Hansen's eccentric vision took shape in the aftermath of the artistic ferment of the 1950s and '60s. At the time of his graduate study at the University of Southern California in Los Angeles, where he received the M.F.A. in 1956, Abstract Expressionism held sway. He adopted its tenets in paintings based on landscape, and later, following his acceptance of a teaching position at Washington State University in Pullman, explored the possibilities of Pop Art and Minimalism with his students. When he realized that he was too far removed from the New York arena to succeed by its criteria, he decided that there was nothing to be lost in doing exactly as he pleased. Ironically, the "outsider" body of works that he has created since that epiphany has brought the national success that eluded him earlier.

Imagery has always been important to Hansen, even when it was submerged in gestural abstractions. During the 1960s, as he abandoned abstraction, he began to develop the inventory of images as well as the formal strategies that continue to serve him. He credits Rajput and Mughal painting, in particular the specific figuration within static, generalized settings, and the distinct divisions of color, as influences in this transition. Assimilating these characteristics into his thorough grounding in Western art history and modern movements, he adopted a simplified drawing style, deceptively naive in its appearance, as a means of incorporating humor and exaggeration in allegorical representations.

Among the images that appear with some regularity is Hansen's alter ego, "the Kernal", who sallies forth from "Fort Bentleg" into wondrous encounters with gigantic insects and plants whose anthropomorphism is funny but also unnerving. As a small, unprepossessing Everyman the Kernal embodies the pleasure, confusion, and apprehension in our human relationships with the natural world. Brought forth from Hansen's anti-art sentiments, the figure was the direct result of a drawing of a free-floating, striped bent leg. In Hansen's words, "it didn't refer to anything, including art." However, it did connect with his enjoyment of the Western literature of mountain men, which triggered the imaginative context for Hansen's — and the Kernal's — vision.

Beneath the humor, Hansen's work conveys a respect for the unrelenting survival tactics in the natural order of things. The ferocity of both species pictured in *Dogs and Bees* portends a disasterous encounter whose outcome seems highly uncertain. With *Bison, Fish, and Tulip* the rigid monumentality of the images suggests even greater ecological peril. Mitigating such intimations of primal terror, however, *Putting Up the Stars* is a reminder of the wonder of the universe, especially when seen in the clear night skies of the Palouse.

In these paintings, as in all his work, Hansen rises above trite sentimentality not only because of the breadth of imaginative subject matter but also through the sheer visual power of his explicit, stage-like compositions, the strong, simple shapes, and most of all, his fluent handling of color. Although colors seem to be drily brushed, they are, in fact, layered and scumbled, creating an energy to match that of the exuberant drawing and whimsical narration.

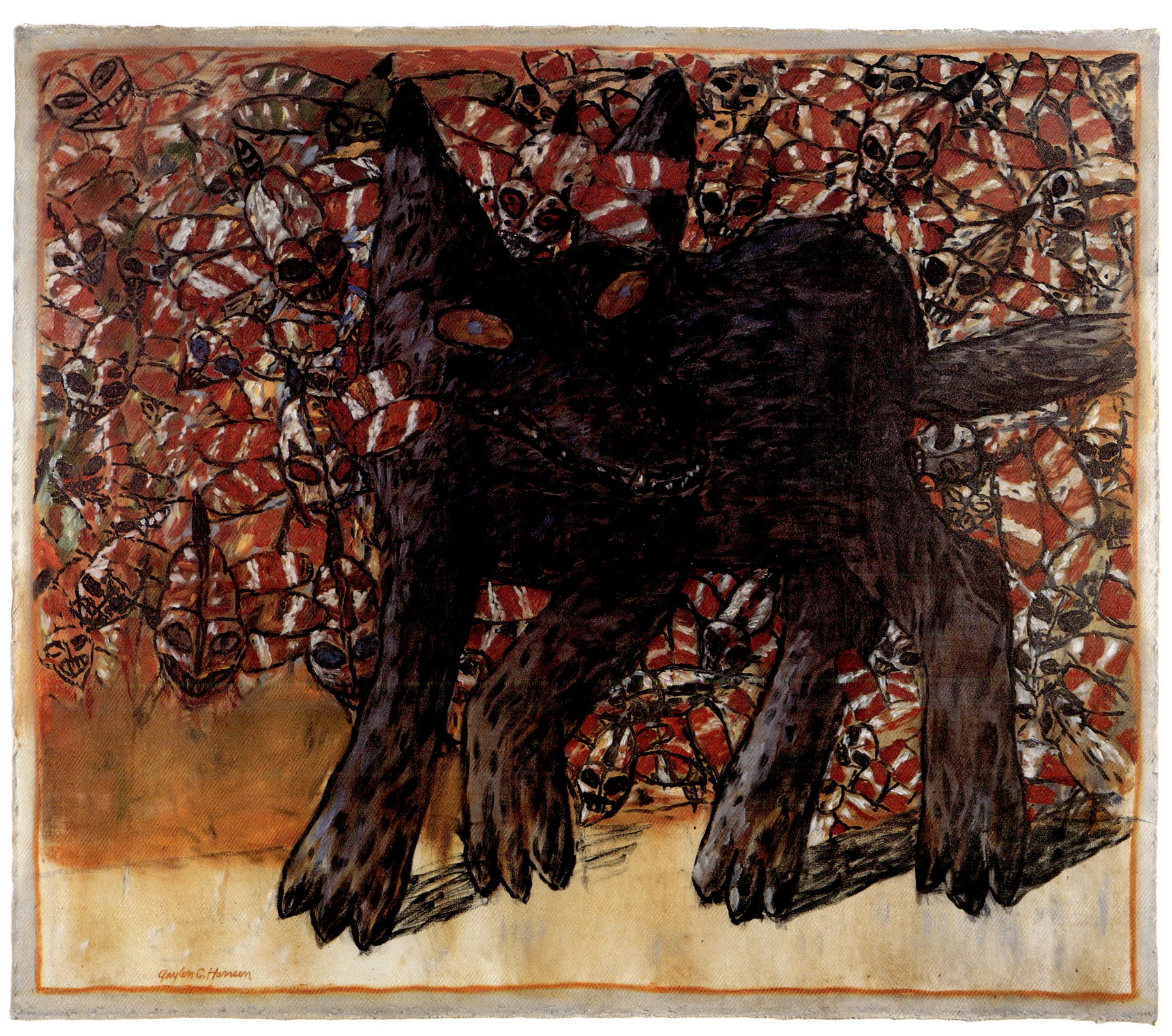

Gaylen Hansen **Dog and Bees**
1987, Oil on canvas, 60" x 72". Private collection. Courtesy Linda Hodges Gallery.

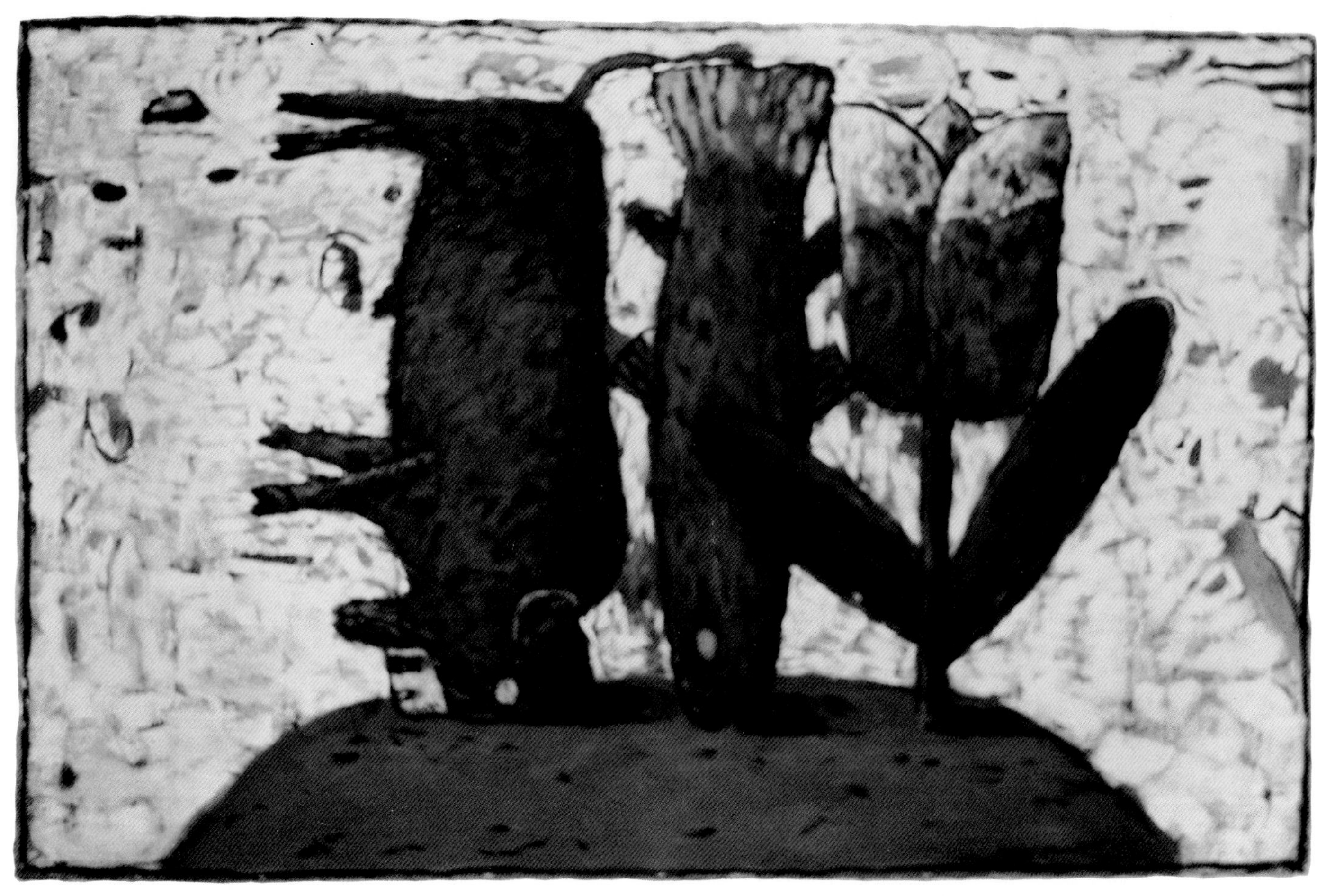

Gaylen Hansen **Bison, Fish and Tulip**
1992, Oil on canvas, 48" x 76". Private collection. Courtesy of Linda Hodges Gallery.

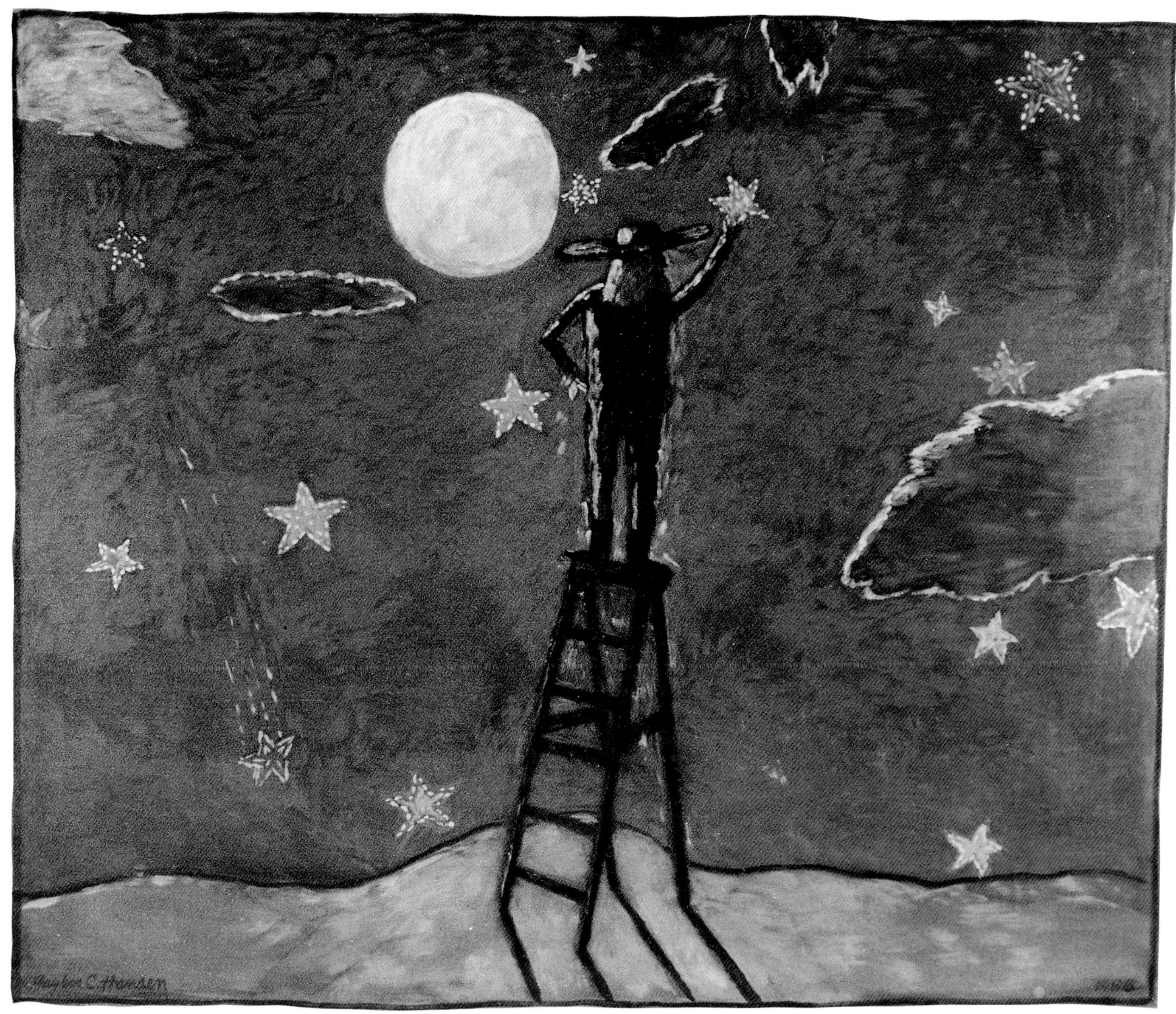

Gaylen Hansen **Putting up the Stars**
1987, Oil on canvas, 60" x 72". Private collection. Courtesy of Linda Hodges Gallery.

Robert **Helm**

Robert Helm's family has lived in the Palouse of eastern Washington since the late nineteenth century. His experience of its stark, open landscape is rooted in memory, history, and daily living, all of which are fused in artworks that transform commonplaces of the visual world into disjunctive, strange manifestations of a mentally constructed world. He depicts ordinary, familiar subjects — twigs, wood planks, rocks and the like — with exact verisimilitude but discomfiting ambiguity. Full of unspecifiable significance, his paintings on wood panels might be viewed as contemporary, secular versions of Medieval icons, speaking not of God, however, but of the rupture between ourselves and nature — and the nature of our experience.

The comparison to icons rests also in the craftsmanship, the shapes, the very objectness of these unusual works. Throughout the 1980s Helm utilized an arch shape for the panels, on occasion grouping them as diptychs or tryptychs. Whether arched or rectangular, all his pieces are enclosed in elaborate frames, which he constructs, that are integral elements of the work. He is a meticulous and versatile craftsman in wood, metal, and leather and considers craft to be indispensable to the meaning and value of a work of art. Frames may be tooled leather, or exquisitely finished hardwood, or wood manipulated to emulate another substance, such as the "rock" frame of *Stone Room.* By their conspicuous presence they disconnect the scene from reality, emphasizing the separateness of a private realm accessed only in imagination.

Helm's use of the arch relates not to architecture, but to vision; the human field of vision, in his opinion, is shaped by the contour of the eye and the plane of the ground. As such, the shape is a psychological link between what is seen and how it is perceived. His attention to perceptual subtleties is at its most intriguing, however, in a *trompe l'oeil* combination of wood inlay seamlessly incorporated into many compositions. The usual sense of *trompe l'oeil* is inverted, however: instead of an illusionary painted surface perfectly duplicating wood objects, actual wood veneer is at times substituted for the painted image. In both *Stone Room* and *Floating Wood,* materiality and illusion are inextricably intertwined.

Dualities also figure importantly in Helm's consideration of time in relationship to his work. Time stands still within the pictures; it is frozen, fixed on seemingly insignificant objects that are forever held in memory. Past existence is represented in the histories of materials he collects and utilizes: rosewood and mahogany beams from a schooner used by Robert Louis Stevenson, floorboards from a girl's school dormitory, a block from the staircase to Ernest Hemingway's first apartment in Paris. There is his own time devoted to the making of each piece and finally, the future time of the work's existence in the world beyond the studio.

Where Birds Go at Night (July), 1993, is one of a sequence of twelve poetic paintings, one for each month. (The title of the series was taken from a poem containing the question, "where do cats go at night?.") Like the other eleven, all of which feature a single bird, *July* is an alluring dream-space of marble and gold. The watchful sparrow is surrounded by images — rocks, twigs, spheres — regularly seen in Helm's work.

Because of its unique physicality and enigmatic iconography, Helm's work defies easy categorization. It has been widely exhibited throughout the country, eliciting such varied descriptions as surrealist, luminist, "outsider," and postmodern. It is deeply rooted in a specific environment, history, and personal memories, yet it is timeless and without place. Like Proust's use of "the little crumb of madeleine" (in *Swann's Way*), Helm summons an extraordinary remembrance of things past with the image of an ordinary small sparrow.

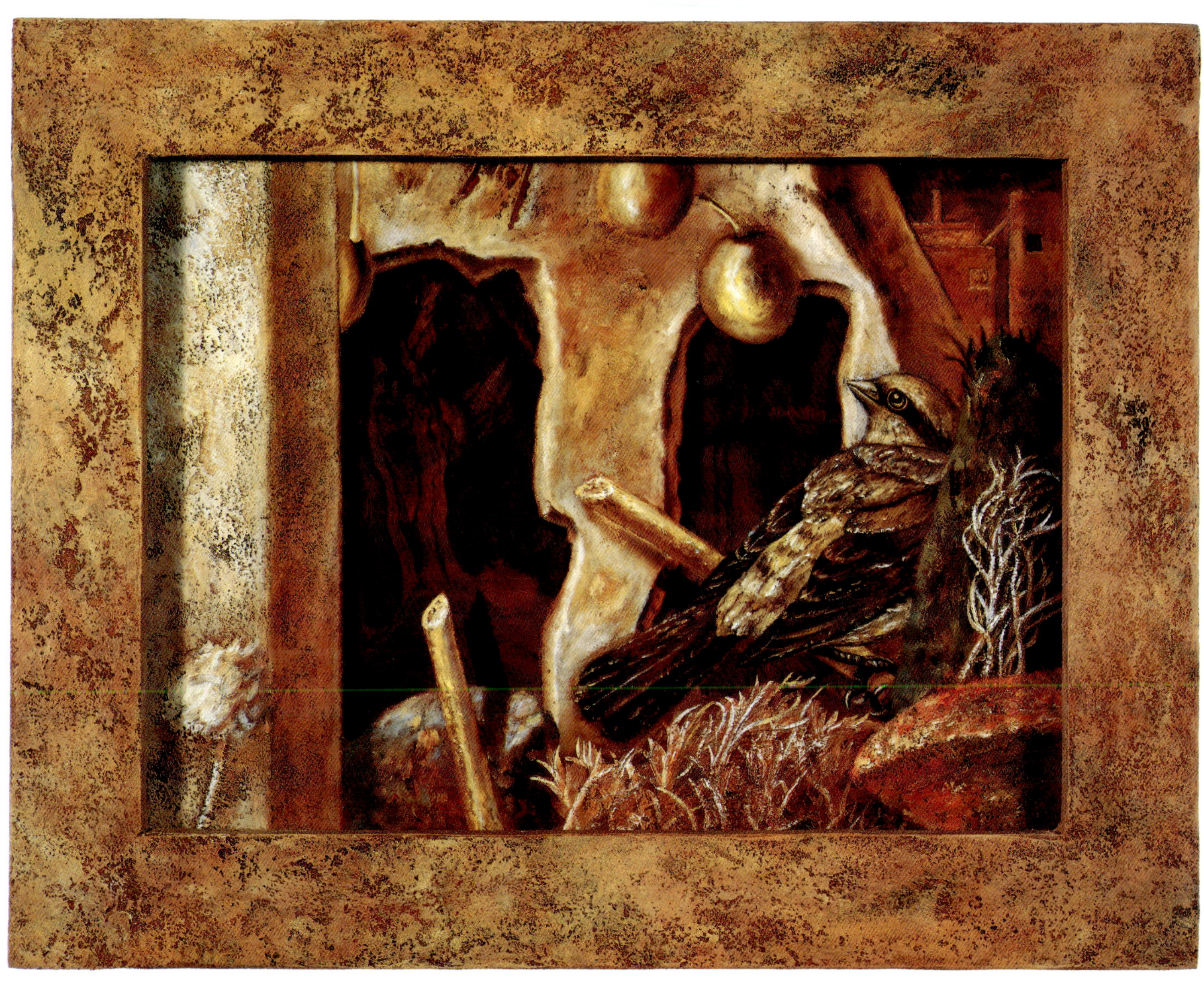

Robert Helm **Where Birds Go at Night (July)**
1992, Oil on panel with wood inlay, 14" x 18" (framed). Collection of The Capital Group, Inc., Los Angeles. Courtesy of L.A. Louver Gallery, Los Angeles. Photograph: William Nettles.

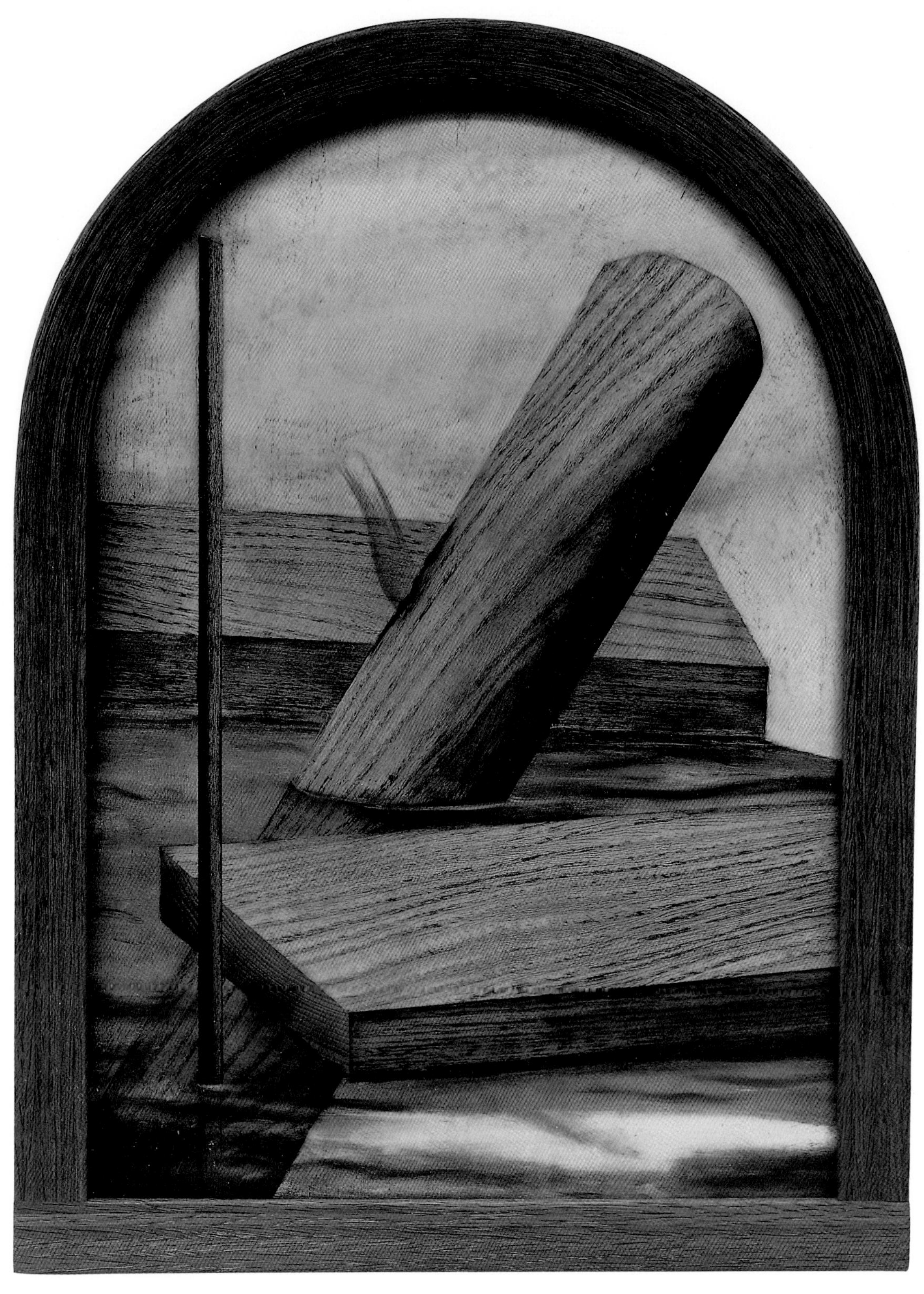

Robert Helm **Floating Wood**
1983, Oil on panel with wood inlay, 20¼" x 15" x ¾". Collection of Pere Alexis. Courtesy of L.A. Louver Gallery, Los Angeles. Photograph: Arthur Okazaki.

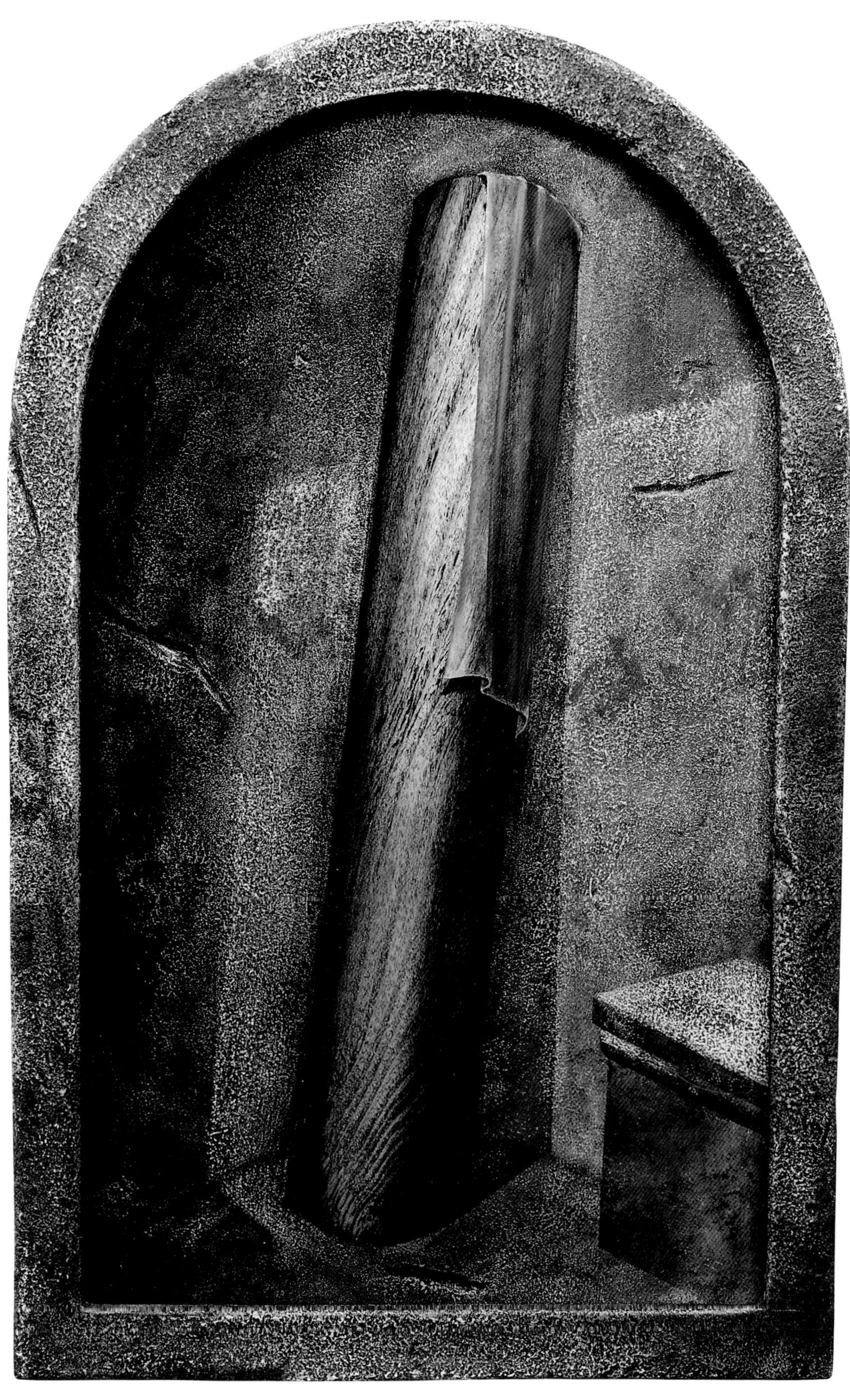

Robert Helm **Stone Room**
1983, Oil on panel with wood inlay, 20¾" x 13" x 1¾". Private collection. Courtesy of L.A. Louver Gallery, Los Angeles. Photograph: Arthur Okazaki

Robert **Herdlein**

Robert Herdlein acknowledges no boundary between art as object and art as social action. After establishing an enviable reputation for his ability to transform big, unsightly industrial cast-offs into the high art of galleries and museums, he changed his practice of art so drastically that many thought he had left the field altogether. Writing for the brochure accompanying an exhibition at the Tacoma Art Museum in 1991, he stated, "I believe in the transformational capabilities of art, and my usage of humble materials, whose origins and functions are questionable, tends to make that idea more evident." He has since chosen to make his idea evident through positive intervention in the lives of children. The two enterprises, although seemingly distinct, are indeed related when considered within the life-encompassing view of art that shapes this unconventional artist's personal philosophy.

A little more than a year after arriving in Seattle in 1987 Herdlein exhibited sculptures constructed from scavenged materials. At this time he combined "found" pieces into cubist-related assemblages, a style irreverently tagged as "Poverty Pop." Very soon, however, he abandoned almost all alteration and let his heroic artifacts of industrial junkyards speak for themselves, their history, their relationship to a profligate consumer society and to the art world's credos. Typically, a 1989 gallery show consisted of four pieces: two fiberglass shower stalls, a tin roof long separated from the shed it once covered, and a huge industrial spool placed on a sheet of vinyl floor covering. In other instances the origins do not dominate the visual impact. *For Patrick Finnucane*, for example, exemplifies a minimalist elegance, yet it also signifies Herdlein's philosophy of transformation. Like Duchamp's "ready-mades," the piece provokes questions of context pertaining to conventions of heirarchy that separate "high" art from the vernacular.

In later work Herdlein's philosophical connections are closer to Joseph Beuys whose "social sculpture" was based in the belief that art is, ultimately, a life lived creatively. Herdlein's project for "In Public: Seattle 1991," though unintended as such, marked his abandonment of studio production to enter the social arena. The guidelines for the city-wide public art projects produced under the aegis of "In Public" stipulated an emphasis on an engagement with the public life of the city. Herdlein's first response was a proposal to give his award money to charity; on reflection, however, he decided to include his time and energy in the contribution. He became a companion and facilitator — officially, "resident artist" — for children being served by Big Brothers of King County, Yesler Community Center, and Yesler Terrace Neighborhood Center. Taking the children into his studio, he introduced them to the creative possibilities that exist in unlikely materials and objects within their environments. At the conclusion of the project an exhibition of the children's artworks, titled "Great Kids' Art," was presented at the Pacific Arts Center. Herdlein's personal contribution was a sculptural pile of new clothing from which the children chose outfits for the first day of school. The final component of the project was a donation to the Make a Wish Foundation.

In 1992, with city funding and Seattle University sponsorship, Herdlein continued his work with low income, inner city children and adolescents. The culmination of the summer project again was an exhibition of their artworks, "Great Kids' Art: Part 2," plus an evening of their performances. For his part Herdlein circled the large atrium of the University's Kinsey Gallery with "clotheslines" hung with new clothes for the children.

In addition to its tangible results, Herdlein's project attracted media attention that stimulated dialogue concerning approaches to the problem of childhood poverty. Is it more productive to advocate political change, as some of the "In Public" projects did, or to take personal responsibility? Herdlein demonstrated that positive results, though miniscule in relation to the problem, are possible from individual effort.

Herdlein, who was born in 1953, views art not as a separate activity but as his way of living. Art, he says, is a verb not a noun. It is not surprising that he recently began an academic program in sociology that will empower his future artmaking work with children. Nonetheless, he does not rule out a return to the studio where ideas can be materialized.

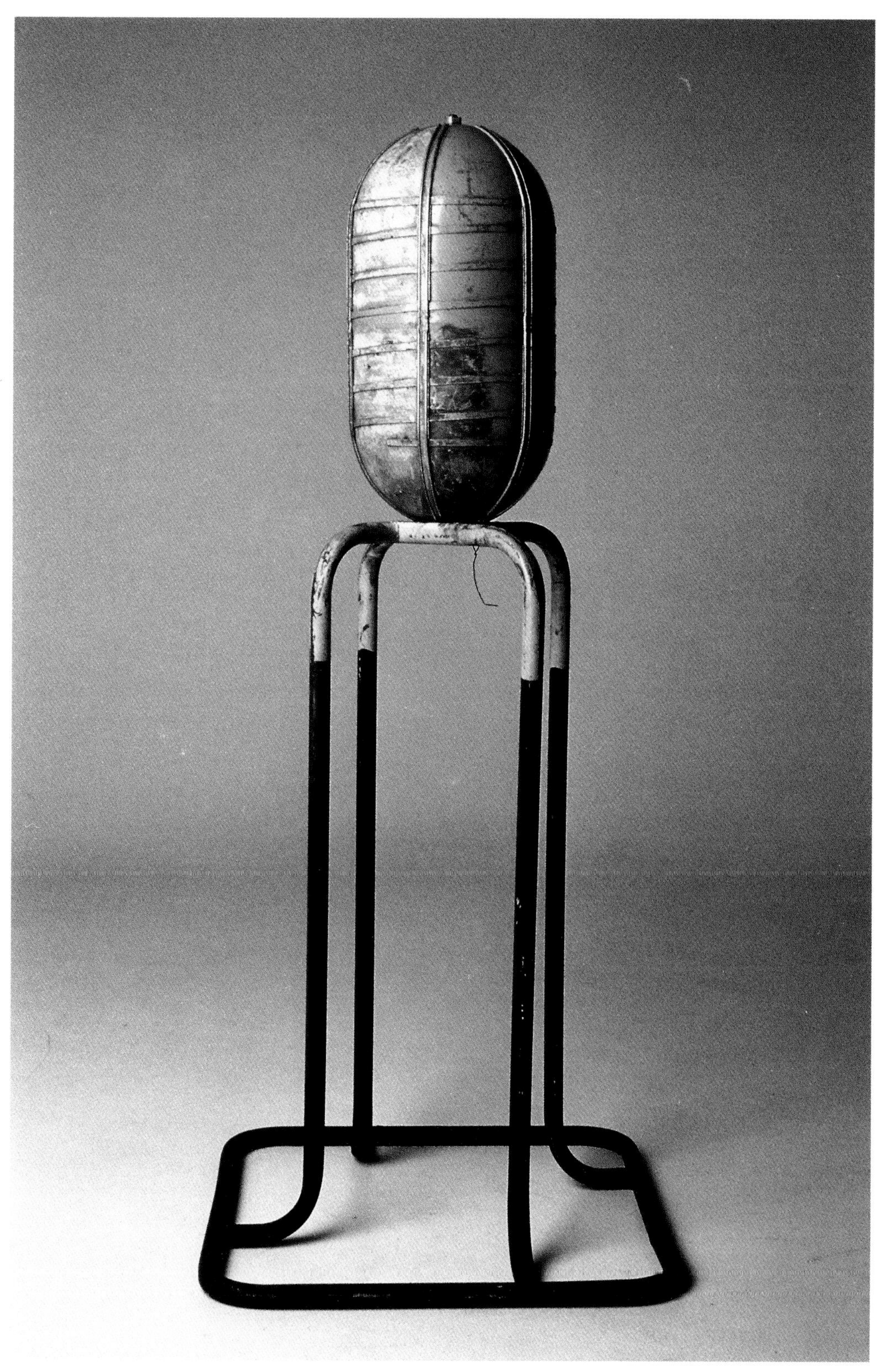

Robert Herdlein **For Patrick Finnucane**
1989, Found object assemblage, 60" x 30" x 30". Courtesy of the artist and Jamison/Thomas Gallery.

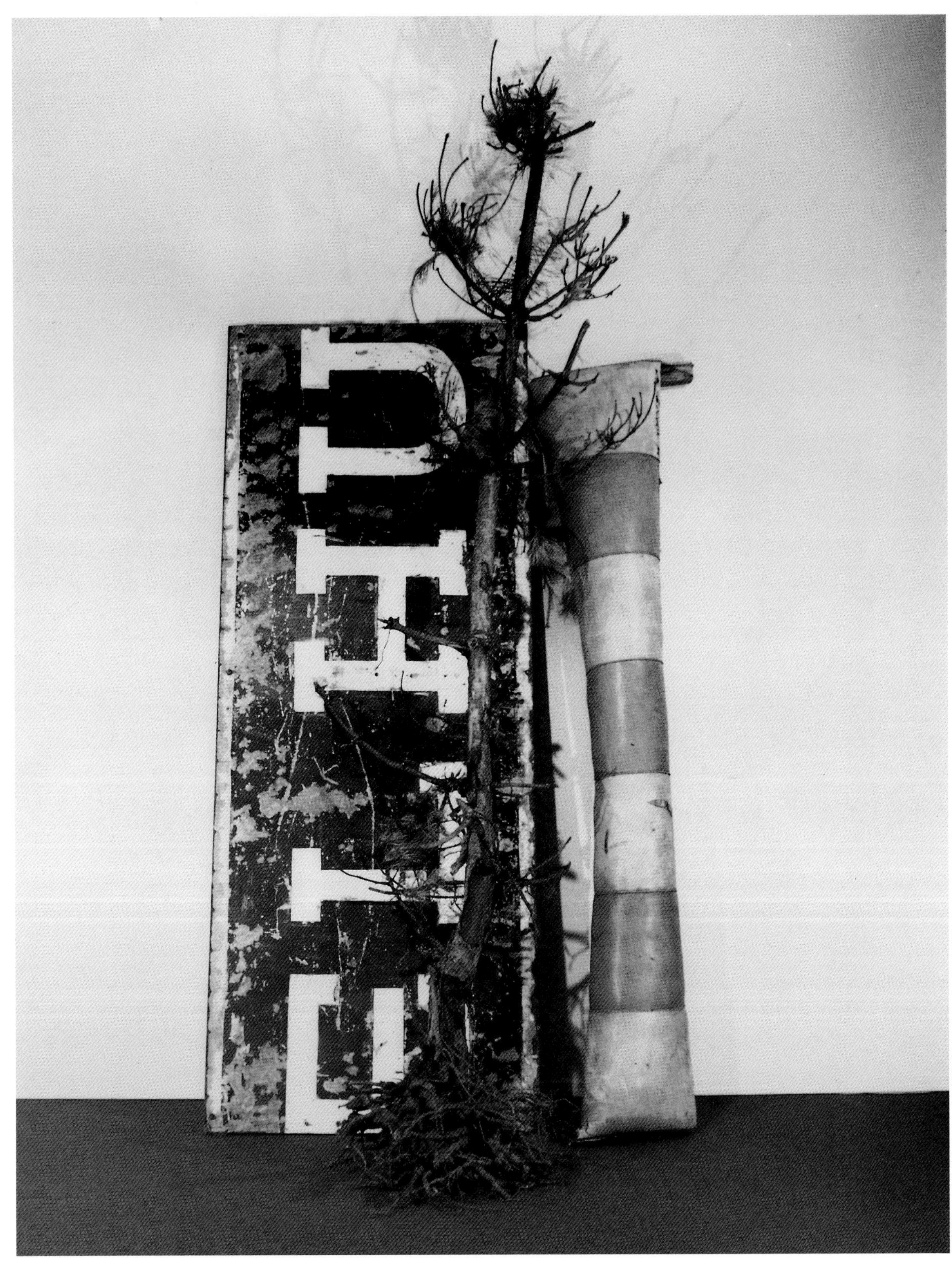

Robert Herdlein **Bayou**
1988, Found object assemblage, 180" x 84" x 48". Courtesy of the artist and Jamison/Thomas Gallery. Photograph: Stephen Reijo.

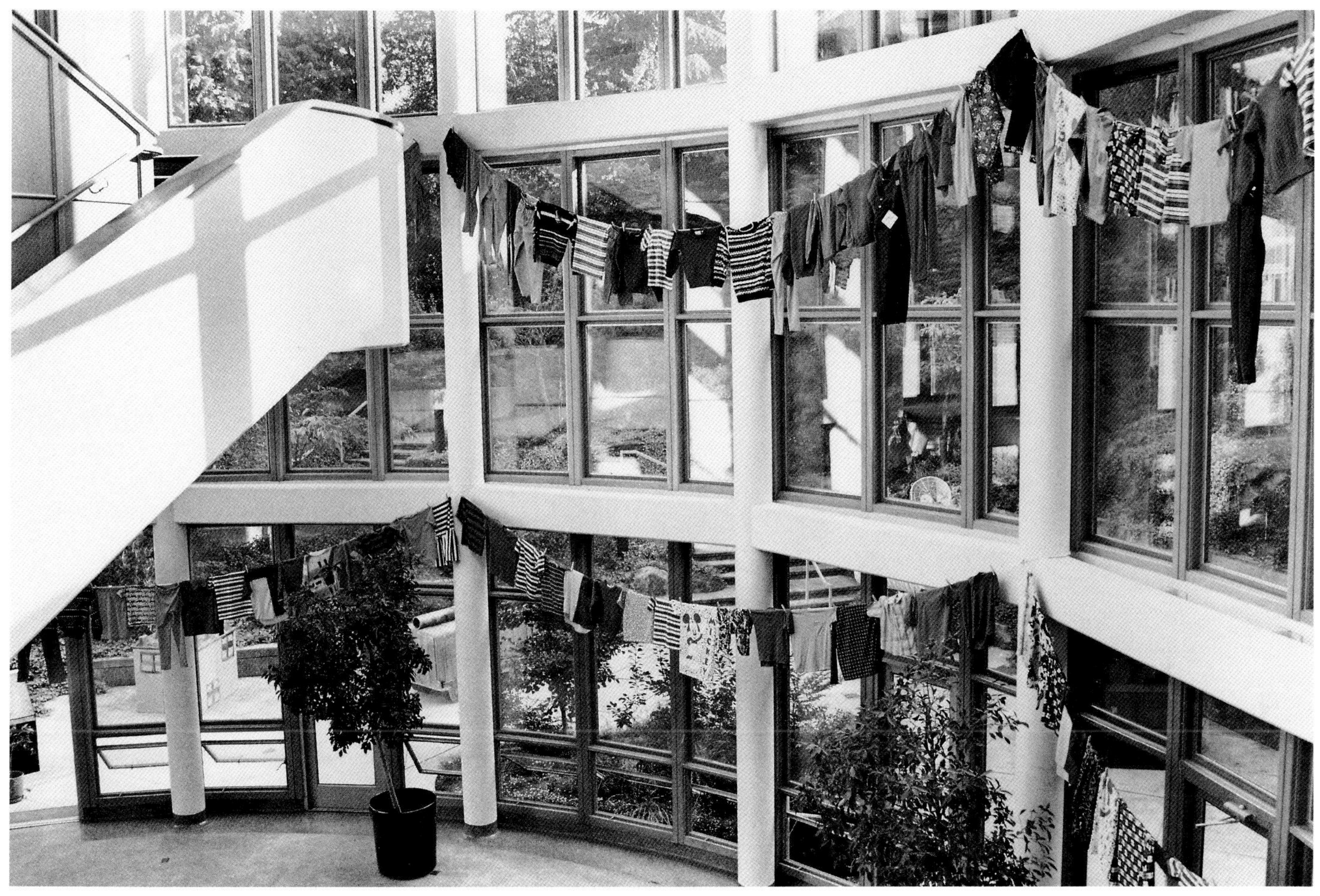

Robert Herdlein **Clothing installation**
Summer 1992, Seattle University, Part of 'Great Kids Art: Part II'. Courtesy of the artist and Jamison/Thomas Gallery. Photograph: Nicholas Hansen.

Malia **Jensen**

Malia Jensen's thesis exhibition at the Pacific Northwest College of Art in 1989 established her immediately as a gifted young painter, not only a fine colorist but also one of conceptual innovation. Her large, atmospheric paintings demonstrated more than a sensitivity to paint for its own sake; they combined broadly brushed muted colors with subtle allusions (a floating hand in one, a glued-on sock in another) to the artist's personal engagement with the painting's creation. The work had consequential effects: It won the top prize in the show, it attracted the attention of critics and galleries, and it caused Jensen to stop painting. She retreated into the studio and two years later introduced a new body of three-dimensional, mixed-media work that was more akin to the eclecticism of post-modernism than to the painterly modernism that was evident in the paintings.

Jensen's dissatisfaction with painting stemmed from an urge to connect more directly to her own life experience, not only in the process and materials of artmaking but also in its conceptual base. A self-described packrat and nature lover, she turned to non-art materials as the means for exploring psychological and cultural aspects of the human relationship with nature. She found the immediacy she sought in cast-off objects laden with their own histories. Although their identities and associations remain in the finished work, their lack of preciousness is completely denied by the meticulous craftsmanship she lavishes upon them. Taxidermied animal-forms are painstakingly upholstered in old inner tubes or wrapped in wasps' nest paper; a block of wood is sanded to the shape and smoothness of a satin pillow; small trees are measured for patterns for the flannelette "garments" she stitches. Her techniques and materials, which have both playful and disquieting overtones, are related to the Minimalist concept of primacy of materials, but not to the exclusion of imagery and potential meaning. In essence, her work turns on the tension between what it is in terms of its tangible, material identity and what it represents in terms of its inherent contradictions.

Perhaps to memorialize her transition, Jensen's first show of sculptures included a skull-like mound of paint blobs scraped from her palette and sealed within a plexiglass box. Then, as if staking out her new territory, *The King of the Forest,* a wall-mounted "trophy" consisting of a taxidermist's form for a deer-head and covered with cut-up flannel yardage reproducing Elvis's likeness, dramatically and irreverently announced its mundane origins and metaphoric affiliations. Like all Jensen's work, "The King" brings about an intuitive, immediate, and visceral response to an object that is familiar but so contextually aberrant it compels thoughtful reflection.

The transference of nature from autonomous phenomenon to the realm of human desire, a common hidden theme in fairy tales, undergirds the somnolent surrealism of "Sleepwalking in the Woods," a 1994 gallery exhibition that included *Beauty Mark* and *Pear, Chokecherry, Apple (tree socks).* Totally encased in black rubber, blinded and smothered, *Beauty Mark's* romantic title mocks the sculpture's dark allusions to the removal of the animal from the context of pure nature to one of trophy, artifact, and fetish. Jensen's penchant for obsessive workmanship, although invisible, is at its height in *Pear, Chokecherry, Apple.* The title refers to the trees she carefully measured at the point where the trunks divide into branches. She then made paper patterns from which the flannelette print "tree socks" were cut and stitched. Suggestions of human loss and alienation notwithstanding, the colorful garments hung limply from a clothesline as if waiting for the tree-fairy to take them down to warm the chilly little trees.

Jensen's preoccupation with psychological connections with nature began early. She was born in Honolulu (in 1966), but since the age of four has lived in Oregon. As a child, living in relative isolation on fifty acres of forested land on the eastern slopes of the Coast Range, she developed an imaginative interaction with the flora and fauna in her surroundings. Now, as an adult Portland dweller, she retains, and in fact, intellectually dredges her childhood fascination with the non-human inhabitants of the woods. With the onset of sophistication, however, irony has replaced innocence. Her art is a reminder that the loss of nature, like the loss of innocence, is irrevocable.

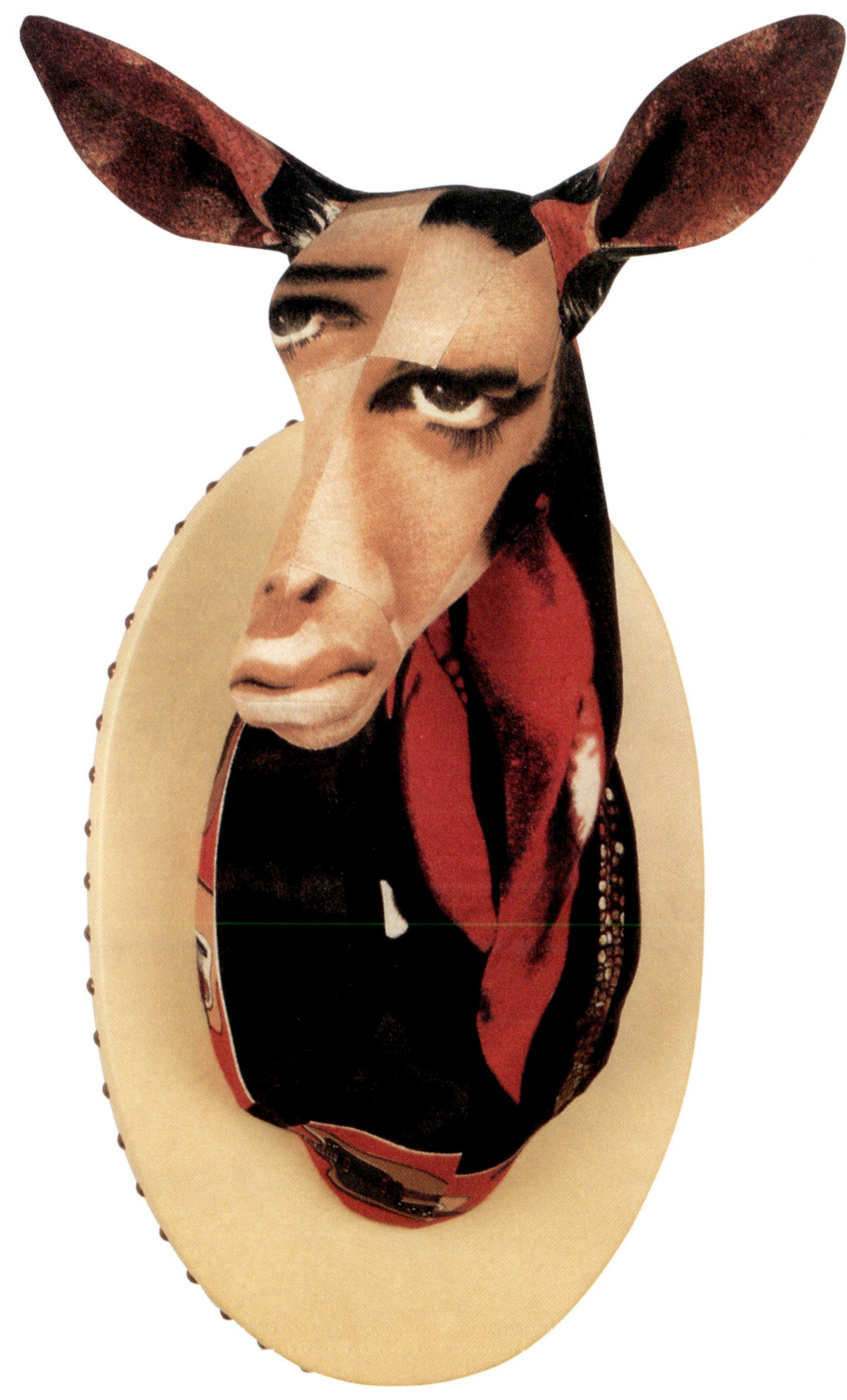

Malia Jensen **King of the Forest**
1992, Mixed media, 31" x 20" x 21". Collection of Rory MacKay.
Courtesy of the artist. Photograph: David Browne.

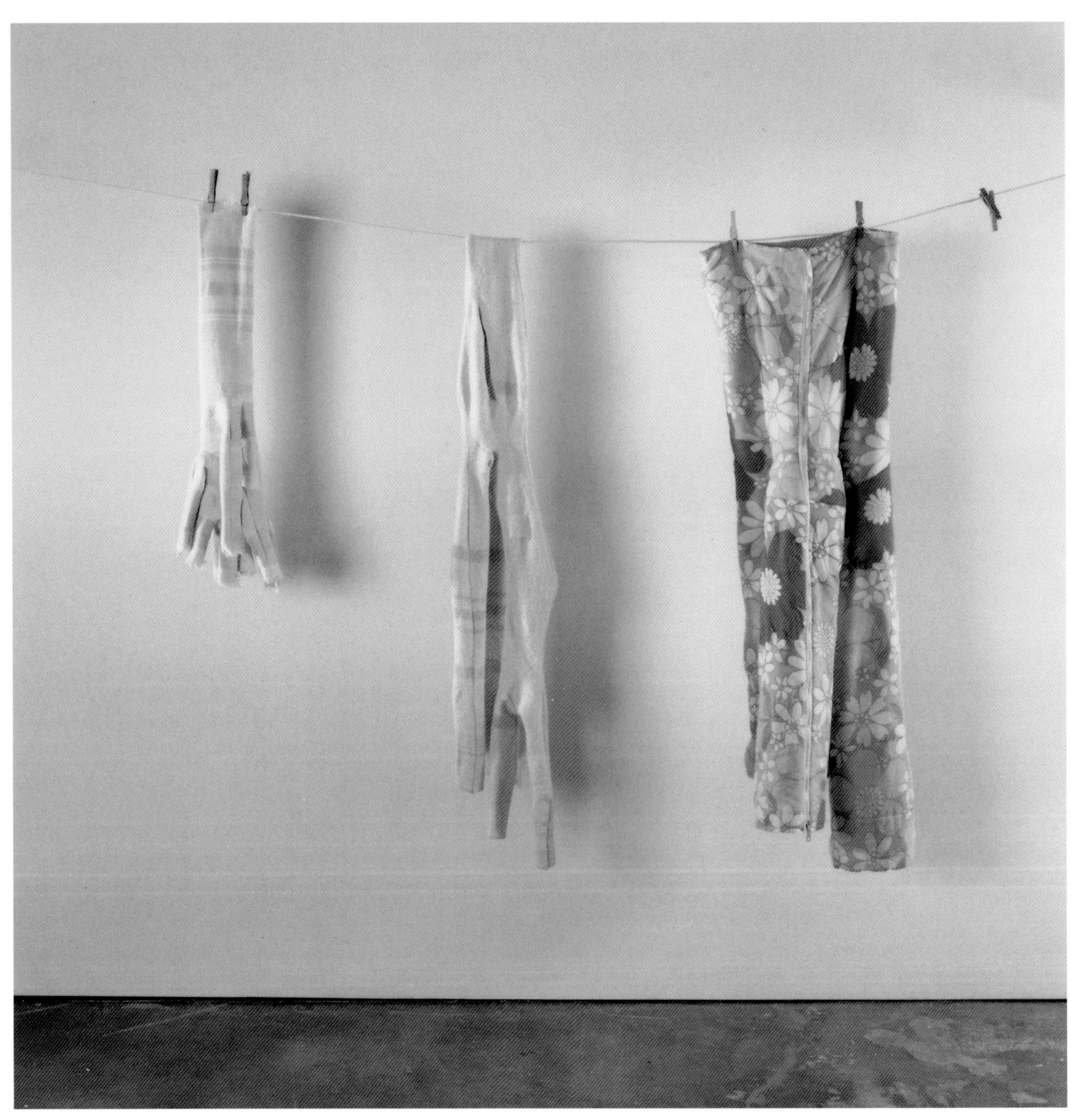

Malia Jensen **Pear, Chokecherry, Apple (tree socks)**
1994, Mixed media, Approx. 58" x 68". Courtesy of the artist. Photograph: Craig Damon.

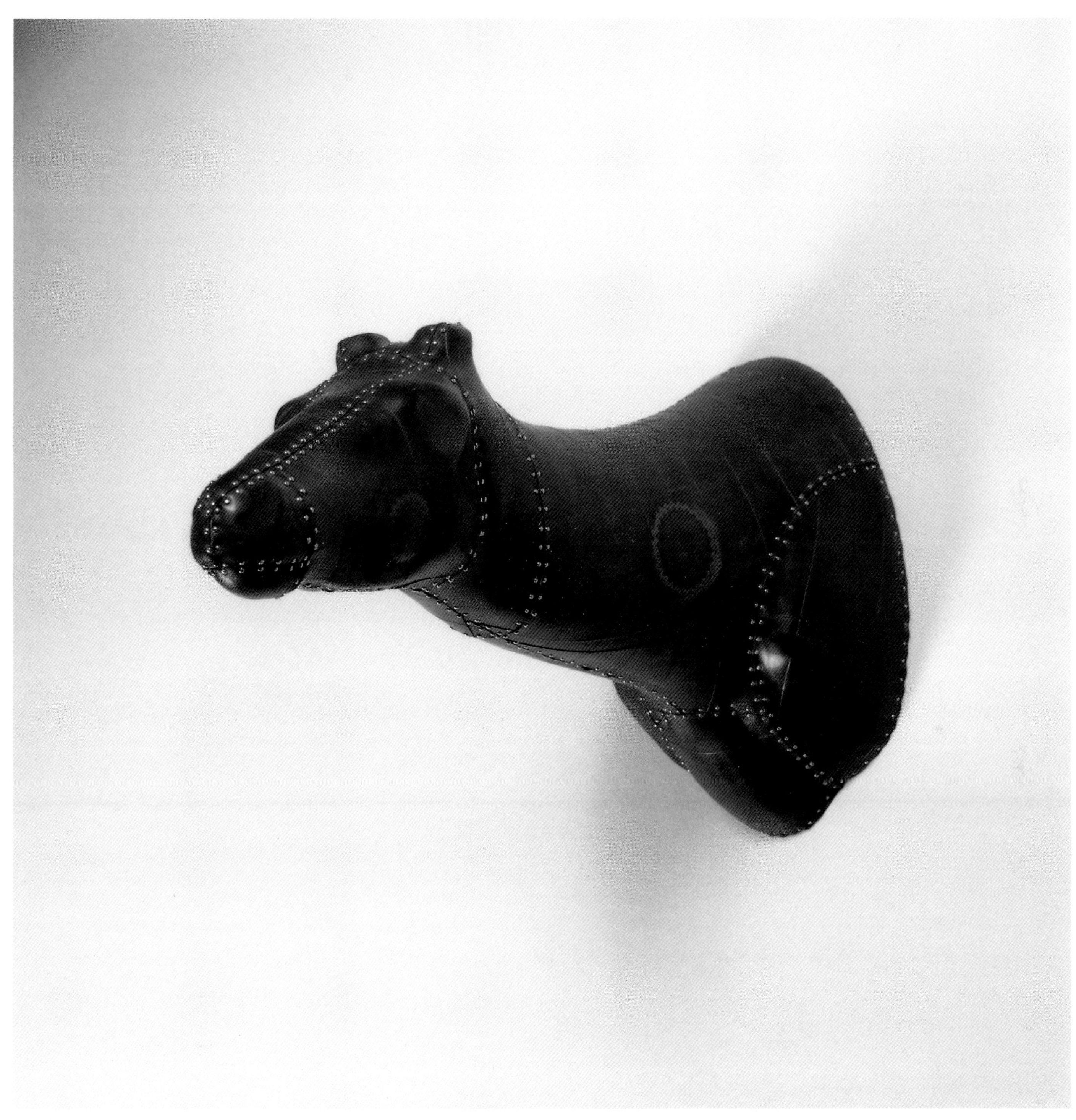

Malia Jensen **Beauty Mark**
1994, Mixed media, Life size. Collection of Henry Hillman. Courtesy of the artist. Photograph: Craig Damon.

George **Johanson**

George Johanson's vivid "psychic landscapes" continue a strong Oregon tradition in a realism that is both painterly and eccentric. Although his work draws directly on personal sources, it illuminates an inner world where dream-like mixes of fact, myth, and fantasy create extraordinary spectacles. Ordinary occurrences, places, humans, and animals from conscious life are recontextualized within a shadowy mental terrain where the free-wheeling unconscious mind asserts itself in puzzling metaphors.

Johanson acknowledges his obvious debt to Surrealism, especially to verists like Magritte who transformed mundane objects and events into unforgettable images drawing on repressed anxieties. Johanson, too, conflates serenity and disquietude, but his interests are less Freudian than pictorial. The luminous and impressionistic coloration of *Regatta With Three Graces*, for instance, infuses the many, seemingly disparate elements of the composition. While the sparkling color arrangement is compelling in itself, the strange mix of images reflects themes and motifs that recur throughout his body of work. Johanson sculls on the Willamette River, which flows through Portland, so it is not surprising that boats and water assume symbolic importance. His deep interest in art history is seen in the central group of three female nudes, the "three graces" of art historical prominence. Here, in a sylvan setting they seem to be guardians of the oars needed to propel the boats carried by the unseeing scullers.

Born in 1928 in Seattle, Johanson was a precocious child artist, as a self-portrait sketched at age ten (which introduced a 1989 retrospective exhibition of his drawings at the University of Oregon) attests. He arrived in Portland in 1946 with a scholarship to attend the Museum Art School (now the Pacific Northwest College of Art), but after three years decamped for New York to study printmaking with Karl Schrag at the famed Hayter Atelier 17 workshop. This period was the heyday of Abstract Expressionism, and Johanson, still a student, was both stimulated and greatly influenced by what he saw. Although he brought that enthusiasm with him when he returned to Portland in 1955, his identification with abstract expressionist painting was not a lasting one. During a 1965 sabbatical from his teaching post at the Museum school, he lived in London where he saw the work of Francis Bacon and David Hockney and was struck with the potency of figurative expression which equalled — and for him, surpassed — that of abstraction. He has not deviated from the figurative since, even though he retains from his earlier improvisational period a conscious, active engagement with the process of painting and the physicality of the paint itself.

Johanson is a noted printmaker whose color intaglios rival the paintings in color complexity. He is also a ceramist, executing large murals in fired ceramic tile. The common denominator, whatever the medium, is drawing. It is both structure and expression, spontaneous and calculated, concerned with the inner dynamics of his subjects as well as description. The strange nocturnal revelry depicted in *The Great Hot Tub*, an etching of 1981, brings all these factors into play. Images are carved out of darkness, formed by patches of white and sinuous white lines. The tilted picture plane, pushing the background forward, compresses space and accentuates the circular motion. As one of many pictures based on an amusement park theme, *The Great Hot Tub* speaks of human mindless activity in an atmosphere of darkness and danger. The swirling rides are like alien space ships hovering nearby while their potential passengers dance, lounge, and plunge into their small, self-contained water world.

Self-portraits have occupied Johanson since the age of ten and they are invariably graphically trenchant depictions. Although he often places himself in the scenic works in the role of an unobtrusive observer, the self-portraits, in contrast, are explicit revelations of the various ways in which he experiences himself, usually with some degree of absurdity. *Galloping Fool*, for example, presents the artist as a centaur, the wild and coarse creature of Greek myth, who now roams the night sky above Portland in Johanson's spirit.

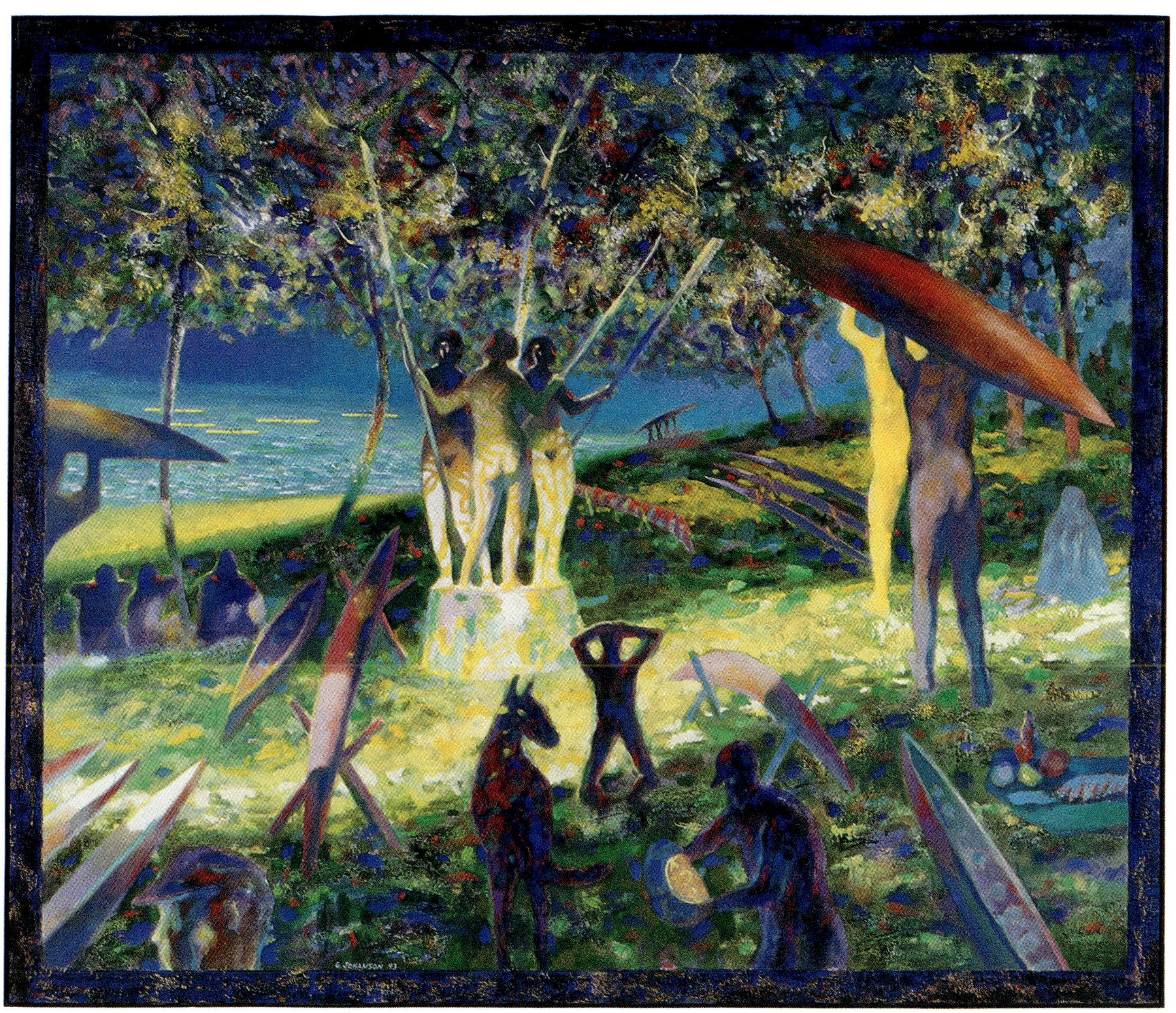

George Johanson **Regatta With Three Graces**
1993, Oil on canvas, 59" x 70". Collection of the artist. Courtesy of the artist and Elizabeth Leach Gallery. Photograph: David Browne.

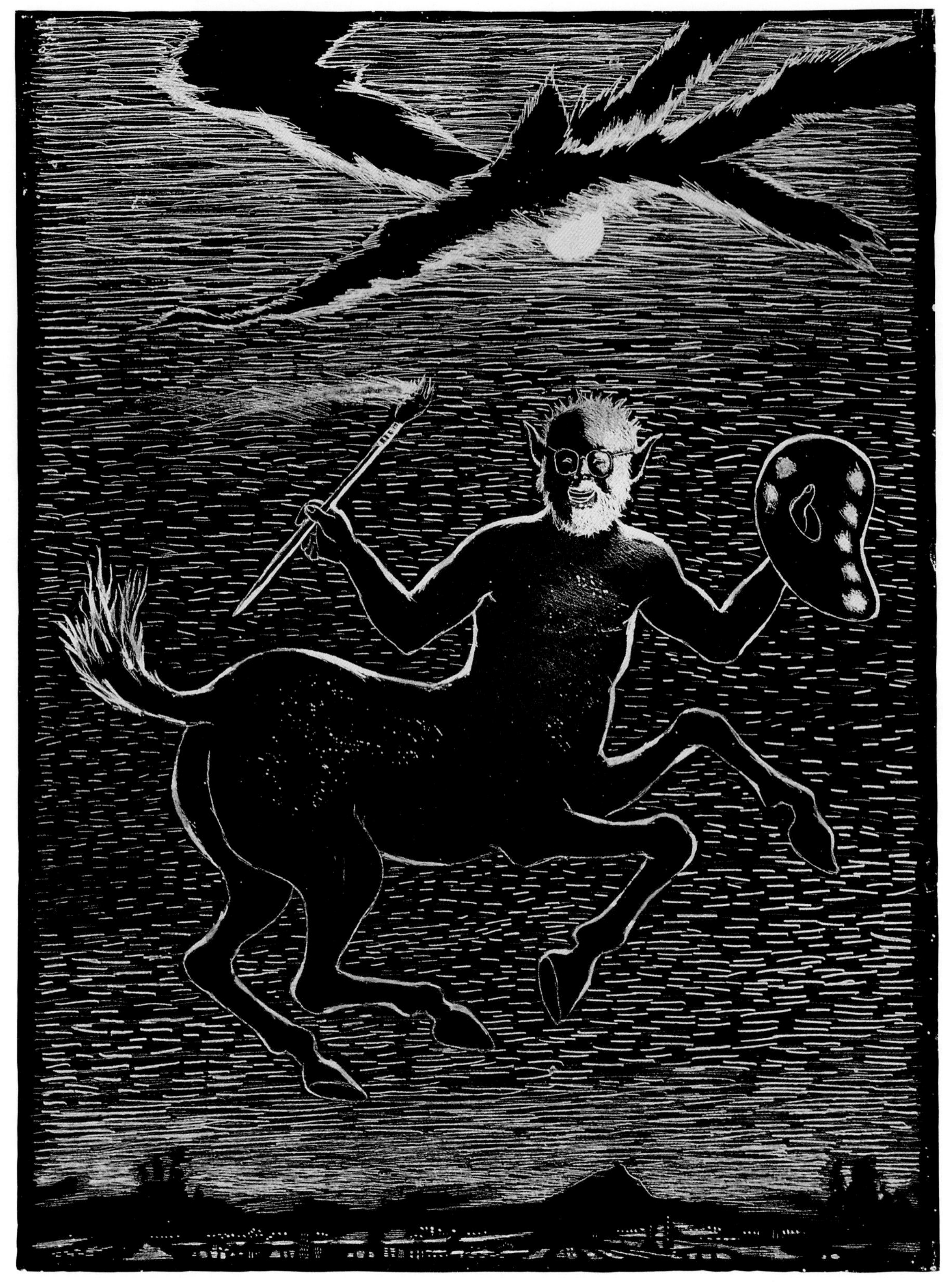

George Johanson **Galloping Fool**
1993, Etching with watercolour, 24" x 18". Courtesy of the artist and Elizabeth Leach Gallery. Photograph: Aaron Johanson.

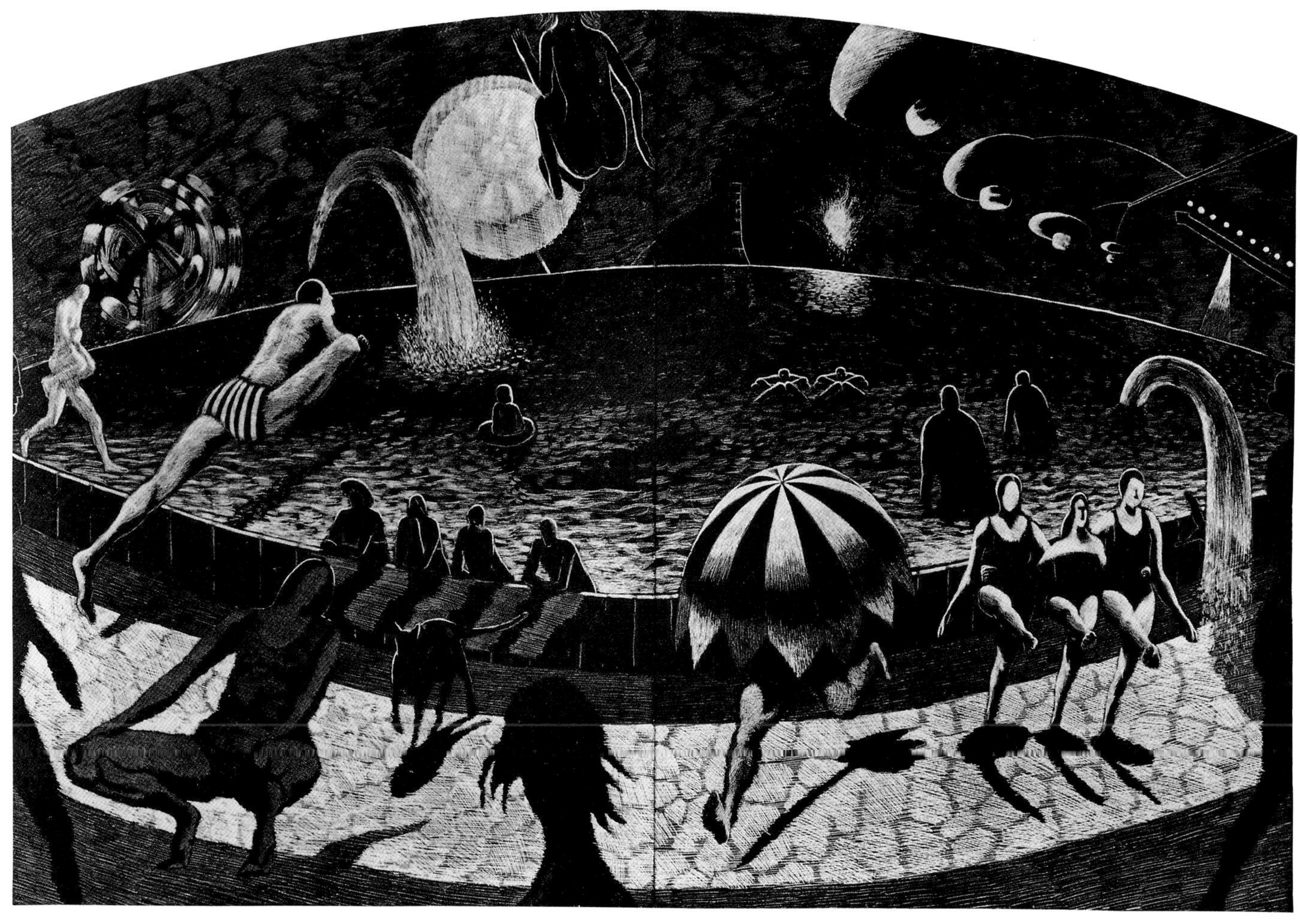

George Johanson **The Great Hot Tub**
1981, Etching with watercolour, 24" x 36". Courtesy of the artist and Elizabeth Leach Gallery. Photograph: Aaron Johanson.

Fay **Jones**

Fay Jones's acrylic paintings on paper are like unfinished mystery novels; they offer many clues but no solutions. Their enigmatic characters and fluid content might also place them as postmodern novels. In either case, they are vivid, pictorial narratives with an immediate, visceral effect that novels cannot achieve. They consist of large casts of characters, animal and human, cavorting in improbable settings. Time and events are compressed into a holistic space where images are clear but meaning is elusive. Few Northwest painters have so consistently and fully developed subjective narration as the means of figurative and formalist innovations. A superb colorist, she controls emotional tension through subtle combinations of hue and tone, creating a charged trialogue among line, shape, and color.

Although she began her career at the time of heroic abstraction, Jones has always preferred figuration and narrative content. For several years after her graduation from the Rhode Island School of Design in 1957 and a subsequent move to Seattle, she concentrated on small formats with the intimacy of a diary. The naive, somewhat cartoonish drawing style, which she developed at that time, continues to characterize the much larger and more complex work of recent years. Content, too, has evolved; personal references are now oblique or metaphoric and subsumed in broader social concerns.

While source ideas are rarely explicit, they are plentiful, often spilling over each other, as in *Two Pools: Riddle and Ghosts.* Images of bald babies, empty dresses, and sailors with huge balls for hands, which appear with some frequency in Jones's pictures, are joined by a variety of actively engaged mouse-people, a tribute to Art Spiegelman, whose books on the Holocaust, *Maus I* and *Maus II*, were created in a cartoon format. Mostly separate and oblivious of each other, the tiny figures, plus frogs, snakes, centipedes, a skeleton, and more, share a field of neutral ochre and are offset by the two large amorphous blue shapes. Within the active surface design, the two pool-like shapes, depicted from a completely different perspective, become reservoirs of calm, a transition from the lively figures to the blank, white, ghostly images below.

As a child who read incessantly and had no parental restrictions on subjects or ideas, Jones developed her imaginative resources at an early age. She recalls a fifth grade assignment to draw a picture with an autumn theme. Instead of the expected pumpkin or colored leaves, she drew a woman in a fancy party dress, highball in one hand and cigarette in the other, sitting at a bar. That flair for theatrical effect continues to surface in scenes made memorable by their odd juxtapositions, discontinuities, and inaccurate perspectives both in imagery and in compositional arrangement.

In 1985 Jones, still a serious bookworm, undertook a series based on a history of her reading. One of the series, *Alice vs Betty*, pits a feisty Betty Freidan against a vaporous, disengaged Alice who stands apart from the world on a pedestal. Pages from *The Feminine Mystique* and *Alice in Wonderland*, densely collaged across the entire surface, are the setting for the two literary icons and their opposing symbolisms. The silhouetted Betty, whose upraised arm sports a red boxing glove, seems to shield her companion who looks back at Alice from Betty's knowing perspective.

Although Jones stresses the importance of drawing in organizing the compositional framework of her paintings, her carefully orchestrated color passages also act as a structural element, and in addition bring about a dominant emotional atmosphere. The cool greens and blues in the large (4' x 5') *Poet's Limbo* divide the composition horizontally, and at the same time establish a serene continuity for the insensate poet's dreaming. While the sharply drawn vertical divisions and disparate images convey the lack of linearity in an unconscious mental state, the chromatic unity suggests the flow of its vignettes.

It is, of course, the visual strength of the paintings that is immediately compelling. Nontheless, what ultimately holds us is Jones's ability to transpose personal experiences and memories into unique representations of the pscyhic ground beneath the posturings in everyday social actions and interactions.

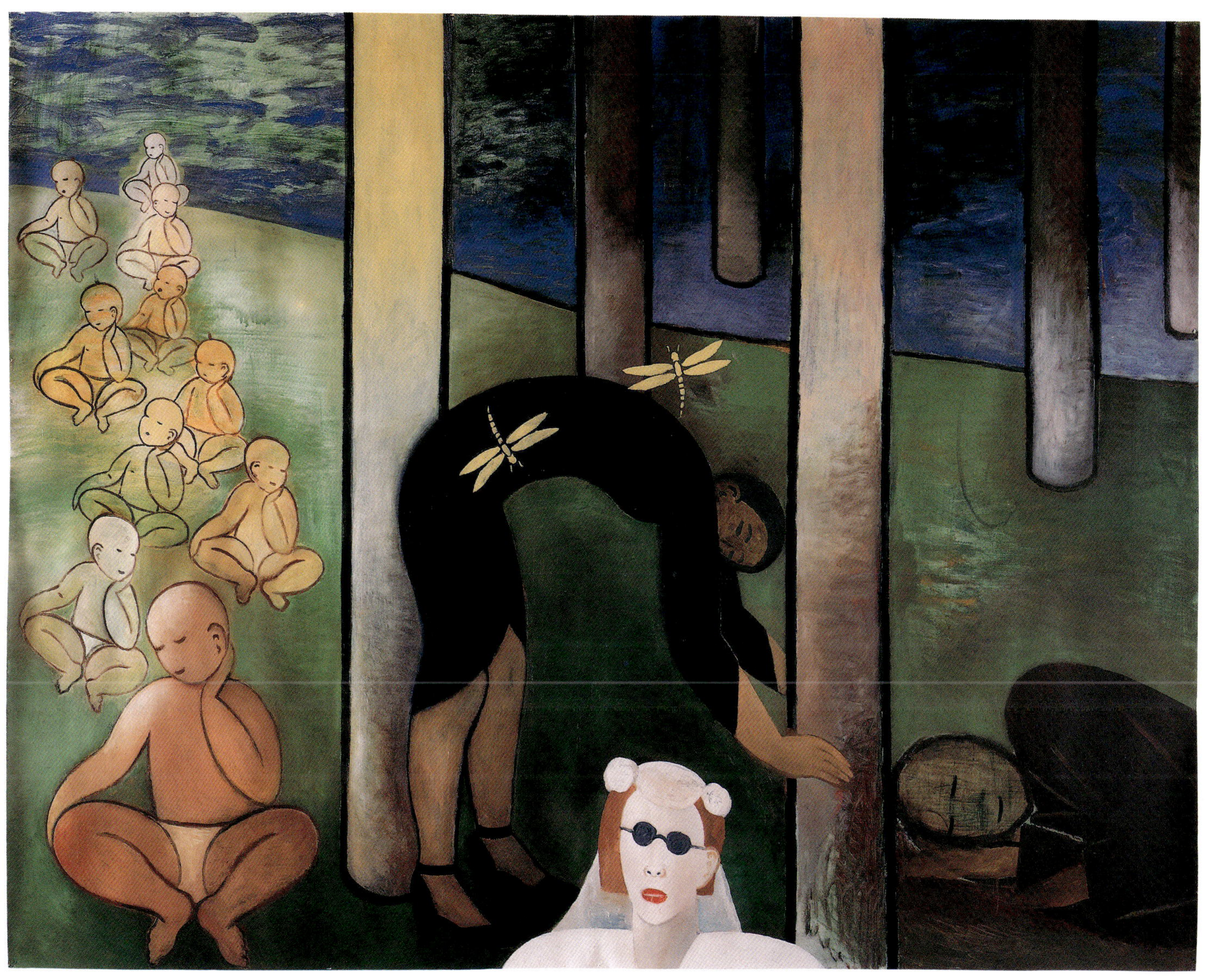

Fay Jones **Poet's Limbo**
1992, Acrylic on paper, 77" x 102½". Collection of Harold and Arlene Schnitzer. Courtesy of Francine Seders Gallery and Laura Russo Gallery.
Photograph: Eduardo Calderoń.

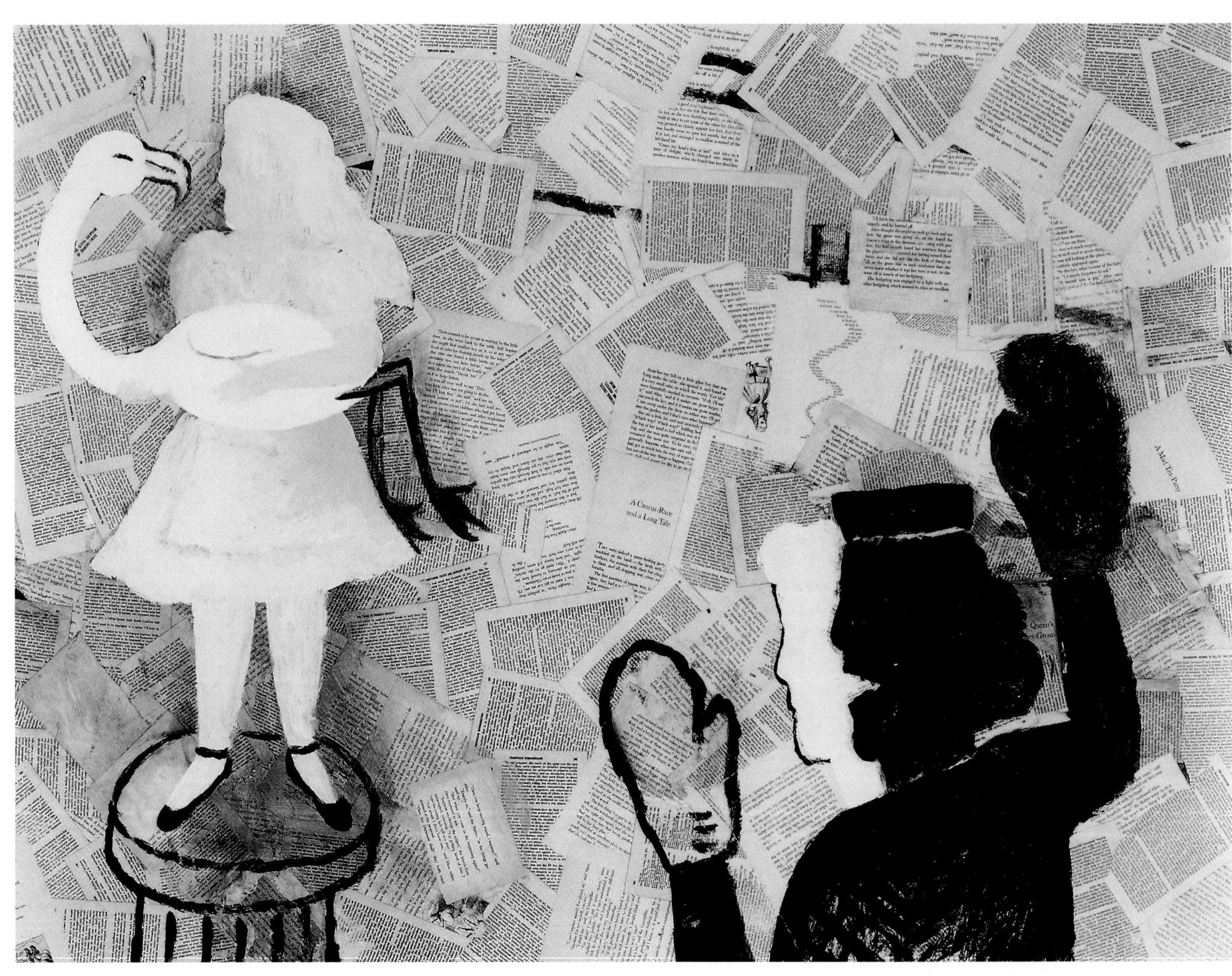

Fay Jones **Alice Vs. Betty**
1985, Acrylic and collage on paper, 39" x 53". Collection of Sonja Blomdahl. Courtesy of Francine Seders Gallery and Laura Russo Gallery. Photograph: Chris Eden.

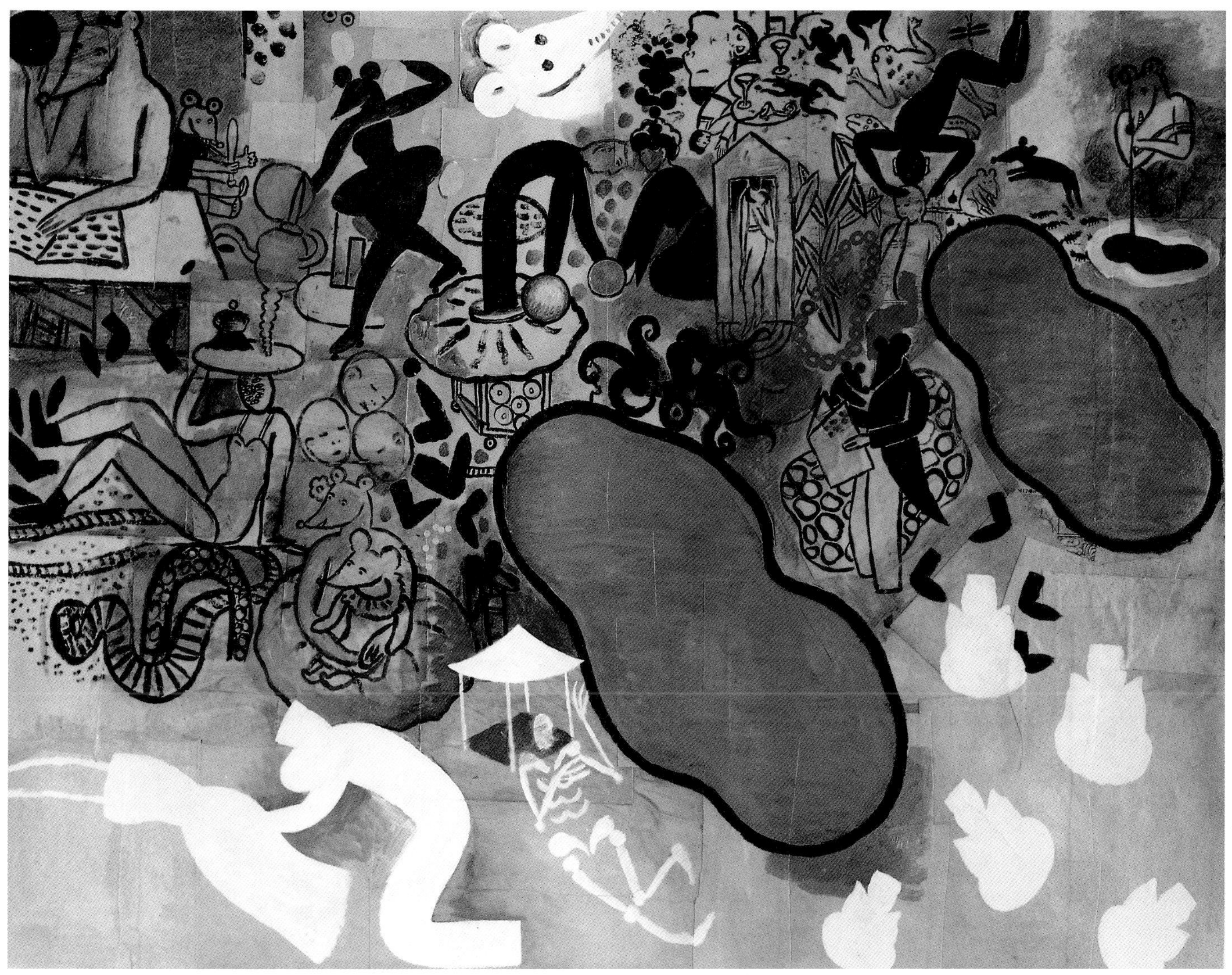

Fay Jones **Two Pools: Riddle and Ghosts**
1992, Acrylic, sumi, collage, 38¼" x 50". Courtesy of the artist and Francine Seders Gallery. Photograph: Eduardo Calderoń.

Mel **Katz**

Mel Katz is one of the Northwest's most original and consistent exponents of totally abstract sculpture. His rigorously reductive structural works have a unique physical presence in which form, color, and mass convey his intellectual as well as aesthetic concerns. Like many artists of his generation, he absorbed Abstract Espressionism, Pop, and Minimalism, and from them formed his own individualistic expression. His sculptures call attention to the materiality of the art object and its relationship to the space it occupies; they borrow from the commercial world of kitsch; their surfaces become areas for decorative, two-dimensional treatment. Ultimately, his work is an inventive mix of shapes, improbable structure, and curious materials that are both substance and symbol. Perhaps because he was a painter before becoming a sculptor, surface design and color are vital elements in the work. In fact, his sculptures often play on the contradictions between two and three-dimensionality.

Katz was born in Brooklyn, New York, in 1932 and studied art at Cooper Union and the Brooklyn Museum. As a young New York painter in the 1950s he found his greatest inspiration in the paintings of Arshile Gorky. At the time of Katz's move to Portland in 1964 to teach at the Museum Art School (for two years and since then at Portland State University) his paintings were heavily influenced by Gorky's refined coloration and sensuous line. By the end of that decade, however, his interest in the dynamics within the painting had led him to reject both the physical and implied constraints of the rectangular format. Playing on the dichotomy between illusion and object-ness, he began a series of transitions, first to shaped paintings, then to wall-constructions, to free-standing sculptures in the 1980s, and most recently, back to wall-mounted pieces. All Katz's progressions are related primarily to investigations of materials and form. He is essentially a formalist, an analytical artist who is guided by empirics but also capitalizes on the inherent implications and associations of materials, color, and process. The vinyl surfaces on the large pieces of the late 1980s, for example, are mass-produced, consumer-oriented floor and counter coverings. Obviously taken from the world of industry and commerce, they are sly assaults on conventional value systems pertaining to materials, to aesthetics, and to heirarchical categories, such as "functional," "kitsch," and "fine" art.

The frontality and shaped edges that are a hallmark of Katz's sculptures have an autobiographical origin. The artist's father was a tailor, and as a child Katz often watched him cut stacks of fabrics from patterns, then fit the pieces together before sewing them into finished garments. Although oblique references to this memory are evident throughout Katz's body of work, they are sometimes explicit, as in the series revealingly titled "Patterns." More often, he prefers to adapt characteristics of pattern pieces to the formal elements of his work.

The large constructions with plastic laminate and vinyl coverings that occupied Katz for most of the 1980s are his most stunning and critically acclaimed sculptures. With their plastic exteriors sporting the exotic colors and patterns of kitchen floors and their vertical, asymmetrical stances suggesting a moving human figure, they seem to be parodies of heroic monuments. Although rigorously formal in their execution, the sculptures are also pointed commentaries on cultural determinants of art, value, and use in our society.

In contrast to these raucous sculptures, Katz has turned recently to steel wall-constructions, like *Extremities*, that are both somber and elegant. Once again the material is pivotal: Sheets of metal are cut with lasers, the pieces then layered and riveted, their overlapping contours appearing as lines. Whether left untreated or coated in very dark colors, the pieces are dense, not only with their actual weight but also with the mental weight of Katz's inventive approach to abstract sculpture in its relationships to materials, to drawing, to form, and to the surrounding space.

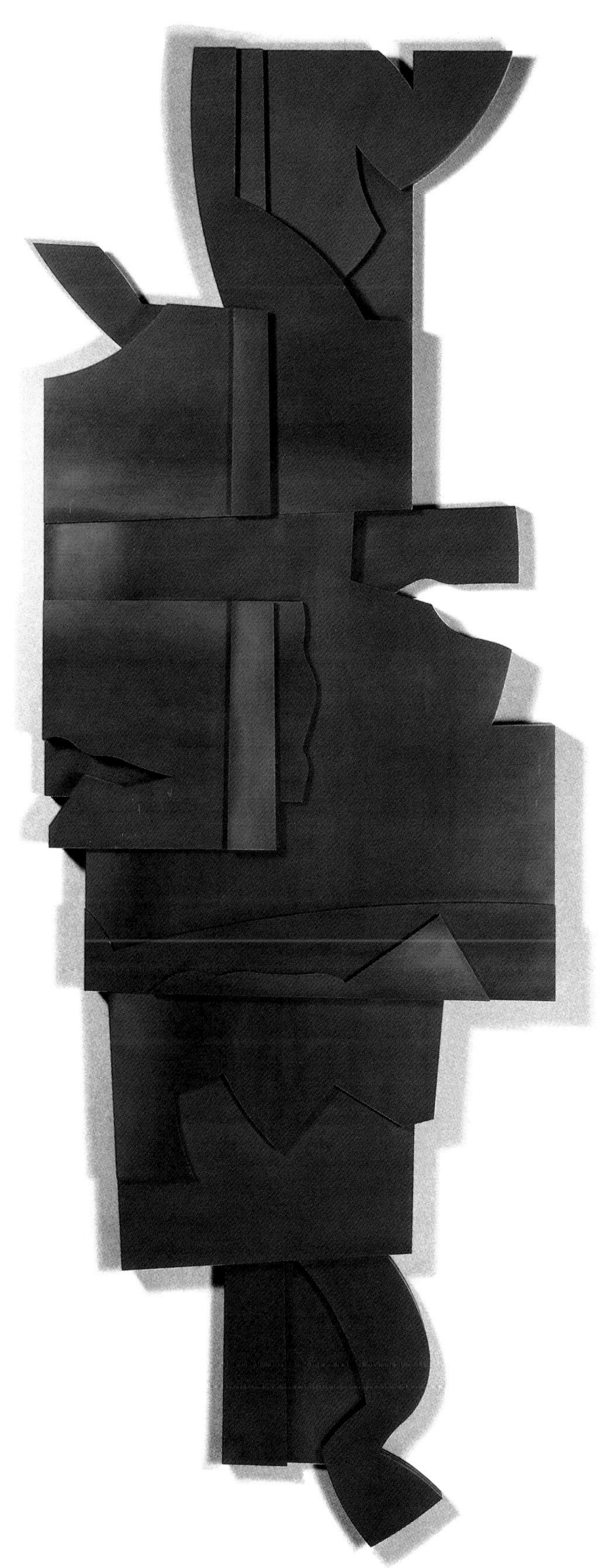

Mel Katz
Extremities
1993, Corten steel, 118" x 41" x 4".
Collection of the artist.
Courtesy of Laura Russo Gallery.
Photograph: Stewart Harvey.

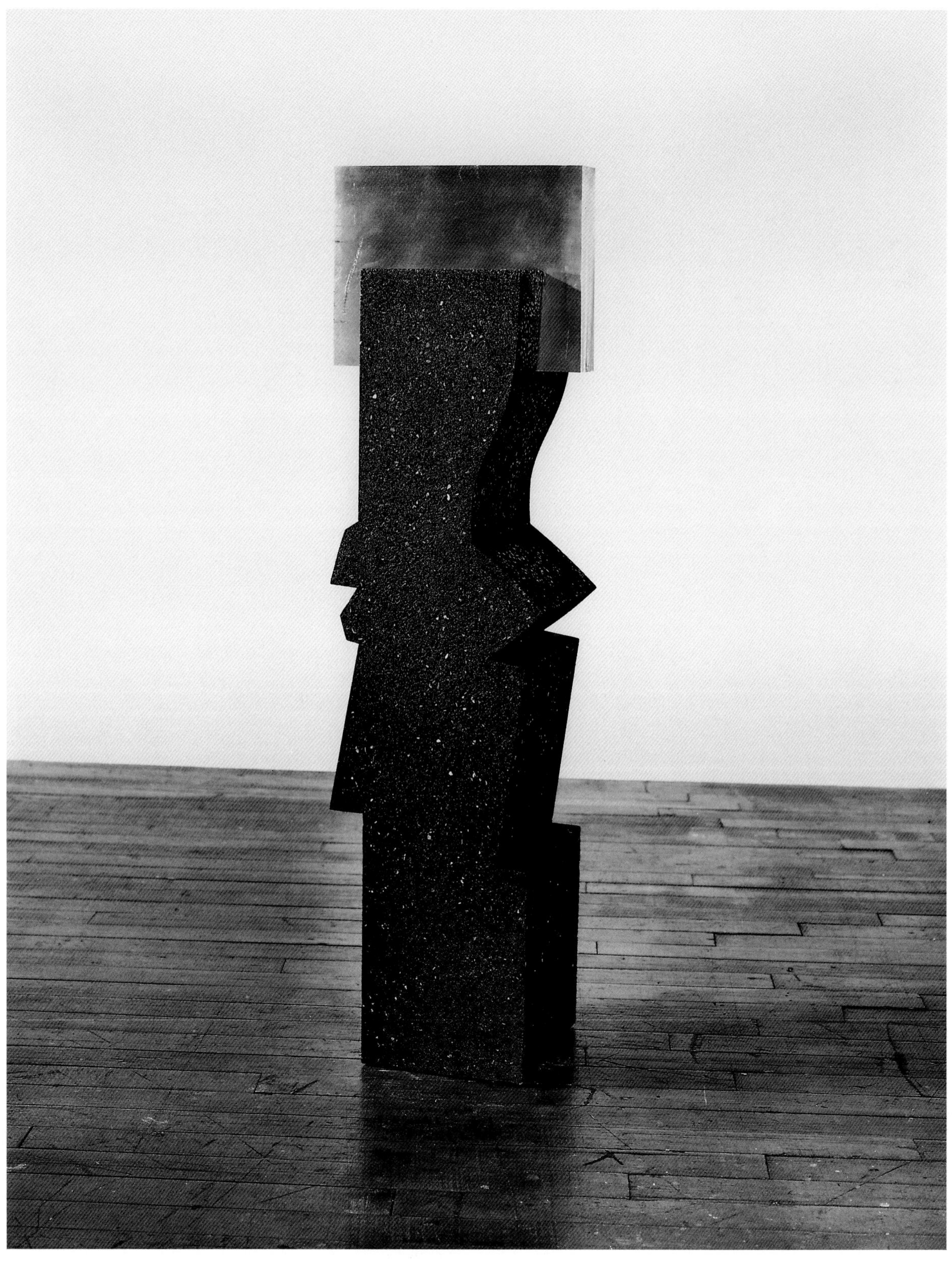

Mel Katz **Black Concrete/Aluminium**
1985, 54" x 16" x 12". Collection of Cascade Estates Corp. Courtesy of Laura Russo Gallery. Photograph: Stewart Harvey.

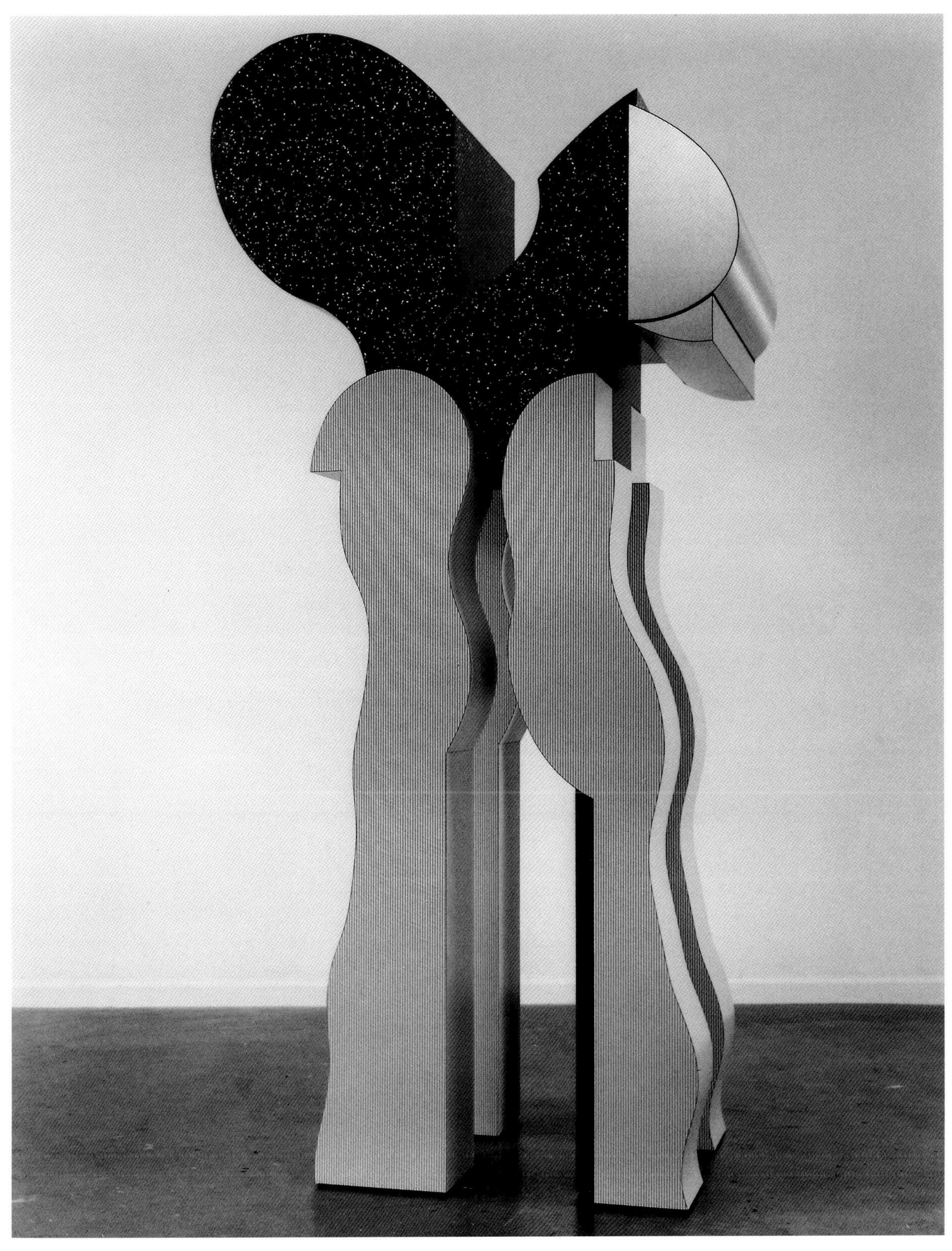

Mel Katz **Confetti, Stripes and Aluminium, Too**
1991, 96" x 46" x 31½". Collection of the artist. Courtesy of Laura Russo Gallery. Photograph: Stewart Harvey.

Ken **Kelly**

At first, Ken Kelly's elegant abstract paintings seem to offer nothing more than the optical appeal of graceful, repetitive patterns undulating over heavily worked fields of thick neutral colors. With a little time, as flickers of brighter hues and vestigal patterns begin to emerge from the murky strata beneath their translucent surfaces, an underlying dark beauty, like that of a black opal, makes itself felt. In addition, visual contradictions come into play — symmetry versus disorder, delicacy versus toughness, the seen versus the merely suggested — and they bring to mind similar contradictions in human experience. Still, there are no stories, no specific references. Kelly's rich fusions of viscid paint and organic images are hauntingly (and on his part, deliberately) nebulous.

Although he has always been heavily engaged in process and physicality, Kelly's evolution from intuitive, aggressively expressionistic painting to the controlled, evocative abstractions that characterize his current work has been gradual. His early exhibitions after settling in Seattle in 1981 featured sketchy figures or letters within luxuriant color fields. He was, he has observed, trying to be as bluntly direct as possible, letting the paint itself carry intellectual content. By the late 1980s he was producing large abstract paintings consisting of vibrant circular shapes placed both under and over demarcated, layered color fields.

After two or three years of such formalist based work Kelly began to doubt its authenticity to the extent that, in his words, he "hit a real dry spell" lasting about a year. During this period of soul-searching, he was influenced by two artists whose working processes he observed, Jeffry Mitchell and Ann Hamilton. Their use of incremental, repetitive elements, laboriously accumulated and composed, represents a life philosophy as well as a particular aesthetic. For Kelly, the concentrated time-consuming process, combined with a love for the sheer physicality of paint, became the catalyst for a new body of work that brings content to an aesthetic of formal abstraction.

In marked contrast to the bright colors and paint slathered disks of earlier times, Kelly took his palette down to muted, somber hues. He turned to stencils for sharp-edged cellular shapes and flowing lines that arc, swell, and stretch across gelatinous surfaces. The process that generates each painting is a long, arduous building-up, layer by scraped layer, of earthy colors until the surface resembles a topographic relief map. The paint gradually accumulates the weight and history, along with evidence of the subterraneum forces, that form the surface and infuse its design.

In the lattice-like *Prong*, the linear symmetry, rhythm, and overall patterning can be read either as ornamental calligraphy or as etchings in nature, rather like the striation patterns on leaves and shells, or perhaps,like fossilized markings. Invariably, however, such references are hazy. The "meaning" in the corroded surface, cheerless colors, and elegaic cadence of the uniformly looping lines is in the visceral and emotional responses they elicit.

As he continues to develop this body of work Kelly is expanding his repertoire of stencilled images and now allows more color to seep through the submerged pockets and layers of paint that have been wiped, coated with acrylic gel, wiped again, and finally overlaid with swooping trails of the gel. The large paintings, *Trance* and *Buck*, are typical in their display of luminous organic shapes that move through the gelled coating, the scraped paint, and each other.

Kelly does not use frames, preferring to adhere canvas to wood supports in order to diminish mental boundaries between the painting and its environment. His choice of forceful one-word titles is still another strategy to offer a point of entry into the work, but one that does not preclude individual responses.

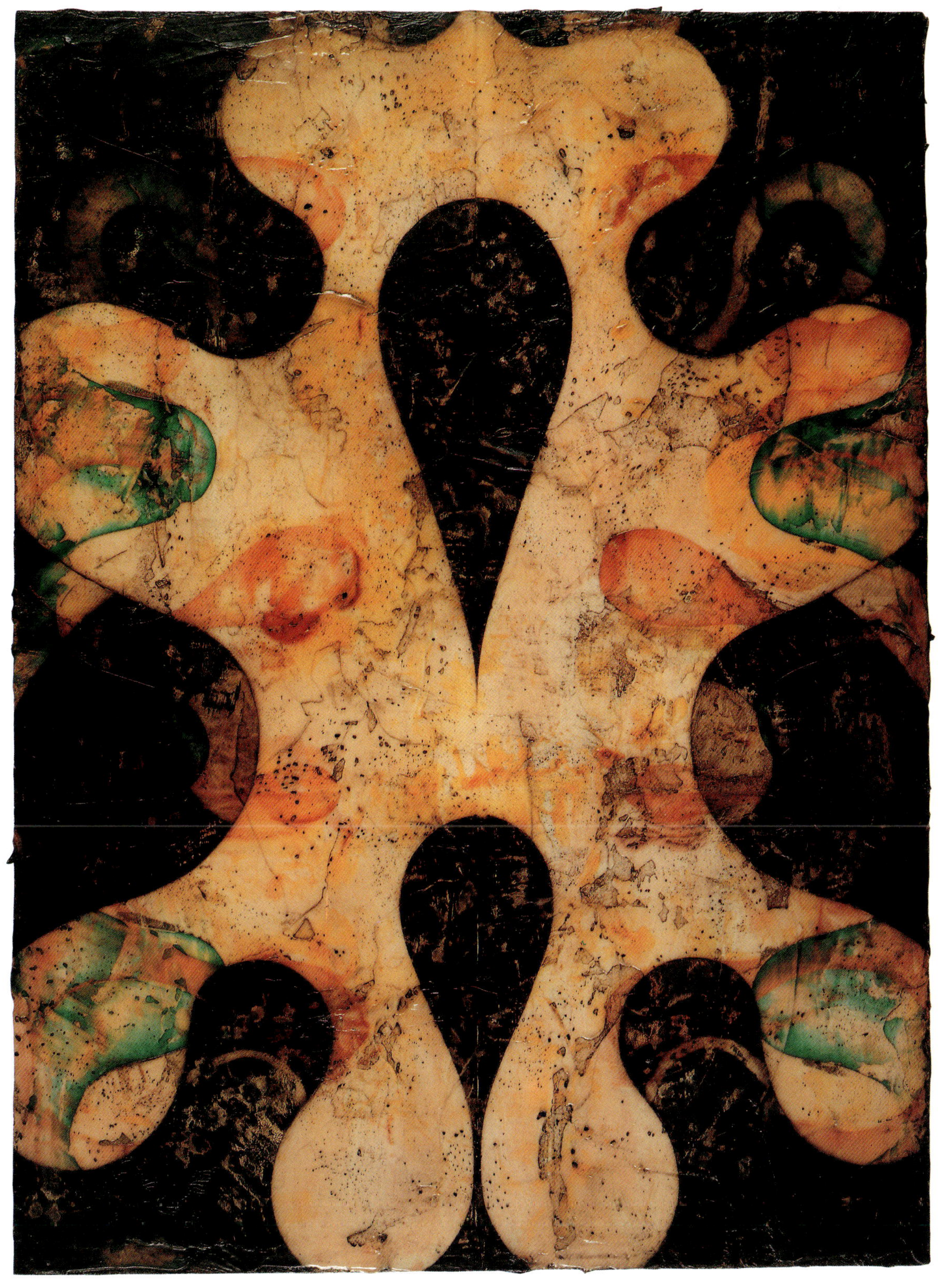

Ken Kelly **Buck**
1994, Mixed media on canvas, 48" x 36". Collection of Michael Schultz. Courtesy of Greg Kucera Gallery and Pulliam/Deffenbaugh/Nugent Gallery. Photograph: Arthur S. Aubry

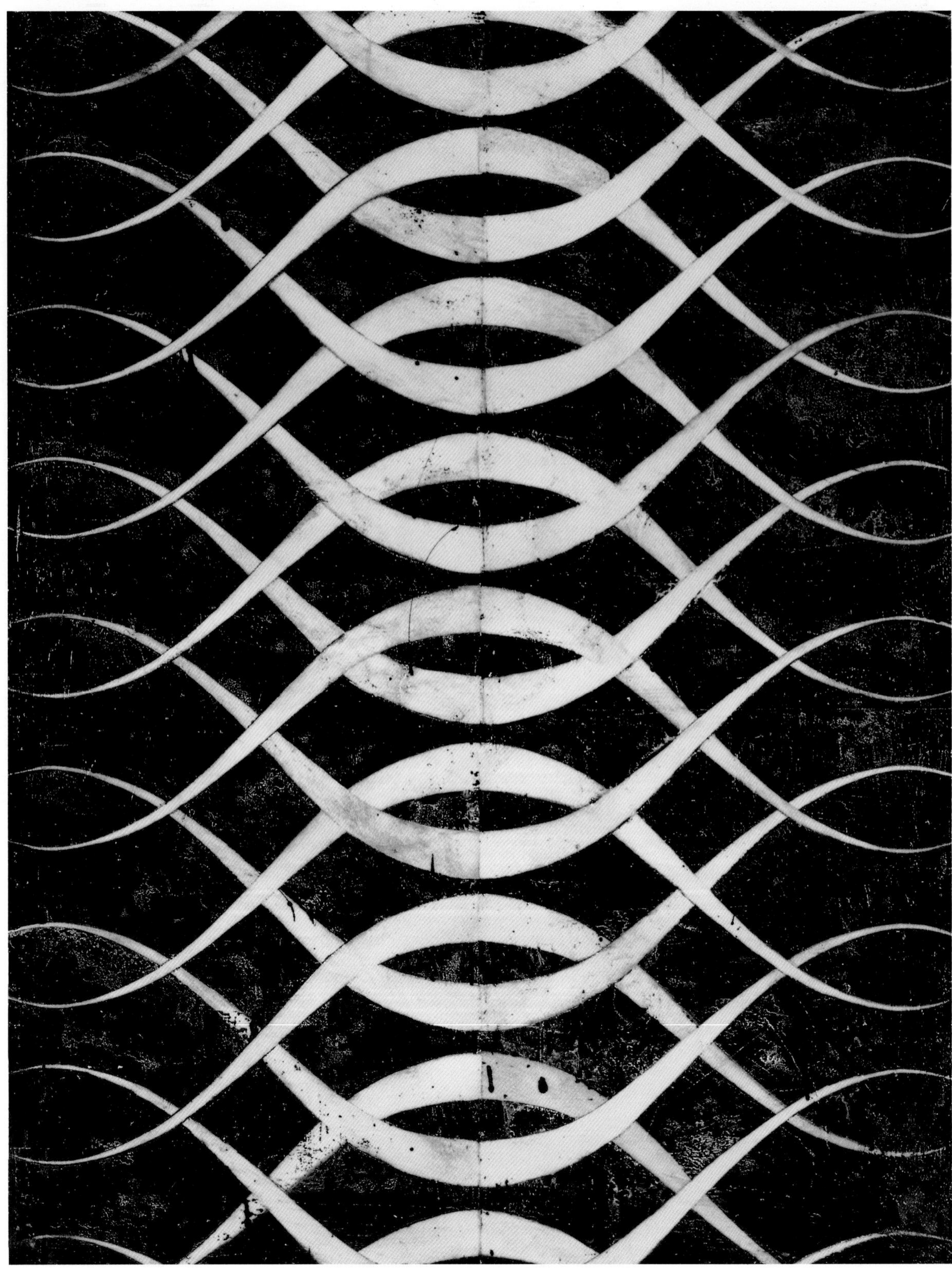

Ken Kelly **Prong**
1992, Oil on canvas, 54" x 42". Courtesy of Greg Kucera Gallery and Pulliam/Deffenbaugh/Nugent Gallery. Photograph: Arthur S. Aubry.

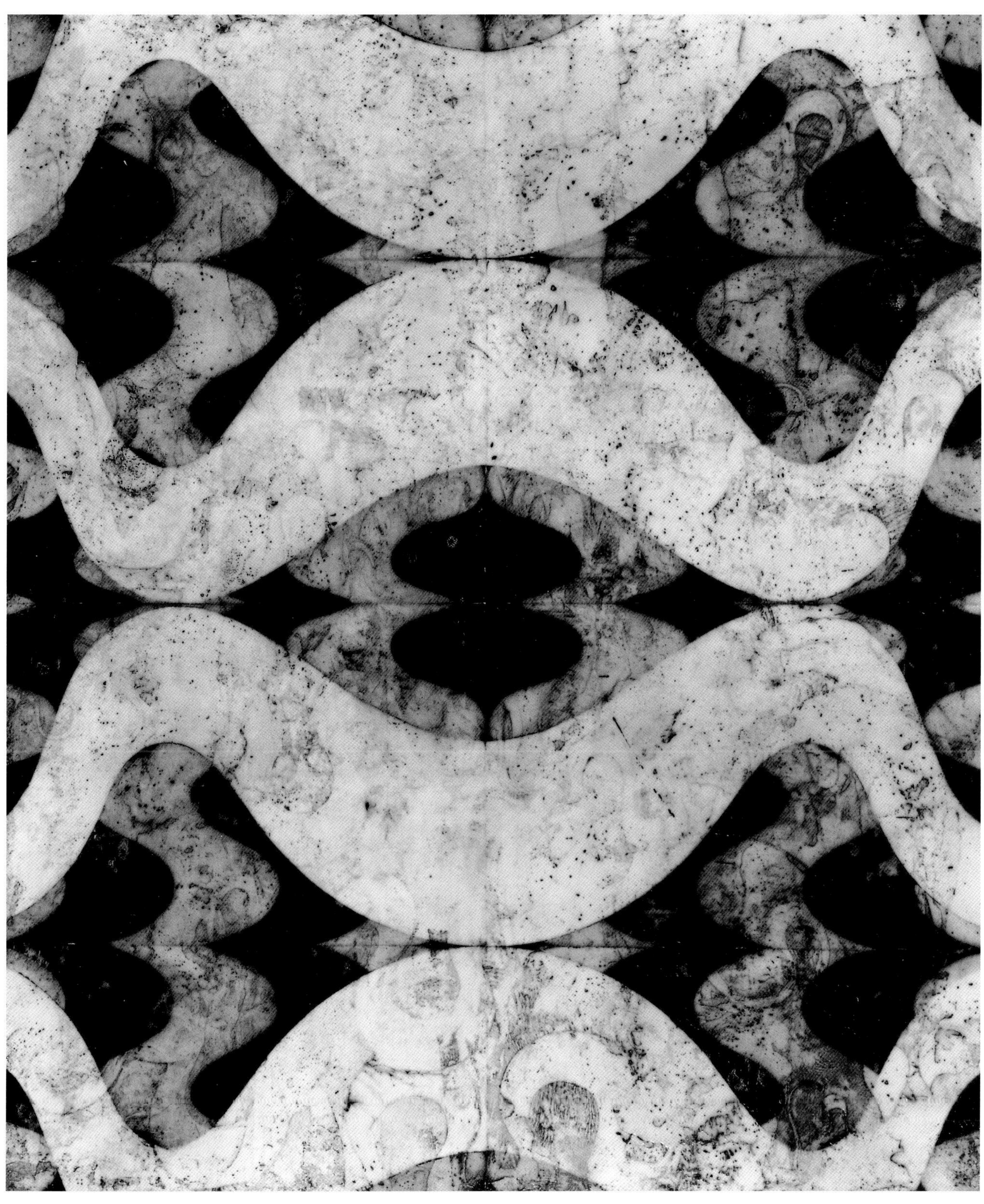

Ken Kelly **Trance**
1994, Mixed media on canvas, 84" x 72". Courtesy of Greg Kucera Gallery and Pulliam/Deffenbaugh/Nugent Gallery. Photograph: Arthur S. Aubry.

Dianne **Kornberg**

Dianne Kornberg's large black-and-white photographs of animal and bird skeletal remains arouse contradictory, and often chilling responses to the cool beauty in what is generally considered to be grisly subject matter. In their clarity of detail her "bone pictures" are reminiscent of scientific documentation, but that is merely the beginning of their associative resonance. Literally images of death, they are powerfully emotive, and at the same time they bring into play stylistic and theoretical issues in contemporary photographic art. Her work challenges the acceptance of images, in particular, photographic images, as signifiers of any absolute truth. As she explores the mental space between the reality of the subject and the reality of the photograph her "truth" becomes one of paradoxes: chaos and order, reality and illusion, intellectual distance and emotional immediacy.

While they are reminiscent of the *memento mori* tradition, Kornberg's subjects appear not in a context pertaining to nature nor to their deaths but as sculptural objects arranged in the studio and re-created in a formalized, two-dimensional idiom. For example, the entire surface of the large gelatin silver print titled *12 Cats* is filled with massed skulls, vertebrae, femurs, tarsals, and all the rest — hundreds of cat bones — as densely composed as the drips in a Jackson Pollock painting. By photographing from directly above the arrangement and lighting it evenly Kornberg eliminated contextualizing references as well as hierarchical values, thereby heightening both visual and associative ambiguity.

Diptychs in a series titled "Bone Stories" and exhibited in 1993 are based on a long stored collection of specimens used in comparative anatomy classes at Reed College in the 1930s. Each diptych, like *Raven Skull*, juxtaposes two images of the same subject, one of the label on the storage box and the other of the box's contents which the label identifies. By using identical lighting, size of print, and close-up, centered compositions in both photographs Kornberg again cancels a hierarchy of importance; the image of the label and the image of the bones are equally weighted signifiers. References to naming, to classifying, preserving, i.e., methods of control, are paired with potent images that represent the ultimate lack of control over nature's most inexorable process. Ironically, the photographs themselves are evidence of the same contradiction; their authority as evidence of the real world is opposed by their authority as artistic inventions.

While almost all the recent work is black and white, Kornberg has used color in the past, and occasionally, when "the subject demands it," as she says, still does. Her academic background is in painting, which made color the obvious choice when she turned to photography, and now undoubtedly influences her orchestration of values and contrasts in black-and-white. Not long after graduation she abandoned painting for the camera's direct relationship with what the eye sees. Self-taught in photographic techniques, she prefers still life because of its potential for "fooling around with ideas," and also because it offers the ability to determine every aspect of the process, from concept to the final printing.

Kornberg's early photographs often were embellished with collage and hand coloring. Gradually, elements added to the print disappeared and instead, were incorporated into the set-up for the photograph. For a portfolio related to the diptychs of "Bone Stories," she photographed small bones distributed and "systematized," within grids she had constructed of white thread on a black background. Emulating archeological practices, she utilizes the grids as a device to focus attention on the significance of placement.

Kornberg grew up in Richland, Washington, home of the Hanford Nuclear Reservation, and as a child was attracted to science. Her large collection of bones, small skeletons, shells, and insects, which began when she was a high school student, holds multiple fascinations, scientific, aesthetic, and poetic. In Native American mythology there is a character called "the old Skeleton Fixer" and like him, she seems to be searching for the soul that once inhabited the bones.

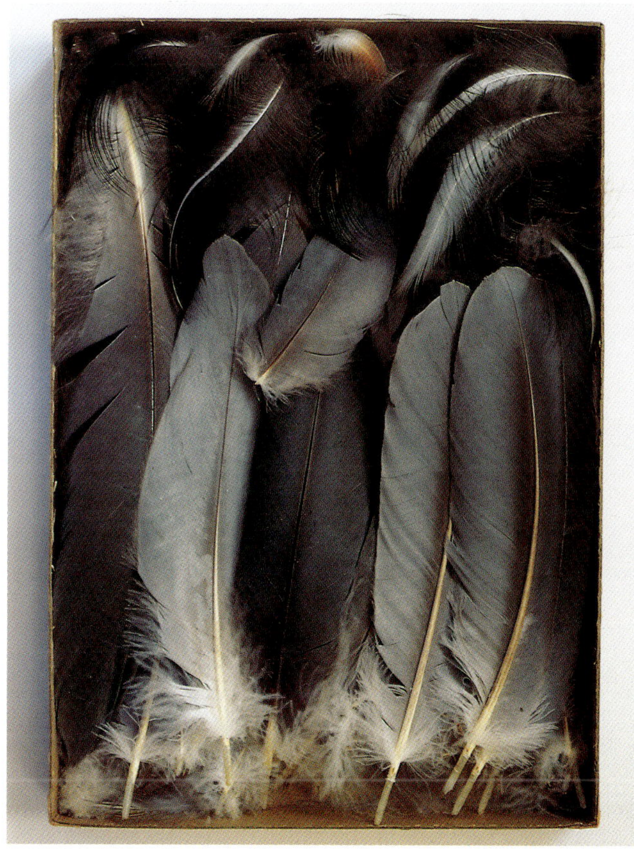

Dianne Kornberg **Feathers of the Great Blue Heron**
1993, Cibachrome diptych, 53" x 78". Courtesy of the artist and Savage Fine Arts. Photograph: Dianne Kornberg.

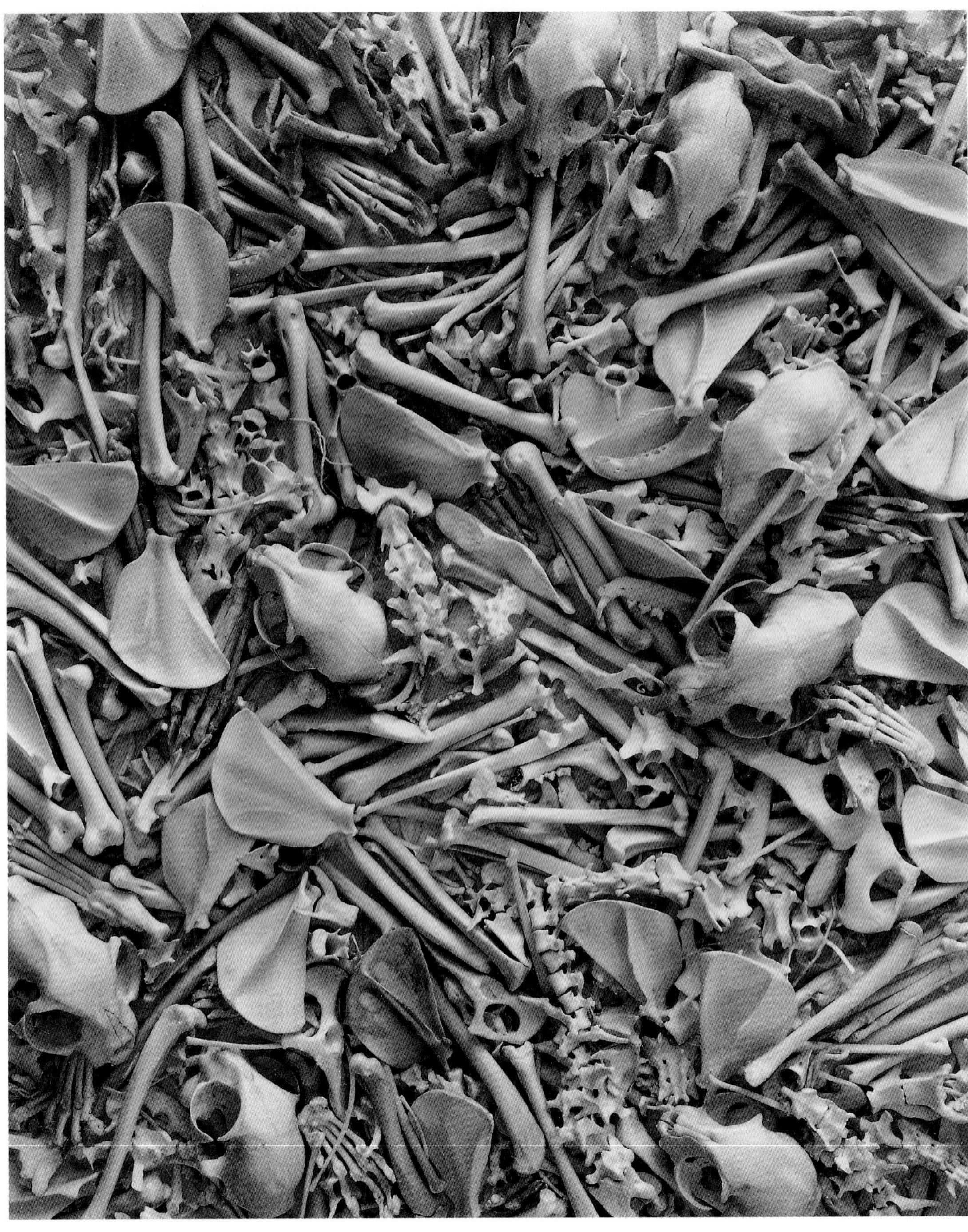

Dianne Kornberg **Twelve Cats**
1992, Selenium toned gelatin silver print, 47" x 38". Courtesy of the artist and Savage Fine Arts. Photograph: Dianne Kornberg.

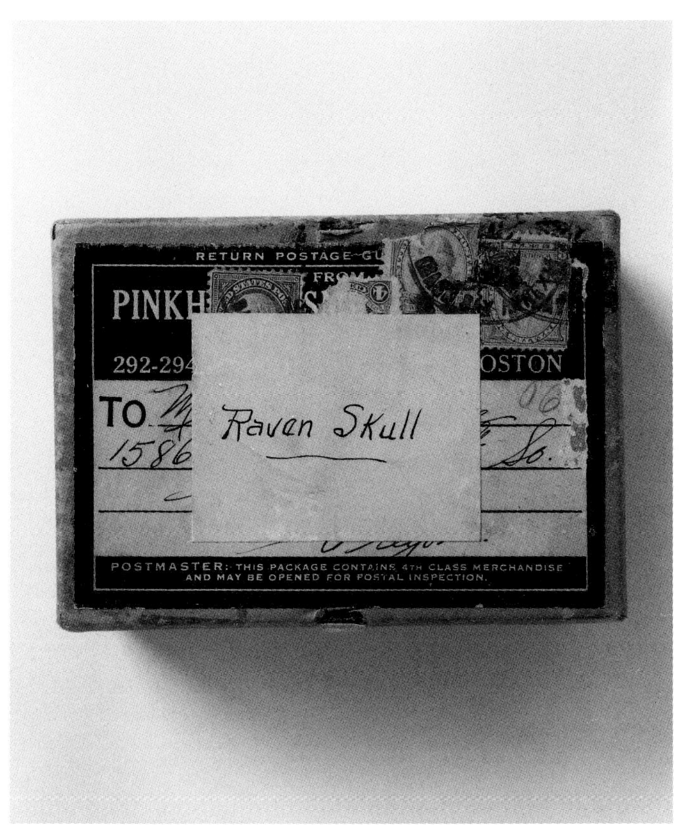

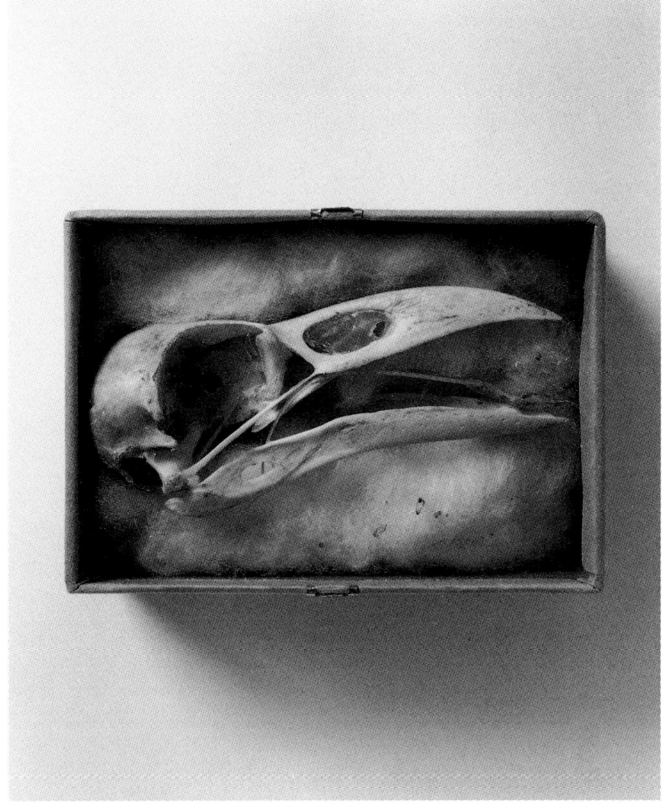

Dianne Kornberg **Raven Skull**
1993, Diptych, Selenium toned gelatin silver prints, 18" x 32". Courtesy of the artist and Savage Fine Arts. Photograph: Dianne Kornberg.

James **Lavadour**

James Lavadour's fiery, visionary landscapes are not about the land as much as they are about his deeply felt responses to it. Although each painting begins as a reference to a specific place, in the process of creation it becomes a powerful embodiment of personal and cultural connections to the earth. He is a member of the Confederated Tribes of the Umatilla Indian Reservation and has lived on the Umatilla Reservation in northeastern Oregon almost all his life. The canyons, streams, and high plateaus of the Blue Mountains are his ancestral domain; the force of their presence in the lives of the people they sustain is the bedrock of Lavadour's art.

Part Walla Walla Indian, Lavadour was aware very early in life of being different, belonging to the "Alima," that is, "the people in between." It was a condition that must have been a formative factor in his reflective nature. He speaks often of finding himself through the many hours spent walking the land, a habit begun during childhood and maintained to this day: "I owe everything about my art to the land. It's where I was educated, where I dreamed, got solace and empowerment." Through his art, tribal traditions and history are fused with this daily, very personal experience.

As he is without formal training, Lavadour at first was dependent on developing his own techniques. His experiments with pigment — letting it drip and move of its own accord, swirling it around — even though inspired by landscape, were abstractions more focused on process than on content. An epiphany of sorts came with a realization that the process was much like that of nature. Art, he believes, simply takes nature from one state to another through the conduit of the human mind.

The earliest exhibited works, from the late 1970s and early 1980s, were ghostly groupings of iconic humans from both the Native American and Euro-American worlds, often boxed off from each other, separate and static. Although these pictures were frequently interpreted as political statements dealing with tensions between the two worlds, which Lavadour knows well, he saw them as a reference to the behavioral and intellectual aspects of the human organism contributing to its inability — or refusal — to accept its consonance with nature. Nevertheless, they are also autobiographical, somberly painted and compartmentalized canvases often incorporating references to the tragedies and problems inherent in life on the reservation.

Gradually, as his signature style evolved, the figure merged with the ground, both literally and figuratively. In such paintings as *Fire and Bones* and *Thunder Head and Bloody Face*, images of "spirit" figures, animals, skeletons, specters of a long lost past, fade in and out of shrouded rocky mountainsides. Gateways and passages through narrow canyons, structural elements in the compositions, extend spiritual connnotations. But even without the mythic references, the works assume metaphysical implications. Thin veils of flowing red and earth hues form massive land masses, scarred and fractured by fire and windswept clouds as if in cataclysmic transformation. When several panels are grouped, as in *Dreamer*, each echoes and reinforces the others, thereby expanding the thematic scope to heroic proportions.

In recent years Lavadour's paintings have become more abstract and more distilled. In an exhibition of 1991, titled "Interiors," the emphasis was on an internalized "landscape" in which the energy of color and brushwork subsume imagery. A further development came in 1993 when he was introduced to printmaking through an artist-in-residence program at the Pacific Northwest College of Art. A series of thirty-seven monotypes produced during the residency are wonderfully free yet condensed manifestations of the paintings' heroic grandeur. Severely limiting color, he relied on dynamic gesture, scraping, and marking to convey the forces that continually re-shape the visible terrain. His passion for the land is unabated but his philosophic dialogue with it becomes increasingly focused.

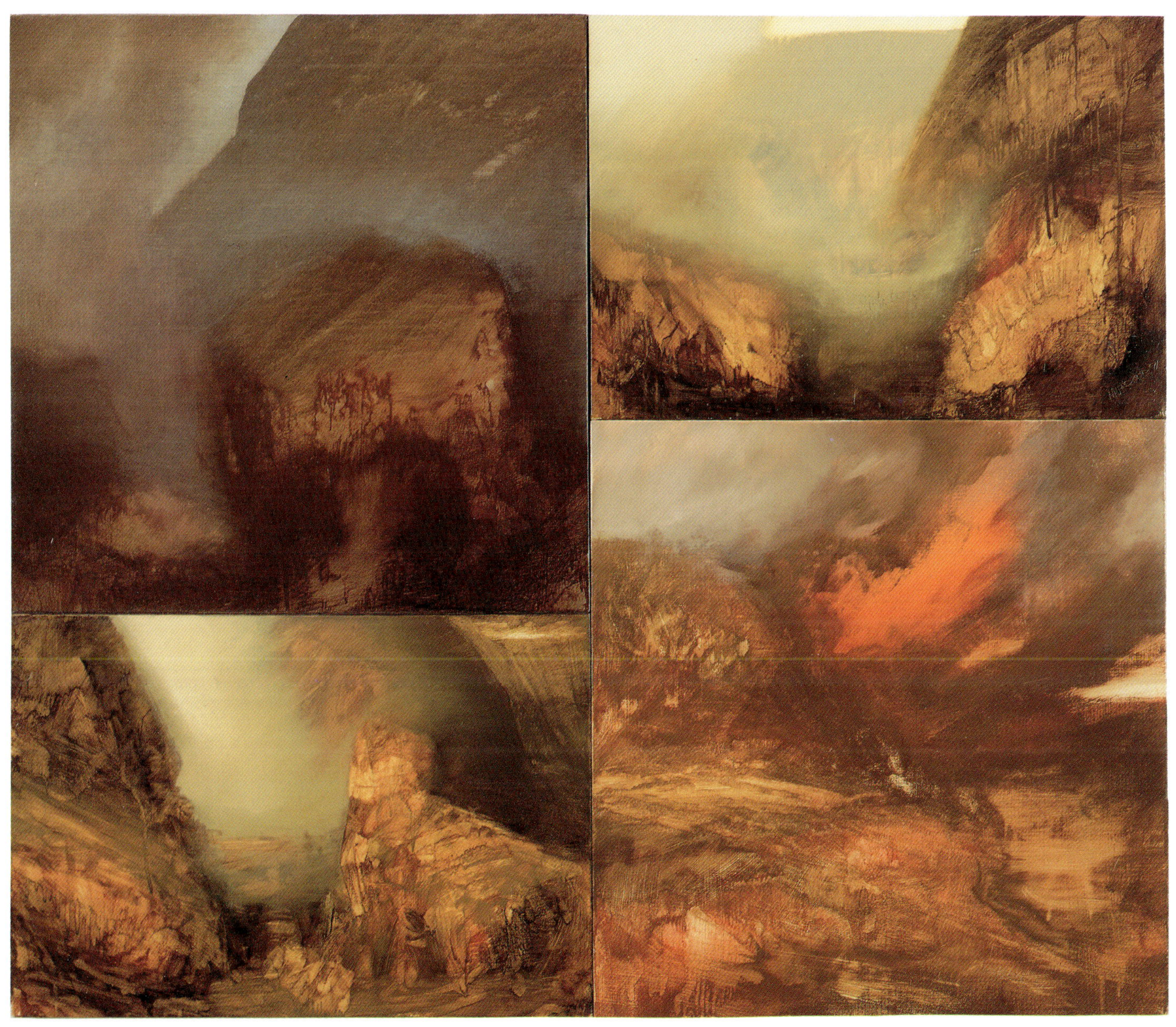

James Lavadour **Dreamer**
1991, Oil on linen, 52" x 62". Private collection. Courtesy of Elizabeth Leach Gallery. Photograph: David Browne.

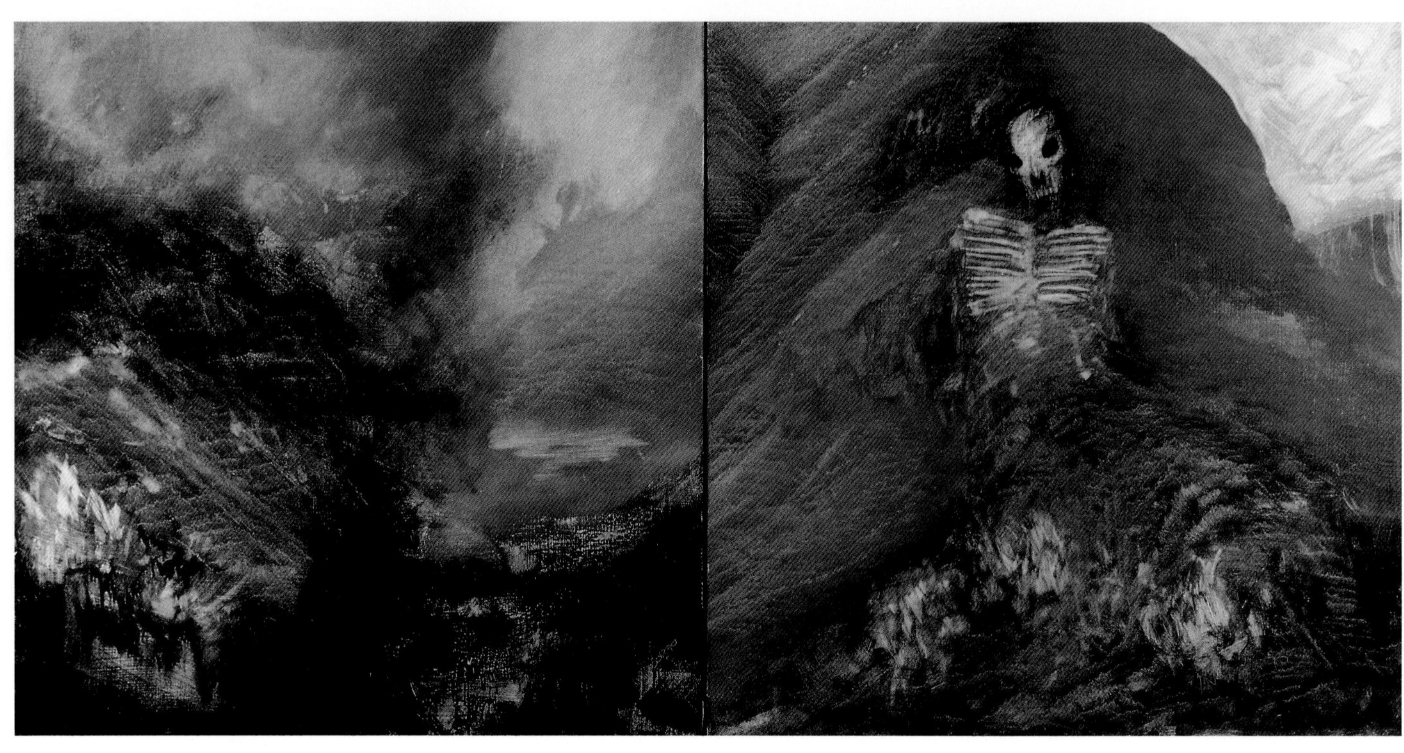

James Lavadour **Fire and Bones**
1990–91, Oil on linen, 31" x 62". Collection of Boise Art Museum. Courtesy of Elizabeth Leach Gallery. Photograph: David Browne.

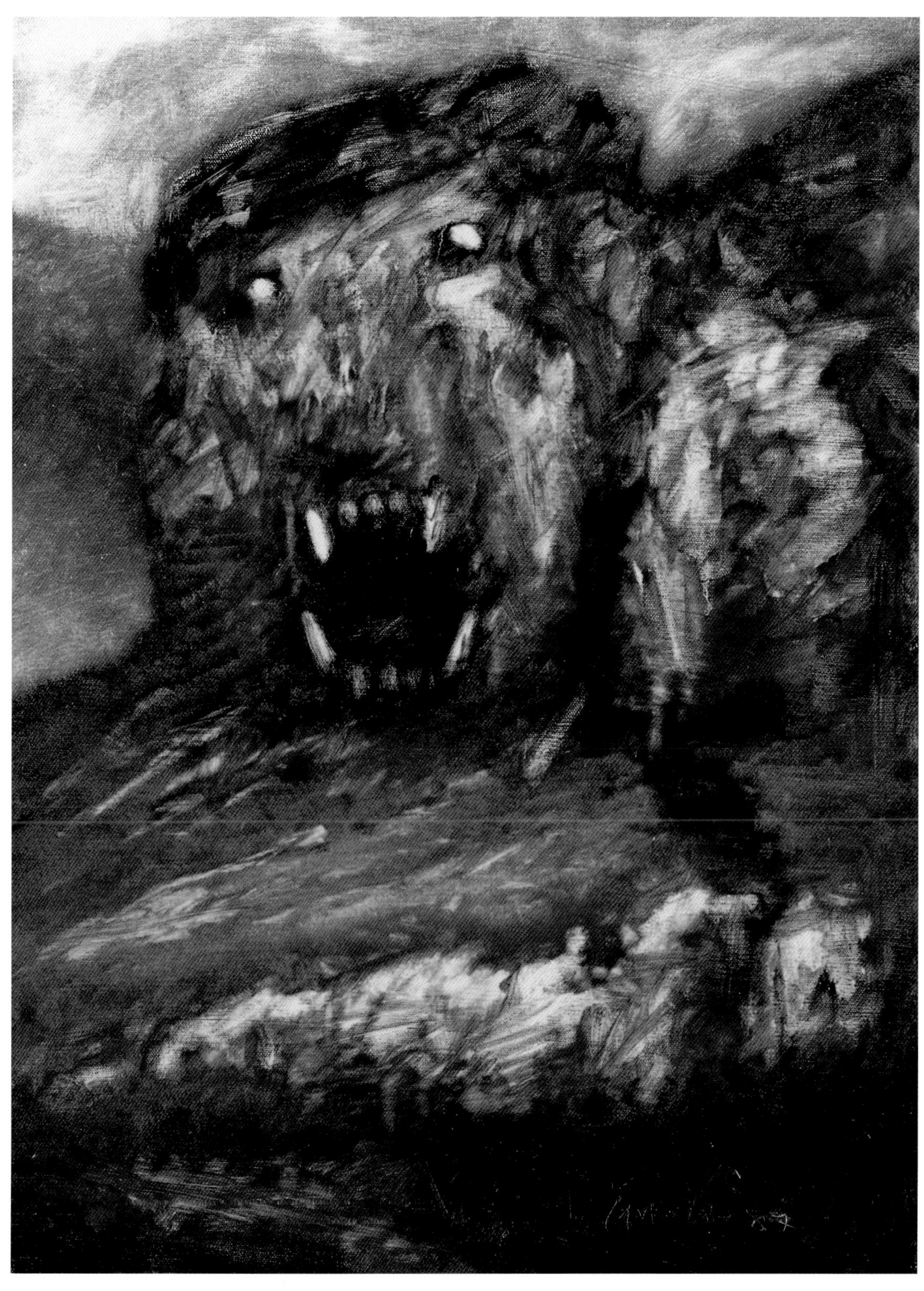

James Lavadour **Thunder Head and Bloody Face** (detail)
1987, Oil on canvas, Three elements: 18" x 72" each, 72" x 54" total. Collection of Frank Russell Company, Tacoma. Courtesy of Elizabeth Leach Gallery. Photograph: Gary Sutto, Seattle Art Museum.

Jacob **Lawrence**

Jacob Lawrence has lived in Seattle since 1970, but in truth he cannot be claimed by the Northwest more than by any other region. Nor can he be described in a limited fashion, as he often is, as the nation's foremost African-American artist. He is, simply, an American master. His many honors, including the National Medal of Arts awarded in 1990 by President George Bush and more than a dozen honorary doctorate degrees, are a tribute to his personal achievement and to his unique body of work which comprises a pictorial epic of human struggle and endurance told through African-American experience. Without any hint of bombast or heroics, he has consistently portrayed his subjects — historical people and events, the lives and activities of ordinary people — with an authenticity that comes from deeply held humanistic convictions. His figurative style reflects that humanism. Formally, it is an adaptation of cubist tenets, densely composed in near abstract areas of bright, unmodulated colors, yet easily read.

Born in 1917, Lawrence grew up in Harlem where his childhood interest in art was developed within a poor but culturally rich community environment. The Harlem Art Workshops (sponsored by the Works Progress Administration during the Great Depression) and the American Artists School in New York City where he took night classes were the sources of his schooling in art. As a teenager he also haunted museums and libraries, independently extending his knowledge of art history and techniques. By the age of twenty-three he was an exhibited, successful artist.

The series that brought Lawrence widespread recognition is "The Migration" first shown in 1941 at the Downtown Gallery in New York. Consisting of sixty panels painted in tempera on gesso, each accompanied by a brief, narrative text, the series is a succinct history of the migration of thousands of southern, rural blacks to the industrial North during the early decades of the twentieth century. The difficult flight from one kind of oppression to another is represented in small (12" x 18") paintings that have the coherence and intimacy of a book. Shunning conventional perspective and chiarascuro in favor of an overall surface arrangement, Lawrence encapsulates layers of meaning within interlocking color shapes punctuated by a few telling touches such as a potently expressive gesture or attitude of a figure.

"Migration's" enduring strength, both aesthetic and as a document of continuing social change was proved again, a half-century after its initial exhibition, in a widely acclaimed 1993–95 nation-wide tour organized by The Phillips Collection of Washington, D.C. Imbued with the passion of an artist who had great personal investment in its subject, the series may well stand as Lawrence's masterwork. His practice of working in series did not begin or end with "Migration," however. Preceding "Migration," he produced series on the historic figures Frederick Douglass, Toussaint L'Ouverture, and Harriet Tubman. He has also grouped paintings around specific events and themes: "World War II" (1945), the "Hospital" (1950) and "Theater" (1953) series, and two later epochal series, one on death and the other on the origin of life, "Hiroshima" (1983) and "Genesis" (1993). Also, in what might be considered a lifelong series, he has recorded throughout his long career everyday scenes of life that he observes around him.

In 1970 Lawrence was invited to the University of Washington as Visiting Artist. At the end of the three month appointment he was asked to join the faculty as a full professor, and in 1971 he and his wife, painter Gwendolyn Knight, moved from New York to Seattle. Lawrence had previously taught for limited times at many colleges and art schools and has often remarked on the importance and satisfaction that stems from teaching. Since retiring from the University in 1987 he continues to visit learning institutions while maintaining vigorous creative activity.

Lawrence's use of gouache — and earlier, casein tempera — and his stylistic manipulation of flat colors are well suited to the bold design of posters, murals, and screenprints that have occupied him at various times. Seattle's Kingdome Stadium is home to ten large porcelain-on-enamel panels (a public art commission of 1979) depicting muscular athletes in action. In pronounced contrast, screenprints created for a children's book, "Eight Sermons of the Creation from the Book of Genesis," published in 1990, are delightfully personal interpretations of the biblical story of creation.

The connecting link in all Jacob Lawrence's work, whether historical, political, or anecdotal, is compassion and a sense that life, in its wretchedness as in its glory, is to be celebrated.

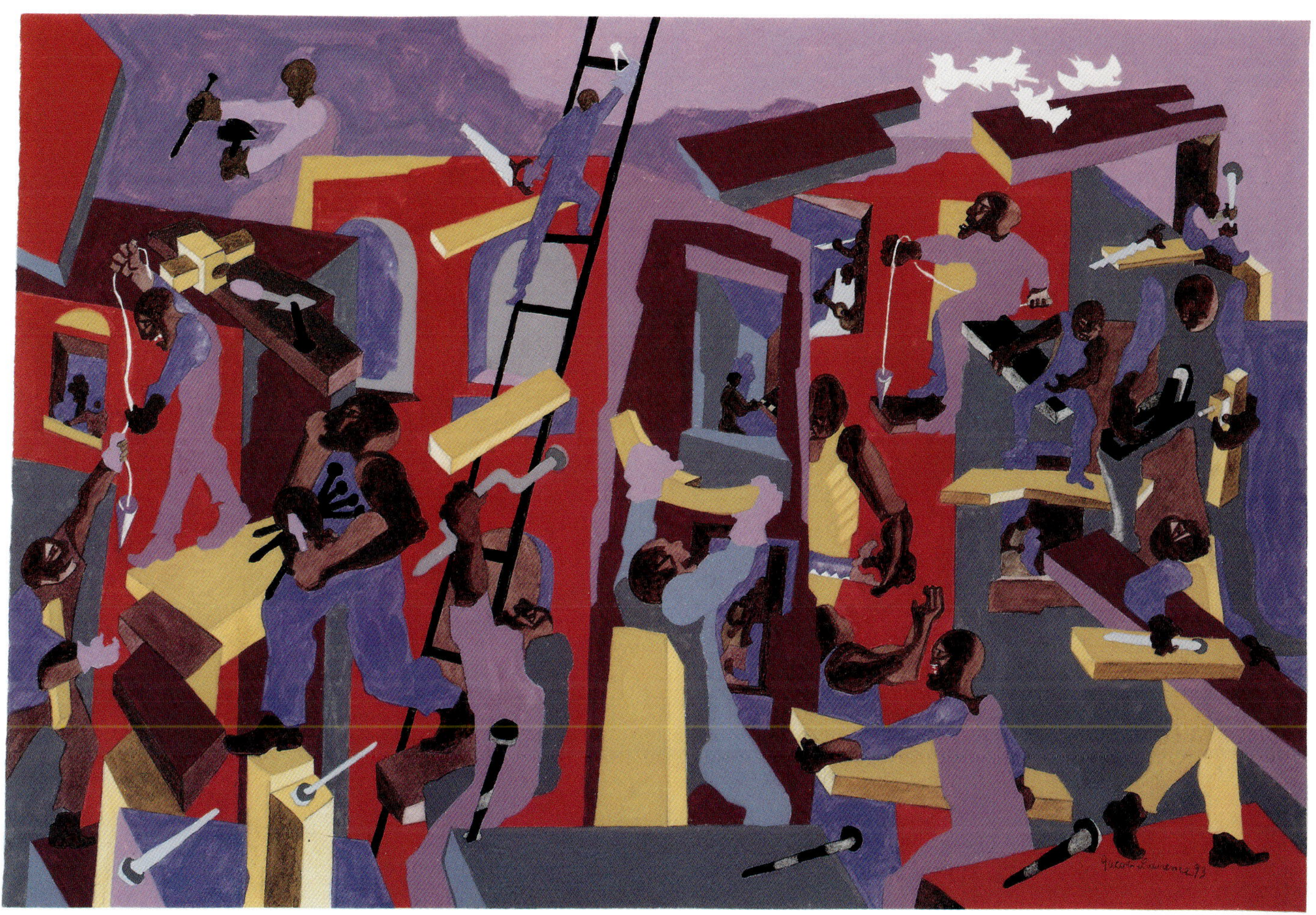

Jacob Lawrence **Builders in the City**

1993, Gouache on paper, 19" x 28". Courtesy of the artist and Francine Seders Gallery. Photograph: Spike Mafford.

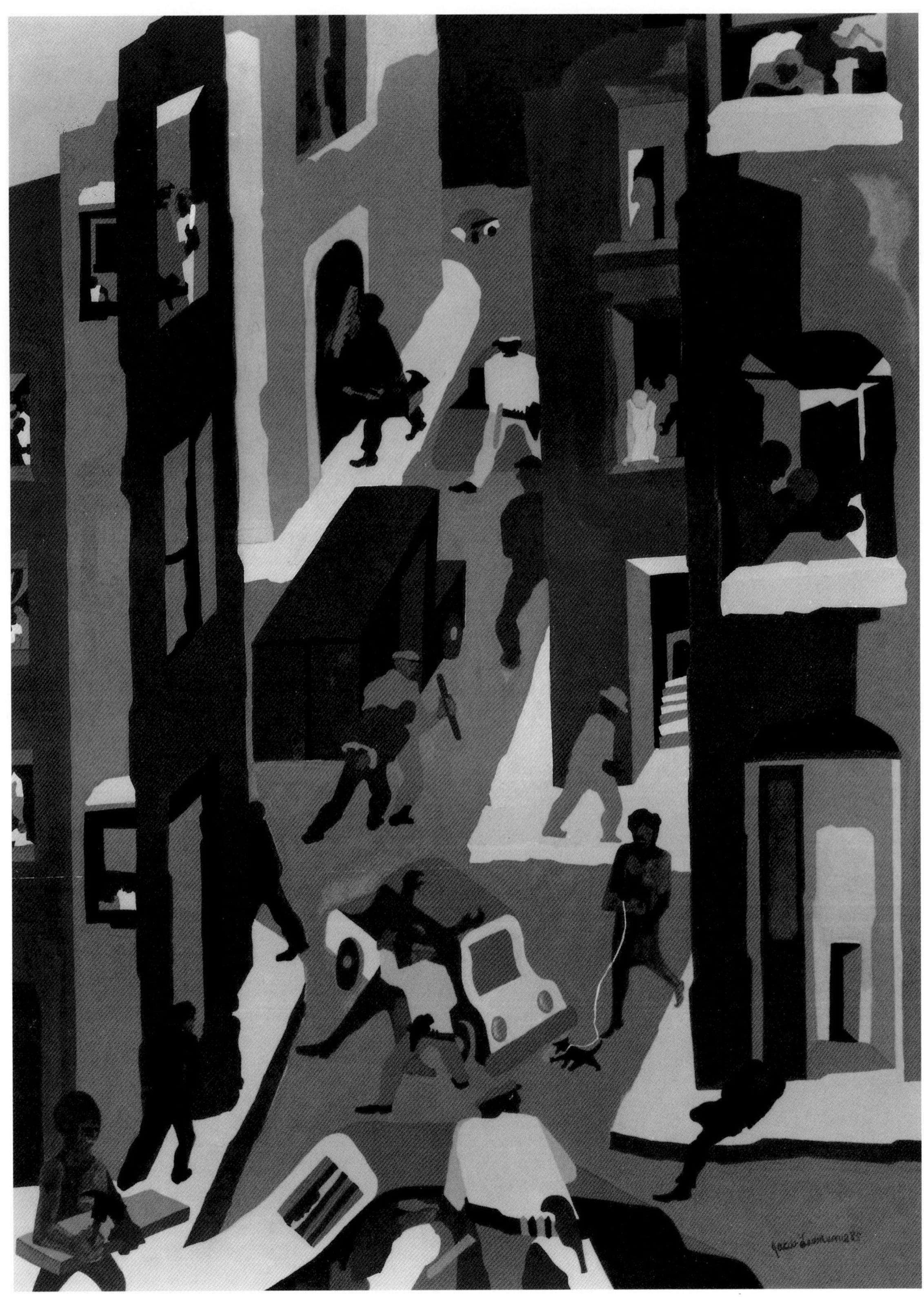

Jacob Lawrence **Street Scene**
1985, Gouache on paper, 30" x 22". Private collection. Courtesy of Francine Seders Gallery. Photograph: Chris Eden.

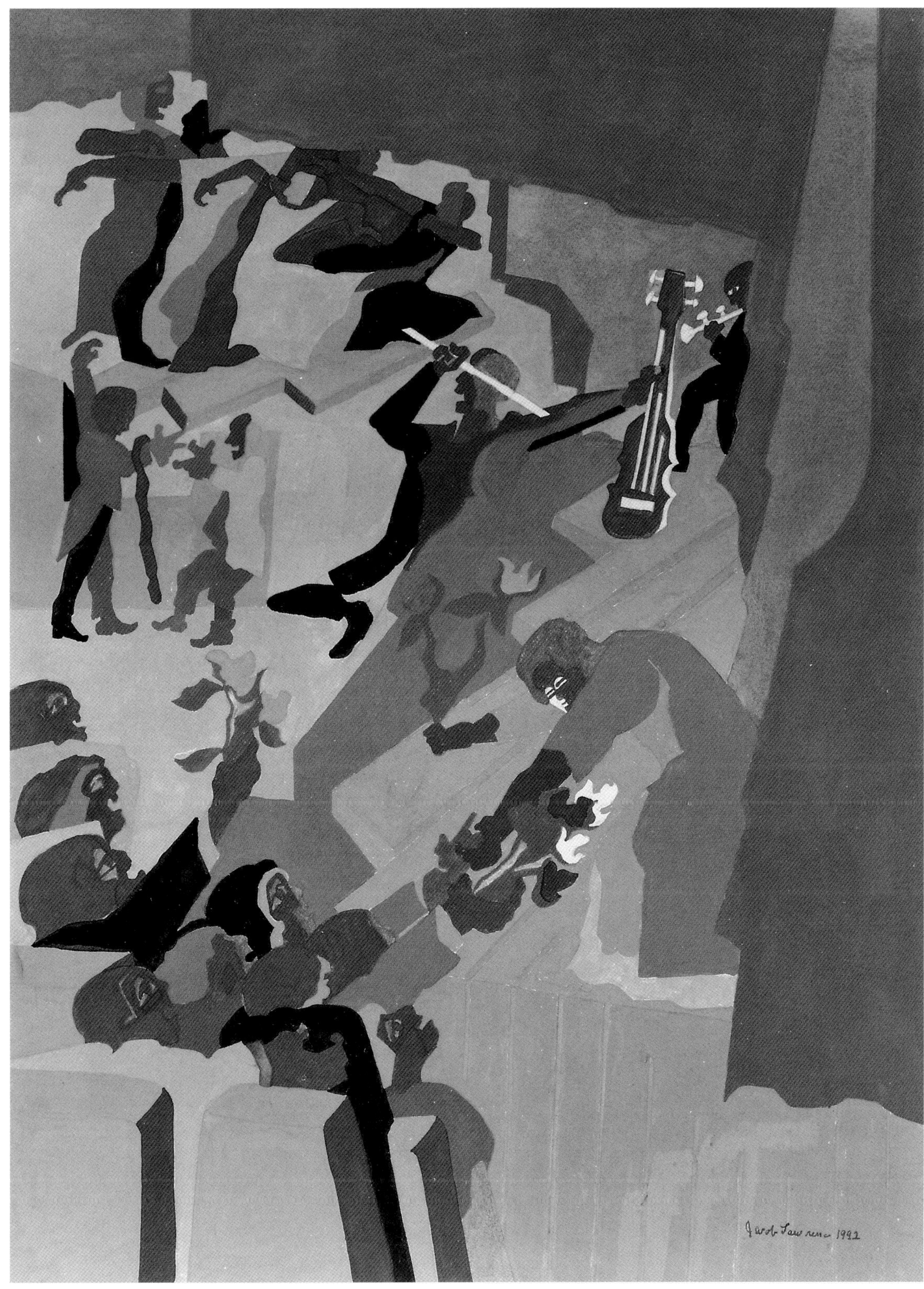

Jacob Lawrence **Grand Performance**
1992, Gouache on paper, 35" x 28". Private collection. Courtesy of Francine Seders Gallery. Photograph: Chris Eden.

Helen **Lessick**

Helen Lessick's remarkably broad, conceptually based art takes surprising forms and appears in unusual, non-art places as, for examples, a cow wandering among a herd in Valence, France, a birch tree house structure in the Hoyt Arboretum in Portland, and a straw bale hut on Sauvie Island near Portland. Gallery works, too, are widely varied in form, encompassing artist's books, installations, paintings, and drawings. Like the larger projects, they turn on personal as well as societal relationships to nature, to culture, and their intermixing. Content may be hermetic, cloaked in references to philosophy, science, and art itself, but visually, the strong physical presence of her artworks compels an attentive reading. A house motif, for example, is central to an extended major series, and no matter what its materials (it has appeared in shimmering lamé floating above one of Portland's busy downtown streets, as shaped birch trees, as open pipe assemblies, and straw bales, among others), it is always in the iconic form of a simple block with pitched roof. Such direct representations of commonplace structures and objects are deceptive, however. Viewers are drawn into a web of associations and responses, a web Lessick carefully weaves around the ambiguities of meaningful signs that discompose our apprehension of the world.

An extensive exploration of the myriad cultural and personal associations attending the word "house" has occupied Lessick for more than a decade. As in all her work, she plays on the capacity of visual signifiers to displace meaning, not only by such devices as metonymy and metaphor, but also by contextual variations. Although all the "houses" in the series are represented by the same simple shape, the materials and the environments in which they are placed generate a thematic framework. There are houses for the seasons of the year, houses that refer to nature's elements, and houses that reflect inner mental states.

Among the seasonal houses *House for Autumn*, which brought story-telling, Native American drumming, the setting, the date and weather into the contextual ambiance symbolized by the sculpture, exemplifies Lessick's multi-dimensional exposition of the nature-culture theme. The work was conceived as a metaphor for the earth and was built of earth's materials — straw bales, sod, and coal — and destroyed by earth's elements — the winter rains and winds. On the evening of its dedication, the autumn equinox in 1991, a group of celebrants gathered in the field surrounding the sculpture to watch the last rays of the sun pierce its dark interior, then to participate in ceremonial performances by Lessick, the story-tellers, and drummers. The placement of the work on Sauvie Island, located at the confluence of the Willamette and Columbia Rivers, referred to the three distinct cultural groups that have occupied the island: Native American, Asian, and European. Stories representing the cultures of these groups were told inside the house to audience members who entered, one or two at a time, and sat on the coal-covered ground to listen and to receive a symbolic "gift" of an ear of dried corn, a gourd, or a starfruit.

Artist's books make up the core of Lessick's work, often spawning ideas for installations and public projects. Most address the ambivalence in communication that affects personal relationships, and utilize objects, both appropriated and created, as a counterbalance to the cryptic text. *Cleavers*, for example, joins menacing objects and ambiguous text that at first seem disjunctive but soon reveal themselves to be wryly and disconcertingly connected.

As artist-in-residence at Art3 in Valence, France, in 1993 Lessick enlisted the cooperation of the Lycée Agricole to produce *Le Paysage Vivant*. Her "living landscape" consisted of a fine looking, black-coated dairy cow with the word "poème" shaved on her left flank. Moving among the herd, thus causing the word to be seen only intermittently, the cow became, until her hair grew out, an elusive and whimsical reference to romantic French landscape painting, to Magritte's surrealism, and to Lessick's own "poetic" conceptualism.

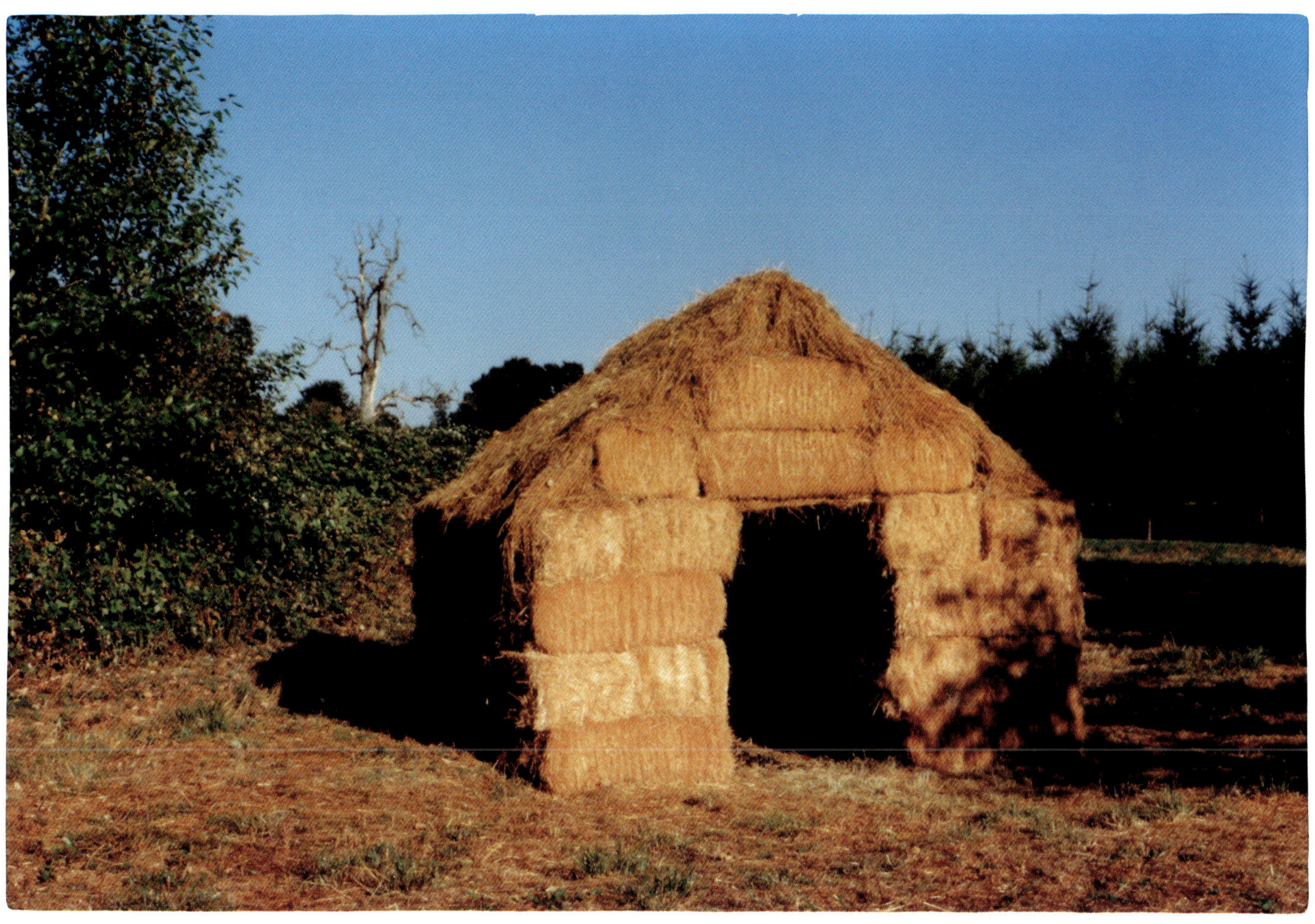

Helen Lessick **House for Autumn**
1991, Sited installation with hay, coal and wood, Sauvie Island, Oregon. Courtesy of the artist. Photograph by David Potter.

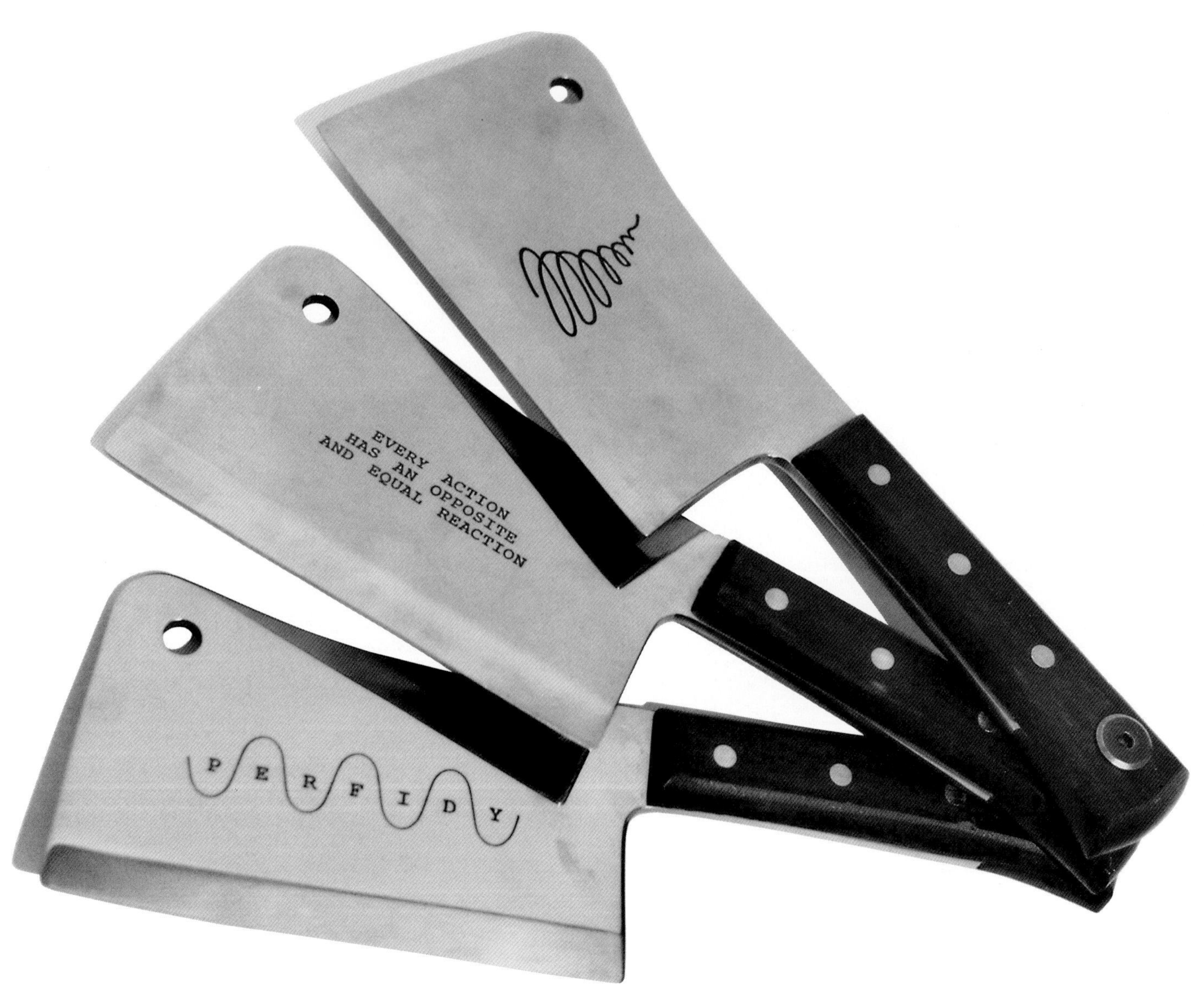

Helen Lessick **Cleaver**

1990, Artist's book on meat cleavers, 13" x 6" x 3 cleavers. Collection of Sackner Archive of Visual and Concrete Poetry, Miami Beach. Courtesy of the artist.

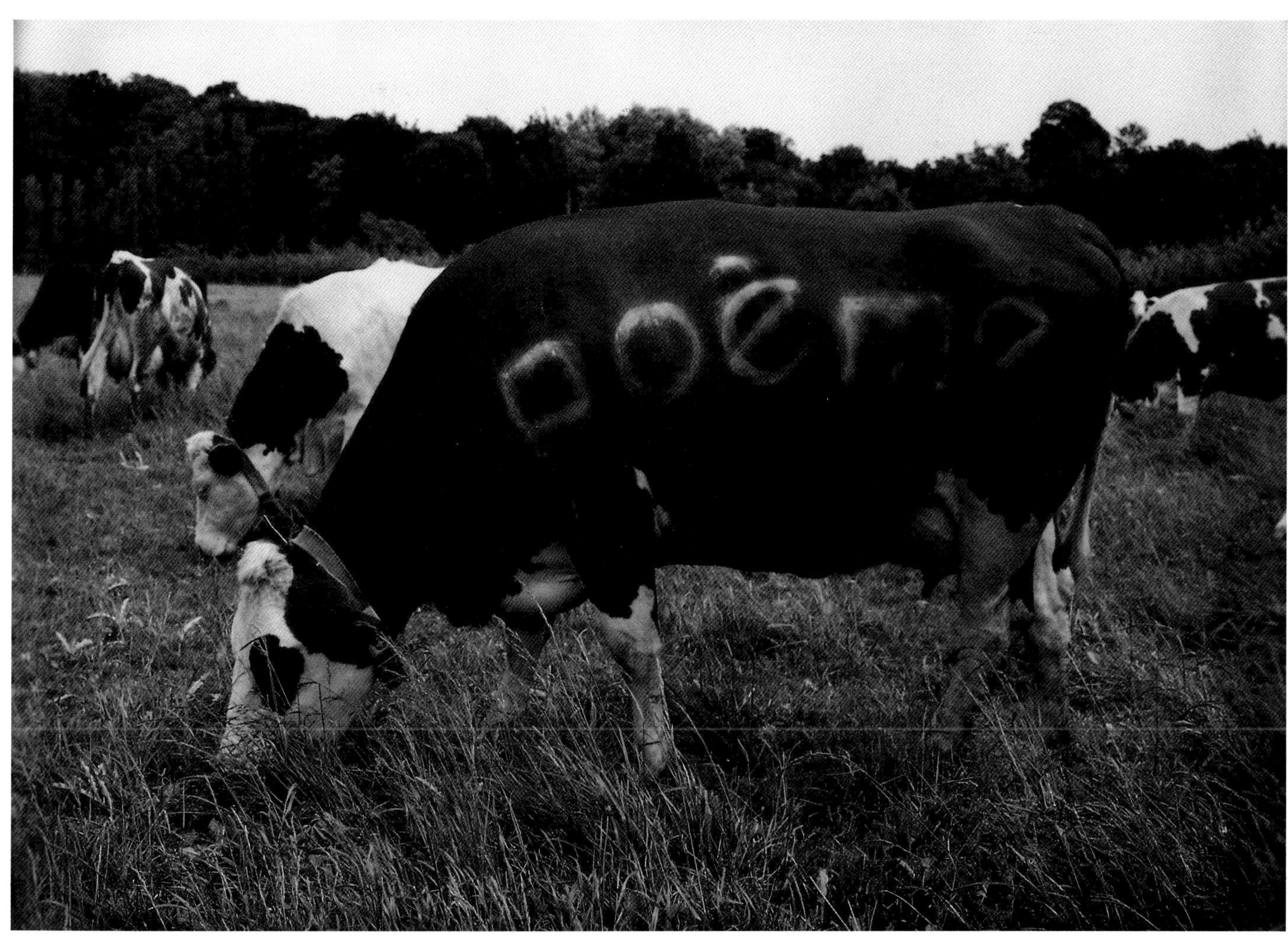

Helen Lessick **Le Paysage Vivant**
1993, Site specific landscape work in Valence, France. Courtesy of the artist. Photograph: P. Plattier.

Sherry **Markovitz**

Sherry Markovitz practices the ancient art of beadwork, incorporating all its associations of cultural histories, decoration, and painstaking handiwork into widely exhibited sculptures that are lauded as much for rich metaphoric resonance as for their dazzling physical presence. First attracted to beadwork as borders for paintings, she has developed from it a singular body of work based on the tension created by the incongruity between the forms and their materials. Wall-mounted sculptures, both representational and abstract, are completely encrusted with beads, buttons, and other ornamental trim, arranged either in intricate patterns or in nuanced tones of a single hue. Explicit celebrations of craft, decoration, and exacting, repetitive work by hand, these complex artworks are also conceptually rigorous, addressing universal concerns of spirituality, death, and one's place in the world.

Markovitz began applying beads to three-dimensional forms about 1981 after a foray in Seattle junk shops produced several taxidermy forms. Using the forms as a base, she molded papier-mâché replicas of the animals represented by the forms, but rather than accepting the resulting head-forms as simplified, direct representations, she adopted the strategies of folk artists, in effect, creating a reverberating tension not only between the underlying form and a highly decorative surface, but metaphorically, between fantasy and reality, interior structure and exterior display, death and vivifying beauty. Separately, the forms and the embellished surfaces are potent signifiers; together they evoke the myriad incongruities that bedevil any sense of order and reason in our lives.

The dynamics of male and female identities are immediately apparent in both *Yellow Bear* and *Marquesa.* As trophies of the hunt the heads are emblematic of masculine ritual and dominance. Their beaded, embellished surfaces place them in a very different context, however, one in which delicacy, beauty, and domesticity undermine the traditional hegemony their forms represent. In addition, there is a terrible poignance carried by these two effigies in their connotations of capture, subjugation, and death. Dark, glowing eyes set into the glittering surfaces poeticize the pathos of irretrievable loss as nature is converted into the means of human gratification.

Markovitz's extraordinary beadwork produces painterly effects, not only in the relationships of colors but also in expressively individualized facial expressions as can be seen in the miens of the pathetic *Yellow Bear* and the haughty *Marquesa.* Complex, multi-colored patterns, as those in Marquesa's resplendent red-spiked tiara above the pale blue head and the flowered design on the shoulder, engender a thematic unity and at the same time suggest folk designs in eastern European cultures. As one might expect, Markovitz is intensely interested in the use of beads in various cultures. Her animal heads pay homage to the respect in many non-Western cultures for the symbolic powers of body ornament and embellishment, not only in ceremonial rituals but also in proclaiming societal status.

In 1990 Markovitz turned to simple, organic forms as unadorned as the animal heads are ornate. Close similarities — process, materials, wall presentation — are obvious, but in appearance and references, the new bead encrusted works, most of which are based on horn and gourd forms, are very different. First, they are not trophies but objects of intimacy suggesting body parts or growing things. Some seem to be suspended, curving against the wall. Others, like *Twins,* are spherical or bulbous forms firmly attached to their support. Most are monochromatic, modulated so closely that the entire surface seems to shimmer. Although less obviously life-like than the heads, their implied movement, gesture, and organic configurations do, in fact, suggest forms of life.

In his essay for the catalog accompanying a 1992 exhibition of Markovitz's work at the Mint Museum of Art in Charlotte, North Carolina, curator Mark Richard Leach captures the essence of Markovitz's work: "… the metaphorical and associative value Markovitz incurs through her use of beads might be best understood as curiosity towards the multiplicity and richness of human identity and expression."

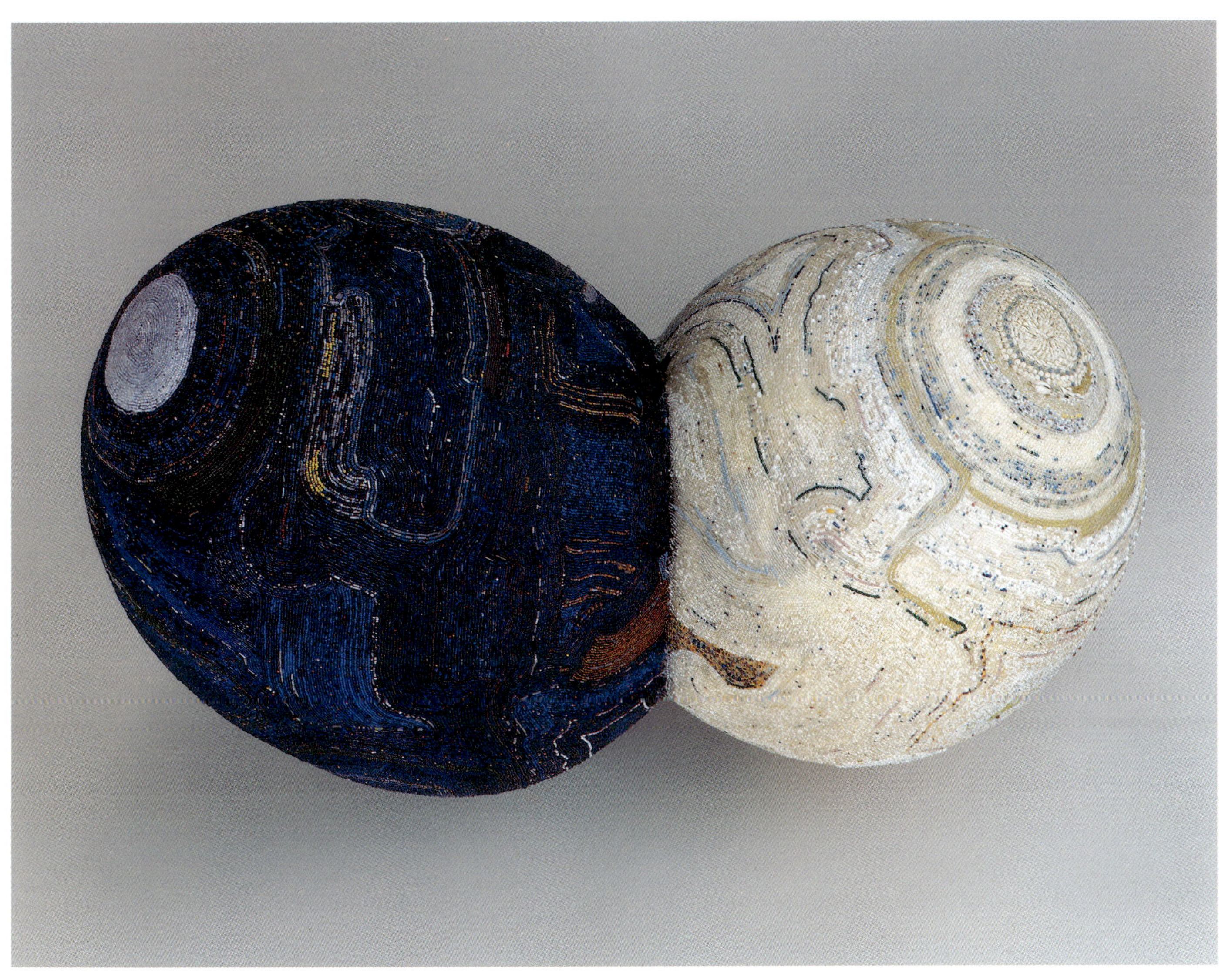

Sherry Markovitz **Twins**
1994, Beads, wax/pigment, fiberglass, papier-mâché, 33" x 17" x 24". Courtesy of the artist and Linda Farris Gallery. Photograph: Nancy Hines.

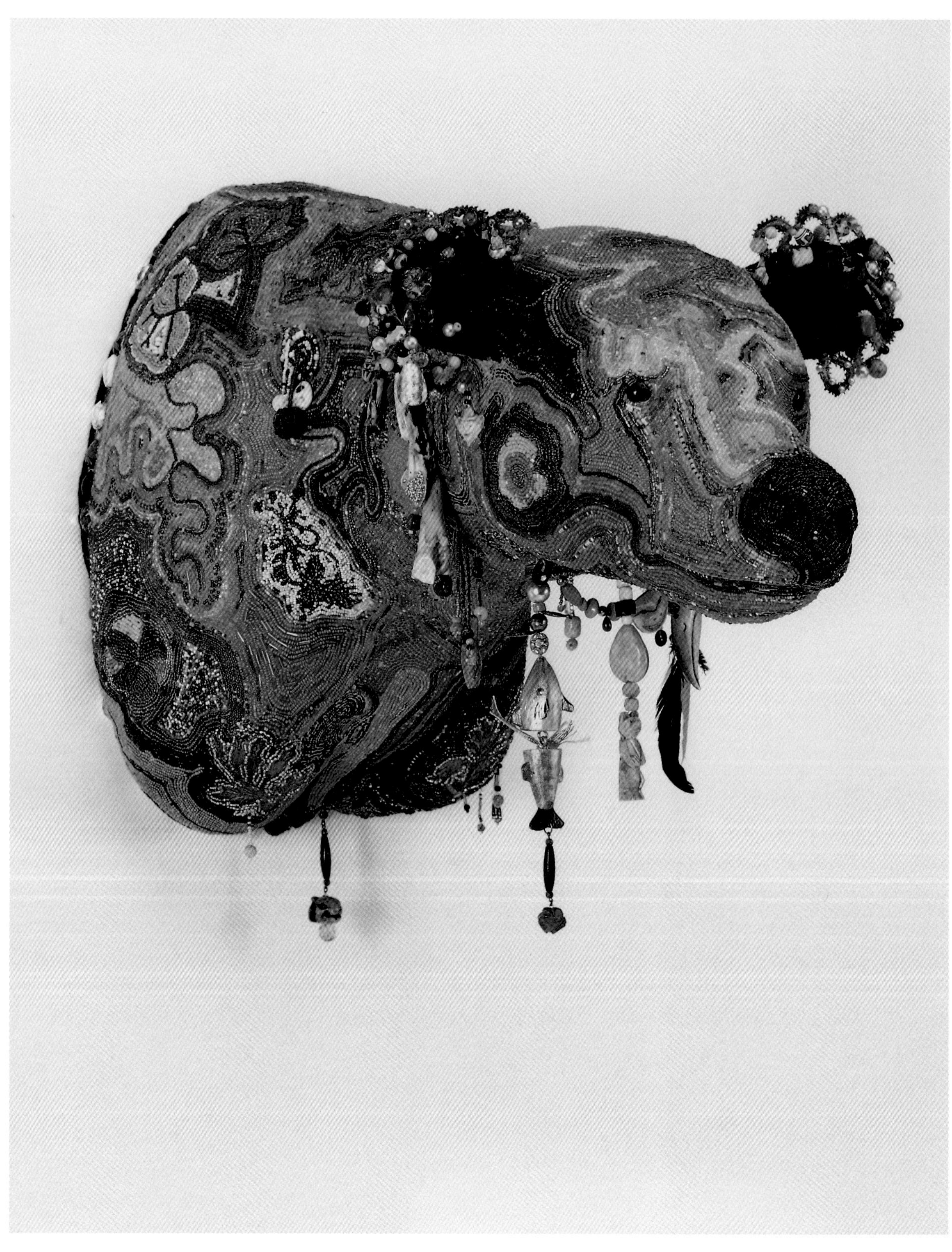

Sherry Markovitz **Yellow Bear**
1994, Beads, papier-mâché, fiberglass, wax/pigment, 19" x 14" x 25". Courtesy of the artist and Linda Farris Gallery. Photograph: Nancy Hines.

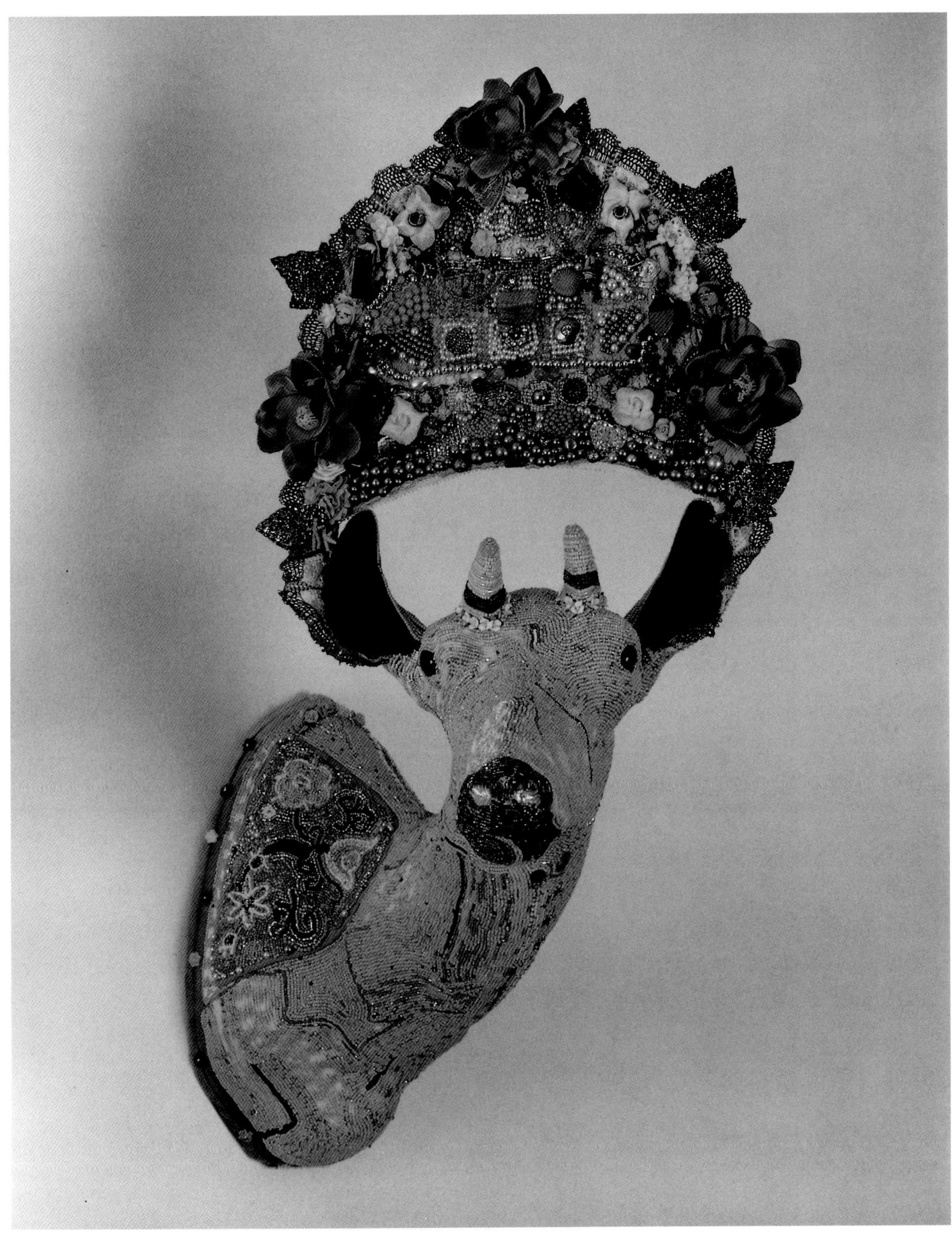

Sherry Markovitz **Marquesa**
1992, Beads, mixed media, 32" x 15" x 25". Courtesy of the artist and Linda Farris Gallery. Photograph: Eduardo Calderoń.

Jeffry **Mitchell**

At first glance much of Jeffry Mitchell's art appears exuberantly decorative, a riot of paper cut-outs, caricaturish drawing, and molded animals, flowers, and blobs that seem to run amuck in his prodigious constructions and installations. Far from uninhibited play, however, the work is a sophisticated blend of low culture materials, a postmodern sensibility, and the artist's spirited musings on religion, sex, art, literature, and the importance of work. Trained as a painter, ceramist, and printmaker who began his career with uncompromising abstractions, Mitchell with great verve challenges all premises of formalist art with his conceptually driven use of materials, processes, and presentation.

When he began exhibiting in Seattle in 1989, Mitchell was already an innovator of materials, techniques, and ideas, which was immediately apparent in puffy free-standing and wall constructions made of glassine (a semi-transparent, glazed paper). Limiting himself to geometric figures executed in both two and three-dimensional versions, he created sculptures such as *Geometry Park,* a playful combination of Japanese, Minimalist, and optical-puzzle influences. The artistry and ephemerality of *origami* (he had recently returned from a residency in Japan) are incorporated into the bulbous forms and their densely patterned surfaces. The surface treatment, consisting of repeated, rubber-stamped patterns, foreshadowed the extensive use of repetition that has become a distinctive feature of Mitchell's work.

In 1991 a major installation for the Poncho Series at the Seattle Art Museum established Mitchell as one of the most inventive young artists in the Northwest. Although it was untitled, Mitchell referred to the work as a "requiem for childhood" and utilized many symbols of childhood and sexual innocence (rows upon rows of identical, upright plaster bunnies, a huge pile of limp, white muslin toy-size elephants, putti) placed within a long, curtained room reminiscent of a mausoleum. As a requiem the installation was clearly related to AIDS and to those whose sexuality is tinged with the awareness of death.

Mitchell also pits playfulness against melancholy in the large, combination wall and floor sculpture, *Jesus in a Crowd,* 1991, which is based on James Ensor's *Entry of Christ into Brussels* of 1889. The carnival atmosphere with its mob of fatuous revelers in Ensor's painting is contemporized by Mitchell, whose relationship to his Catholic background is a frequent theme, into a multitude of clowns. The primary figure, a truncated clown, stretches its overly long arms and huge flabby hands along the floor as if in supplication. Ensor's indifferent onlookers become Mitchell's tinted plaster, goofy clown faces lined up in rows along the wall like assorted cake decorations.

Mitchell traces his love of repetition and accretion to his experience in learning to knit as a child in his grandmother's care. Creating a finished garment, over time and from a long sequence of individual stitches, symbolizes, in his view, the value of labor, which he celebrates in his purposely labor-intensive art. The process of producing and assembling each increment of a complex piece, even though it may result in a haphazard appearance, is as essential to the work's intent as knitted stitches to a sweater.

Possibly the most personal of his large sculptural pieces, *Growth Afterwards — Like a Valentine* of 1994 is also the most absurd in its appearance and problematic in its interpretation. Like a huge colorful piñata in the shape of an elephant it is, physically, a flimsy wood structure covered with all sorts of "trimmings:" paper flowers, drawings, quotations and notations, small toys, and hanging from a string draped above, block letters spelling "I LOVE MOM DAD." Unlike a piñata, it does not spill out treats, but rather, through the snippets of text and the many scribbles and sketches, it is a compendium of longing and libidinous impulses, of ephemeral notations such as telephone numbers, of ideas and musings on whatever subject held his interest at a particular moment.

His impressive sculptural works notwithstanding, Mitchell's primary and constant artform is drawing, which flows in torrents from his fertile imagination. Cartoonishly expressive drawings, which supply the basis for an on-going body of etchings, precede the sculptures in his imaginative attempts to bridge the gap between enchantment and self-knowledge.

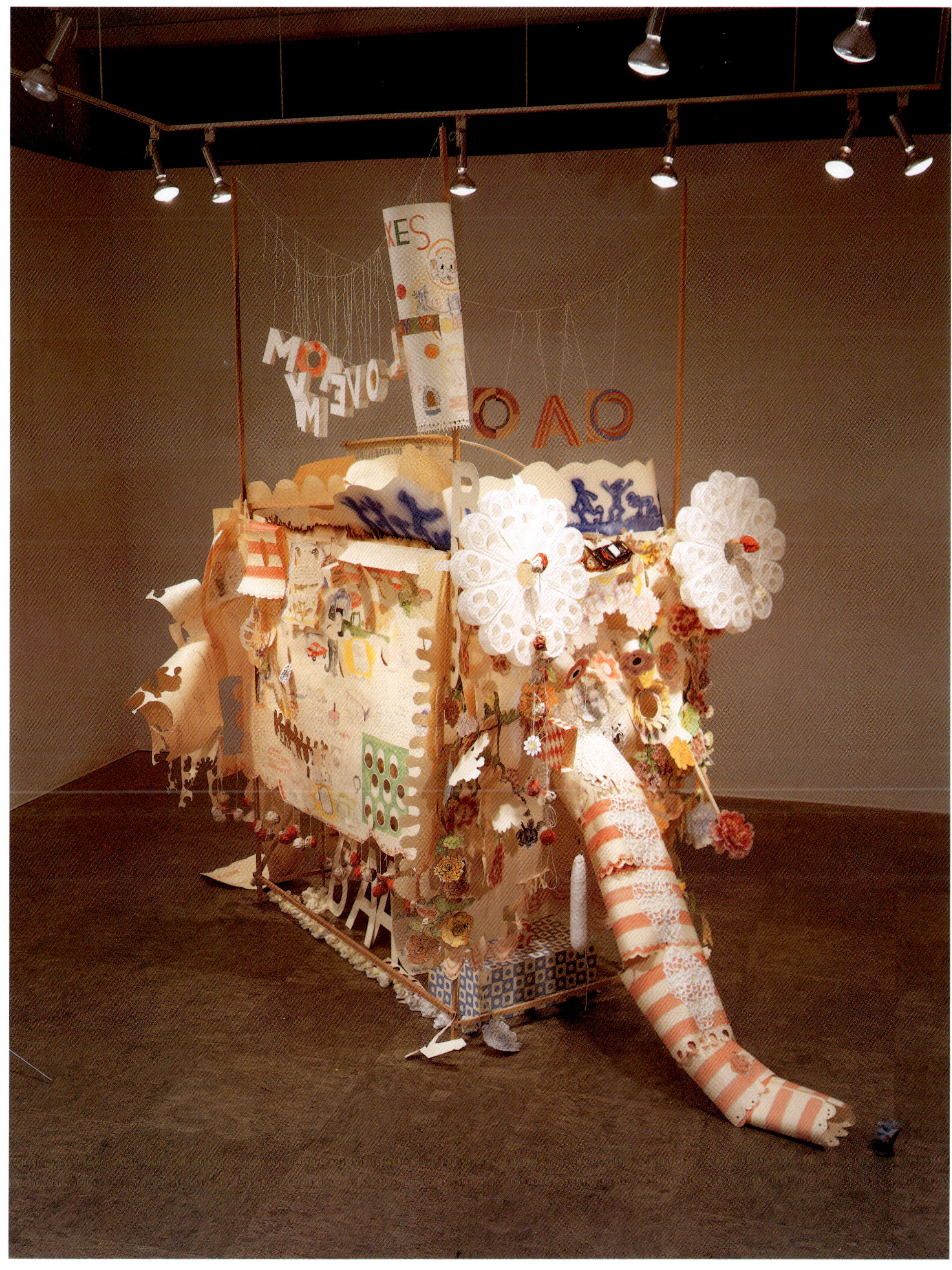

Jeffry Mitchell **Growth Afterwards — Like a Valentine**
1993, Mixed media and paper, 120" x 72" x 80". Courtesy of the artist, Greg Kucera Gallery and Pulliam/Deffenbaugh/Nugent Gallery.

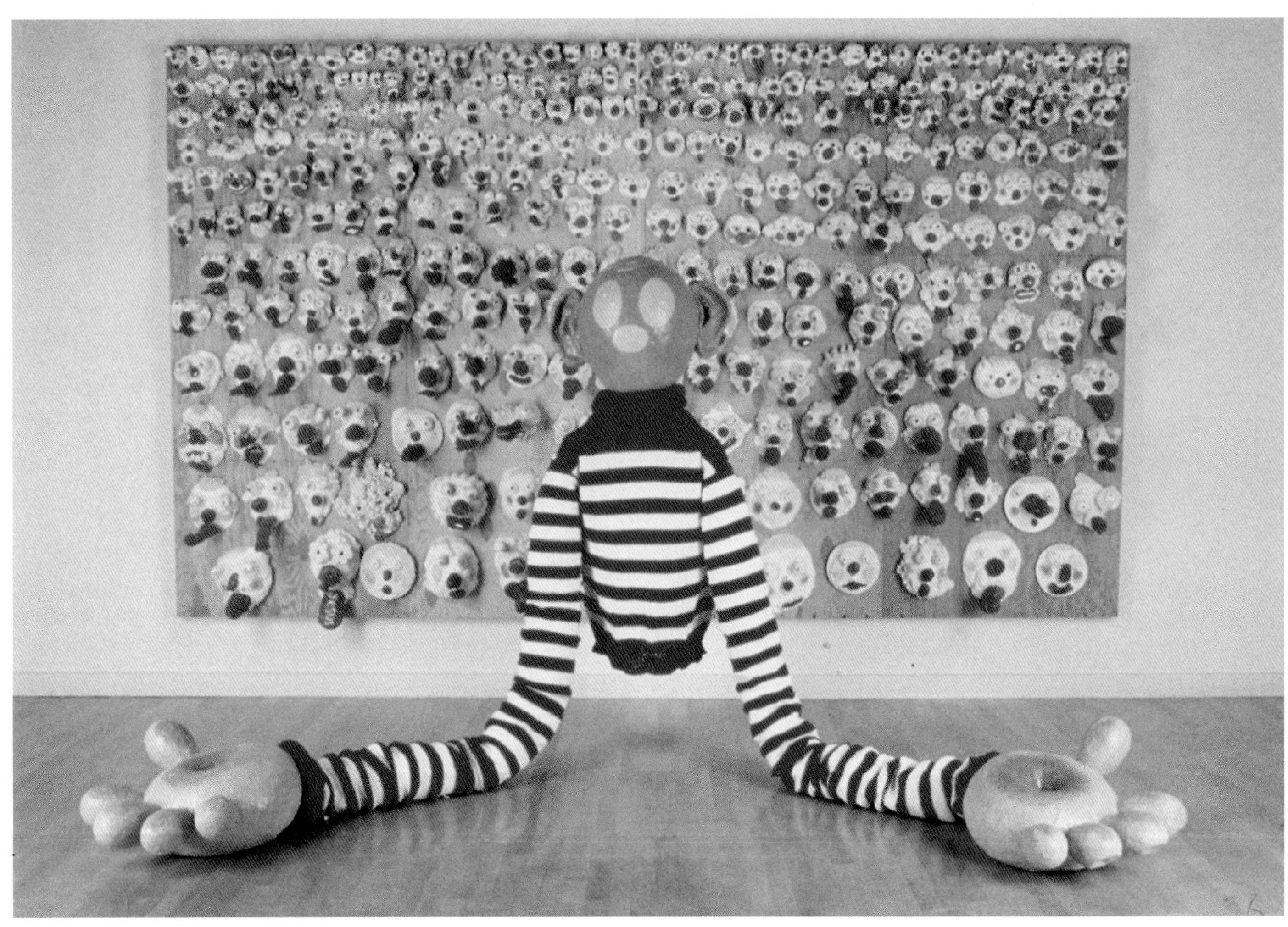

Jeffry Mitchell **Jesus in a Crowd (after Ensor)**
1991, Mixed media, 8' high x 12' long x 10' deep. Collection of Seattle Art Museum. Courtesy of Greg Kucera Gallery and Pulliam/Deffenbaugh/Nugent Gallery.

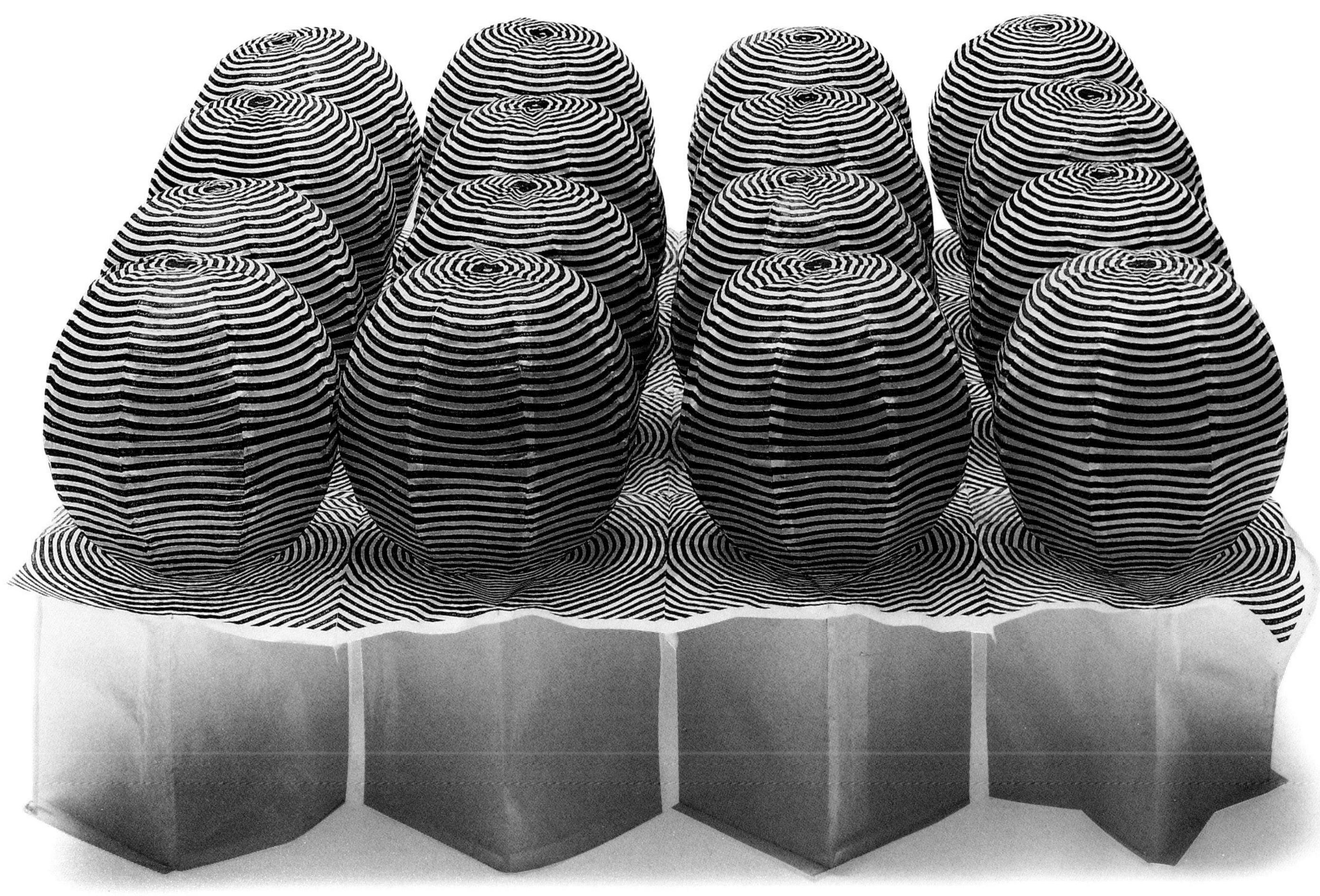

Jeffry Mitchell **Geometry Park**
1988, Rubber stamp on glassine, 48" x 48" x 24". Private collection. Courtesy of Greg Kucera Gallery. Photograph: Ken Wagner.

William **Moore**

William Moore's sumptuous, wood vessel-objects recall a time when art was not separated from daily life or from religious belief. Like ceremonial objects of august rituals, they reaffirm the potency of certain objects, in particular, vessels, as manifestations of symbolic, functional, and aesthetic significance. Moore, who is academically grounded in art as well as in woodcraft, celebrates the transcendental potential of both the form and his materials, including the lowly burl that becomes the "vessel" of his works. Spiritual, emotional, and historical associations permeate the physicality of irresistibly sensuous sculptures crafted from a variety of woods and embellished with metals and minerals.

Moore's purposeful combination of craft and art has deep roots in his personal history. His college years in the early 1970s coincided with the dominance of Minimalism, and his M.F.A. project at the University of Michigan consisted of large, austere fiberglass constructions within its paradigm. Beneath the sculptures' theoretical and formalist based superstructure, however, was a foundation put in place much earlier by his mother, a woodworker and a rockhound, who taught him to use a lathe and to enjoy "making things." Hobby and craft thus became the paths that led years later to his meticulous attention to materials when he turned to "making things" in the context of sculptural form.

Upon arriving in Portland in 1972 to teach at the Pacific Northwest College of Art, Moore was immediately attracted to Oregon's abundant supply and prominent use of woods. Worried about the toxicity of fiberglass and also, re-discovering his childhood fascination with wood, he began to think of the wood supports in his fiberglass forms as autonomous structures. It was a productive investigation that proved to be the end of his use of fiberglass. For the next several years he produced exquisitely finished wood sculptures that suggested furniture but aggressively denied function.

In the late 1970s Moore created a series of shrines, each with a vessel at its center. Although the vessel was at first a means for articulating the space within the shrine, its presence raised the problem of the space within the vessel. The tension between interior and exterior, which pertains to the entire range of metaphorical and historical significations of the vessel form, became the basis of the new work.

Burls, those peculiar bulbous outgrowths on tree trunks and branches, determine the form of most of Moore's pieces. While their morphology is consistent, the range of sizes, colors, and surface markings make the burls infinitely varied without losing their natural identity. In the finished works most are polished inside and out, like the cone shape of *Pompeii.* Some, however, are left close to the natural state. The burl's extraordinary shape in *Cyclades* and its pitted, "moonscape" surface are exploited to dramatize the contrast with the precisely formed and finished copper pedestal.

Moore's work since 1980 has been strongly influenced by two events. A trip to Greece to see ancient art and artifacts *in situ* brought about his strong sense of the link between certain special objects and their culture, not only their immediate culture but those that are far removed in time and place. Second was a commission to create a crozier, a crucifix, and a reliquary cross for the Mt. Angel Abbey in Oregon's Willamette Valley. In the process of fulfilling the project, Moore felt himself to be a link in the very long, cross-cultural tradition of artists whose production of ceremonial objects is honored, the equivalent of the respect paid in modern, secular cultures to paintings and sculptures.

Both these influences are apparent in the three illustrated works. Although timeless in their simple, classic forms, their titles, *Euphrates*, *Pompeii*, and *Cyclades* also suggest the kinship Moore feels with ancient cultures. *Euphrates*, in particular, not only exemplifies the timeless universality of certain objects as testimony to spiritual needs, it is also the individual expression of an artist conversant with the ideas and values of late twentieth century American art and culture.

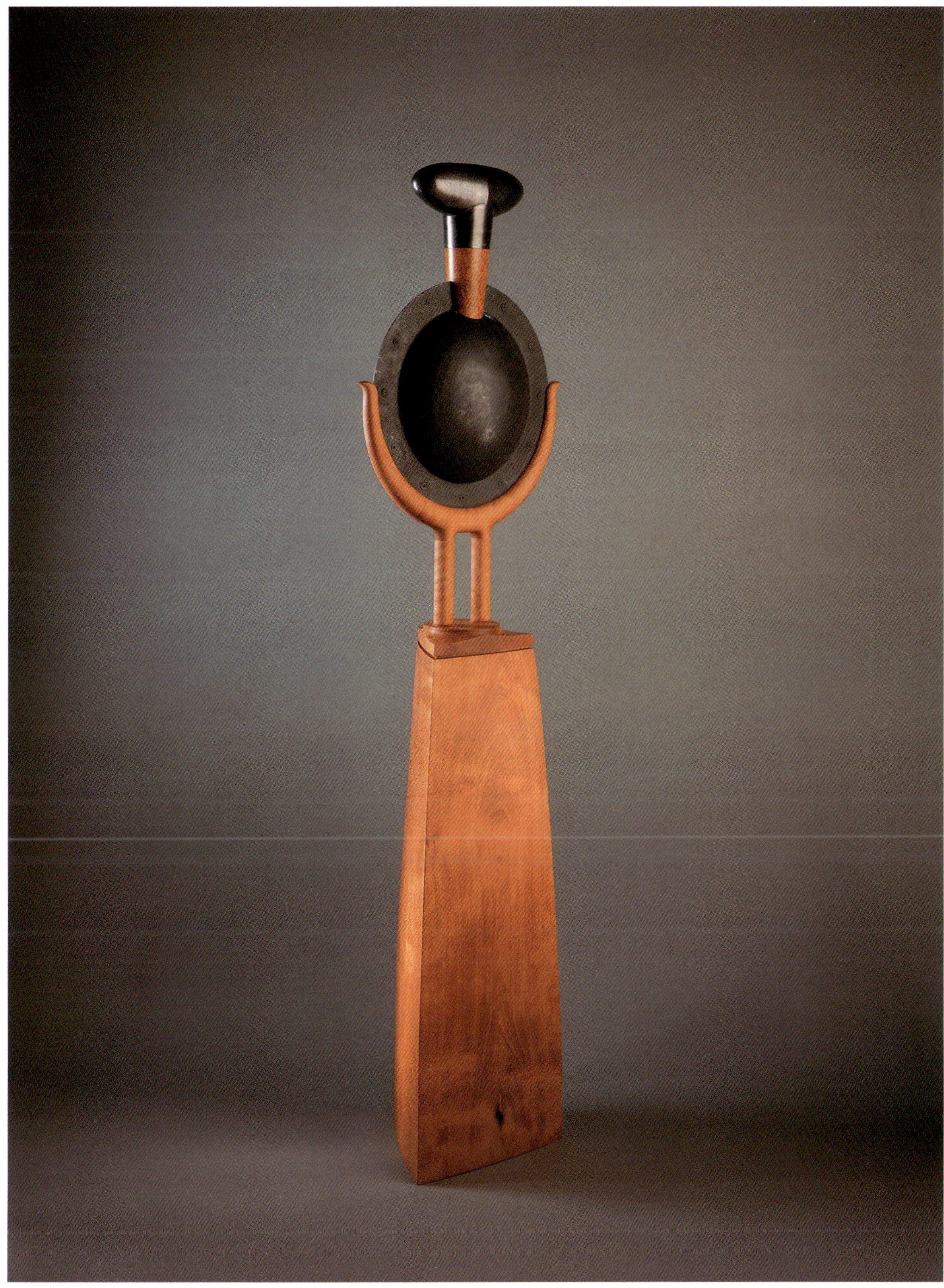

William Moore

Euphrates

1990, Spun copper, Madrone, 65" x 18" x 12". Collection of E. Kenneth Hederson, Longview, Washington. Courtesy of the artist and Laura Russo Gallery. Photograph: Harold Wood.

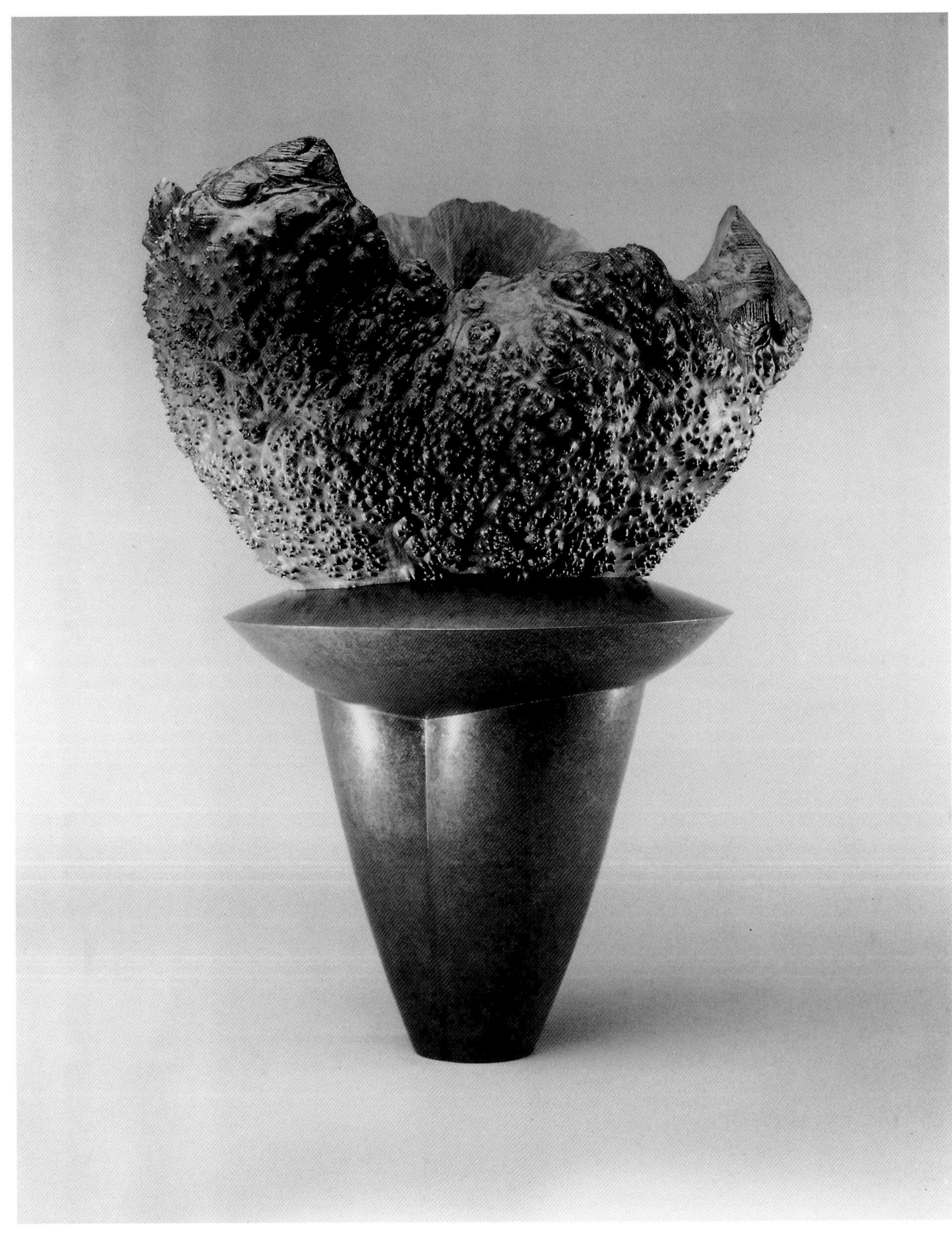

William Moore **Cyclades**
1994, Spun copper, Madrone burl, 16" x 9" diameter. Courtesy of the artist and Laura Russo Gallery. Photograph: Harold Wood.

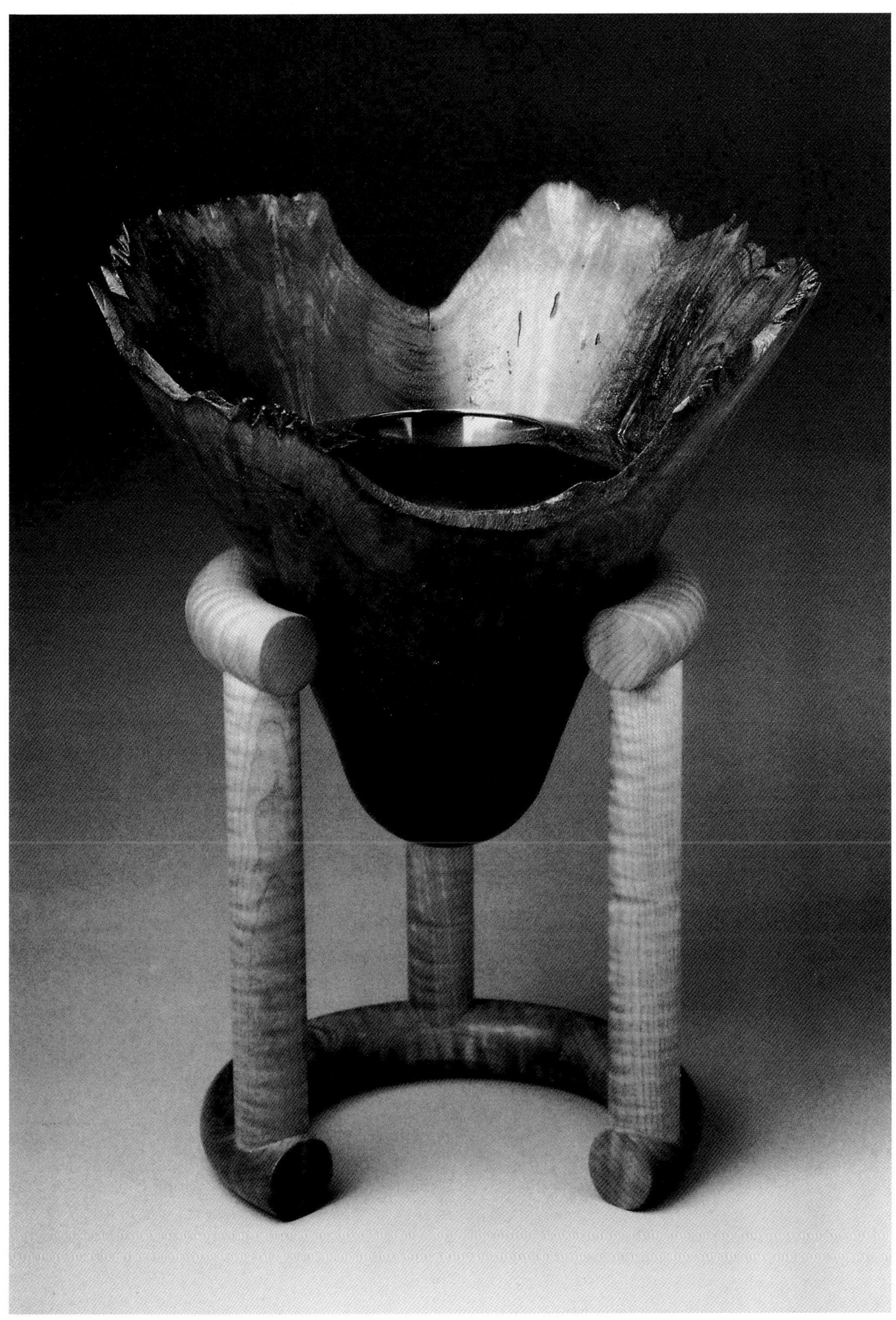

William Moore **Pompeii**

1990, Spun copper, Black Walnut, Maple, 13" x 10" x 8". Collection of Irving Lipton, Encino, California. Courtesy of the artist and Laura Russo Gallery. Photograph: Harold Wood.

Carl **Morris** and Hilda **Morris**

Carl and Hilda Morris were Oregon's preeminent artists until their deaths, hers in 1991 and his in 1993. Although his paintings and her sculptures are rooted formally in the tenets of Abstract Expressionism, they also reflect a sensitivity to the rich diversity in the Northwest natural environment. Both were intellectually inclined, interested in all the arts plus the philosophical and scientific underpinnings of society, and these, as well as their ideas about art, were of crucial importance during the post-World War II years in establishing the liberating context in which today's art flourishes.

Their mutual interests and shared life notwithstanding, in their artmaking they were separate, neither collaborators nor advisors. There was an underlying symbiotic relationship, however, as Barry Johnson noted in a biographical essay on Carl, "... their work converses — about calligraphy, philosophy, the desert, the ocean, ancient and future shapes, planes, and colors — in the language of abstract art and in the language of a shared half century of life."[1]

Carl Morris and Hilda Grossman met in 1938 when she arrived in Spokane, Washington, to teach at the Federal Arts Project art center which he headed. Both were the same age — born in 1911 — and brought highly cultivated backgrounds to their isolated outpost. Their rapport was instantaneous. He was a Californian who had studied at the Art Institute of Chicago and at the Kunstgewerbeschule: Werkbund in Vienna. She was a native New Yorker trained at the Arts Student League and the Cooper Union School of Art and Architecture. Both had absorbed art history in the great museums of the United States and Europe. Following their marriage in 1940, and some months later, the demise of the art center, they lived for a short while in Seattle where they were among the group of artists led by Mark Tobey and later referred to as the "Northwest School." In 1941, when Carl accepted a Federal Arts Project commission to paint a mural in the Eugene, Oregon, Post Office, they moved to Portland, their home for the rest of their lives.

The origins of the sweeping, light filled canvases that made Carl Morris's national reputation are clearly visible in his early figurative paintings of the late 1930s and early 1940s, in which monumental unspecific figures are encircled by blocky sweeps of color. By the 1950s the canvases had exploded both in actual size and in the scope of their painterly prowess. The cycling color blocks of earlier works now were fractured and seemed to be illuminated from within, shining through surfaces striated with line and texture. The fully abstract paintings proclaimed Morris's often-stated belief that the process and materiality of the paint eliminated any need for subject. In that opinion, he aligned himself with the New York promulgators of Abstract Expressionism, many of whom — Mark Rothko, in particular — he knew through his frequent visits, with Hilda, to New York. Hilda's assimilation of the formalistic precepts of Abstract Expressionism was expressed in rough-textured, gestural sculptures that, like Carl's paintings, reached beyond materials and process to intimations of cosmic time and organic change.

Although he chose to live apart from the New York "eye of the storm," Carl Morris achieved nation-wide recognition, exhibiting regularly from 1940 onward in San Francisco, Seattle, and New York. In 1960 a retrospective exhibition was organized by the American Federation of Arts and circulated nationally for two years. The Portland Art Museum mounted the next and definitive retrospective in 1993. Organized with his active participation until his sudden death less than four months before the opening, the exhibition was stunning evidence of the creative unfolding of a singular artist, culminating in huge, vibrant paintings of the last few years.

Although Hilda Morris's work is not as widely known as her husband's, it, too, has been exhibited internationally, commissioned for many public venues, and included in major museum and private collections. Like Carl's paintings, her bronze sculptures and the sumi paintings that absorbed her in later years as her health declined track the development of an oeuvre that is representative both of its era and of her own thematic concerns. The "hidden correspondences" that she attributed to her work are sensed in their powerful gestures and crinkled surfaces, both evoking the mysteries of an archaic past.

1. *Carl Morris: Paintings 1939–1992,* catalog with essay by Barry Johnson (Portland Art Museum publication, 1993), p. 8

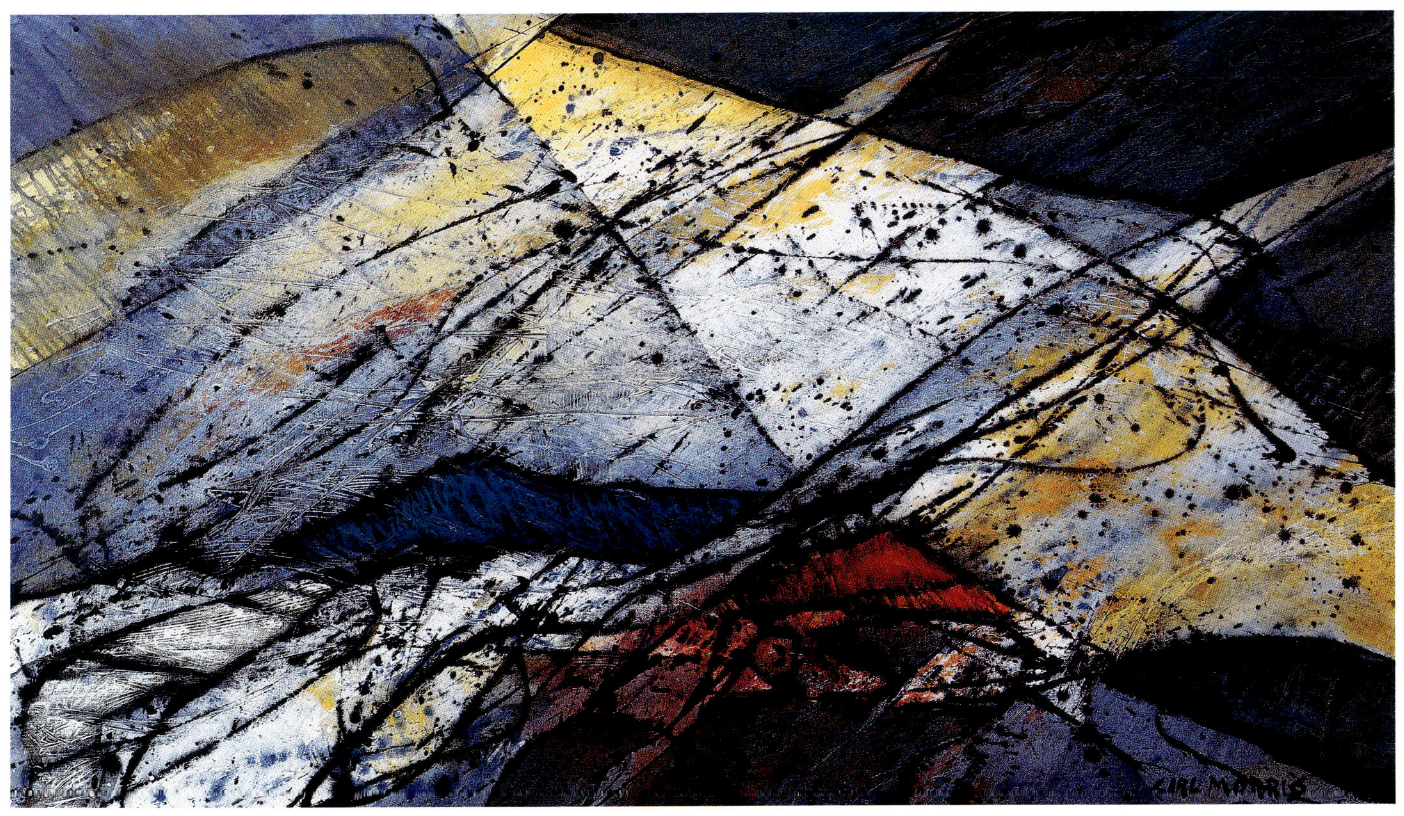

Carl Morris **#773 Beacon**
1992, Acrylic on canvas, 41" x 72". Collection of Maribeth Collins. Courtesy of Laura Russo Gallery. Photograph: David Browne.

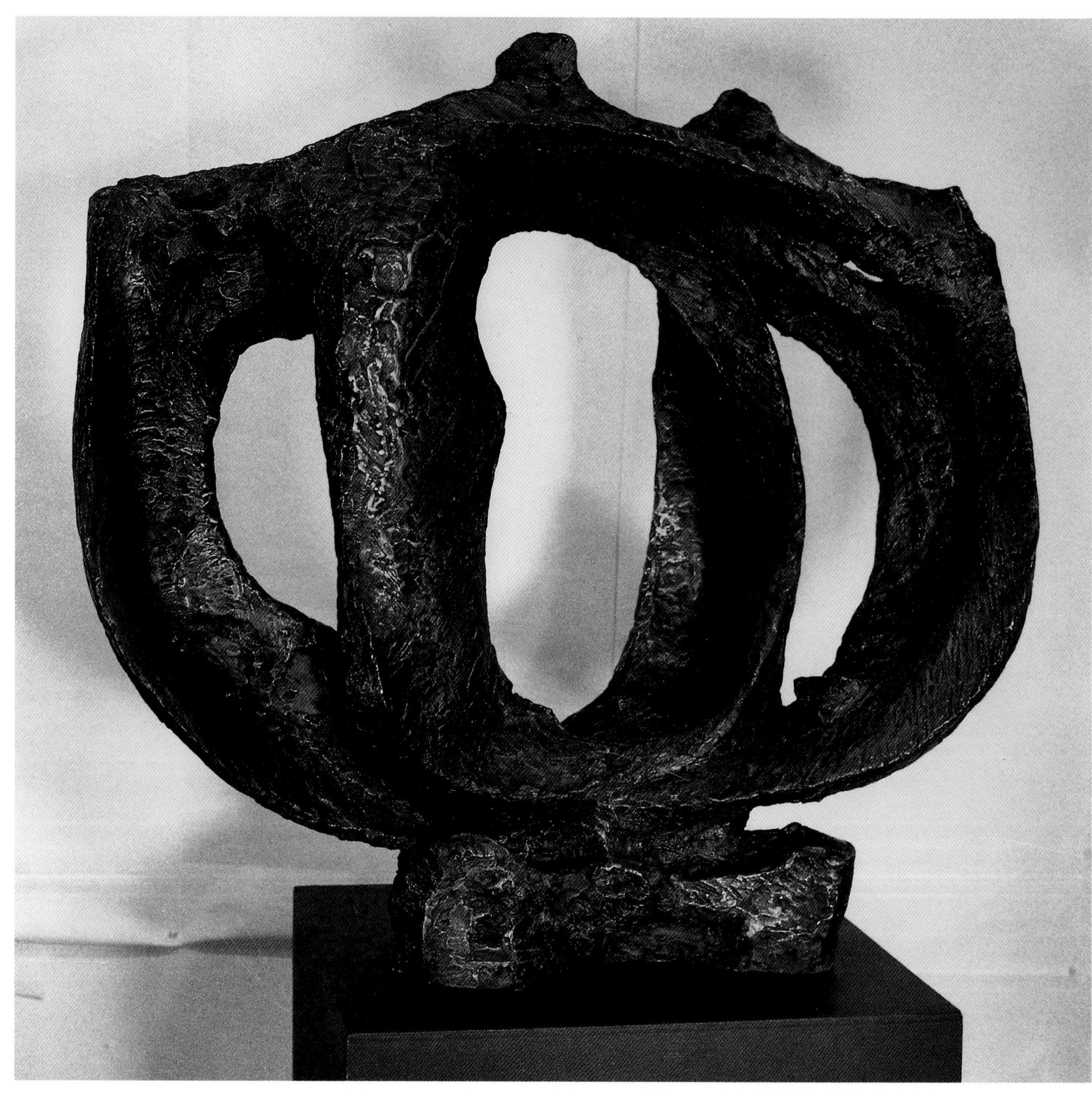

Hilda Morris **Double Round V**
Cast bronze, 37" x 38" x 19". Private collection. Courtesy of Laura Russo Gallery. Photograph: Carl Morris.

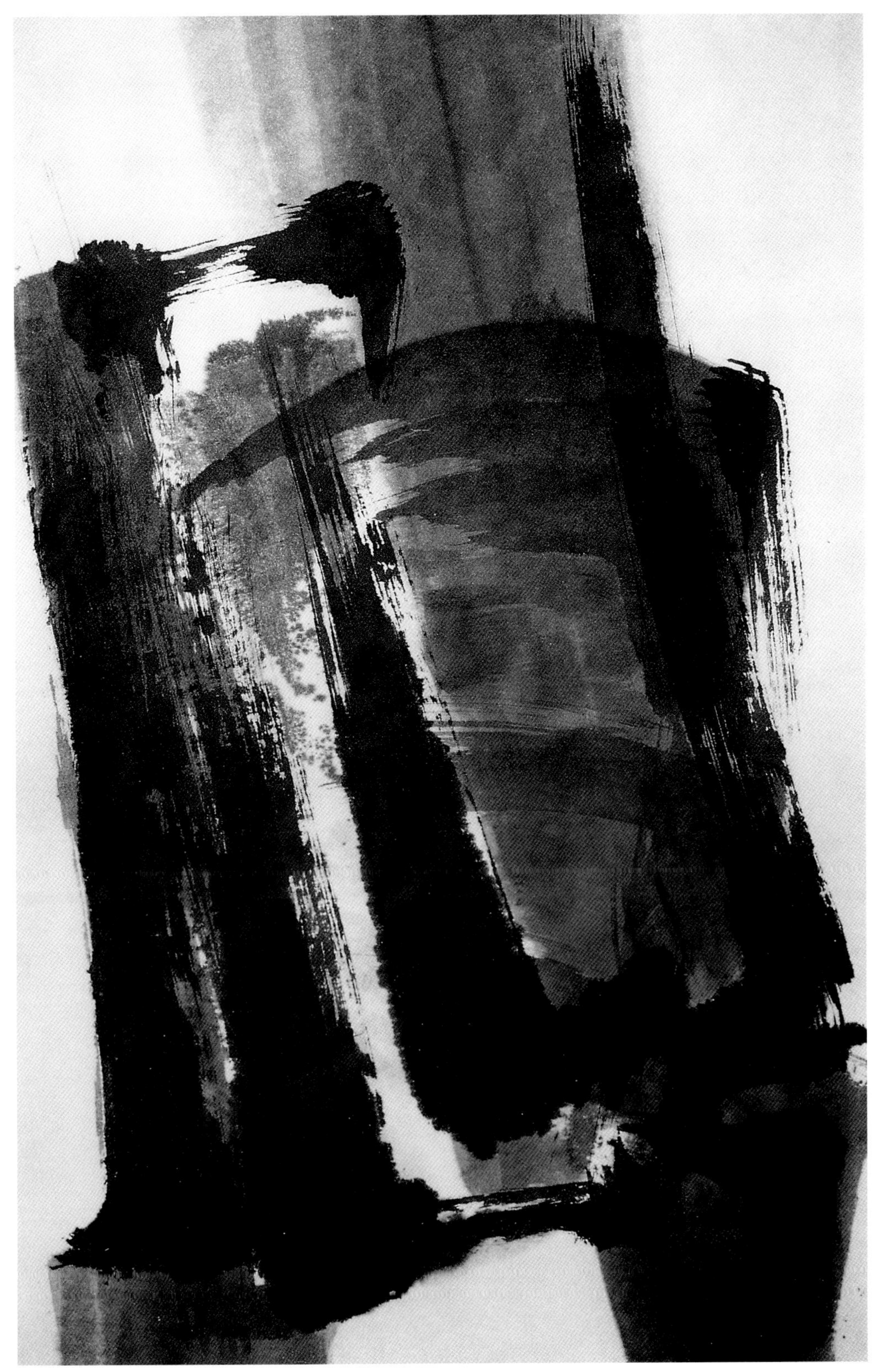

Hilda Morris **LR #8**
1987, Sumi painting, 39" x 25". Courtesy of Dr. and Mrs. James Fearl. Photograph: Carl Morris.

William **Morris**

William Morris converts reminders of death — bones, tusks, weapons, canopic jars — into glass works so stunningly beautiful they are life-affirming, the very antithesis of the somber subjects they represent. In fact, they are not about the pain and loss of death, but about ritual, memory, and continuity. These modern-day talismans of primordial rituals embody eternal mysteries in thoroughly contemporary objects. By combining the seductively beautiful qualities of glass with iconographic creativity Morris brings an exciting and fresh approach to his artform, one that dispels any lingering notion that would limit glass to craft.

A Californian, born in Carmel in 1957, Morris was introduced to glass as a medium in high school, then experimented with both ceramics and glass at California State University, Chico, before re-locating to Washington in 1978 to train at the Pilchuck Glass School under Dale Chihuly. So gifted that he became an instructor the next year, he has since become independent but continues his association with Pilchuck as an artist-in-residence. His early work, dating from the mid-1980s and which consists of blown, somewhat flattened cylindrical vessels often surrounded by a scattering of glass "stones," attests to a Chihuly influence. Morris's emphasis on drawing, however, was a differentiating factor even at that time, and it was the beginning of a process that led from drawing on the form to the form itself as the vehicle of meaning. The small stones became solitary standing stones, and these evolved into elongated forms simulating skeletal fragments, which Morris frequently grouped horizontally in the manner of a still life.

A 1990 installation at the Renwick Gallery in Washington, D.C., marked yet another transition in Morris's thematic development. The assembly of tools, antlers, human skulls, and animal bones, which conjured up a cave entombment of the aftermath of a pre-historic hunt, presaged the artist's turn to forms related to archeological artifacts, both natural and human-made. Among the most direct, *Antler Stack*, of 1992, is an inventive freestanding sculpture, marvelous in both its construction and materiality and in its evocation of the ancients' acceptance of the intertwining of life and death. It is an attitude, Morris seems to suggest, that might be emulated today.

In a continuing series titled *Suspended Artifacts* Morris suspends a few objects of related shapes and colors above a simple black base. In these the familiar bones, tools, and arrows are accompanied by a biomorphic, seemingly ossified vessel sometimes containing an arrow. As opposed to the specificity of *Antler Stack's* ancient burial site, the *Suspended Artifacts* are emblematic, their significance located in the forms themselves.

With the series titled *Canopic Jars* Morris places his underlying theme of the interconnectedness of life and death in the context of dynastic Egyptian art. The jars, which simulate the containers that preserved the viscera removed from bodies during mummification, are topped with heads of animals, such as elk, coyotes, and deer, that are now hunted as sport. The heads are individualized, each shaped from molten glass. The drawings of animals that decorate the jars are achieved by an unusual process of laying out the drawing in powdered glass on a heated steel tabletop with the transfer occurring when a hot bubble is rolled in it, then blown to full size.

Morris has more than an aesthetic and cerebral interest in his subject matter. As a child in Carmel he was fascinated by nearby Indian burial grounds and excavations. Today he is an avid outdoorsman who now and then leaves his log home in a rural wooded area about fifty miles north of Seattle to hike, climb, and hunt with bow and arrows in the mountains of the Northwest. His love for the natural world encompasses a deep respect for the meaning of death as a force in its perpetuation, and which he brings to luminous "life" in his art.

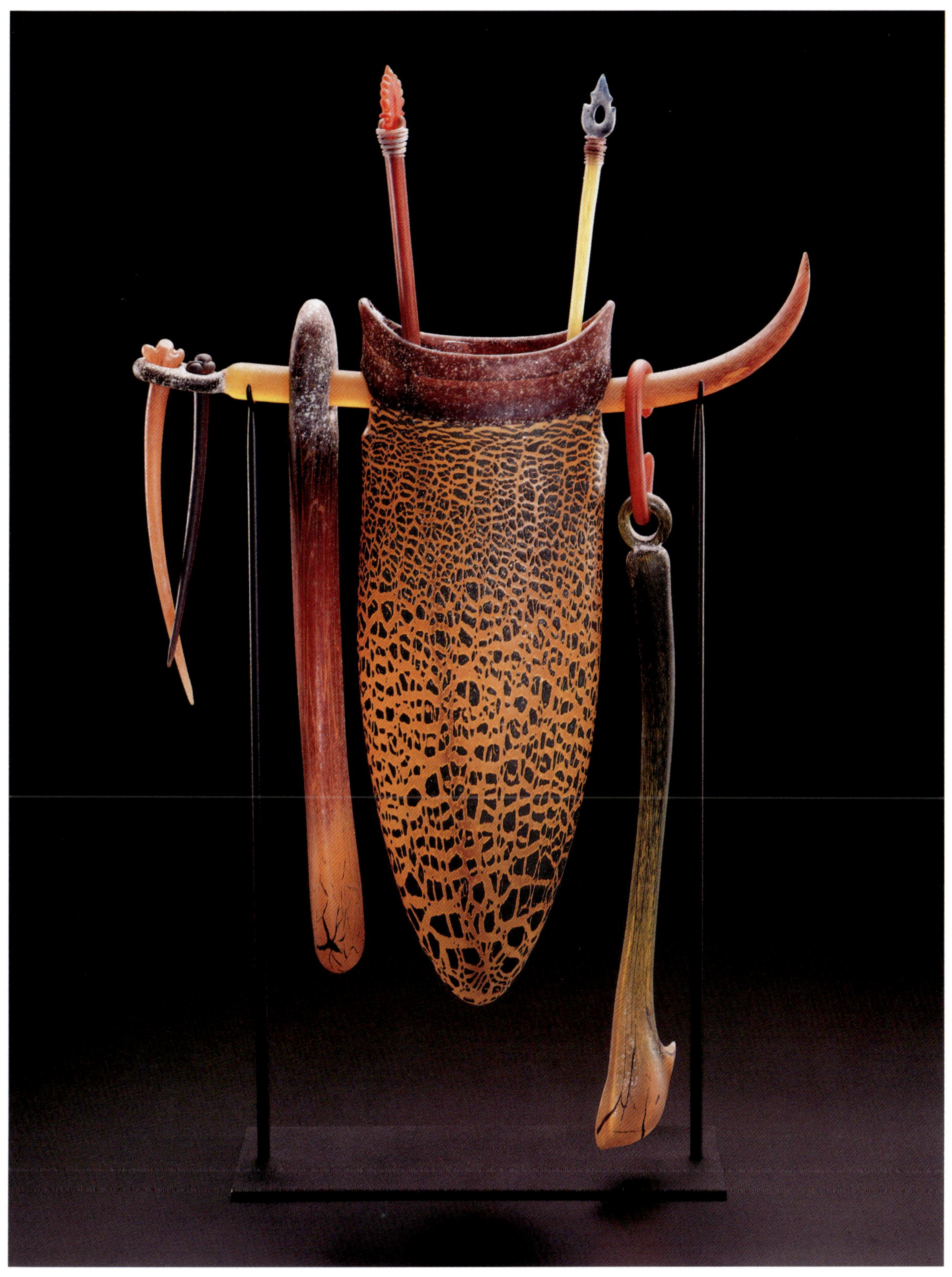

William Morris **Suspended Artifact**
1993, Blown glass, steel, 37" x 24" x 5". Courtesy of the artist and the corporate offices of Keith W. McCaw. Photograph: Rob Vinnedge.

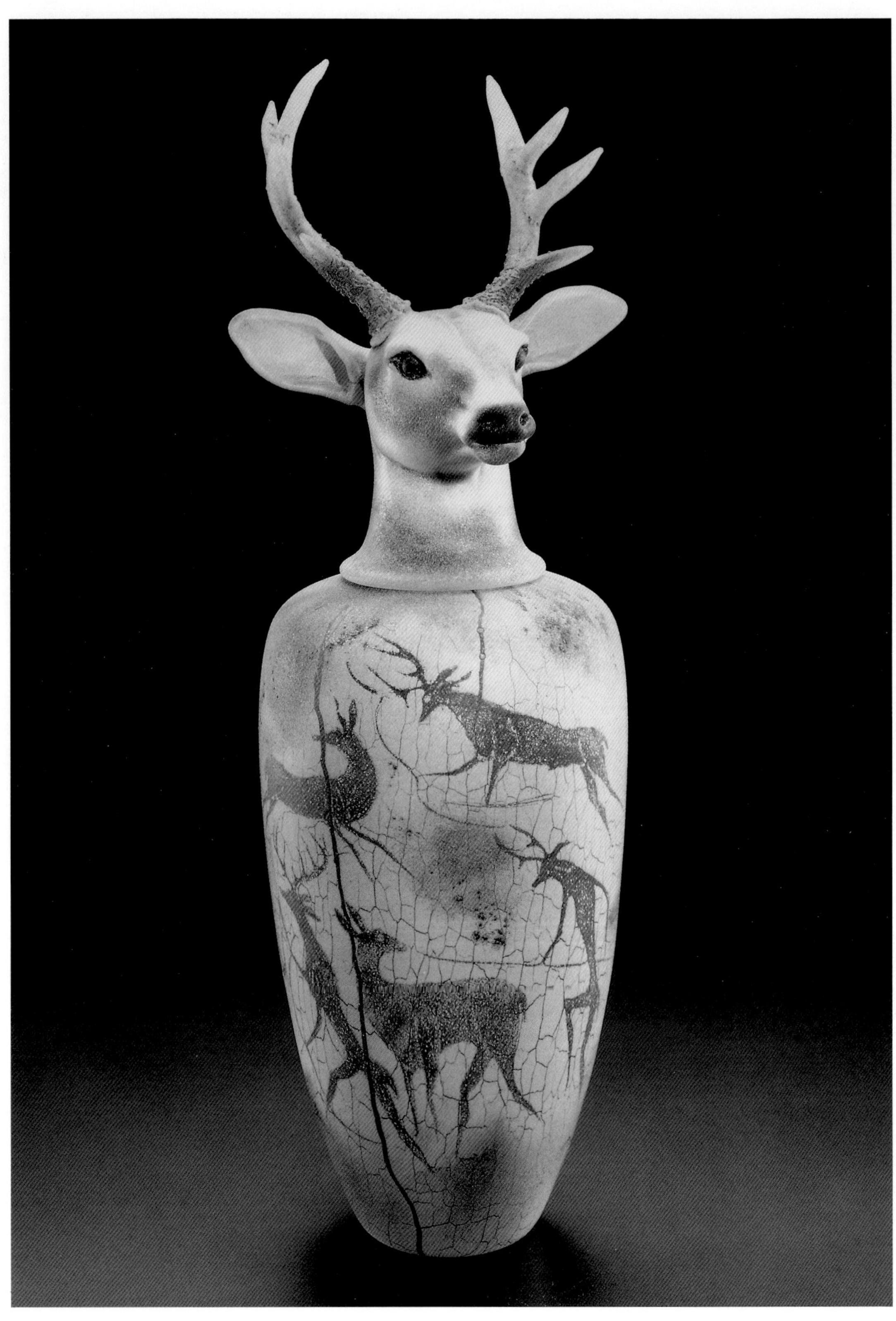

William Morris **Canopic Jar: Buck**
1993, Blown glass, 41" h x 12" diameter. Courtesy of the artist. Photograph: Rob Vinnedge.

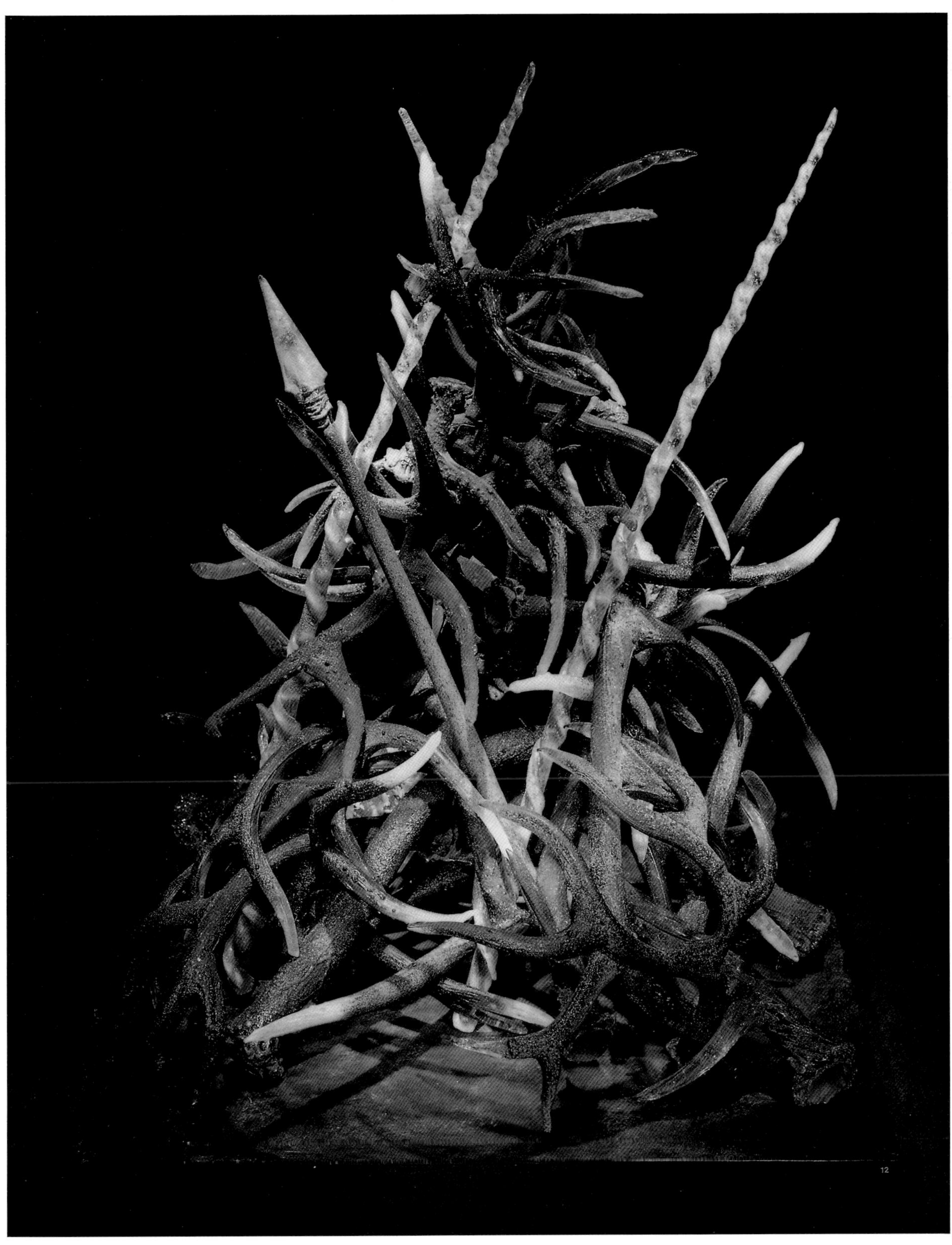

William Morris **Artifact: Antler Stack**
1992, Hand blown and manipulated, 42" x 36" x 36". Courtesy of the artist. Photograph: Rob Vinnedge.

Ronna **Neuenschwander**

Ronna Neuenschwander's sculpture, as her life, is grounded in two very different cultures. Married to a native of Mali, West Africa, where the couple spends extended periods with his family, this native of Kansas and resident of Portland blends motifs, materials, and aesthetic traditions of her two countries in clay figures that capture a universal, indomitable human spirit. She does not simply borrow from an African culture; she assimilates Mali's stories, customs, and values, expressing them through fetishistically charged figures.

The primitive appearance of the figures, typified by *To the Bone* of 1990, is also a blend of African and Euro-American attributes. A dominantly African aesthetic seen in the stylization and exaggeration of the adobe torsos is counterposed by the smooth surface and refined detail in the expressive faces of the earthenware heads. Neuenschwander blurs distinctions in the use of materials as well; the "stick" legs and truncated arms are clay simulations; the spikes in the base of *To the Bone* and the nails that form the hair are real.

A later figure, *Blue Boy* of 1993 incorporates an even more expressive head above a body covered with a colorful mosaic "garment". Fairly vibrating with optical energy, the sitting figure's roundness is dominated by the prominent large belly and the glistening head with its open mouth. The vivid mosaic of ceramic shards, atypical in Neuenschwander's predominantly earth-hued figures, was produced from her ceramist husband's broken plates and inspired by her admiration of Antoni Gaudi's mosaics and by the famous "blue boy" of Thomas Gainsborough's eighteenth century painting.

Neuenschwander's unusual career track, from her beginnings as a University of Kansas educated ceramist to bi-continental, mixed-media sculptor, took a definitive turn with a trip to Africa in 1984. She had been working with animal themes, creating a series based on the relationship of beasts of burden to societal development, and eagerly took advantage of an opportunity to view camel caravans. Her travels took her through the arid, land-locked country of Mali where her interest in the local use of adobe and earthenware overcame language and cultural barriers. In Bombaka she met Baba Wagué Diakité, a student and storyteller, who is now her husband and a ceramics artist with a growing reputation of his own.

Not only is Neuenschwander's work true to Mali's social culture, it also reflects that country's poverty. It is a country with a poor economy; the water table is shrinking and the desert is expanding. The brown earth provides meager food but ample clay, which has multiple uses. In spite of hardships, however, daily life goes on much as it always has. Gardens are planted, the compound is swept, and stories are told. This is the world of Neuenschwander's figures. With stoic dignity they convey the joys, the playfulness, and the sorrows of village people.

In 1992 Neuenschwander began a series of vessels that had a personal reference beyond the usual poetic symbolism. Swollen jugs sprouted heads and limbs, long boats became recumbent figures; for nine months the metaphor of woman as vessel became personal in her pregnancy. Since the birth of her daughter, the vessel theme has evolved to include children. Many of these figures, as in *Blue Boy*, are as rounded in the middle as jugs, a stylization with strong visual and symbolic impact.

A large multiple sculpture that refers to the effects of industrialization as it encroaches on agrarian ways of life, *Les Enfants Terribles* (French is the colonial language of Mali) is made up of three sitting figures taking their comfort atop a five foot long, low table. Reminiscent of the legendary three wise monkeys, each displays a referential attribute: a blue fish, a red apple, and a white bone. The table, a product of developed countries, is covered with a patchwork of sheet metal pieces on which Neueunschwander has hammered text in English, French, and Bambara (the native tongue of Mali), stories concerning the boys' mischief.

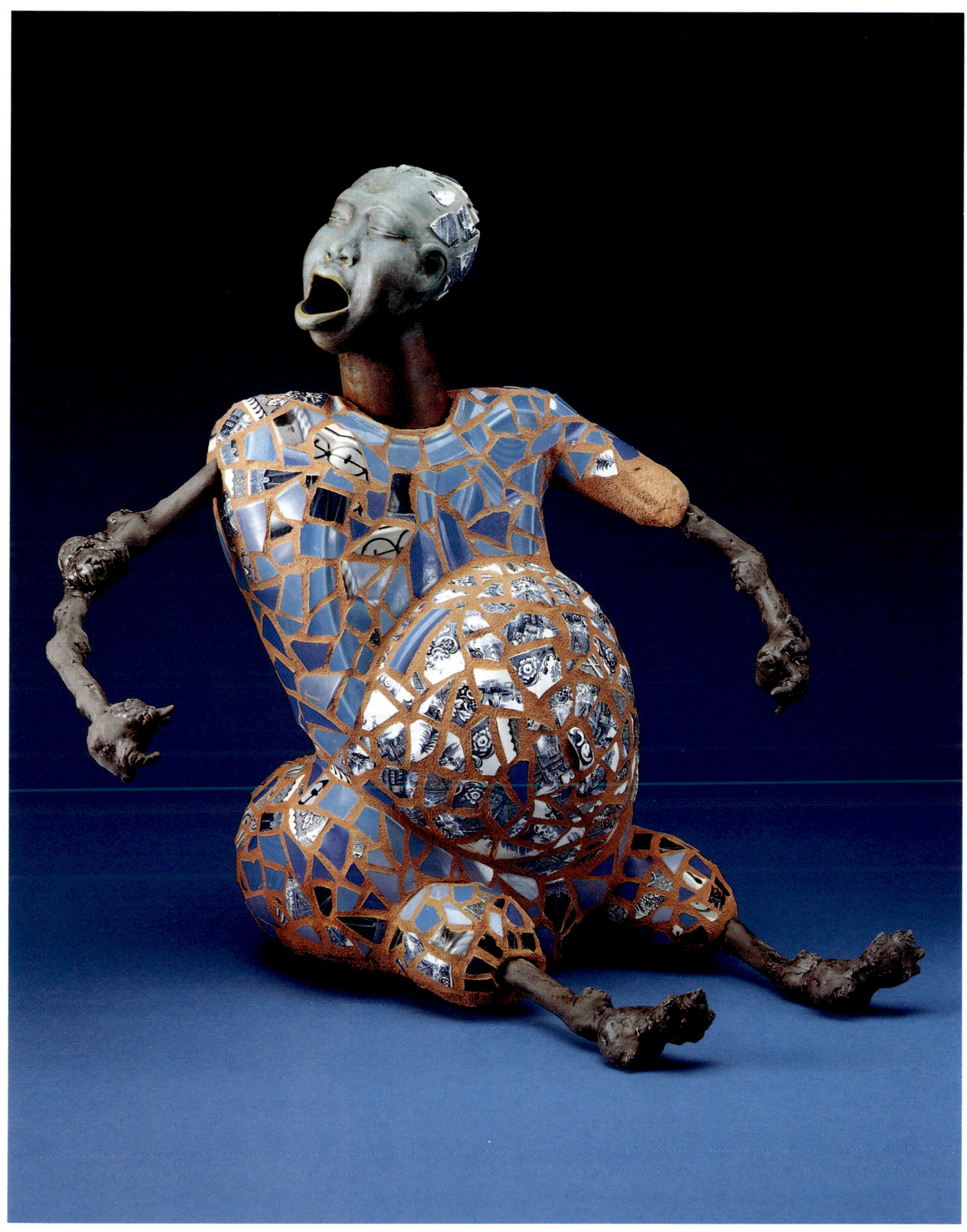

Ronna Neuenschwander **Blue Boy**
1993, Earthenware, adobe, shards, 18"h x 20"w x 12"d. Collection of Martin and Judy Bloomfield, New York. Courtesy of the artist. Photograph: David Browne.

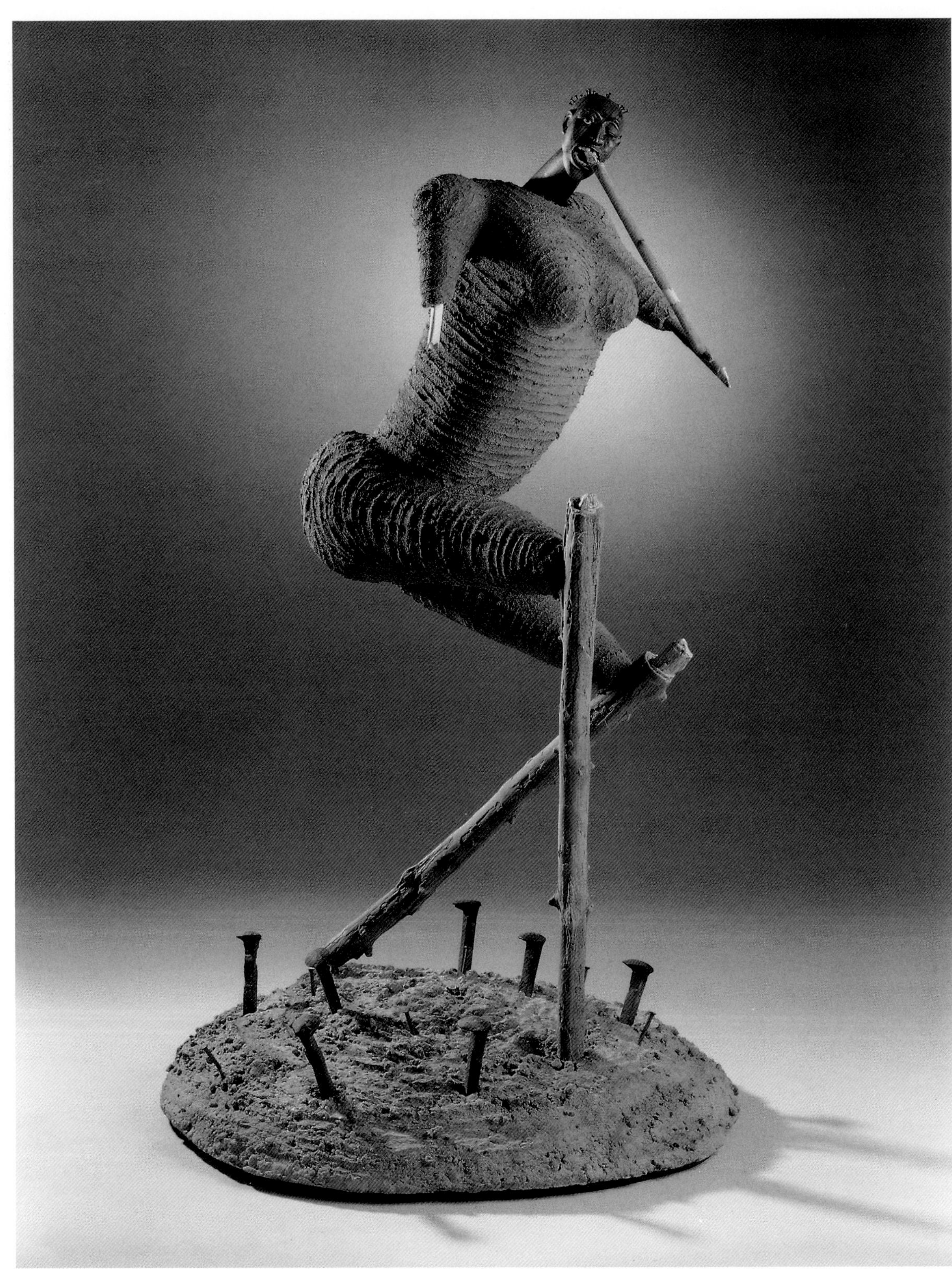

Ronna Neuenschwander **To the Bone**
1990, Adobe, earthenware, concrete, metal, teeth, 52"h x 32"w x 32"d. Collection of David Browning and Kay Altman, Portland. Courtesy of the artist. Photograph: David Browne.

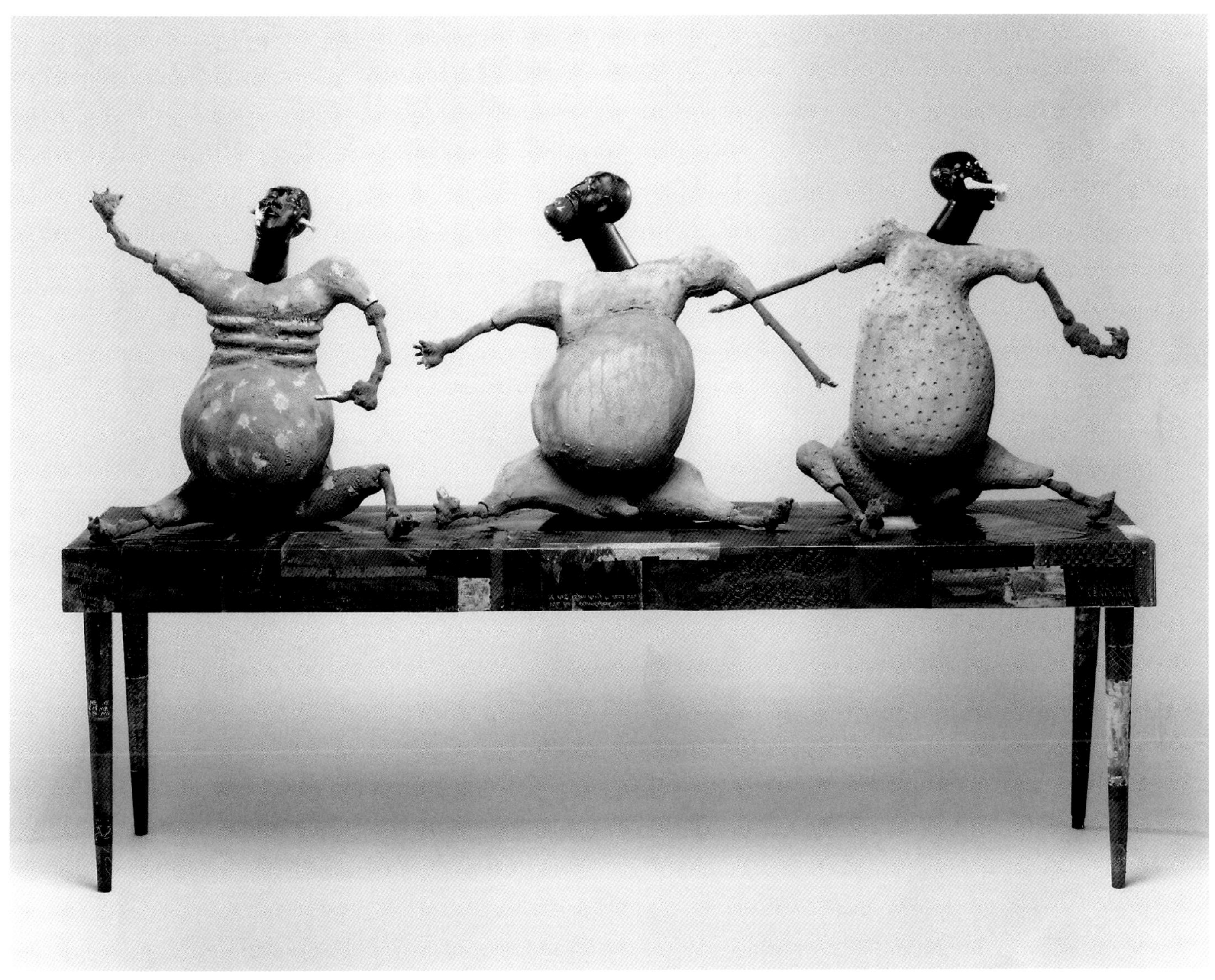

Ronna Neuenschwander **Les Enfants Terrible**
1992, Adobe, earthenware, wood, embossed sheet metal, 41"h x 62"w x 13"d. Private collection. Courtesy of the artist. Photograph: David Browne.

Lucinda **Parker**

Lucinda Parker's physical response to the viscosity, plasticity, and most of all, the chromatic energy of her medium is palpable, plainly visible in paintings so visually stimulating they seem to be a natural force in themselves. Even as a precocious sixteen year old art student painting a self-portrait, she showed her predilection by using a palette knife to build up a thick surface of color blocks in which figure and ground are enmeshed. Since abandoning representation, while she was still in college, she has developed a distinctive gestural style that is equal parts bold colors, sweeping motion, and volumetric forms.

Although Parker has been described as a formalist, a decorative painter, and a neo-expressionist, none is wholly accurate. She is those and more. The primary impact of her paintings is indeed optical; many paintings, especially those of the 1980s, are a cacophony of colors. Nonetheless, her work is never without content beyond the effects of its materiality. The very simple shapes that function formally in an ambiguous relationship of figure and ground are rife with symbolic evocations. Elongated ovoids, such as those in *Saraband*, have multiple references in nature. These, as well as spirals and circular forms, are archetypal and carry universal psychological impact. The tension between them and the great energy of Parker's painting suggests an unending process of regeneration.

In recent work, particularly a series of black and white acrylic-on-paper paintings of 1994, Parker shows a newfound interest in a central figure. A literal representation, frequently, a leaf, is flanked by emblematic shapes sketchily brushed into a white field. Parker has always used black and white freely to push colors, to turn forms, to emphasize a sense of volume, or to confuse positive and negative areas. In these small studies, without color's diversion, the images move back and forth between positive and negative, exposing the structural permutations that are hidden in the fury of color and brushwork in the polychromatic paintings.

Parker's approach to art encompasses her keen interests in literature, music, and the natural world. She sometimes refers to the velocity of her brushstrokes as a metaphor for the flow and movement of water. Images, even when reduced to geometry, are based on natural forms. She frequently includes words and phrases in the painting's body, border, or frame, crudely brushed as if they were a sudden afterthought. Whether as a play on words, a musical term, or a Latin name for a plant, the text initiates a lively interaction of interpretive signs.

The daughter of a scientist and a professional musician, Parker's creative and intellectual energies were encouraged throughout her childhood and early education in Boston where she was born in 1943. While a student at Reed College in Portland she took art classes at night at the Museum Art School, then returned, after graduation, to the east coast where she earned the M.F.A. at Pratt Institute in Brooklyn in 1958. After working for a year in New York she returned to Portland for both personal and career reasons. Then and now, Parker finds Portland's livability and the Northwest natural environment conducive to developing the total authenticity that she sees as the indispensable condition of effective art. "My job," she observes, "is to counter the superficiality in life, to make something that causes people to take time to reflect."

If her paintings are to be grasped, reflection is indeed necessary. Underlying their sheer physical presence are timeless existential conflicts between chaos and order, spontaneity and control, what is visible and what is sensed. While her work is an obvious celebration of painting as painting, it is also a provocative blend of emotion and thought.

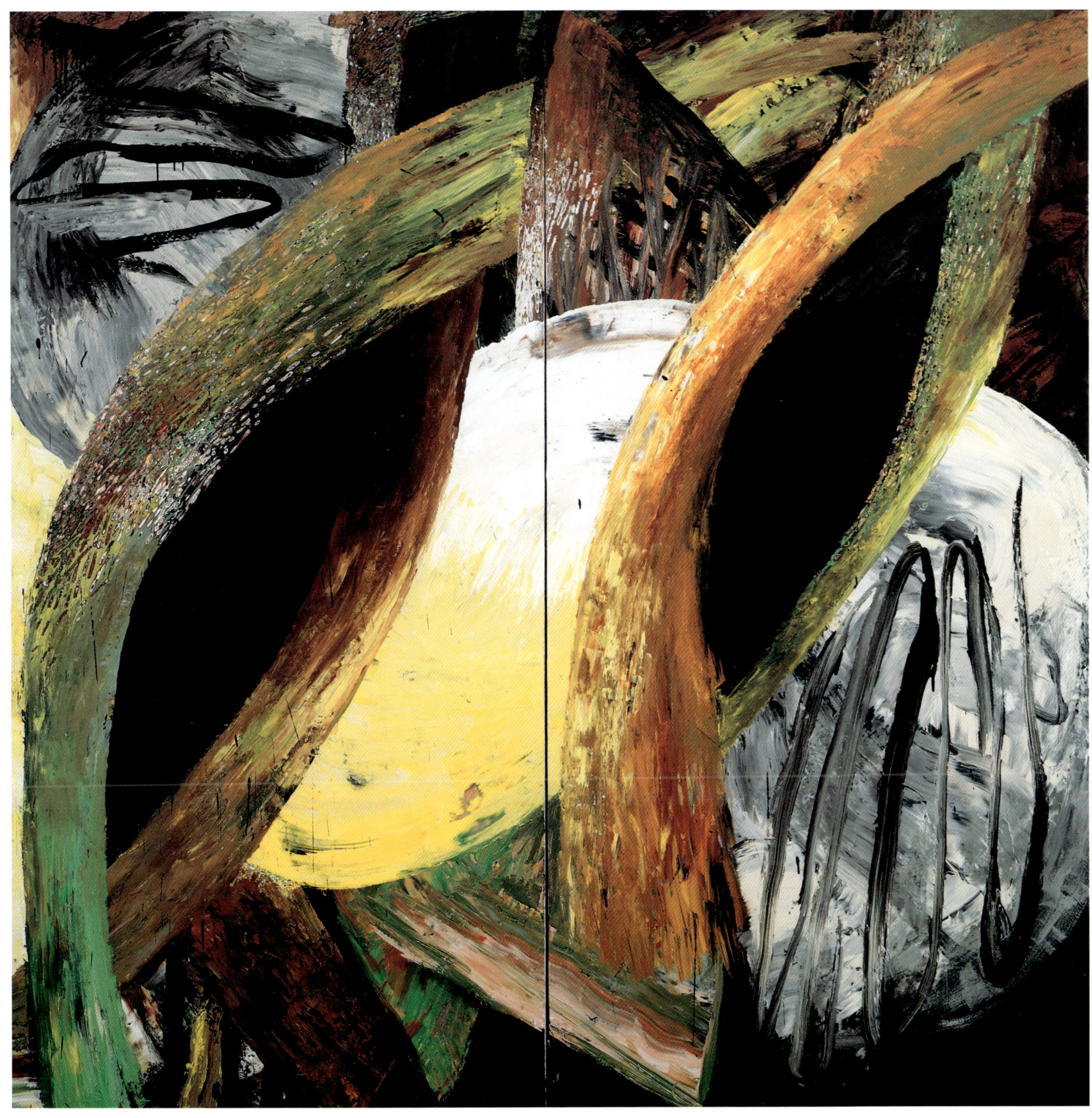

Lucinda Parker **Saraband**
1994, Acrylic on canvas, 8' x 8'. Collection of the artist. Courtesy of Laura Russo Gallery.

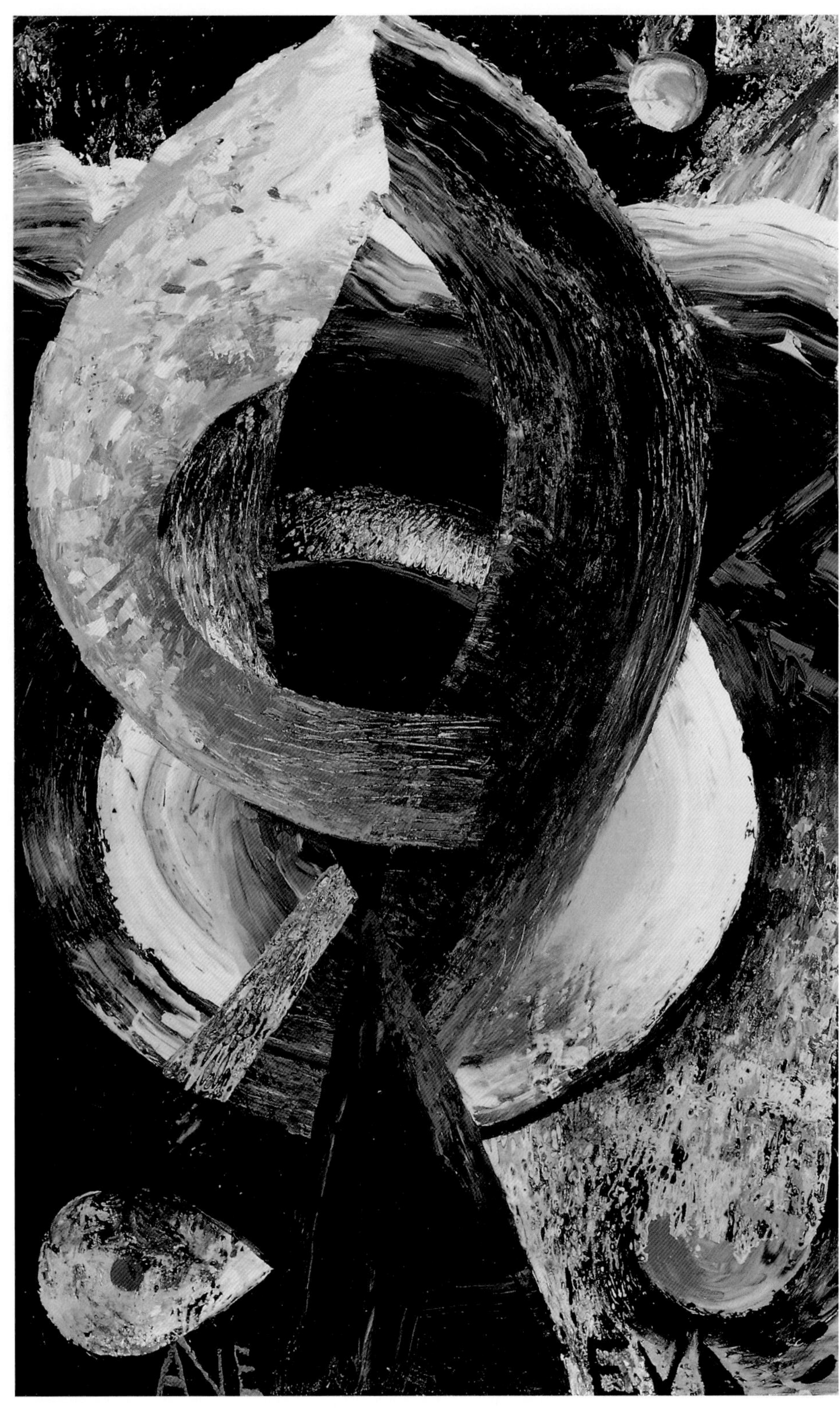

Lucinda Parker **Ave Eva**
1991, Acrylic on canvas, 78" x 48". Collection of the artist. Courtesy of Laura Russo Gallery.
Photograph: David Browne.

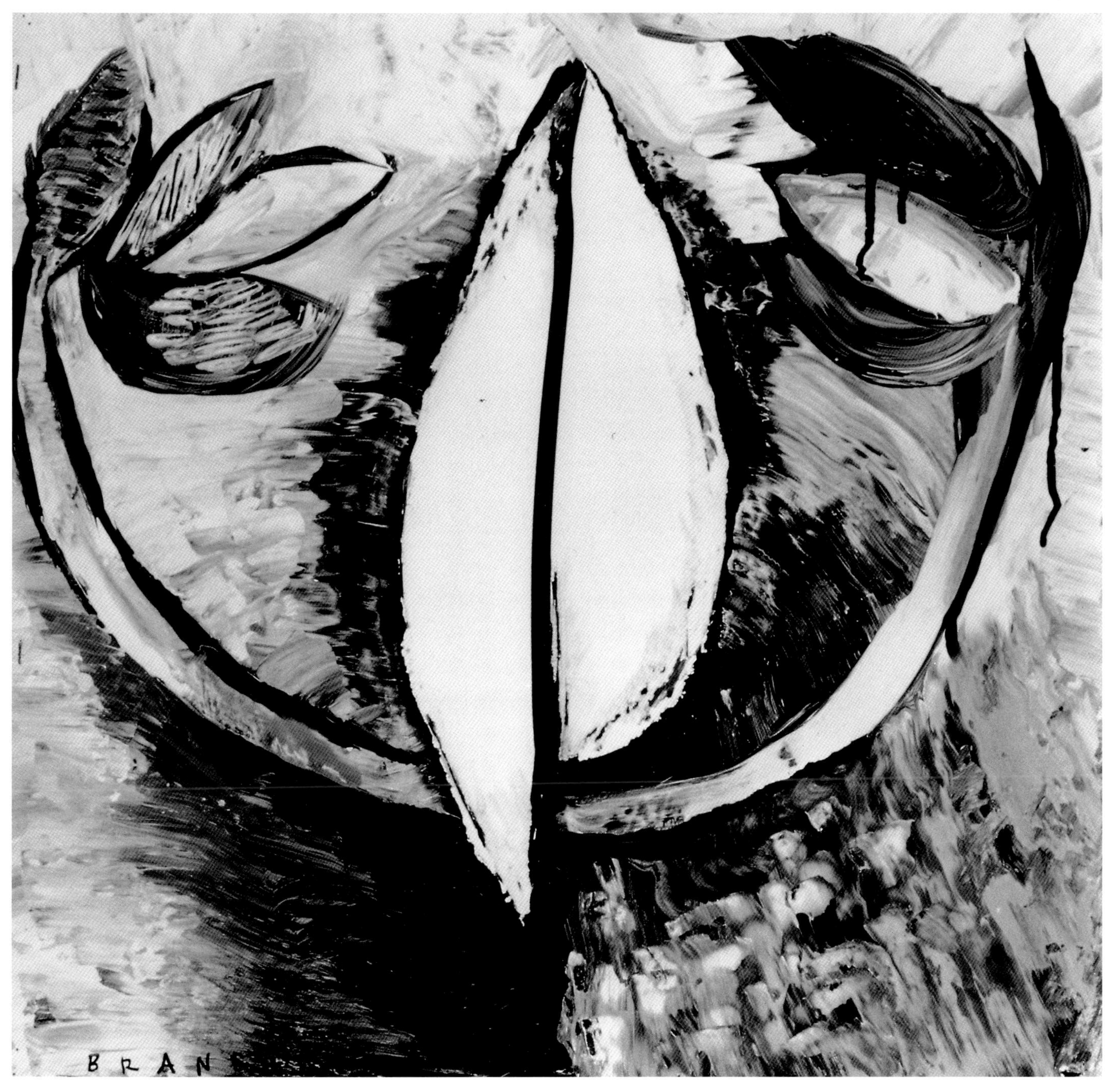

Lucinda Parker **Branching**
1994, Ink and acrylic on paper, 19" x 20". Collection of the artist. Courtesy of Laura Russo Gallery. Photograph: David Browne

Laura **Ross-Paul**

Laura Ross-Paul's dynamic paintings, fusions of symbolic colors, enigmatic figures, and vaporous settings, are visual equivalents of emotional states. While her work has been exhibited in thematic contexts of narration, landscape, figuration, and expressionism, it might be better described as visionary. The strange scenes she creates are psychodramas, acted out by gesturing figures, nude and bald, often actively engaged with nature in its most elemental forms. "Plots" are ambiguous, intended to trigger associations, emotions, and memories that may be particular to the individual viewer but are universally human.

When Ross-Paul began her career just after acquiring the M.F.A. at Portland State University in 1976, she painted quite realistically from direct observation, and was immediately successful. Soon, however, a desire to engage directly with the physicality of painting led her to abstraction and a technique that consisted of troweling a mixture of rhoplex and plaster over the entire surface of large canvases. This phase of her development ceased in 1981 when she gave birth to a son. The experience of childbirth, in her case deepened by memories of her mother who died when Ross-Paul was an adolescent, compelled her to seek an expression that is capable of touching the depths of human experience, a goal which she could not reconcile with abstraction. The first painting in the ensuing transition, *What Was It Like For You?*, (two merged figures, one light, one dark standing in aqueous, muted blue-greens and violet) was a reference to that lost relationship.

As the figure took on renewed importance in the content of her work, Ross-Paul eliminated many individualizing details in order to concentrate on gestures and attitudes that clearly convey emotive states. Her choices of coloration and composition, as well as her forceful, expressionistic painting style, intensify and sustain the desired mood. Notably evident of this strategy, *Beating Back the Icebergs* is also among the most psychologically suggestive, dark both in its appearance and in its evocations. The red figure, hip-deep in a black and green sea, seems futilely engaged in striking out against insurmountable odds; a narrative suggested by the image but as open to personal interpretations as a Rorschach test.

Because her art is an outgrowth of her personal conscious and subconscious experience, it is not surprising to find a frequent use of feminine imagery. In particular, *Buds and Fruit*, a predominantly blue painting of 1993, is strongly suggestive of feminine introspection. The yellow spheres, which the woman holds close to her body — and are echoed in the glowing spherical stomach — are archetypal symbols of fertility and growth. An other-worldly light both suffuses and dramatizes the scene and, as in almost all her paintings, plays an important role in establishing a mental, rather than a physical, space.

Like most Northwest artists, Ross-Paul is influenced subliminally if not explicitly by the cool climate, spectacular landscape, and soft light that characterize the region. From her hillside studio she has a sweeping, one hundred-eighty degree view of the city and sky, and her sensitivity to the sky's "moods" permeates her canvases. The energy of her brushstrokes, the diffused and shifting colors, and the surreal light she favors have counterparts in her daily experience of the ever-changing sky, which in her work is a metaphor for the fluidity of thought. Like the sky, her frequent images of water and boats are employed primarily as metaphors, but they, too, have special relevance in an area laced with bodies of water.

Ross-Paul regularly works from models and has an unusual relationship with the women and men whose poses and gestures vivify the paintings. It is, in fact, a creative collaboration instigated by a rapport between the artist and her models established over long periods of working together. The models are so attuned to Ross-Paul's intent that they bring their own innovations to such details as a hand motion or a body attitude that can inform the content. The use of multiple arms and hands in *Arms and Limbs* stems directly from that interaction. More important, however, is the pictorial interaction in which the couple, waving their arms ineffectively in their primordial surroundings, suggest the passionate struggle to find one's place — and self — within the uncertainties inherent in our relationships with each other and with nature.

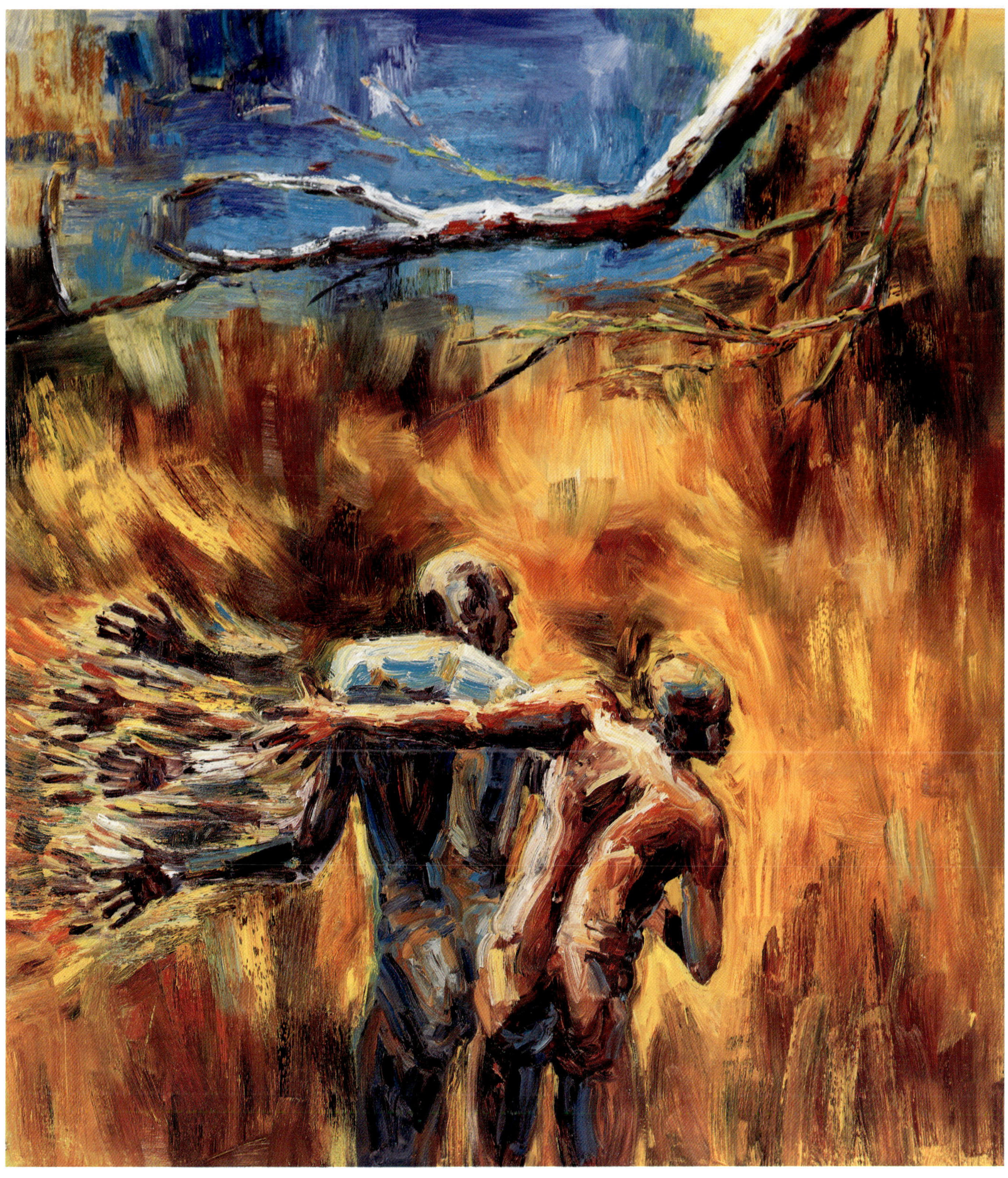

Laura Ross-Paul **Arms and Limbs**
1994, Oil on canvas, 54" x 48". Courtesy of the artist and Elizabeth Leach Gallery. Photograph: Jim Lommasson.

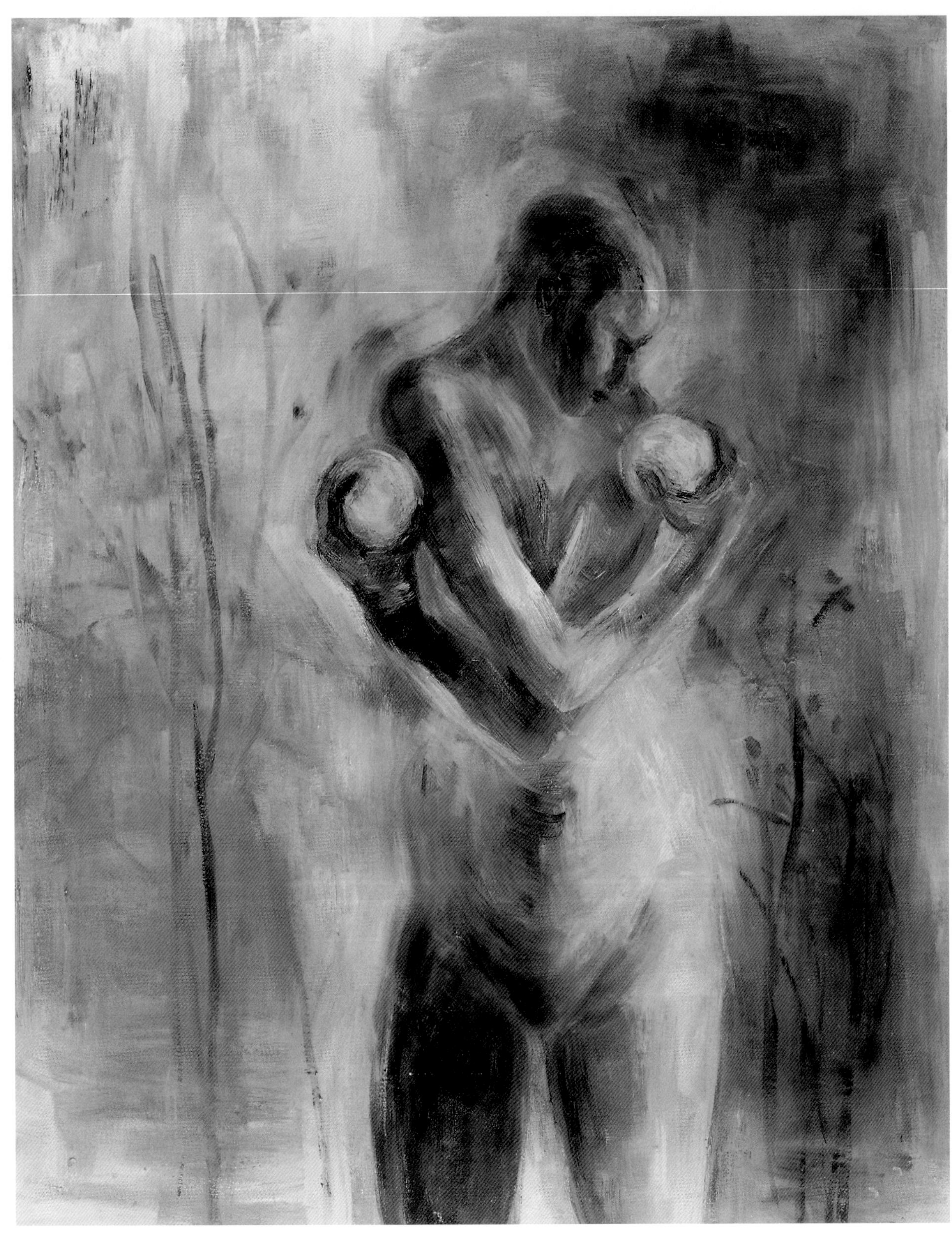

Laura Ross-Paul **Buds and Fruit**
1993, Oil on canvas, 50" x 40". Courtesy of the artist and Elizabeth Leach Gallery. Photograph: Jim Lommasson.

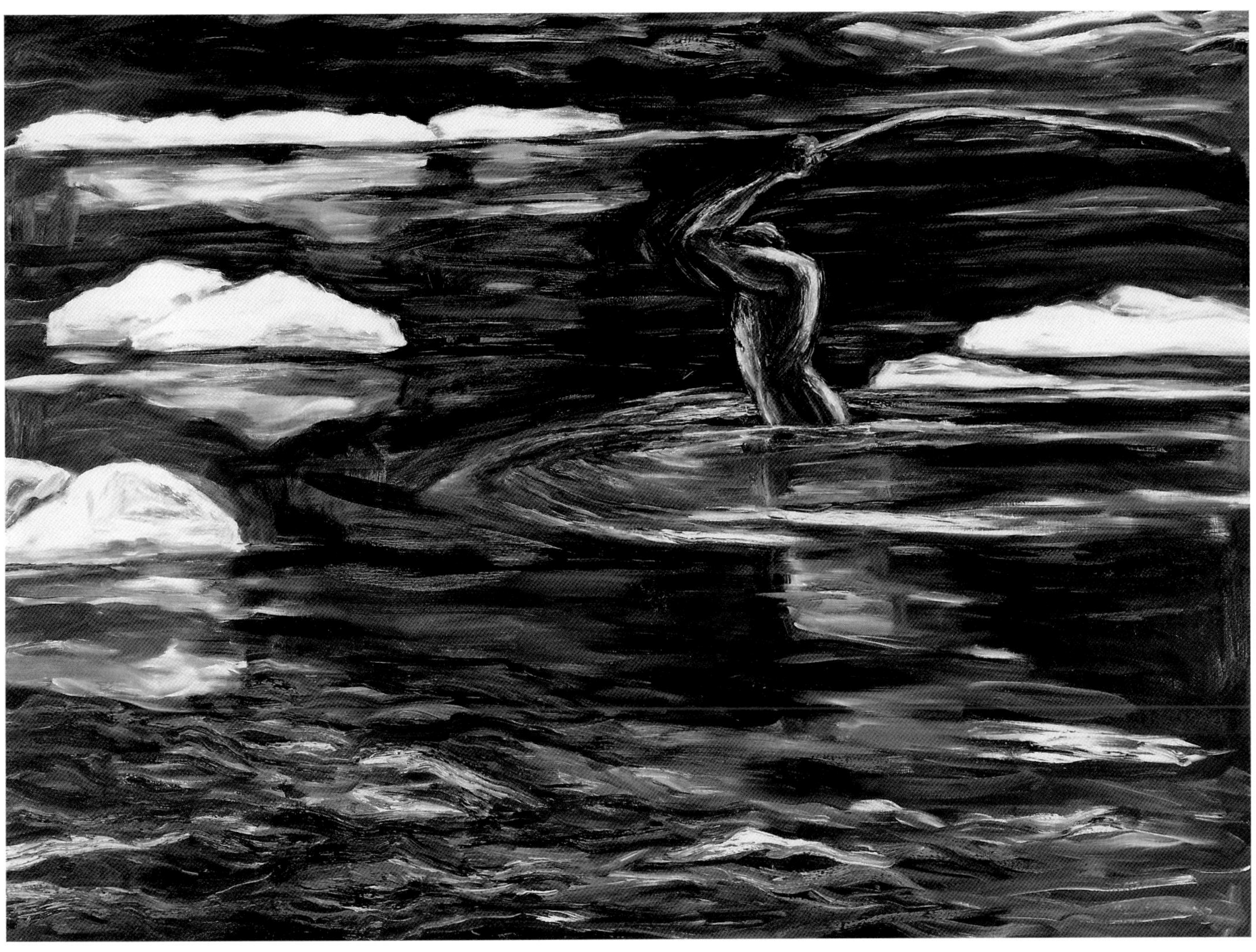

Laura Ross-Paul **Beating Back the Icebergs**
1987, Oil on canvas, 70" x 96". Courtesy of the artist and Elizabeth Leach Gallery. Photograph: Jim Lommasson.

Glenn **Rudolph**

Glenn Rudolph's wide-ranging body of work, consisting entirely of black and white photographs, memorializes social and environmental change in the Northwest. He possesses a carefully honed instinct for unusual subjects whose images speak of disappearing identities: abandoned railroads as they are reclaimed by the forest, neighborhoods in the process of change, small town festivals, and aging bodies. Subjects are followed over extended periods, photographed again and again in his effort to capture the nuances that charge each photograph within a series with the intensity of an exact, unique moment. Even though his work has the clarity and coherence of documentary photography, his aesthetic is that of a visionary. Moody or witty, the work is too subjective to be considered as documentaries; in his definition it is, simply, "nonfiction" photography. His empathic relationship with both his subjects and his medium results in photographic art that is a provocative combination of information and emotion, evanescence and substance.

Formally, Rudolph's crisp, silver gelatin prints are marked by his control of tonalities to define the high points of the compositions. Beautifully choreographed passages of light and dark are so painterly in depth, range, and contrast that they have been compared with Rembrandt's chiaroscuro. Like many northern European painters of Rembrandt's time, he is acutely aware of the emotive content that can be conveyed by the silvery light of overcast skies and dark, water laden clouds. As a case in point, the eerie drama of *Milwaukie Road* is heightened by just such atmospheric conditions.

As he holds a B.F.A. in painting (University of Washington, 1968), Rudolph's painterly tendencies are hardly surprising. Soon after graduation he discovered, in his words, "that a camera could do what I wanted better than painting." Since that time he has become almost a legendary figure, seldom seen in art circles, pursuing his art in the woods, byways, and neighborhoods of the Northwest in an old truck, always accompanied by his Leica camera and his dog. Long periods of observing and establishing close relationships with his subjects result in innumerable rolls of exposed 35mm film from which he extracts a mere handful of prints — "ten or twelve per year if I'm lucky" — that meet his standards for exhibition.

Among his many series the darkly romantic photographs of remnants of abandoned railroads, including both *Milwaukie Road* and *Twin Tunnels*, best exemplify Rudolph's thematic and aesthetic priorities. On one level the series is a record of old tracks and trestles, bridges, and tunnels in the process of disintegration. It may also inspire nostalgic reveries of the long-gone trains steaming through the wilderness over Snowqualmie Pass on their run between Chicago and the Puget Sound. In today's concern with ecology the photographs are reminders of a profligate, frontier society in which human effort and natural resources seemed infinite. Or the pictures may not be about railroads at all but about memory, changing values, about the need to acknowledge and to embrace the past.

While most of the photographs in the railroad series depict the old railroads in a losing battle with the wilderness, some reflect social changes related to its demise — a forsaken station town, the encroachment of suburbia, a golf course stretching along the tracks. It is the railroad's architectural and aesthetic relationship to its surrounding landforms, however, that most fascinates Rudolph, as is evident in *Twin Tunnels*. Visually, the photograph plays off the sunlit, cascading landslide against the tunnel's dark arch. It reflects social history as well, redolent of the tunnel in its past glory which has now deteriorated into nothing more than a curiosity for urban hikers.

A series comprising annual nude portraits that follow the aging process in several middle-age women friends is an ongoing project of considerable personal as well as aesthetic significance. Citing Courbet's treatment of the female nude as an influence, Rudolph also observes his subjects unsparingly but without sacrificing emotive and symbolic content. In *Rudy's Kitchen* mundane details of domestic intimacy, as much as the woman's body, contribute to her sexual identity. Rudolph's investigations of what he terms "the myth of loss of sexuality" not only challenge the cultural bias with regard to female sexuality, but also, the conventions of nude imagery.

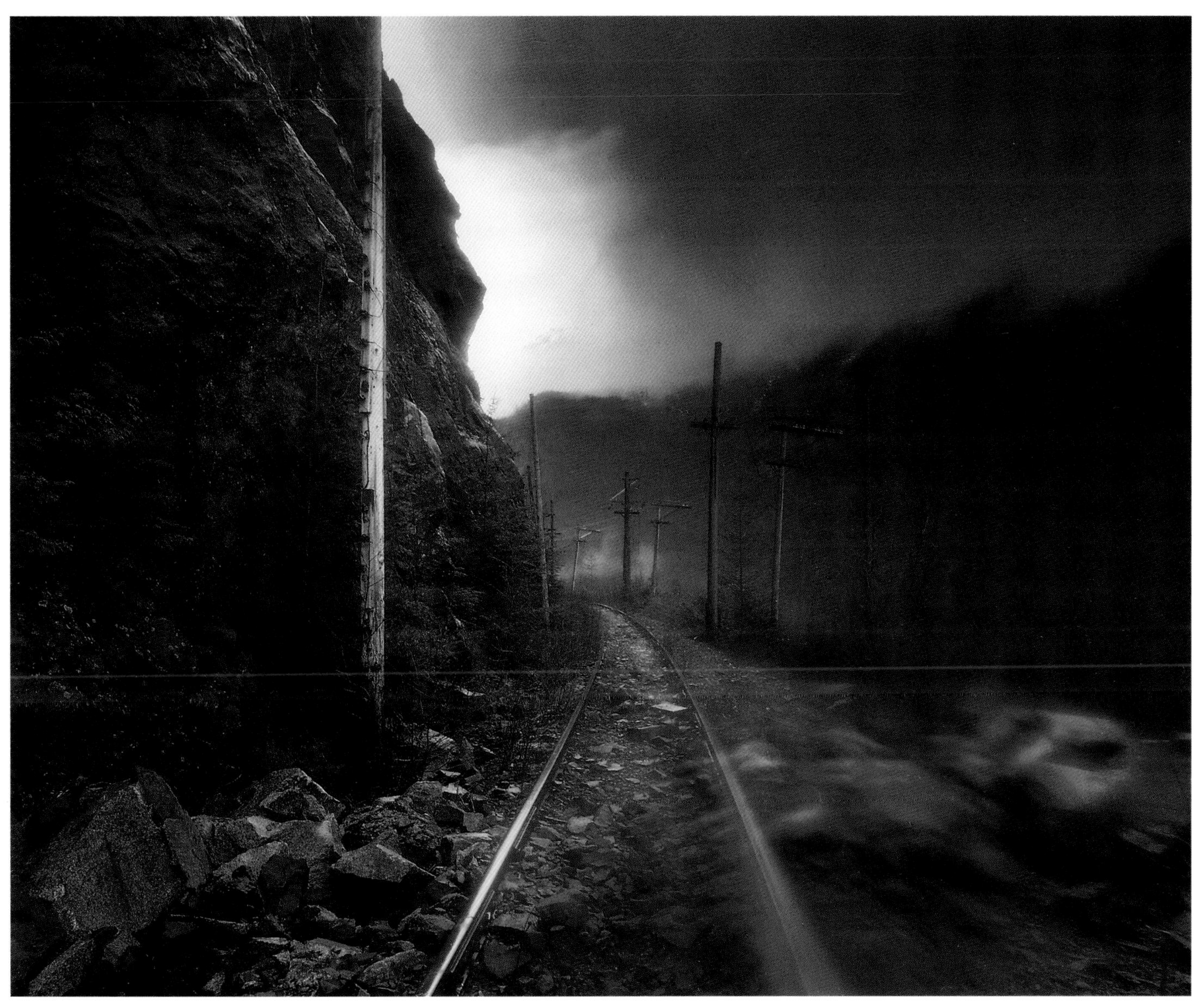

Glenn Rudolph **Milwaukie Road**
1987, Silver gelatin print, 30" x 40". Courtesy of the artist. Photograph: Glenn Rudolph

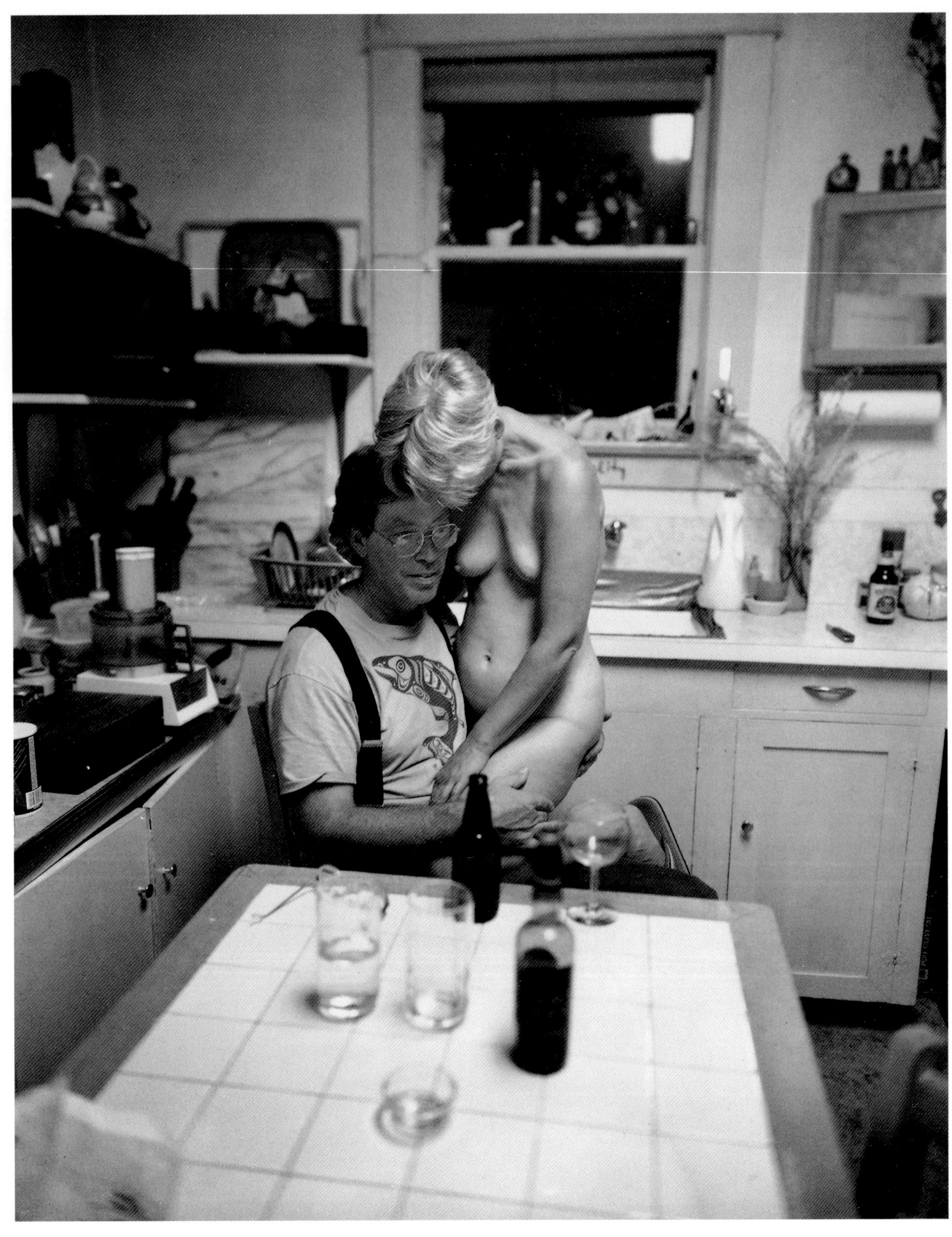

Glenn Rudolph **Rudie's Kitchen**
1992, Silver gelatin print, 40" x 30". Courtesy of the artist. Photograph: Glenn Rudolph.

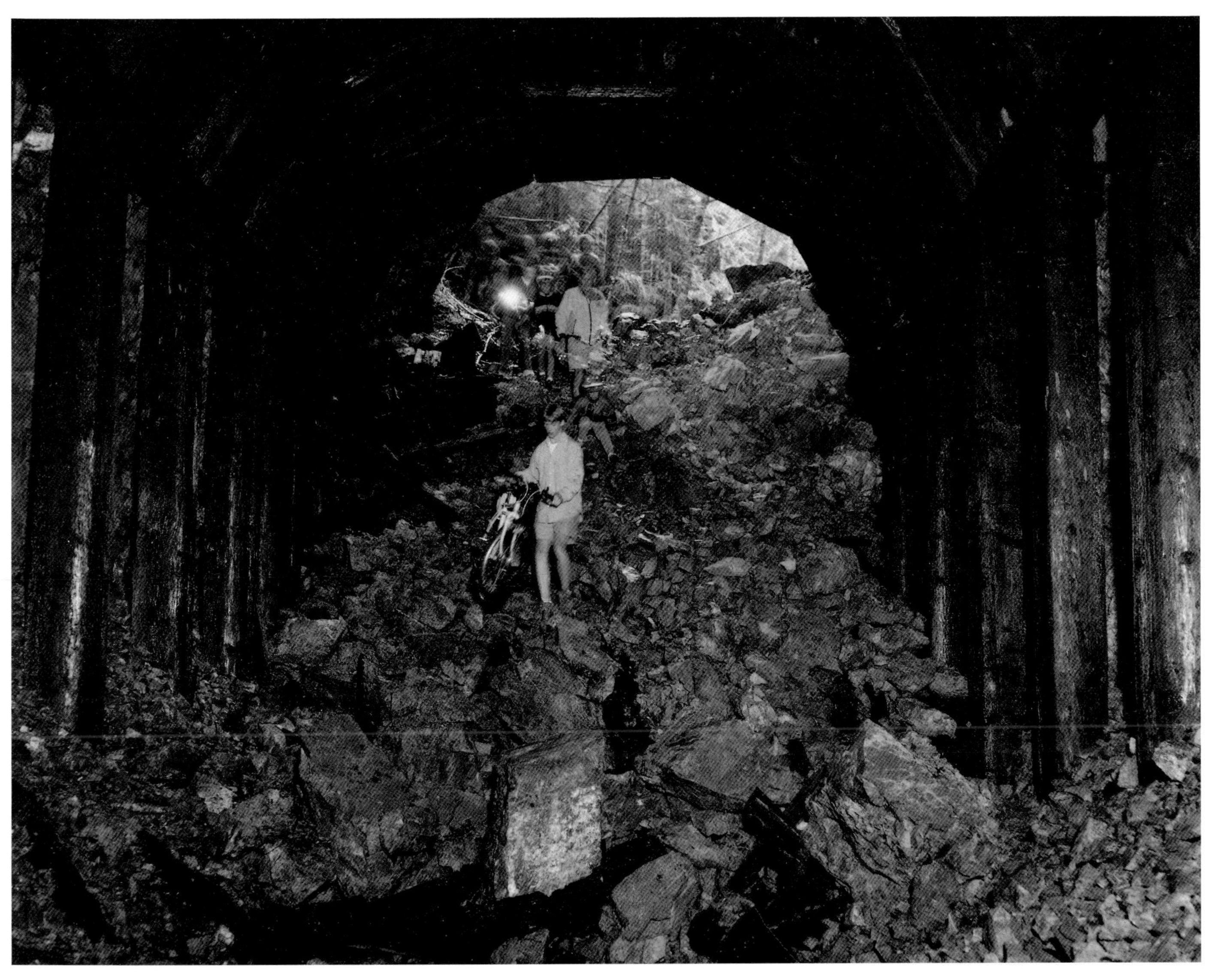

Glenn Rudolph Twin Tunnels, Great Northern Railroad
1993, Silver gelatin print, 30" x 40". Courtesy of the artist. Photograph: Glenn Rudolph.

Michele **Russo**

Michele Russo, the octogenarian dean of Oregon's painters, has been influential in the development of art in Oregon since World War II. A teacher for twenty-seven years, from 1947 until 1974, at the Museum Art School (now the Pacific Northwest College of Art) and an effective activist and advocate for art throughout his adult life, his prominence stems from the humanist principles that permeate both his art and his personal life. His formalized figurative paintings are firmly based in a dedication to communicating, as he says, "the dilemma of the individual." The art of Europe is steeped in various interpretations of this dilemma, and like many of his historical predecessors, Russo uses the female nude as its visual text. Well aware of the political and moral implications of the nude, he purposely exploits its sexuality to explore themes of isolation and the placement of power in female-male relationships. Formulaic contour drawing and the elimination of facial features depersonalize the figures allowing them to function as symbols representing ideas and psychological states.

Few artists' work is as immediately recognizable as Russo's, not only for its unsettling content but also for its singular style in which objective depiction and abstraction are bonded. Stylistically, the dominant innovations of Modernism — flatness, altered perspective, and expressionistic color — are incorporated into an aesthetic based on geometric figuration. The acrylic paintings comprising Russo's mature work are characterized by thinly applied, muted colors, angular delineation of flat, iconic images, and minimal backgrounds. His search for a direct and graphic expression led to a reduction in a large store of images and in the means of their depiction. Hats, umbrellas, shoes, and other ancillary symbols are, like the figures, players in the artist's ironic commentaries on the psychodynamics of sex in contemporary life. His best known series, "Mockeries and Ecstasies on a Chauvinist Theme," to which he frequently returns, features suited men and naked women, such as the couple in *Hop, Skip & Jump*, cavorting with flying bowler hats and umbrellas.

While "The Mockeries" best define Russo's sense of the absurd in male-female relationships, many paintings, neither as provocative nor as caustic, are equally rooted in the human condition and formally, to historical precedents. References to a classical monumentality are seen in solitary, self-absorbed nudes; nudes in pairs are distanced and turned away from each other in empty settings; in groups, as dancers and bathers, they are reminiscent of Matisse's exuberant treatment of identical subjects. The many drawings that Russo has executed throughout his career are elegantly distilled explorations of these themes. In expressive lines that blur as they start and stop on absorbent rice paper, the drawings capture vulnerability, flashes of introspection, and moments of joy.

From the beginning Russo's work has been emphatically figurative. Social realism was at its height when he left Yale in 1934 with a B.F.A. and a yen to experience the great new modern movements that had been omitted from the conservative Yale program. His early experimentation in impressionist and cubist techniques was applied to subject matter that reflected his political engagement with the labor movement. Soon, however, he was drawn to the reductive strategies of Abstract Expressionism, and by the 1960s he had found a balance between naturalism and abstraction that he has maintained ever since. Early paintings of softly rendered generic figures against indeterminate backgrounds evolved gradually into the familiar hard-edge shapes that have dominated his work for more than two decades. The application of color, too, has moved from overlapping, expressionistic patches to subtly nuanced blues, grays, and earth tones banded by black outlines.

Although Russo is an American, born in Connecticut in 1909, he lived for five years during his childhood in his immigrant parents' ancestral village in Italy. His devotion to art began there under the tutelage of a priest who was an artist as well as his teacher. As an adult Russo returns to Italy periodically with his wife, the painter Sally Haley, and never fails to be reminded of the universal and timeless potency of the painted image. Like the *quattrocento* painters he admires, he conveys matters of human urgency in terms of his own time and place.

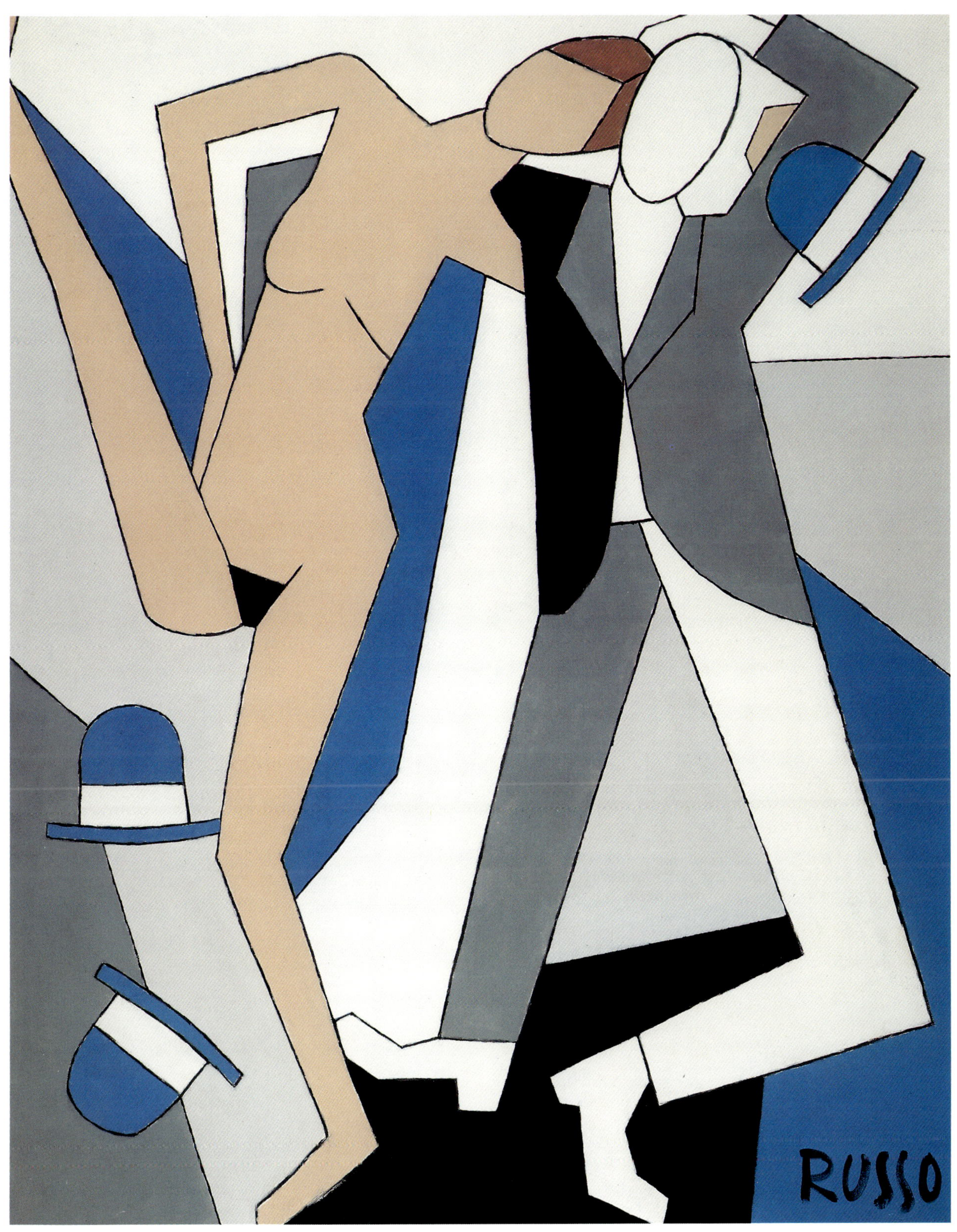

Michele Russo **Hop, Skip and Jump**
1991, Acrylic on canvas, 69" x 55". Collection of the artist. Courtesy of the artist and Laura Russo Gallery. Photograph: David Browne.

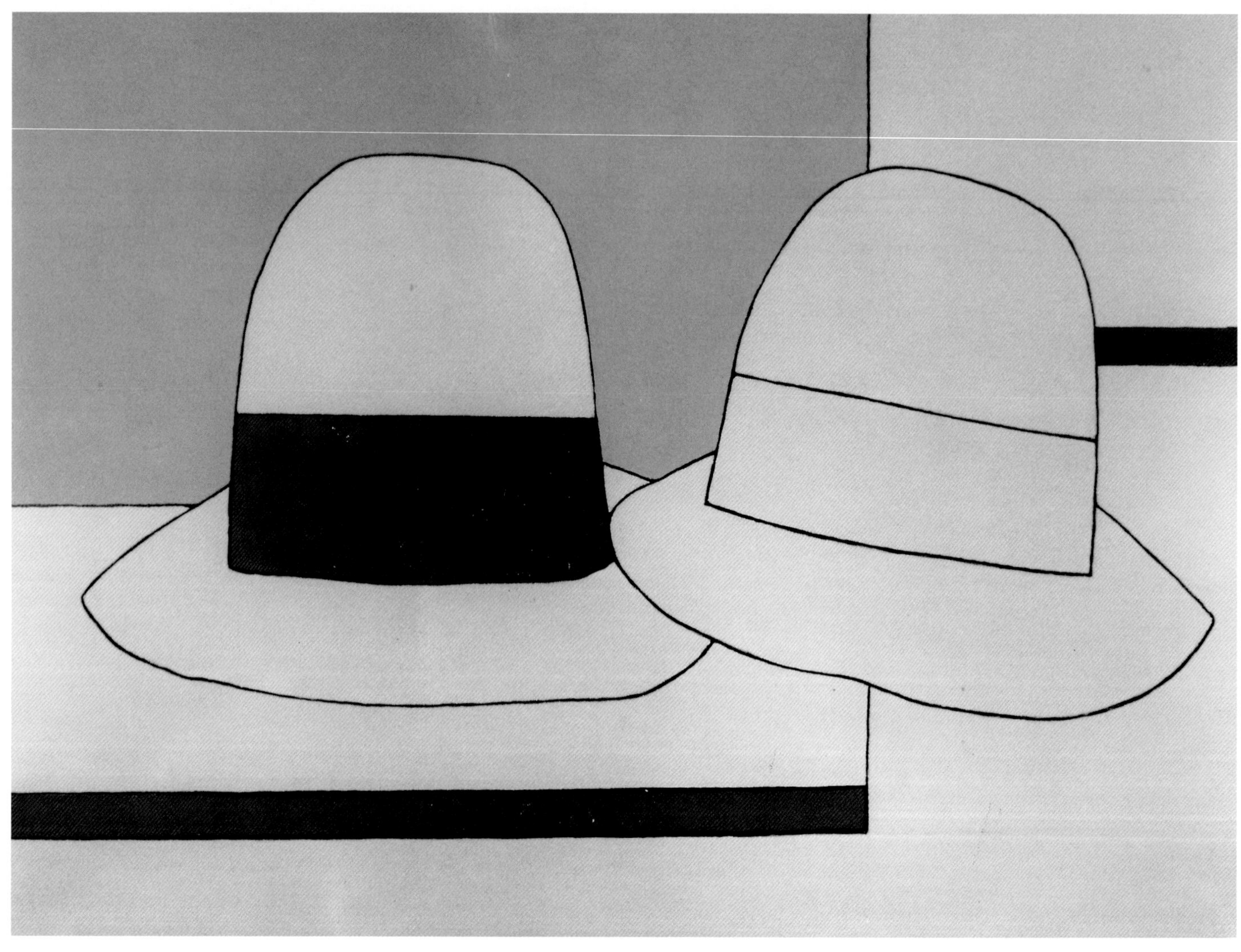

Michele Russo **Two Hats**
1986, Acrylic on canvas, 38" x 52". Collection of Clifford and Doris Carlsen. Courtesy of the artist and Laura Russo Gallery. Photograph: David Browne.

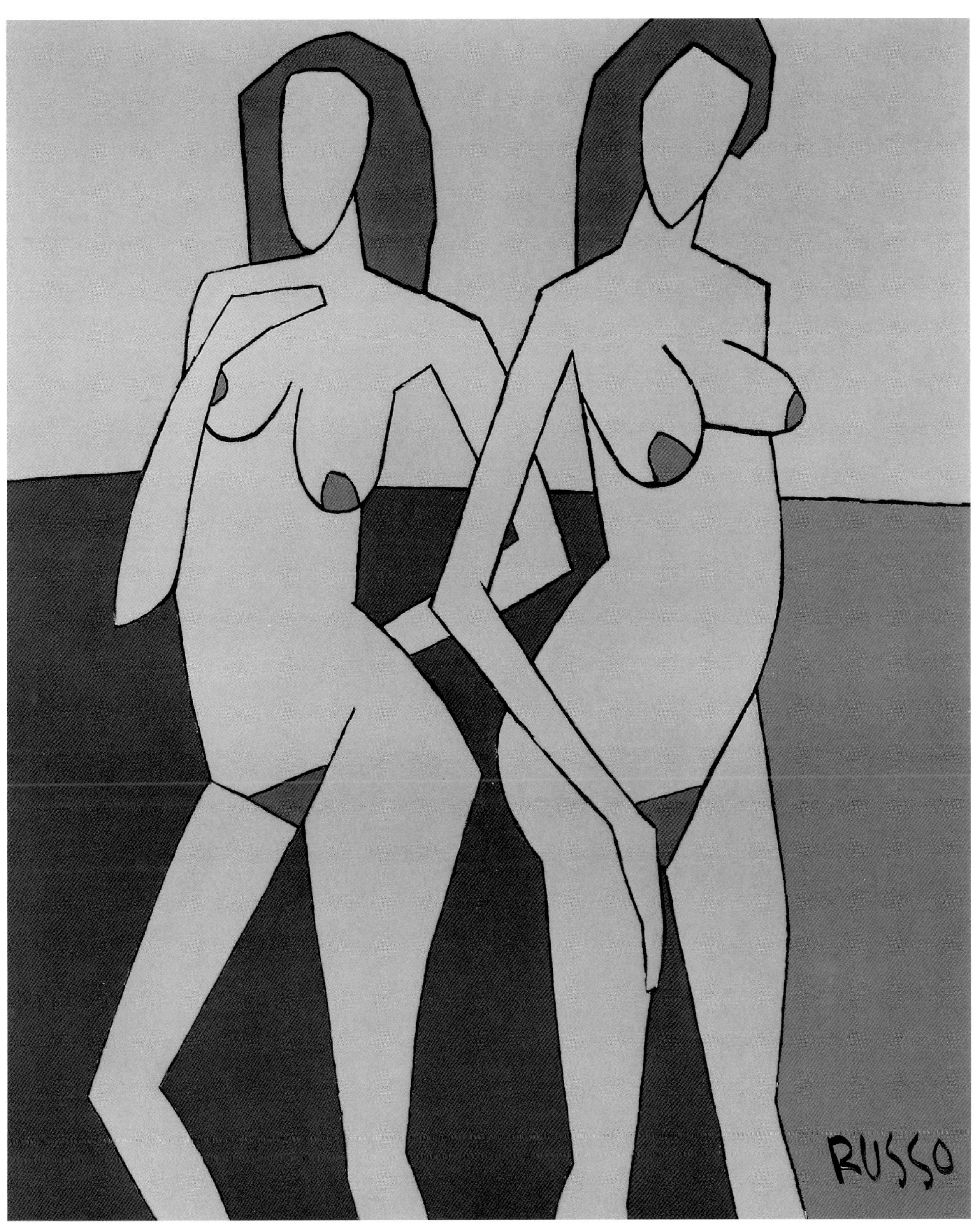

Michele Russo **Subsequent Thoughts**
1988, Acrylic on canvas, 69" x 55". Courtesy of the artist and Laura Russo Gallery. Photograph: David Browne.

Norie **Sato**

Norie Sato speaks of her art as being about "transitions and edges." She might have phrased it to include transmissions and transience as well. Since the early 1970s, when she was introduced to video while in graduate school, she has explored the interactions between electronic processes of communication and human cognitive reception. The fugitive quality of video images, the lines and dots on untuned monitor screens as they come into resolution as visual information, the superimpositions, flashes and flow of visual elements are in certain ways analogous to mental processes of perception and memory. Ephemeral effects such as these are the departure point for Sato's videos, prints, sculptures and sculptural installations in which sensuality and metaphor frame investigations of perceptive processes.

Sato's early work, after obtaining her M.F.A. at the University of Washington in 1974, played on the strong relationship she saw between printmaking and video. Both are dependent on mechanical processes, both are the means of multiple representations and of mass communication. At the time, her graphic compositions, composed of horizontal markings and layered colors, utilized aluminum powder as a referrent to the phosphorescence of the television screen and also to zinc printmaking plates. The videos of the period, like the prints, employed elements of the medium itself — interference patterns, snow and other electronic glitches — in exploring the fleeting quality of images, their lack of demarcation (in Sato's term, "the blurred edges") that must be sorted out, much as the brain operates, in order to bring coherence to what is seen.

"Virtual Imaging," a Documents Northwest exhibition at the Seattle Art Museum in 1984, was composed of static objects, moving images, and optically confusing representations, all within an environment of visual vagaries. In approaching the main space viewers passed through a "forest" of square column "trees" ranging in height from six to eleven feet that were crowned with glass "branches." Monitors inside the columns projected video images upward, causing them to appear as fragments of images or markings on the transparent shards. Beyond the rows of columns a three-part installation of thirteen wall-size panels of varying widths created an enveloping visual atmosphere. The panels, mixed-media works on paper, were arranged in such a way that viewers were obliged to proceed slowly from one to the next in order to discern images within the shifting planes of neutral colors. Sato's use of pastels, colored pencils, watercolor, and metallic powders in layered and subtle juxtapositions created surfaces that shifted from glowing reflections of light to flat planes of absorbed color as one's viewpoint changed. Like television screens, the compositions, made up of thin lines and specks of color on paper, played close views (for seeing details) against the distance required for piecing together the total "picture."

Nearness and distance in a personal context informed Sato's contribution to Seattle's ambitious public art project, "In Public: 1991." From her own experience as an immigrant arriving in Seattle from Japan, she created *Transience of Memory*, four see-through screens placed on the concrete balustrade along the waterfront at Pier 50, very near the spot where as a child of two she entered the United States. Layers of screen were sewed together to create ghost images to suggest Sato's fading memory of the experience. The four screens were accompanied by aluminum etched texts in which she wrote of transience in life, stating in part, "Memory is the screen through which we view the present ... (it) is the after-image of life's experience."

Sato's innovative methods of achieving the effect of depth in translucent materials now center on glass, which is both materially and metaphorically suited to her thematic concerns. In addition to its embodiment of opposites, i.e., transparence and solidity as well as strength and fragility, there is one other that especially appeals to her: Glass is, she says, "all edges and no middle." The glass sculpture titled Book (one of a group of glass and stainless steel mesh works exhibited as "Transformations and Ghosts") is a compilation of etched "pages," each of which is obscured by all the others. The information it contains, Sato suggests, is subject to the processes of its transmission and reception.

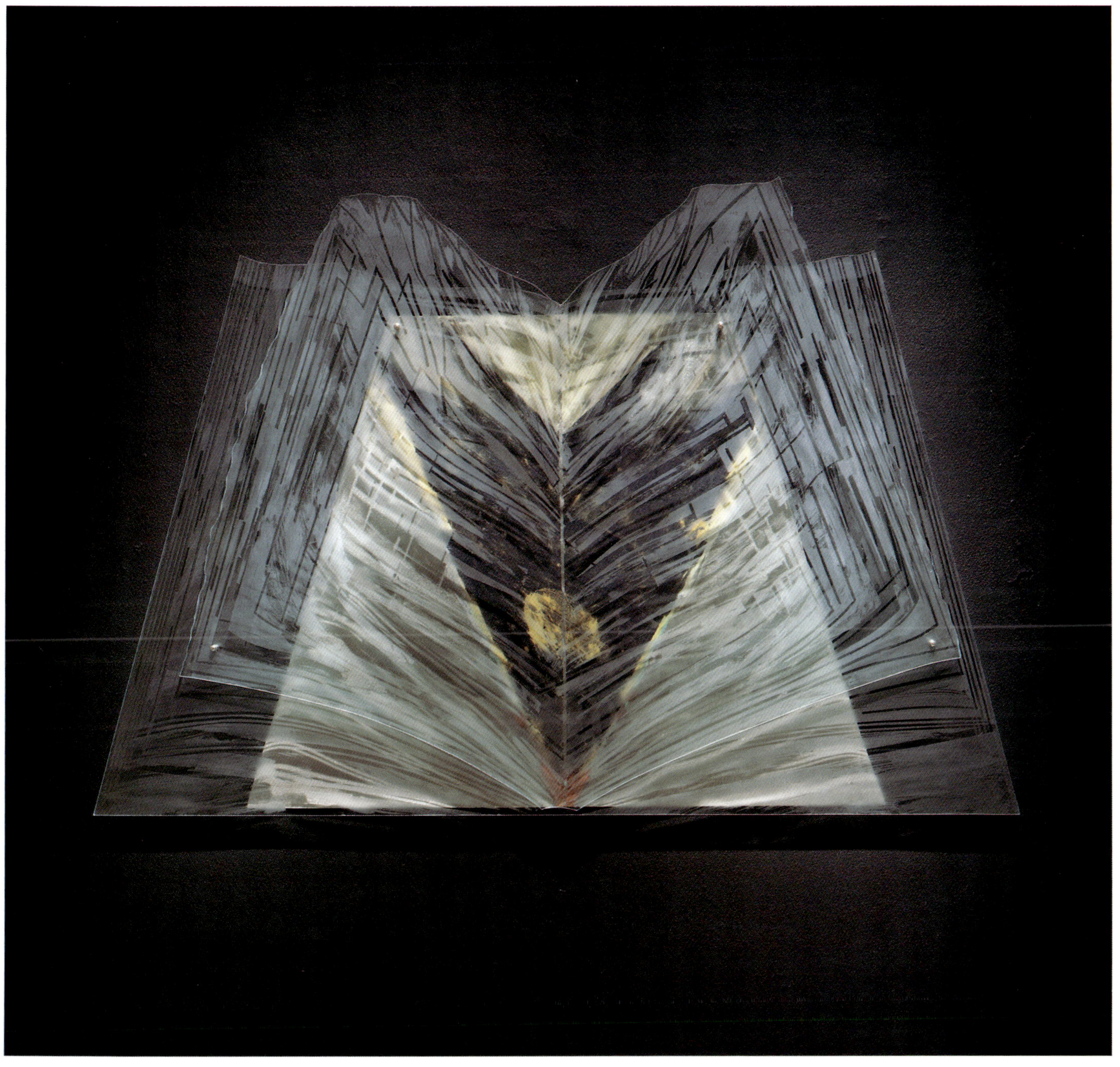

Norie Sato **Book**
Etched glass, stainless mesh, wax and pigment, oil pastel, 68" x 45" x 2". Courtesy of the artist and Elizabeth Leach Gallery. Photograph: Tom Collicott.

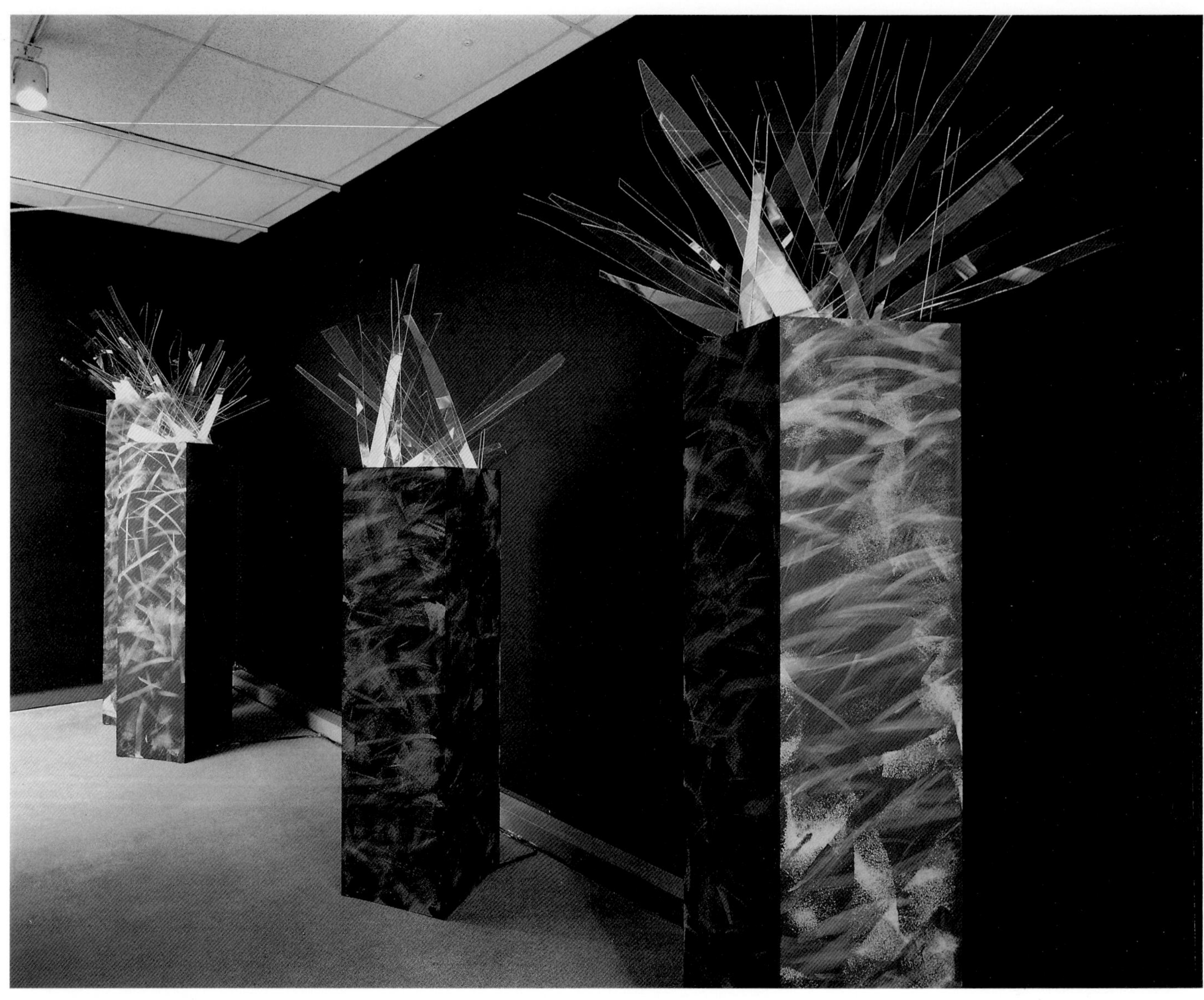

Norie Sato **Virtual Imaging: Phospor Response**
1984, Video installation at Seattle Art Museum. Courtesy of the artist, Linda Farris Gallery and Elizabeth Leach Gallery.

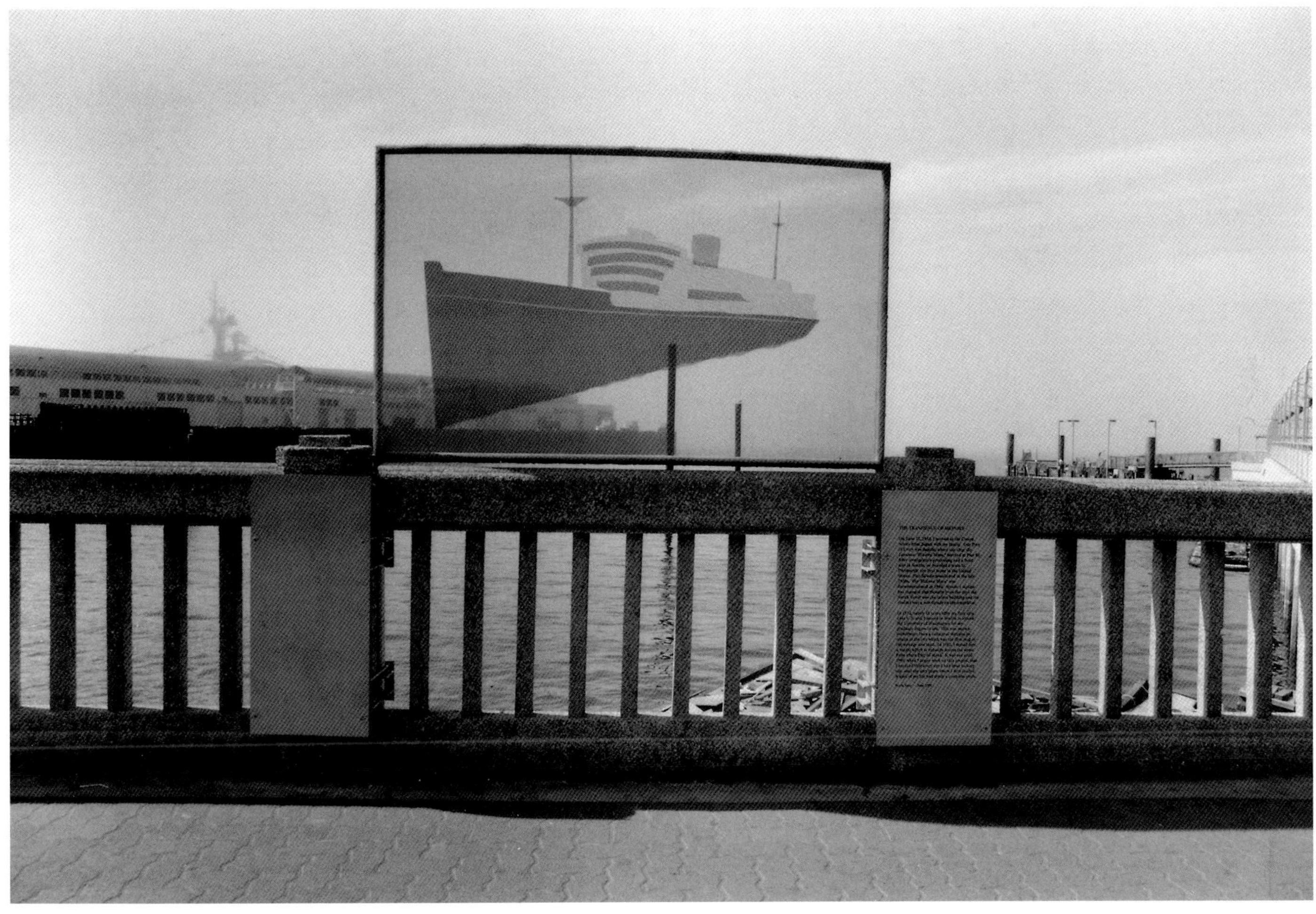

Norie Sato **Transience of Memory**
1991, 1 of 4 screens, stainless mesh, Seattle waterfront. Courtesy of the artist, Linda Farris Gallery and Elizabeth Leach Gallery. Photograph: Norie Sato.

Tad **Savinar**

Tad Savinar sometimes describes himself as a reporter rather than an artist. Inasmuch as his art consists of studied, often bemused commentaries on attitudes, obsessions, and vulnerabilities of urban dwellers of his age group — including himself — he is indeed a pundit, and one of unusual dimensions. His ideas come to fruition not only in art objects, the subject to be considered here, but also in public design projects, civic planning, and in the theater (he is the author of six published plays). Schooled as a painter and printmaker, he now moves among these various disciplines, circulating ideas within their expressive modalities. If there is a common denominator, particularly in his two-dimensional work, it is in his fascination with the relationship between word and image, a relationship that he expresses in the psychologically charged communication tactics of the media. He is, as he says, a product of his time, "and I see this time as a very manufactured thing." Pairing pithy words, epigrams, aphorisms — television's sound-bites — with equally terse pictorial elements, he forges images, text, and materials into a gestalt of contemporary mores.

Although he is a native and lifelong resident of Portland, Savinar's work does not relate in particular to life in the Northwest as much as to his age and class. Born in 1950, he is of the "baby boomer" generation, the first to grow up with television as a ubiquitous presence, the mediator of war, politics, entertainment, and marketing. Not surprisingly, his early work, after completing a B.F.A. at Colorado College in 1973, the year the Vietnam War ended, was politically oriented, consisting of very large, bold wall paintings scaled to dominate both the space and viewers in an allusion to the enormity of television's influence in the social upheaval of the time.

In the ensuing years he continued to address social issues while developing a distinctive style in which wordplay, appropriation of a commercial aesthetic, commercial materials, and commercial processes of fabrication underscore aspects of depersonalization in urban culture. Recently, as his annual gallery exhibitions of the 1990s attest, he is permitting personal experience to inform the work, not only through subject matter but also through production by his own hand. The mixed media drawing, *Daytimer*, of 1994, epitomizes this transition as it is based on his newly acquired mid-life status. The wry accounting of day-dreaming priorities, past and present, encircling the boy may be autobiographical, but it is also representative of the confusions, mixed emotions, and inner battles of most American men as they enter this period in their lives.

The black and white screenprint, *4 Attempts to Order Chaos*, of 1993, is timeless in its implications of a basic human urge. The chalkboard markings by three sophisticates and one innocent are a whimsical reminder that from the Paleolithic Era to the technological age, humans have attempted to explain, understand, and control their environment, including themselves, through the symbolic marks they produce on various surfaces, from rocks to computer screens.

The aggressiveness of Savinar's early work has been replaced by more benign but equally trenchant statements, all the more so for their multiple implications. The visual clarity evident in *Daytimer*, *4 Attempts to Order Chaos*, and *Juggernaut (Action Painting)* cloaks overlapping, underlying, and subliminal significations. The very large *Juggernaut (Action Painting)*, partially finger painted in black on a white background, has the appearance of a diagrammatic depiction of three unattached but synchronized gears rolling at an angle through space. Red letters spelling "brain" are spaced across the gears near the bottom of the canvas. The effect is that of a multiple choice puzzle: Is it a reference to identical human cogs in the social machinery? To runaway brain power? An art historical reference also seems to apply. The title, the scale, and the drips and finger prints on the canvas evoke the heroics and egos of Jackson Pollock and his colleagues who made "action painting" the driving force (juggernaut?) of post World War II art. The probable answer to the puzzle, in terms of Savinar's own use of language, is "all of the above."

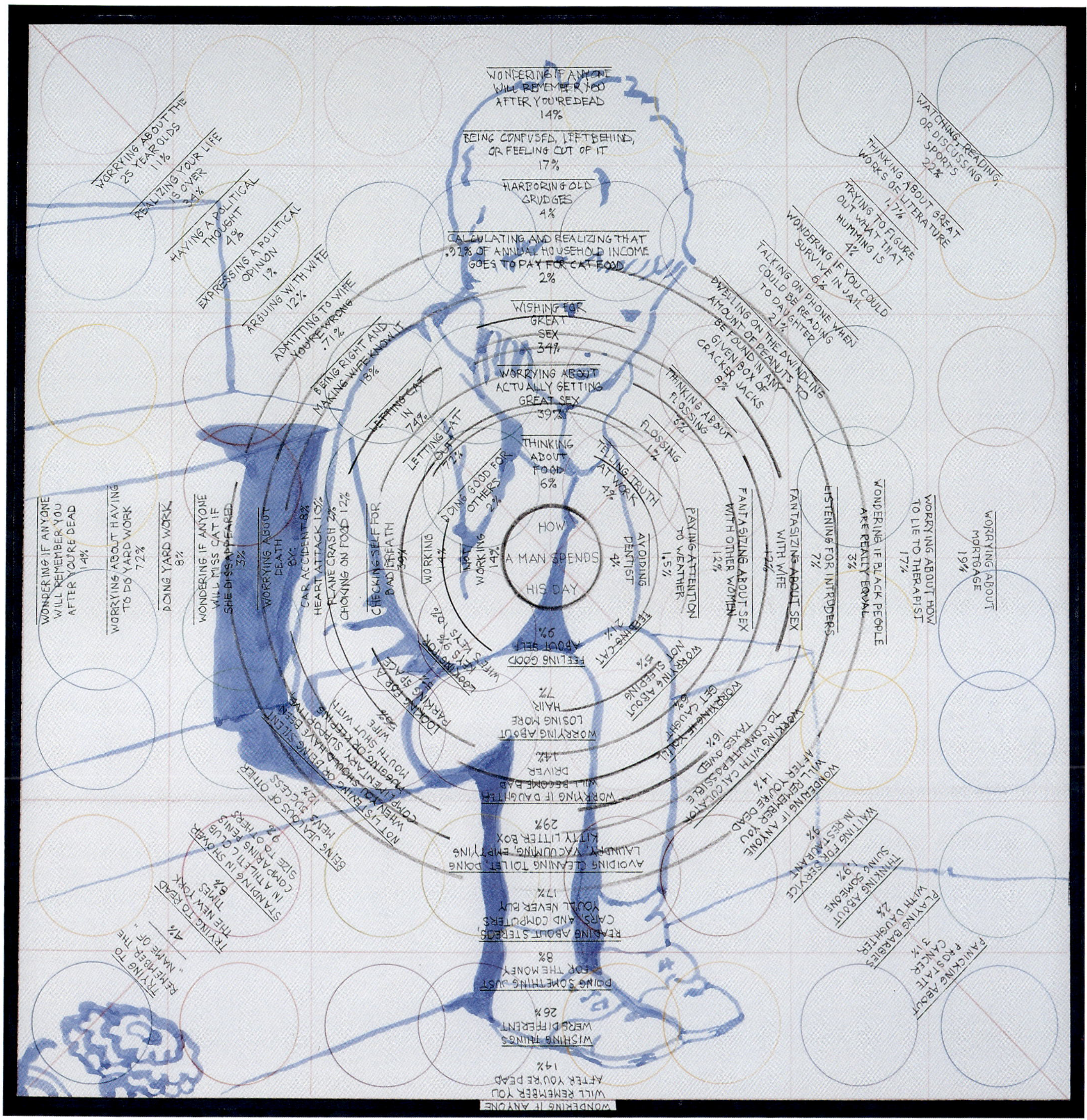

Tad Savinar **Daytimer**
1994, Mixed media on paper, 35" x 34". Collection of Gordon Thompson III. Courtesy of the artist and Savage Fine Arts. Photograph: Bill Bachhuber.

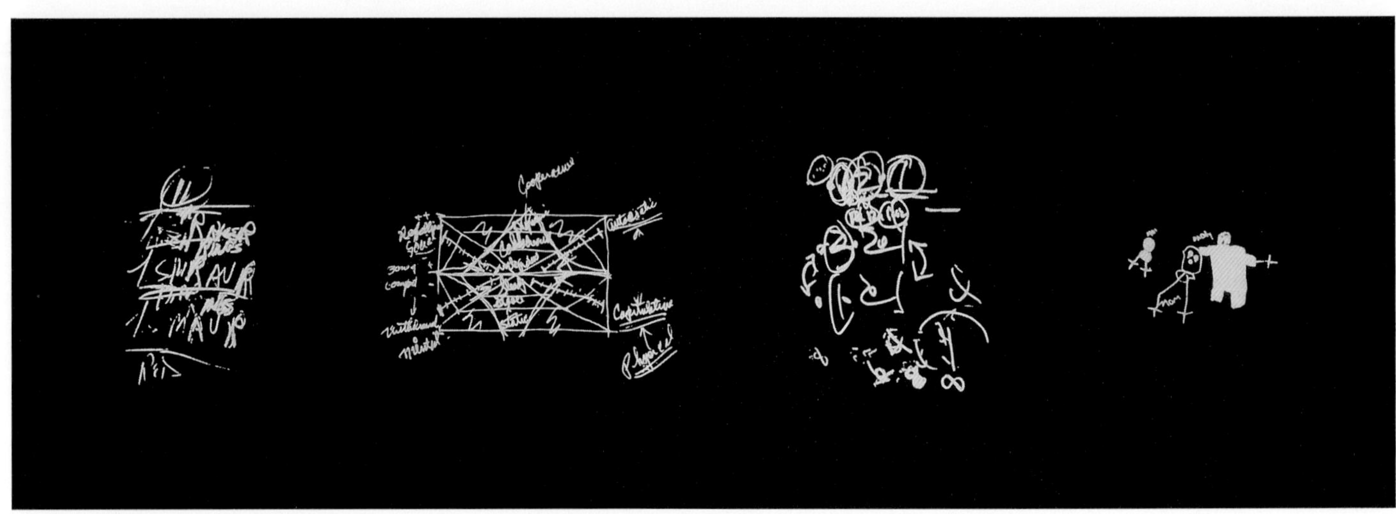

Tad Savinar **4 Attempts to Order Chaos**
1993, Serigraph, Edition of 25. Courtesy of the artist and Savage Fine Arts. Photograph: Wayne Aldridge.

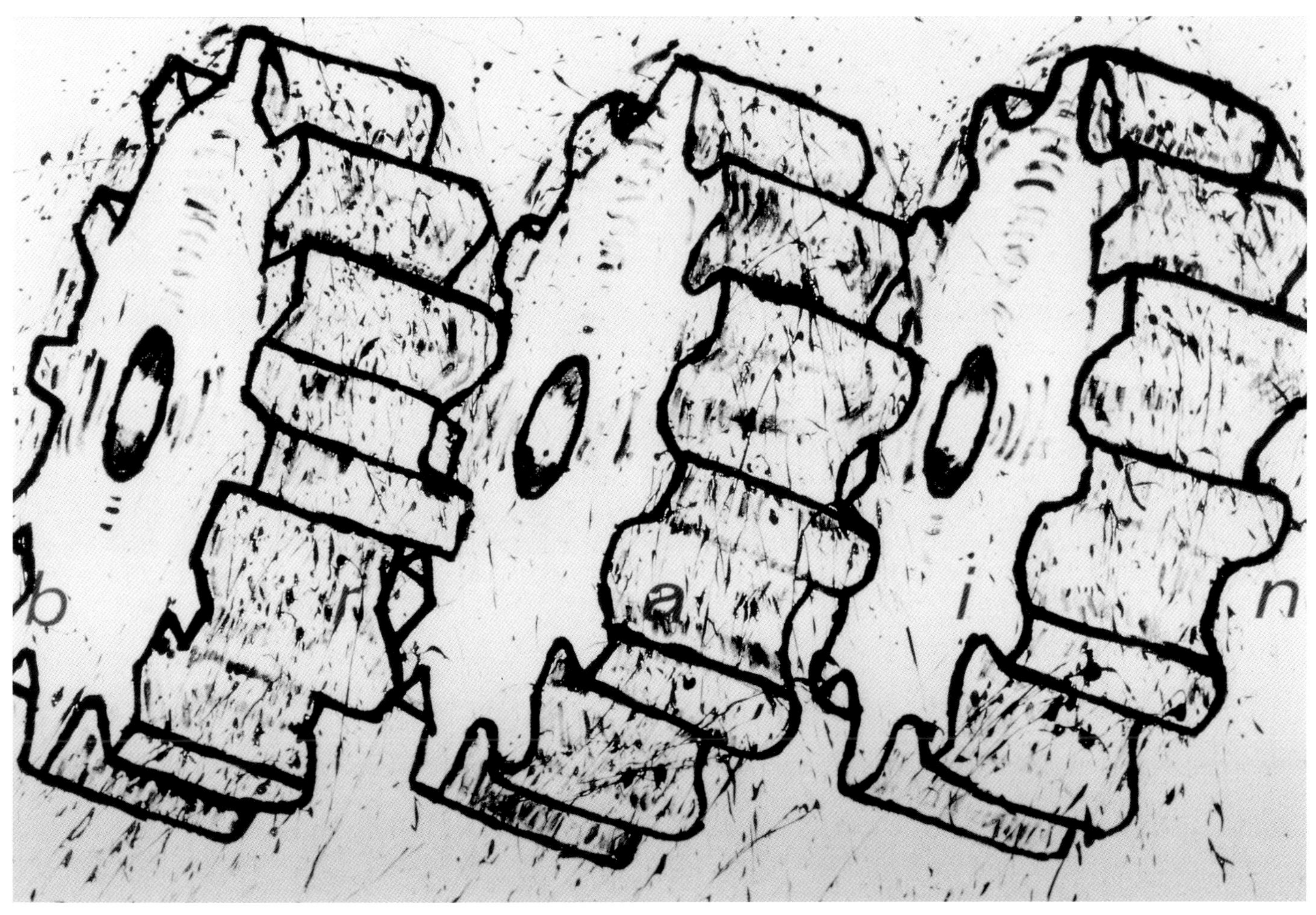

Tad Savinar **Juggernaut (action painting)**
1991, Acrylic on canvas, 60" x 96". Collection of James Winkler. Courtesy of the artist and Savage Fine Arts. Photograph: David Browne.

Buster **Simpson**

Buster Simpson's public art projects are imaginative, sometimes audacious, solutions to social and environmental problems. He describes his approach as "non-linear;" it can also be described as poetic, free-wheeling, and, on occasion, ingeniously witty. His many commissioned public works throughout the country are consistently relevant to issues that are quite specific to the geographic area and the community in which they are sited. By design they bring the human element into the socio-political equation, critiquing the status quo and advocating active participation by citizens. An artist with an intense social consciousness, Simpson considers art an effective means for bringing about change.

Two Northwest works that have become instantly identified with their cities are the *Seattle George Monument*, commissioned for the outdoor park at the Washington State Convention Center Plaza in Seattle, and *Host Analog* at the Oregon Convention Center in Portland. The twenty-eight foot high *Seattle George Monument* of 1989 simultaneously portrays Chief Seattle (originally Chief Sealth) and George Washington. The tripod base, which refers both to surveying and Native American lodge architecture, supports the monument's head, twenty-four aluminum profiles of Chief Seattle fanned out to create an armature for English ivy planted in a Boeing 707 nose cone. A sharpened template, which is also a weathervane, gradually trims the ivy overgrowth to form an evergreen bust of George. On the other side of the head, the growing vines will ultimately obliterate Chief Seattle, symbolizing the disappearance of the area's first culture and the ascendance of the second.

Host Analog is an old growth Douglas fir felled by wind in the 1950s in the Bull Run watershed adjacent to Mt. Hood, Portland's primary water source. Cut into eight segments, each measuring eight by eight feet, it rests near the main entrance to the Oregon Convention Center where it decomposes and offers nurturance to new plant growth germinating from seed and seedlings of cedar, fir, and hemlock that were broadcast over the host — or "nurse" — log. A water system installed over the segmented log in order to keep it wet enough to induce plant growth enables the log, as Simpson says, to continue to drink from the same waters that nurtured it for more than fifteen hundred years.

Simpson's decision to make art with a social purpose was the result of his experience at Woodstock in 1969. Just out of art school (University of Michigan, B.A. and M.F.A.), he and several other artists were commissioned to create sculptural recreational equipment for the festival site. Upon competion the structures were almost immediately dismantled for their materials, which were put to more practical uses in the campsites by festival attendees — literally, "appropriated art." The result, for Simpson, was a revaluation of purpose and a thoughtful examination of the meaning of social value in the context of use value.

The combination of service and public participation is nowhere better exemplifed than in the installation Simpson created for "In Public: Seattle 1991." *Composting Commode*, an open pit toilet intended to be located adjacent to the new Seattle Art Museum, was to provide a service for downtown transients, a service to the city in helping to solve a defecation problem, and finally, to fertilize the soil for a future tree planting. After a three year process to obtain a permit Simpson was unable to install the work because of a determination that its proximity to a water main constituted a health risk. However, in 1992 it was gratefully accepted at the ORCA school and community garden where it will be moved annually, creating the soil for a future grove of fruit trees.

Exchanger Fountain of 1993, similarly adresses a city and environmental need simultaneously. Located in Anaheim, California, it is a sculptural drinking fountain in the form of a concave disk mounted on a leaning tufa column and placed in a pit containing a willow tree. While the tree, the disk and the text inscribed upon it refer to the area's agrarian history and hot, dry climate, the work functions as a water supply for humans and the willow tree. Simpson's design puts the spent water in motion, spilling it through the disk to saturate the absorbent tufa column, thus cooling the incoming supply line as it spirals up the column. The remaining water drips into the pit to nourish the tree that shades the fountain. As users bend to drink, they see their faces and the tree's foliage reflected in the chrome plated brass disk and as they rise, they read the words on the disk: "Santa Ana your water nurtures and your hot winds cool. The water kissing your lips is an offering."

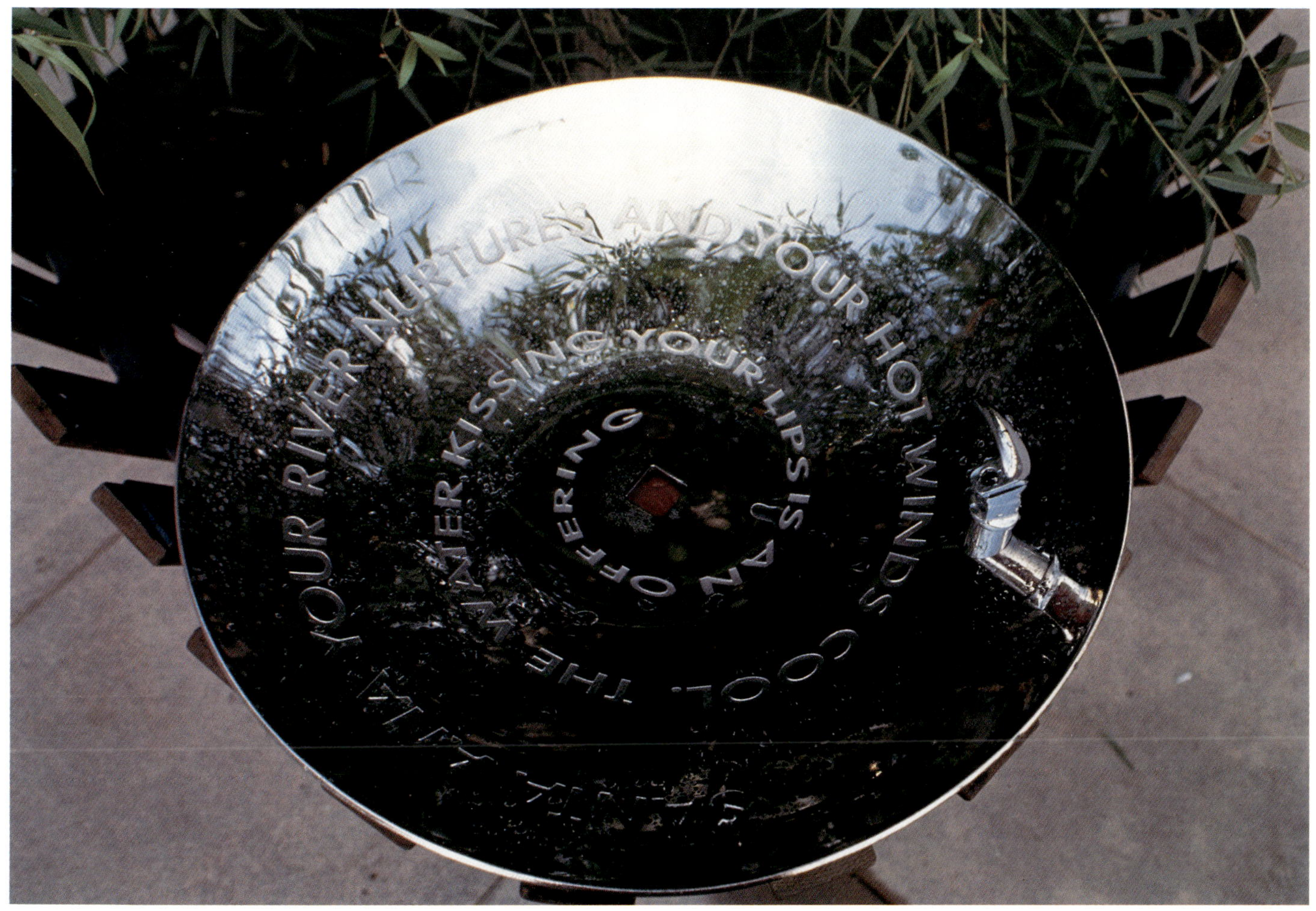

Buster Simpson **Exchanger Fountain**
1993, Anaheim, California, 6' x 6' x 30"h. Anaheim Redevelopment Agency. Courtesy of the artist.

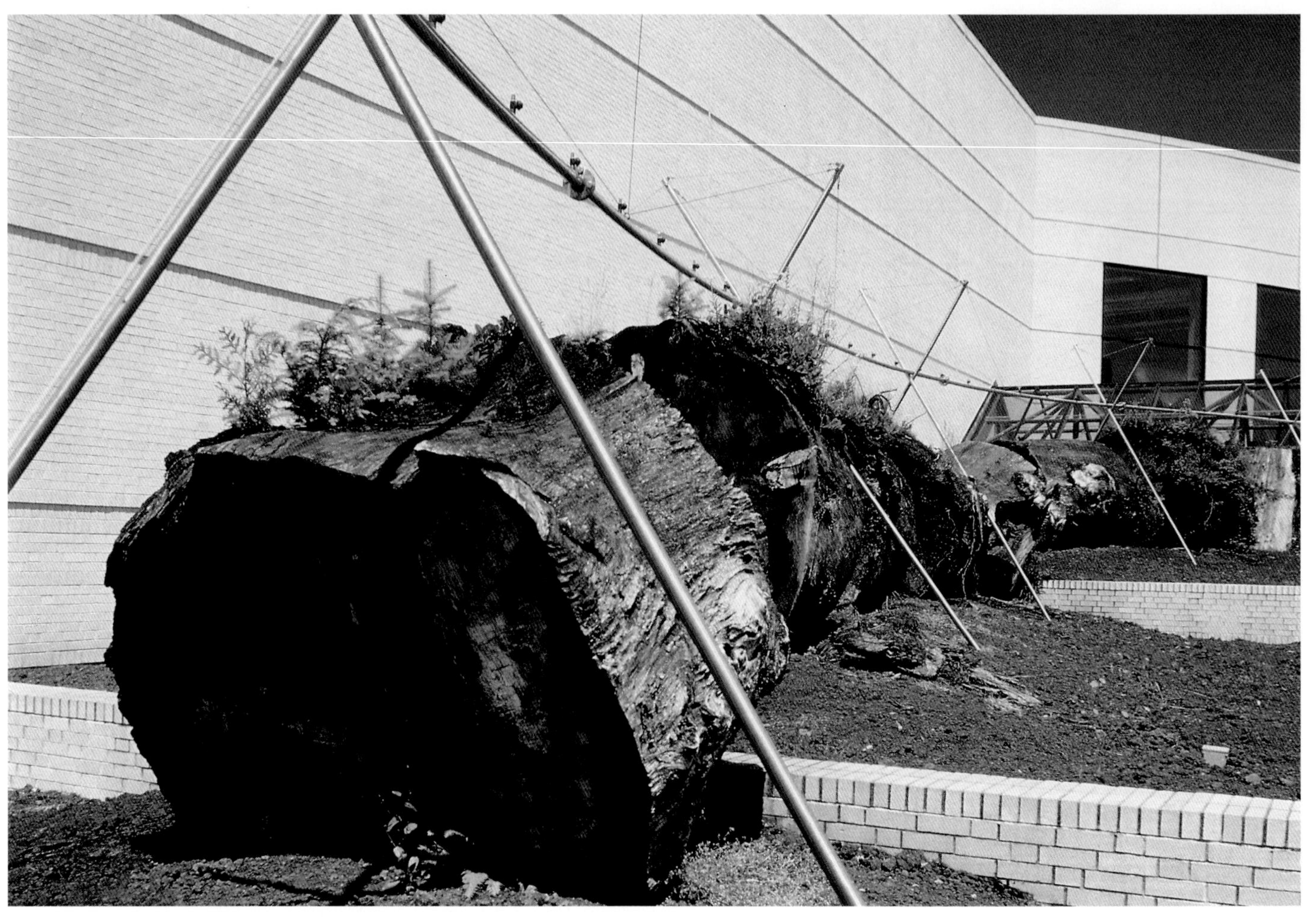

Buster Simpson **Host Analog**
1991, Oregon Convention Center, Portland, 30'w x 70'l x 18'h. Metro One Percent for Art. Courtesy of the artist.

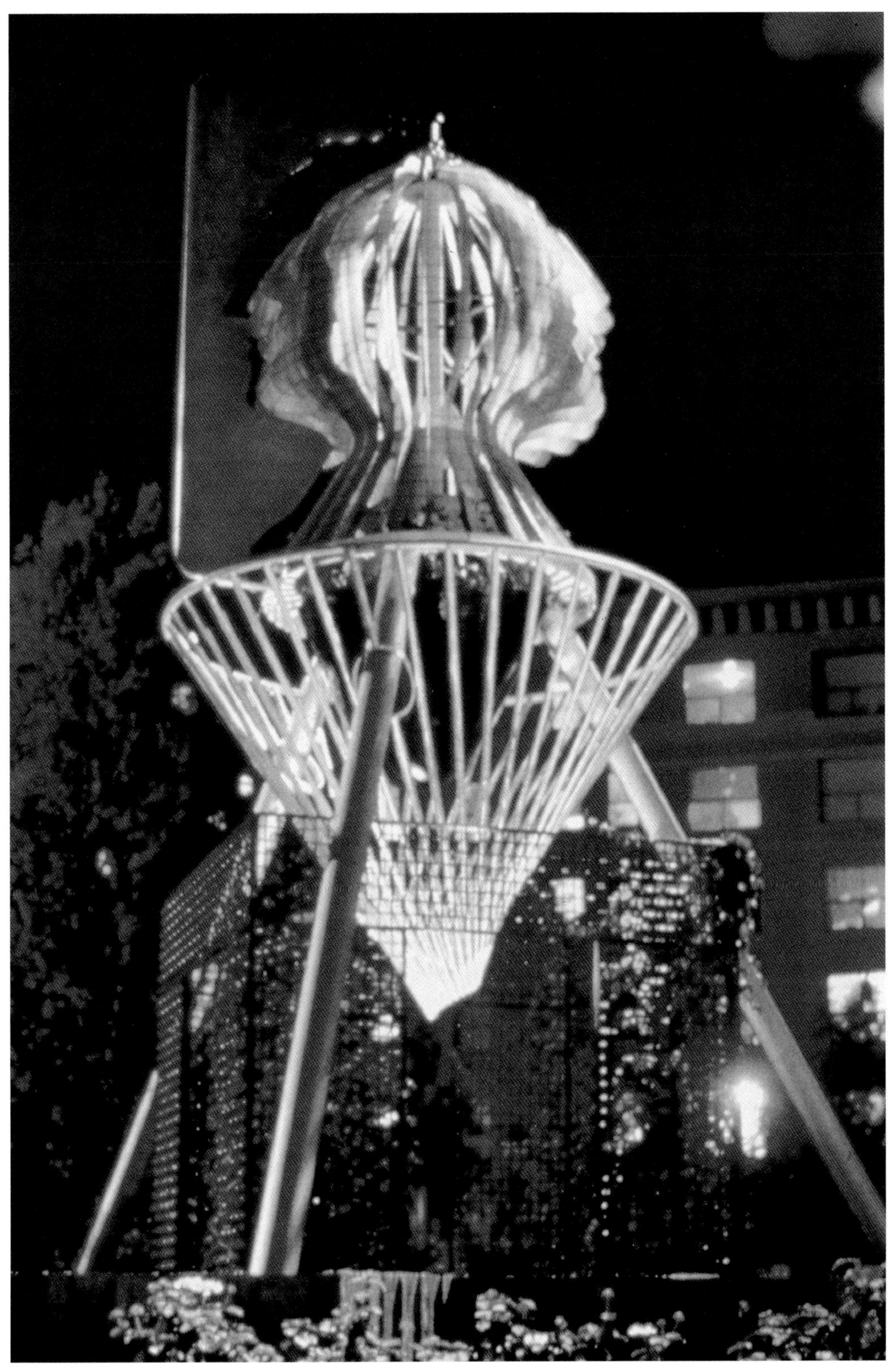

Buster Simpson **Seattle George Monument**
1988, 28'h x 12'diameter, Washington State Convention Center, Seattle. Washington State Arts Commission Percent for Art Program. Courtesy of the artist.

Paul **Sutinen**

Paul Sutinen's art falls into no single conventional category of artmaking, but rather, skips through all of them. He is a conceptual artist whose ideas take form through whatever medium or technique is most appropriate. He has produced large, outdoor public art commissions and indoor gallery installations, performances, sculptures, drawings, and paintings. A lifelong resident of Portland, where he was born in 1949, he uses his immediate environment as both source and laboratory for his investigations of art, *qua* art, and more important, as a way of experiencing the world.

Many of Sutinen's works are based on his close observation of small phenomena, the kind usually deemed unworthy of notice. In a performance piece of 1979 he swept a sidewalk in downtown Portland, not to clean but to "gather material," an assortment of leaves, gum wrappers, cigarette stubs, broken glass and dirt, that were pushed into a pile and left to be dispersed again by the breeze and pedestrians. Fifteen years later, in a 1994 exhibition, he mounted (from many years of accumulation) about twenty small objects, some made, some found, plus photographs, all of which similarly question boundaries between art and non-art. In contrast to Claes Oldenburg who monumentalizes mundane objects such as a cigarette butt or a typewriter eraser, Sutinen often targets an actual object in such a way that it triggers a mental jump in scale. The dinner plate in *Spencer Meets Giacometti*, for example, becomes a vast plaza for the tiny, painted epoxy cube (inspired by his observation of a bit of cheese flung by a child) in what the artist terms as a "notation" for sculptural ideas.

During the 1980s Sutinen created a number of outdoor constructions using a tree as the focus. The first, *The Tree in the Tower*, 1982, consisted of a wood tower built around the trunk of a pin oak tree with openings for the tree limbs. The relationship of the tower to the tree changed with the seasons as the foliage hid or revealed the construction. As Sutinen described it, "The tower effectively 'imprisoned' the tree. But that is a ridiculous notion. The tree wasn't going anywhere. The tree limbs did 'reach'out through windows in the tower. That, too, is silly. The limbs don't reach through the windows. The windows were built around the tree branches. We knew that. Is that what we felt?"[1]

One of the most subtle and delightfully surprising public art pieces among the many in downtown Portland is Sutinen's *In the Shadow of the Elm*, a public art commission of 1984. Approximating a shadow of the trees above, it is a tree image inlaid in the pavers of a wide walkway through the South Park Blocks near Portland State University where Sutinen had studied art a decade earlier. The use of the site as an integral part of the artwork is again dominant in his 1994 design for a fence and walk to be constructed as part of Portland's in-progress West Side Light Rail system. Landscaping and construction are designed to direct attention to elements in the landscape, in the process minimizing the barrier effect of the six hundred foot fence.

Sutinen's black and white drawings and acrylic paintings also deal with process, relationships, and scale as is evident in *Constellation of Drawings — Memory*. It is also a consideration of systems. Consisting of twenty graphite drawings on polyester drafting film, the piece appears to be a grid of randomly placed geometric shapes. Each drawing is, in fact, a different perspective of a cube, flattened and produced in graphite powder so densely applied it seems to carve the shape out of the white space. The relationship of the edges of the shapes to those of the drafting film on which they are rendered, the smudges resulting from the action of the graphite, the variations on a simple, preexisting form; all are carefully considered in Sutinen's search for the "bare bones" of art.

1. Portland Center for the Visual Arts catalog, 1989. "Twenty Seven Installations."

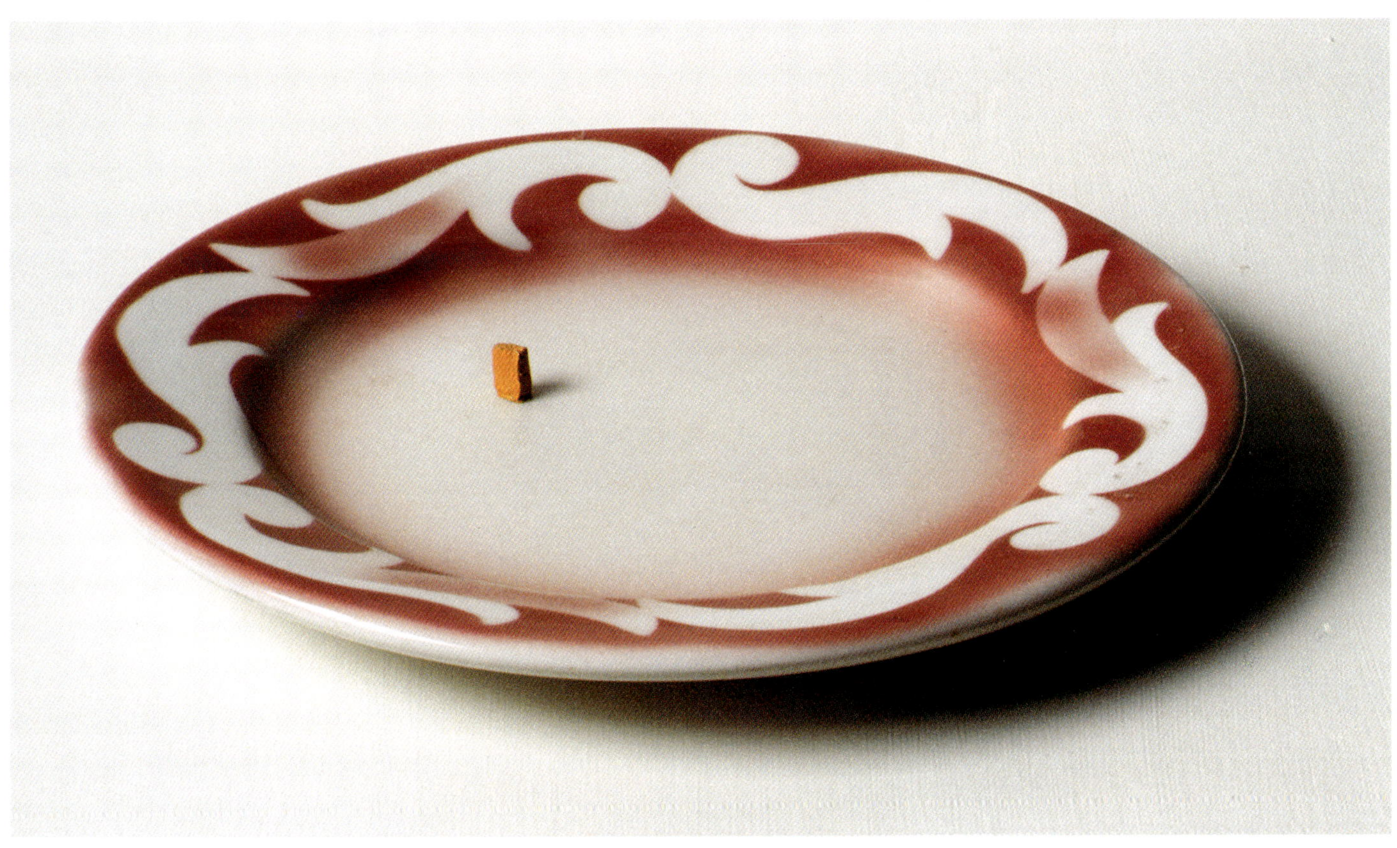

Paul Sutinen Spencer Meets Giacometti
1992, Painted epoxy on plate. Courtesy of the artist.

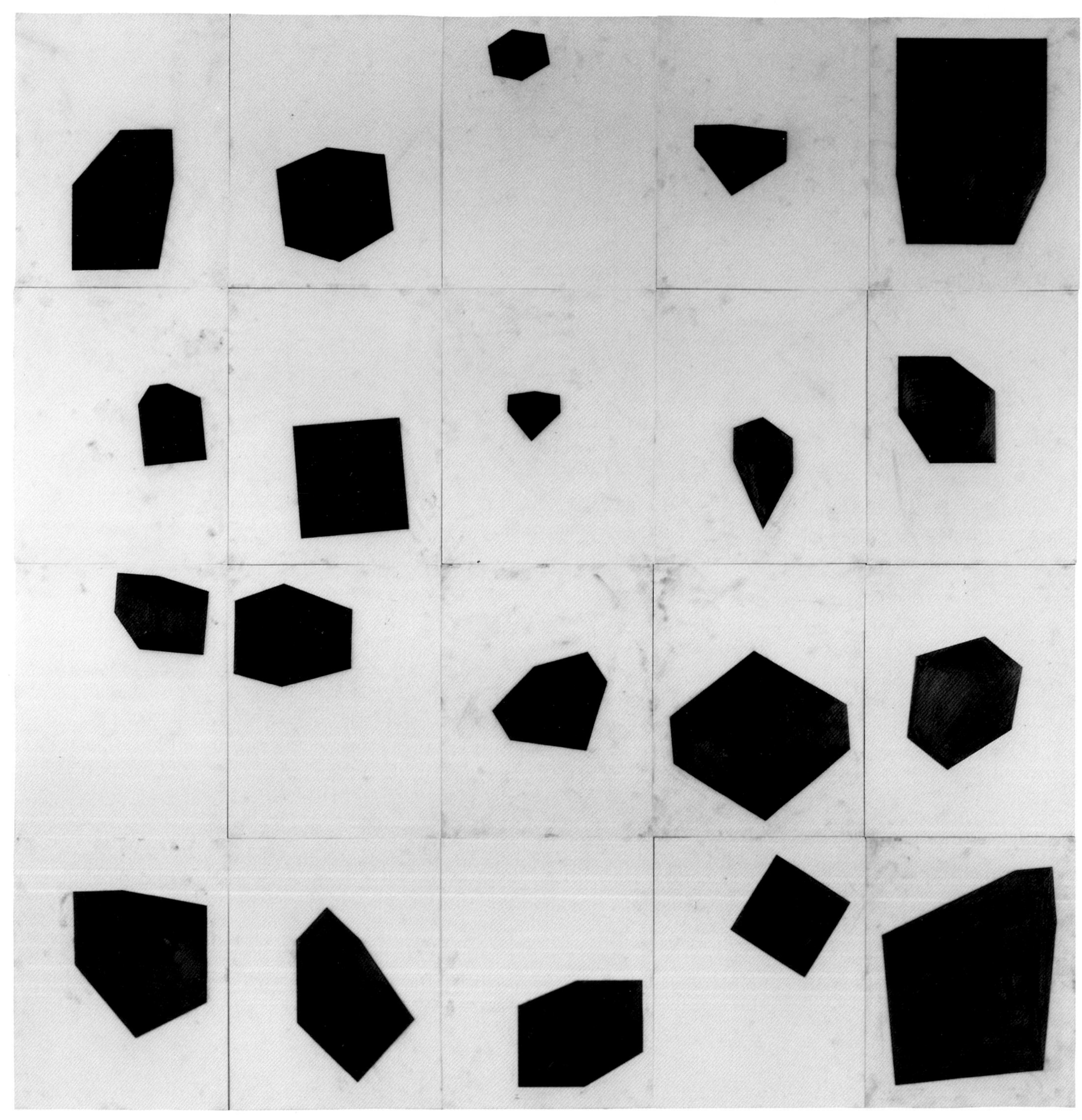

Paul Sutinen **Constellation of Drawings — Memory**
1990, Graphite on polyester drafting film, 20 drawings, 20" x 16"; total size: 80 1/2" x 80 5/8". Collection of Oregon Health Sciences University. Courtesy of the artist.

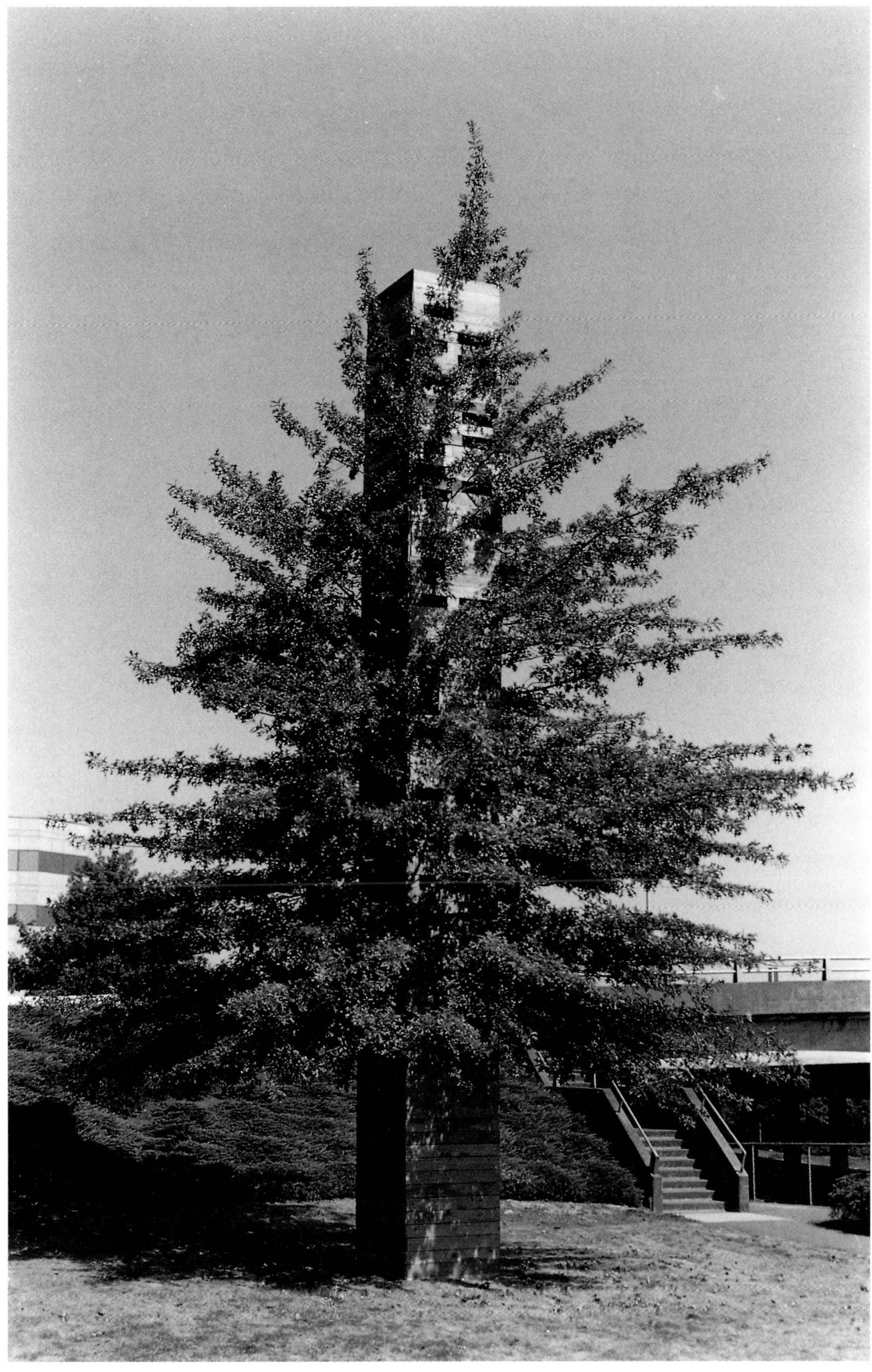

Paul Sutinen **The Tree in the Tower**

1982, Temporary wood construction around living tree in Portland, Oregon, Construction dimension: 40' x 4' x 4'. Project sponsored by Portland Center for the Visual Arts. Courtesy of the artist.

Mike **Taylor**

Mike Taylor's extensive background in graphic design and visual communications is a significant factor in the communicative strategy of his paintings, drawings, and sculpture. The two-dimensional work, in which he employs a schematic drawing style to create visual analogues to language, is based on advertising techniques. The sculptures, in their spare forms and aggressive materiality, are clearly related to minimalist abstraction, but also borrow from advertising's concentration of information into a single strong image. These are the formal strategies undergirding Taylor's cryptic expositions of the complex perceptual processes that come together in the ideas that form our apprehension of the world.

In most of his work Mike Taylor, an African-American who has lived in Africa, draws on the interplay of visual and mental perceptions pertaining to racial stereotypes and class status, as evident in *Top Joe*. It is one of a group of diptychs in which distinctly different but easily recognized images challenge notions of linkage. On one side the simple line drawing of a male head against a bright yellow background is a straightforward depiction; on the other, cylindrical pipes against black are configured as a visual paradox. Taken together, they seem to suggest that the head image is no more amenable to a definitive reading than the puzzle. The series was inspired by a barbershop signboard that Taylor saw in Ghana which illustrated various styles offered by the barber and identified each by a title: "Top Joe," "Master Ponk," "Flat Top," and "Ebony." Taylor was immediately attracted by the political implications as well as the illustrative strength of the signboard.

Although he has lived in Portland since 1982, Taylor is in truth a citizen of the world. He was born in Houston, Texas, in 1947, but from the age of ten through graduate school, lived in Los Angeles. At the University of California, Los Angeles, he earned a B.A. in Design in 1970, the M.A. in Graphic Design in 1972, and the M.F.A. in Graphic Communication in 1973. His academic history notwithstanding, he soon found commercial design boring and in 1975, went to Nairobi, Kenya, as a lecturer in design. The experience of living for three years in Kenya plus travel in Africa and Europe, followed by a stint of teaching in the American South, have been important in the evolution of Taylor's art. Like many American artists of African descent, he draws on both his heritages, and more than most, he addresses his primary concerns — race and class — with a personal awareness of the shift in context and manifestations from culture to culture.

Taylor's assimilation of African art and Euro-American art history is particularly evident in his sculpture. Reductive, shaped and textured forms are amalgams of American abstraction and motifs from African art and history. The massive, carved concrete *Ba*, in a horizontal presentation, resembles an ancient talisman. However, when it was suspended by heavy ropes from a giant block-and-tackle in a 1993 gallery exhibition, evocations of American slavery and lynchings were inescapable.

In 1992 Taylor created a series of four related sculptures based on a pair of gold goddess figures found in King Tutankhamen's tomb. The four, titled *Sarcophagus for Khenememti, Kharsatha, Kher,* and *Selket,* are almost identical in their biomorphic shape although different in materials, size, and allusions. The smallest, *Selket,* suggests a precious tomb furnishing, perhaps a golden idol. Progressively larger, the other three are realized in a variety of materials that, like *Selket,* suggest transformative processes.

Since moving to Portland to accept a position on the art faculty of Lewis and Clark College, Taylor has found no reason to alter the primary concerns of his art, which have always been related to race and class. What has become important to him in the Northwest is the soft, usually diffused light. The bright colors of the "haircut" series define their African context, while the muted and monochromatic surfaces of current work reflect the place of their origin.

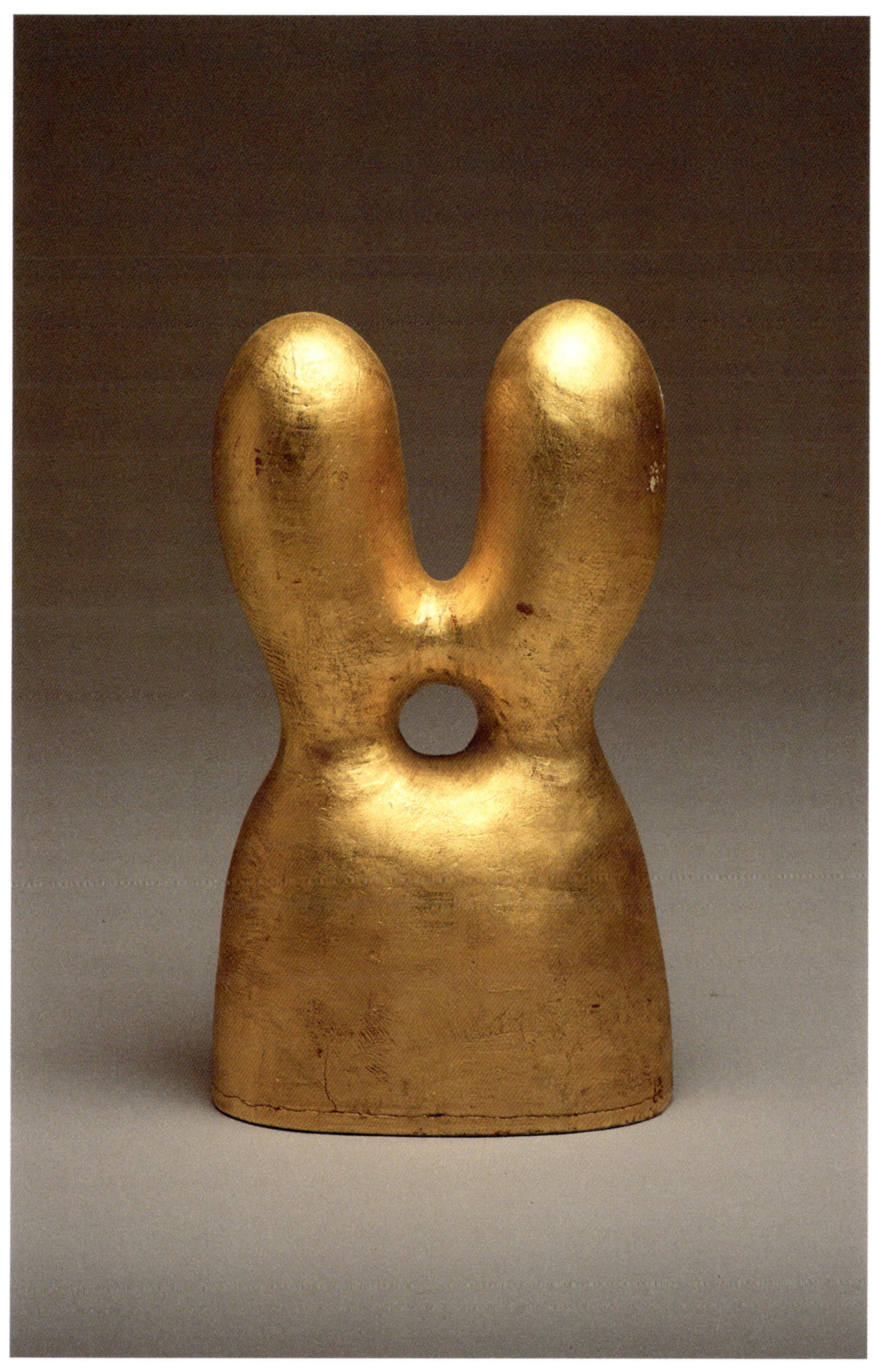

Mike Taylor **Selket**
1993, Hydrocal, gold, 21"h x 12"w x 6"d. Collection of Kally Thurmond, Hope, Idaho. Courtesy of the artist.
Photograph: Pat Burt.

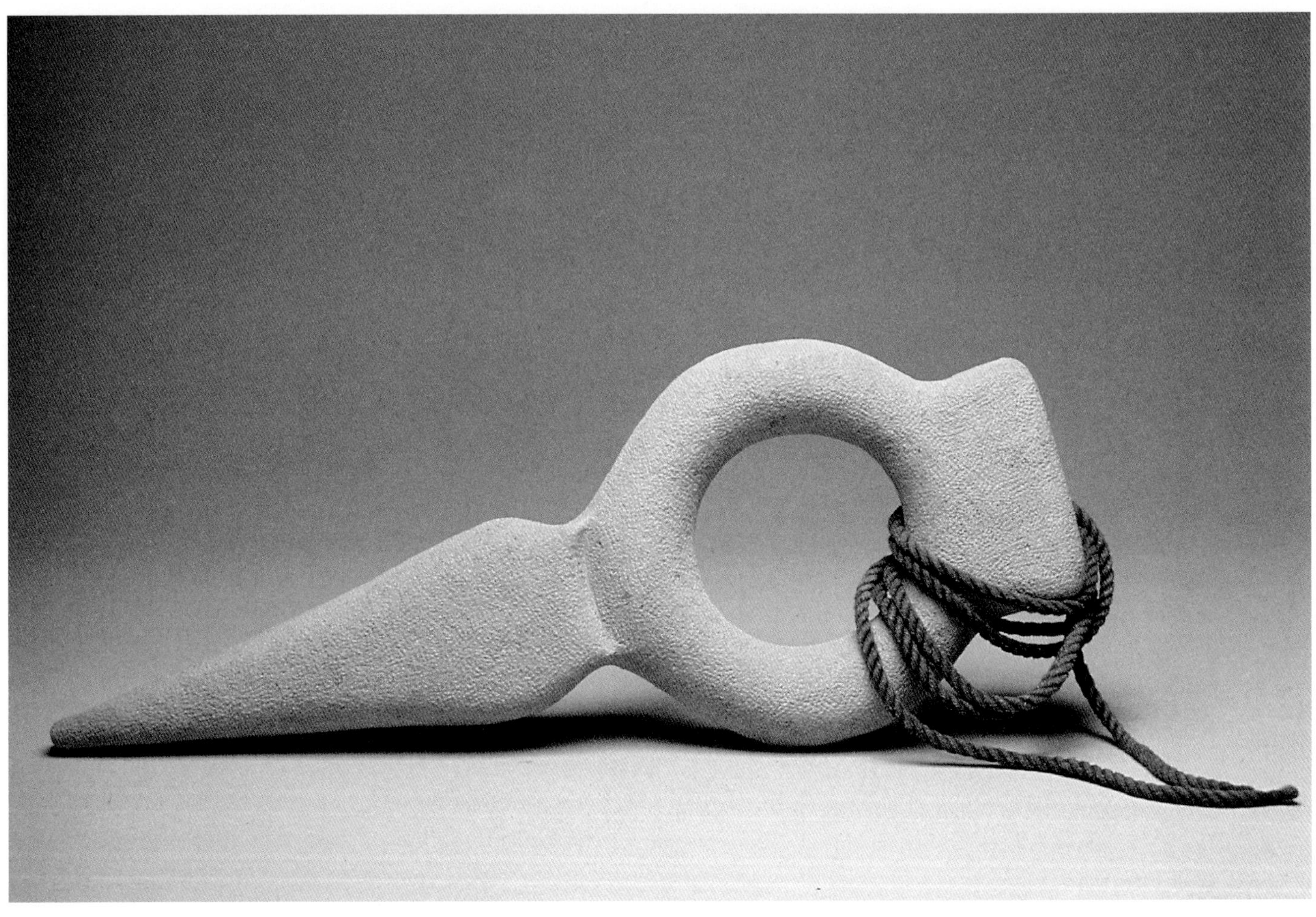

Mike Taylor **Ba**
1992, Carved concrete, block and tackle, rope, 52"h. x 32"w. x 50"d. Courtesy of the artist and Pulliam/Deffenbaugh/Nugent Gallery. Photograph: Pat Burr.

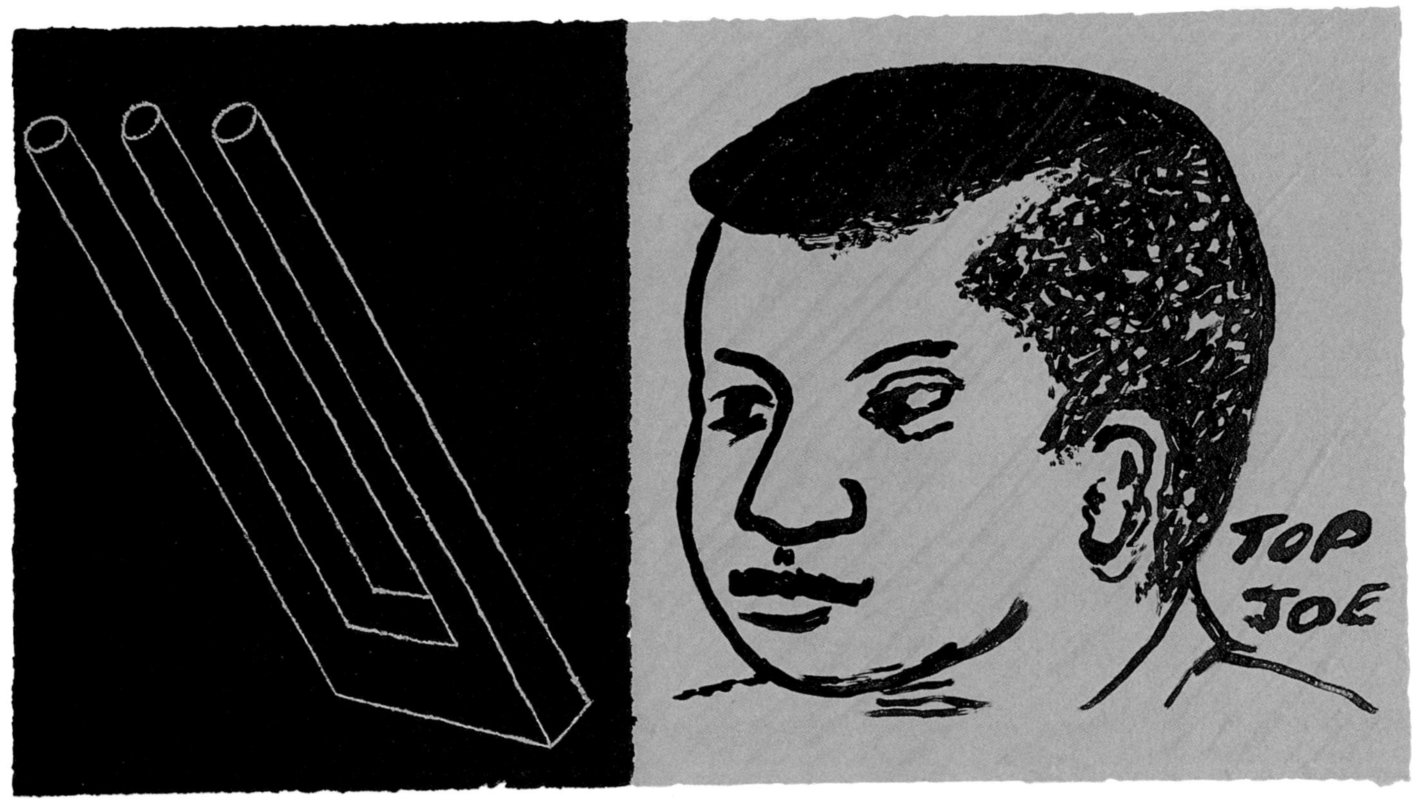

Mike Taylor **Top Joe**
1992, Oil on paper, 24" x 36". Courtesy of the artist and Pulliam/Deffenbaugh/Nugent Galery. Photograph: Pat Burr.

Terry **Toedtemeier**

Terry Toedtemeier's idiosyncratic, black and white photographs of Oregon's land formations extend the premises of both landscape and regional art. Although he is as impassioned in his love of the land as earlier Western romanticists, those epitomized by Ansel Adams, and his photographs are often equally dramatic, his work is always informed by the geologic processes that have given rise to the appearance of specific sites. Landscape, he has observed, is a thin skin stretched over the working forces of the earth. In seeking out evidence of these forces, whether in the form of a tiny, humble pothole or a magnificent basaltic arch, Toedtemeier acknowledges the vast, relentless forces far beneath the "skin" as well as the wind and water erosion and climatic atmosphere that cause the skin's wrinkles, scratches, and gouges. He has staked out a photographic domain uniquely his own where science, history, and art intersect.

During the early 1980s Toedtemeier concentrated on the Columbia Gorge. His interest had been sparked by a historical project for an exhibition at the Portland Art Museum where he is Curator of Photography. Research on the work of 19th and early 20th century photographers who had documented the Gorge led him to explore the same terrain with his own camera. Unlike the early pictorialists who imposed their ideas of spirituality and narrative on grand vistas of the Columbia River, the steep palisades, and the waterfalls, Toedtemeier looked for clues to the Gorge's geologic history and found them in sedimentary outcroppings, the deposits and flow of creeks, the unprepossessing nooks and crannies of nature's domain.

An exhibition of this series in 1986 at Reed College demonstrated the two most significant aspects of Toedtemeier's work: a low-key, almost documentary approach to his subject sites and an aesthetic sensibility that results in photographs of uncommon clarity and tonal richness. Although imagery is composed with meticulous consideration of classical balance and dynamics, the resulting beauty is purposefully somber. In both photographing and devloping his pictures he manipulates contrasts and shifts within the range of grays that will serve to reinforce the tension between the tangibly visible landscape and the unseen actions that form it.

A trained geologist and a fifth-generation Oregonian, Toedtemeier has a fascination with his immediate terrain that is as personal as it is intellectual. Born in 1947, he was a rockhound as a child and as he progressed through the education system, found himself drawn to all the earth sciences. When he settled on a geology major at Oregon State University he found himself approaching his discipline in terms of art as well as science. The camera, which at first was used to aid memory, enabled him to create a perception of the land as he experiences it in terms of its unifying forces and its awesomeness. The photographic challenge is, in essence, a matter of choosing what to photograph and how to see it, a procedure that requires much time in the field. He often re-visits a site many times in order to follow seasonal and atmospheric changes.

Toedtemeier's preferred camera, a Linhoff Technorama 612 PC with its 6 cm x 12 cm negatives, produces narrow, rectangular prints that are ideally suited to his 1992 series based on basalt formations found throughout Oregon. Enlarged and mounted as diptychs and tryptychs as well as singly, the silver gelatin prints convey an almost tactile sense of a particular place and at the same time, a formidable pictorial drama. The players in these geologic sagas are fissures and fractures, arches, caverns, chasms, and boulders, all of them bearing the weathered evidence of their participation in the earth's relentless, implacable re-forming of itself.

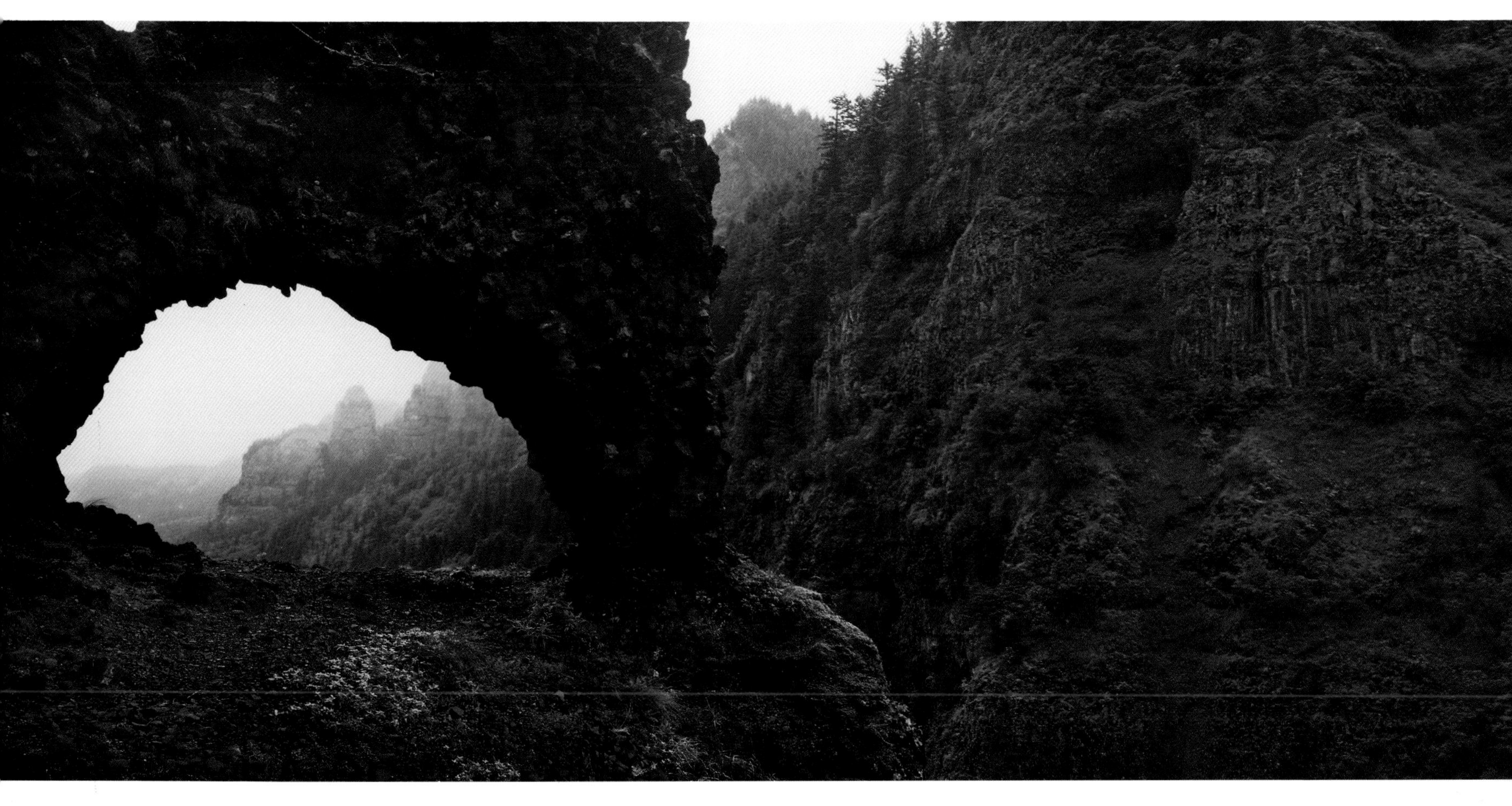

Terry Toedtemeier **Arch in Pillow Basalt, Multnomah County, Oregon**
1986, Silver gelatin print, 9" x 18". Courtesy of the artist and Elizabeth Leach Gallery.

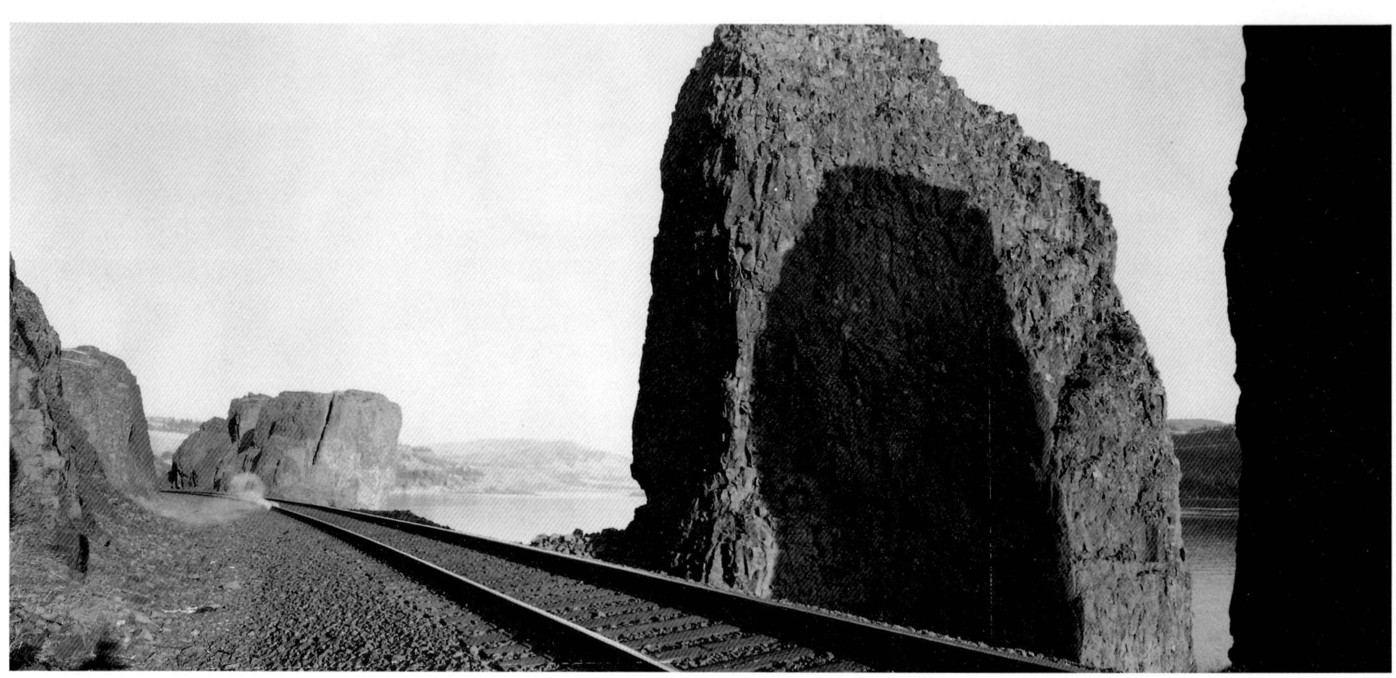

Terry Toedtemeier Burning tie, Rail-cut near Catherine Creek, Klickitat Co., Washington, October 6, 1987.
Courtesy of the artist and Elizabeth Leach Gallery.

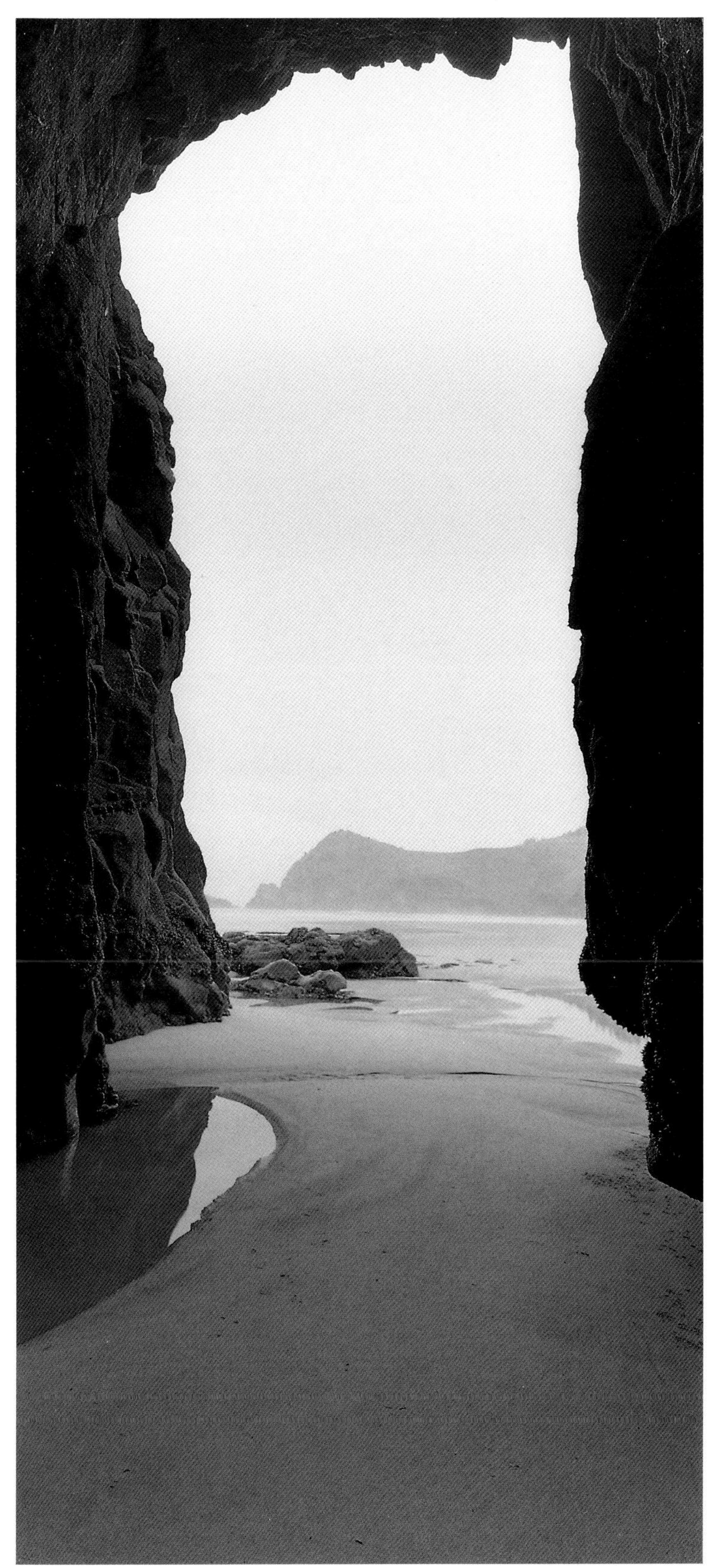

Terry Toedtemeier
Archway, Curry County, Oregon
1994, Gelatin silver print, 18" x 9".
Courtesy of the artist and Elizabeth Leach Gallery.

Patti **Warashina**

Patti Warashina's innovative forms and virtuosic handling of that most elemental of materials, clay, place her work in the vanguard of Northwest clay sculptors. From miniature narrative tableaux to monumental single figures, the refined technique and extraordinary vitalism that mark her work bring to mind very different but impressive historical precedents: Chinese grave figures, delicate, eighteenth-century European colored figurines, and in a more recent context, California "funk" ceramics. In fact, Warashina credits leading artists in the style, Robert Arneson and Ken Price, in particular, for motivating her generation to experiment with non-traditional techniques and aesthetics in establishing their own individual identities. Her experimentation, necessitated by a desire for multiple elements and glistening glazes, led to molds and the low-fire electric kilns ordinarly used by hobbyists. In extending these modest means far beyond the norm, she creates sculptures that are a unique blend of craftsmanship, social relevance, and visual energy.

Although the figures for which Warashina is best known were inspired by her personal experience as a working mother and female artist, they are witty and telling commentaries on the roles of women in American culture. She unmasks the absurdities of conflicting societal expectations as they confuse women's expectations of themselves. The result is a world of clashing rational and irrational impulses. Representational figures are placed in disjunctive contexts of fantasies and dreams, obviously surrealistic as they take playful, deconstructive aim at the Freudian symbolism that pervaded mid-century European Surrealism.

The huge — up to fourteen feet high — figures comprising her recent output are a radical departure from the preceding miniature, all white figures that populated her work for more than a decade. Although such shifts in the formation of her sculptures are routine, all the major series are related, thematically and by the humor in her perspective on cultural mores.

In 1978 Warashina began making small white, nude figures cavorting in strange tableaux or environments. With few exceptions the figures are female, recklessly animated, and laughing. The first, *Splash of Reality*, 1978, depicts a "Godiva" gleefully riding her steed, a household iron. *Flying Shrouds*, 1979, is a tableau in which a group of uninhibited sprites, partially covered with flying sheets that magically fuse with their faces, dance around a fire and plant a shepherd's crook in its center. Tableaux and figures are placed in transparent boxes, for the practical purpose of protection from breakage, but in their scale, delicacy, and isolation, they represent a Lilliputian world that is fascinatingly unreachable.

After more than a decade of continuous production, the series climaxed — and ended — in 1986 with a major piece incorporating seventy-one diminutive figures for the Seattle Opera House. Titled *Procession*, it depicts members of the city's art community as they brandish artists' tools, including brushes much longer than themselves, and climb over and around a line of toy-size white automobiles.

On completing this long, labor-intensive project Warashina was physically and mentally exhausted. Seeking creative renewal, she abandoned both monochrome and small scale works and went to the opposite extreme. The stylized, monumental, polychrome figures that resulted retain an off-beat expressiveness, but as single figures, no longer participate in surreal scenarios. A contextual placement is suggested through ornamental details and a base that makes use of legs and feet. *Woman with Birds* of 1991, for example, seems to be walking through a field of grass while the fourteen-foot-tall *Mercurial Miss* of 1994, a female Mercury created for Bellevue's Meydenbauer Center, strides across mountains, her credit card securely in hand.

Concurrently, Warashina has produced a series called *Jar Heads*, reconnecting her work to the vessel tradition in ceramics. These are thimble-shaped, larger-than-life heads featuring hair ornaments as handles for lids that cover the empty heads. The ornaments and other details convey the identity of each. The soap and soap dish on the head of *Speak No Evil*, along with the protruding tongue, suggest a certain old-fashioned, disciplinary measure for profane speech.

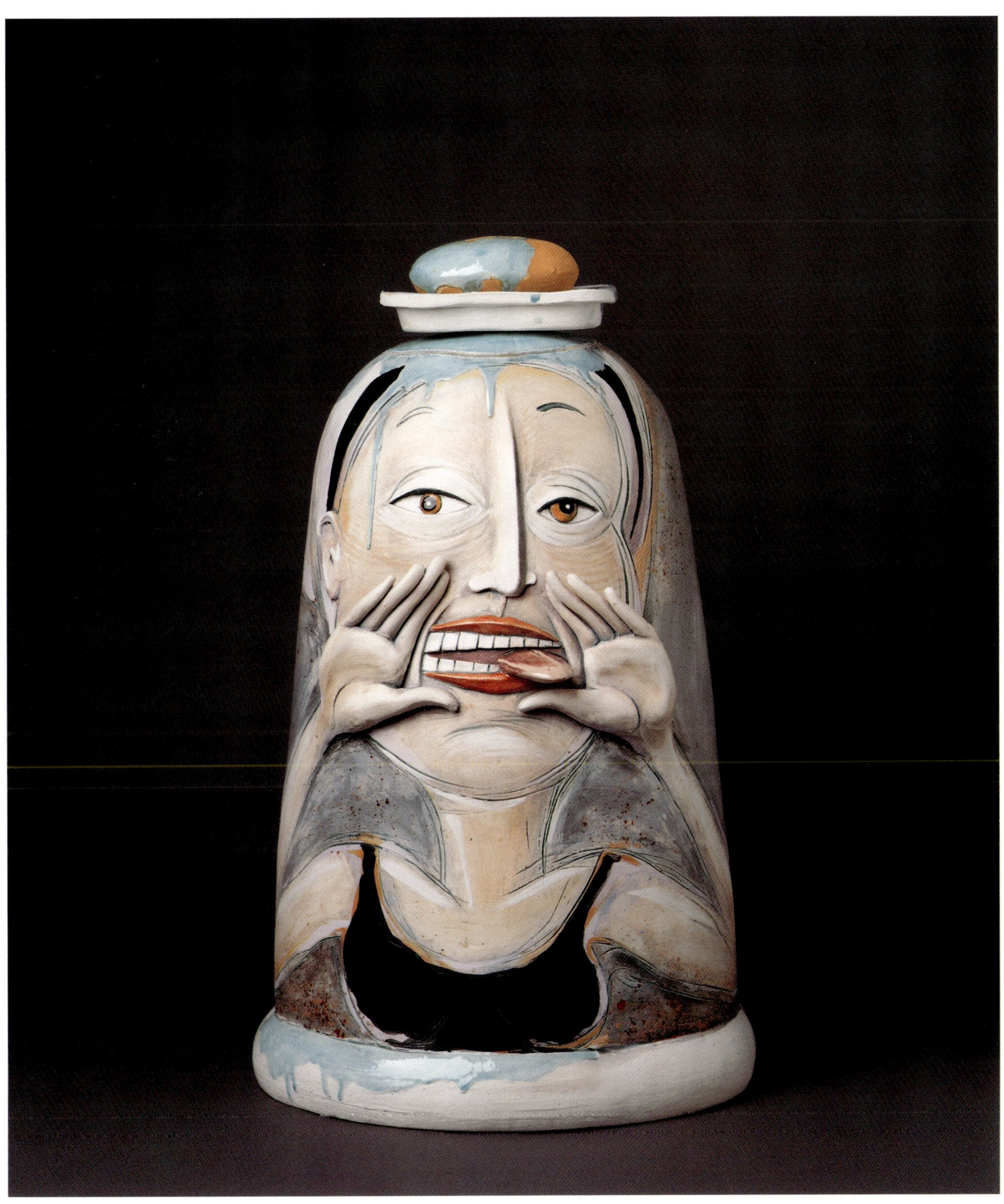

Patti Warashina **Speak No Evil**
1993, Clay and glaze, 25"h x 15" x 13". Private collection. Courtesy of the artist. Photograph: Paul Macapia.

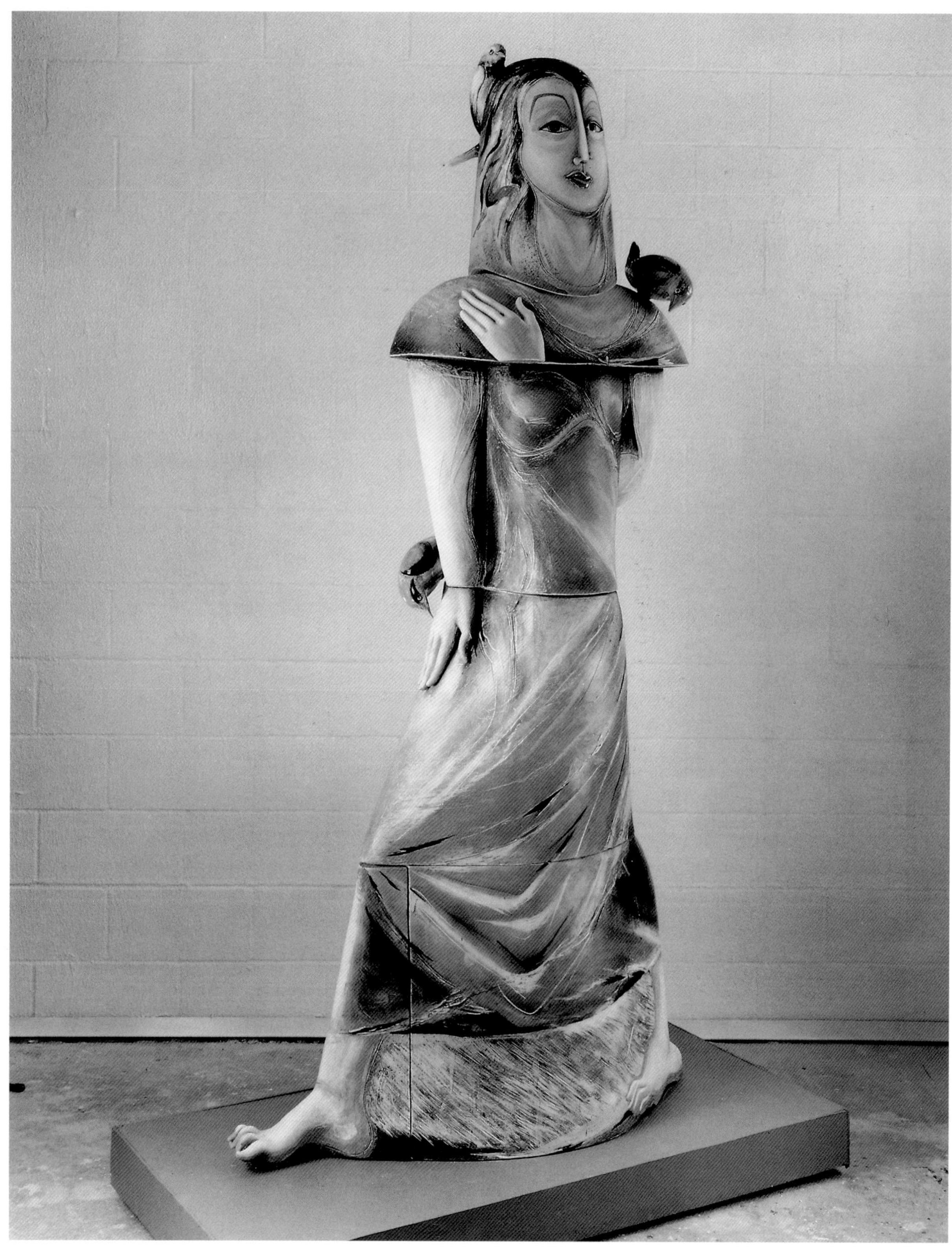

Patti Warashina **Woman With Birds**
1991, Lowfire white clay with underglaze and glaze, 95" x 46" x 25". Courtesy of the artist. Photograph: Roger Schreiber.

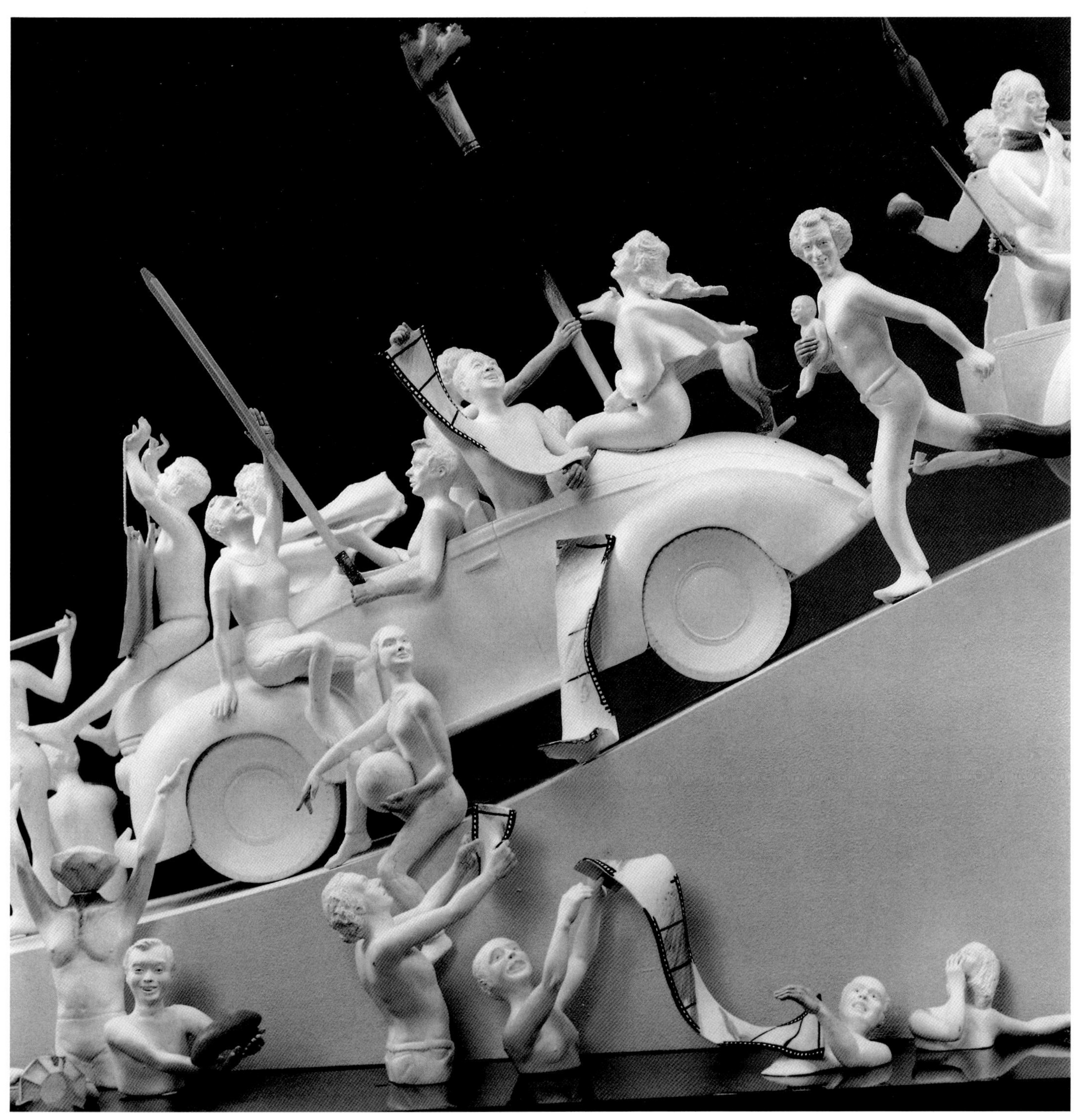

Patti Warashina **A Procession** (detail)
1986, Ceramic, 10' x 3'w. Seattle Opera House. Courtesy of the artist. Photograph: Roger Schreiber.

Artist **Biographies**

Cecilia Concepcion **Alvarez**

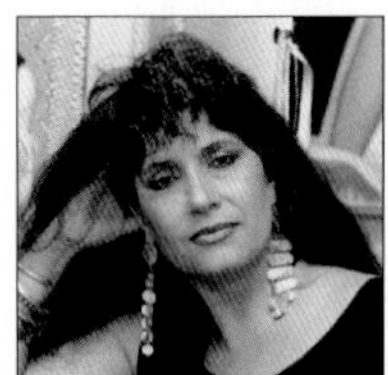

Photograph: S. Valencia

1950 Born in National City, California
Lives in Seattle

Education and Awards

San Diego State University, Sociology
1986 Juried Award, Fiestas Patrias Art Competition
1987 Certificate of Recognition, City of Seattle, Mayor Charles Royer
1992 Commission Award, Washington Arts Commission, Seattle Central Community College

Solo Exhibitions

1992 *Cecilia Alvarez*, Chase Gallery, Spokane, Washington
1991 *Sacrifices*, Whatcom Museum, Bellingham, Washington
1990 *Origins*, Goodwill Arts Festival, Seattle
1980 Women's Center, Eastern Washington University, Cheney, Washington
1973 Kaiser Foundation, San Diego
1969 Galeria Marsol, Ensebada, Mexico

Group Exhibitions

1993 *Recuentros* (international touring show), NW Touring Exhibits, Museo de Artes Contemporeanos, Santiago de Chile
1992 *1492–1992*, Seattle Art Museum
1991 *CARA*, Smithsonian Institute, Washington DC
1990 *In-Transition* (touring exhibition), Goodwill Arts Festival, Seattle
Chicano ART: Resistance and Affirmation (international touring show), Wight Art Gallery, University of California, Los Angeles
1989 Acevedo Gallery, San Diego
1987 Pacific Northwest Bell, Seattle
Bumbershoot Festival, Seattle Center
Whitman College, Walla Walla, Washington
1985 Galeria de la Raza, San Francisco
1984 *Chicano/Latino Artists in the Pacific Northwest*, Evergreen State College, Olympia, Washington
1983 Viking Gallery, Western Washington University, Bellingham, Washington
1979 Cheney Cowles Museum, Spokane, Washington
1970 Chicano Park, San Diego

Public Collections

1993 Mexican Museum, Permanent Collection, San Francisco
1992 Seattle Art Museum, Permanent Collection, Seattle

Guy **Anderson**

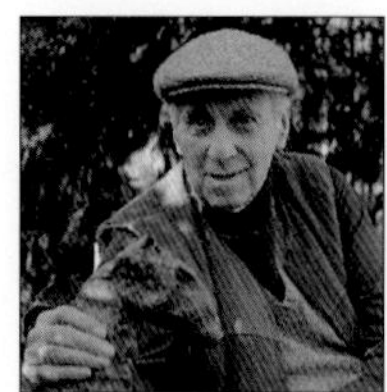

Photograph: Spike Mafford
Courtesy of Francine Seders Gallery

1906 Born in Edmonds, Washington
Lives in LaConner, Washington

Education and Awards

Private study with Eustace Ziegler, Seattle
1929 Tiffany Foundation Resident Scholarship
1969 Governor's Award of Special Commendation
1975 Solomon R Guggenheim Fellowship
1983 Governor's Art Award
1987 King Country Arts Commission's Honors Award

Solo Exhibitions

1994 *Guy Anderson & The Sea, Tracing a Theme Through Twenty Years of Work*, Francine Seders Gallery, Seattle
1992 Pulliam Deffenbaugh Nugent Gallery, Portland
1991 Pulliam Deffenbaugh Nugent Gallery, Portland
1990 Francine Seders Gallery, Seattle
1989 1001 Fourth Avenue Plaza Building, Seattle
Francine Seders Gallery, Seattle
1987 Port Angeles Fine Arts Center, Washington
Valley Museum of Northwest Art, Port Angeles, Washington
Francine Seders Gallery, Seattle
1984 Francine Seders Gallery, Seattle
1982 Francine Seders Gallery, Seattle
1980 Francine Seders Gallery, Seattle
1979 George Belcher Gallery, San Francisco
Francine Seders Gallery, Seattle
1978 Francine Seders Gallery, Seattle
1977 *Guy Anderson: Retrospective Exhibition*, Seattle Art Museum and Henry Art Gallery, University of Washington, Seattle
Francine Seders Gallery, Seattle
1975 Francine Seders Gallery, Seattle
1974 Whatcom Museum of History and Art, Bellingham, Washington
1973 Tacoma Art Museum, Washington
Francine Seders Gallery, Seattle
1971 Francine Seders Gallery, Seattle
1970 Francine Seders Gallery, Seattle
1968 Tacoma Art Museum, Washington
1965 Otto Seligman Gallery, Seattle
1963 Kenmore Gallery, Philadelphia
Otto Seligman Gallery, Seattle
1962 Smolin Gallery, New York
Michael Thomas Galleries, Beverly Hills
Orr's Gallery, San Diego
1960 Seattle Art Museum
Tacoma Art League Gallery, Washington
Harvey Welch, Portland
1959 Otto Seligman Gallery, Seattle
1957 Otto Seligman Gallery, Seattle
1954 College of Puget Sound, Tacoma, Washington
Otto Seligman Gallery, Seattle
1952 Zoe Dusanne Gallery, Seattle
1945 Seattle Art Museum
1936 Seattle Art Museum

Selected Group Exhibitions

1993 *Landscapes*, Pulliam Deffenbaugh Nugent Gallery, Portland
Northwest Masters, Foster/White Gallery, Kirkland, Washington
1992 *Skagit Valley Artists*, Valley Museum of Northwest Art, LaConner, Washington
It Figures: The Human Image in Art, Index Gallery, Clark College, Vancouver, Washington
1991 *25th Anniversary Exhibitions: The Early Years 1966–1972*, Francine Seders Gallery, Seattle
Masks of God, St Mark's Cathedral, Seattle
1990 *Views and Visions in the Pacific Northwest*, Seattle Art Museum
Northwest by Southwest: Painted Fictions, Palm Springs Desert Museum, Palm Springs, traveling to Yellowstone Art Center, Billings, Montana; Western Gallery, Western Washington University, Bellingham, Washington; Sarah Blaffer Campbell Gallery, University of Houston
1989 *In Retrospect: Twenty Five Years*, Governor's Invitational Art Exhibition, State Capital Museum, Olympia, Washington
Decade of Abstraction 1979–1989, Bumbershoot Festival, Seattle Center
1920–1960: Our Northwest Art History, Skagit Valley Museum, LaConner, Washington
1988 *A Trip Through the USA*, Francine Seders Gallery, Seattle
Contemporary Survey: A Visible Presence in the Northwest, Cheney Cowles Memorial Museum, Spokane, Washington
1987 *Seattle Style*, Musee des Beaux-Arts, Carcassonne, France
A Cameo of Northwest Watercolors, Bellevue Art Museum, Washington
1986 *Northwest Impressions: Works on Paper*, Henry Art Gallery, University of Washington, Seattle
1985 *Seattle Painting 1925–1985*, Bumberbiennale, Seattle Center, Seattle
East/West/East: The Public Art Space, Seattle Center House
Myth in Primitive and Contemporary Artists, John Pence Gallery, San Francisco
1984 *Figurative Works by Artists of the Francine Seders Gallery*, Francine Seders Gallery, San Francisco
Figurative Works, North Seattle Community College Art Gallery
Northwest Art from Corporate Collections, Waterfront Park, Pier 57, Seattle
1982 *Spiritualism in Northwest Art*, Henry Art Gallery, University of Washington, Seattle

Pacific Northwest Artists and Japan, National Museum of Art in Osaka, Japan; Seattle Art Museum
1981 *The Mind's Eye: Expressionism*, Washington Year Exhibition, Henry Art Gallery, University of Washington, Seattle
Portopia '84, An Exhibition of Washington Artists, Kobe, Japan
Governor's Invitational, State Capital Museum, Olympia, Washington
1980 *West Coast: Art for the Vice President's House*, San Francisco Museum of Art
1978 *Northwest Traditions*, Seattle Art Museum
Group Exhibition, Olin Gallery, Whitman College, Walla Walla, Washington
1977 *Northwest '77*, Seattle Art Museum
1976 *Two Centuries of Art in Washington*, State Capital Museum, Olympia, Washington
Northwest Priorities, Seattle Art Museum
Artist Friends of Mark Tobey, Francine Seders Gallery, Seattle
Figurative Works, Francine Seders Gallery, Seattle
Landscapes, Francine Seders Gallery, Seattle
1975 *Northwest Masters*, Seattle Art Museum
Northwest Painters Invitational, Museum of Art, Washington State University, Pullman
Guy Anderson, Philip McCracken, Anacortes Arts and Crafts Festival, Anacortes, Washington
Birds, Beasts, and Monsters, Francine Seders Gallery, Seattle
Governor's Invitational, State Capital Museum, Olympia, Washington
1974 *Art of the Pacific Northwest: From the 1930s to the Present*, National Collection of Fine Arts, Smithsonian Institution, Washington DC; Seattle Art Museum; Portland Art Museum
Skagit Valley Artists, Seattle Art Museum
Governor's Invitational, State Capital Museum, Olympia, Washington
1973 *Governor's Invitational*, State Capital Museum, Olympia, Washington
1972 *Anderson, Lundin, Moss, Nicholson*, Francine Seders Gallery, Seattle
1971 *The Artist and the Sea*, Whatcom Museum of History and Art, Bellingham, Washington
73rd Western Annual (Inaugural), Denver Art Museum
1970 *Drawing Society National Exhibition*, circulated by the American Federation of Arts
1969 *Annual Exhibition of Northwest Painting and Sculpture*, Seattle Art Museum (regularly since 1926)
Governor's Invitational, State Capital Museum, Olympia, Washington
1966–68 *A University Collects: Oregon-Pacific Northwest Heritage*, sponsored by the American Federation of Arts, toured USA
1966 *Thirty-Five Seattle Artists: An Exchange Between the Sister Cities*, Seattle and Kobe, Kobe Municipal Art Museum, Kobe, Japan
Governor's Invitational, State Capital Museum, Olympia, Washington
1964 *Tacoma Selects*, Tacoma Art Museum, Washington
1963 *First Governor's Annual Invitational Exhibition of Washington Artists*, State Capital Museum, Olympia, Washington
Northwest Art, University of Puget Sound and Department of Art, Tacoma
Kittredge Art Gallery, Tacoma, Washington
Governor's Invitational, State Capital Museum, Olympia, Washington
1962 *Holiday Exhibition*, Seligman Gallery, Seattle
1961 *Northwest Painters*, Museum of Art, University of Oregon, Eugene
Religious Dimensions/Art 1961, Brigham Young University Fine Arts Festival, Provo, Utah
1960 *Guy Anderson Exhibition*, Tacoma Art League Gallery, Washington
1959 *Paintings and Sculptures of the Pacific Northwest: Oregon, Washington, British Columbia*, Portland Art Museum
1957–58 *Eight American Artists*, organized by US State Department and Seattle Art Museum, and circulated in Europe and Asia
1957 *Guy Anderson with Leon Applebaum*, Otto Seligman Gallery, Seattle
Vincent Price Collects Drawings, Oakland Art Museum, Oakland, California
1947–48 *Ten Painters of the Pacific Northwest*, Addison Gallery of American Art, Philips Academy, Andover, Massachusetts

Documentaries

1983 *Upfront*, profile produced by Nancy Schewdop, KOMO TV
1982 *American Skyline*, National Public Television: contains portions of the KCTS Channel 9 documentary, *Three Artists in the Northwest* (see below: 1976)
1978 *Northwest Visionaries*, directors: Ken Levine and Nancy Keith
1976 *Three Artists in the Northwest*, production of KCTS Channel 9, producer: Jean Walkinshaw; cinematographer: Wayne Sourbee

Selected Public Collections

Art Gallery of Greater Victoria, British Columbia
Bank of California, Seattle
Betts Patterson & Mines, Seattle
Bogle & Gates, Seattle
Bothell Library, Bothell, Washington
Boymans-Van Beunigen Museum, Rotterdam, The Netherlands
Brooklyn Museum, New York
Cairncross & Hempelmann, Seattle
City of Seattle, Seattle
Danmor Company, Bellevue, Washington
Davis Wright Tremaine, Seattle
Edmonds Library, Edmonds, Washington
Foster Pepper & Shefelman, Seattle
Henry Art Gallery, University of Washington, Seattle
Hillis Clark Martin & Peterson, Seattle
Hilton Inn, Seattle-Tacoma International Airport
Junior League of Seattle
Karr Tuttle Campbell, Seattle
King Country Arts Commission, 1987 Honors Award Commission (Washington State Convention Center)
The Lakes Club, Bellevue, Washington
Meany Hall, University of Washington, Seattle
Metropolitan Museum of Art, New York
Microsoft Corporation, Redmond, Washington
Mills & Cogan, Seattle
Minor & James Medical, Seattle
Mundt MacGregor Happel Falconer Zulauf & Hall, Seattle
Municipal Gallery of Modern Art, Dublin
Munson-Williams-Proctor Institute, Utica, New York
National Museum of American Art, Smithsonian Institution, Washington DC
Opera House, Seattle Center
PACCAR, Bellevue, Washington
Pacific Northwest Bell, Seattle
Polyclinic, Seattle
Port of Seattle International Trade Center, Sea-Tac International Airport
Preston Thorgrimson Ellis & Holman, Seattle
Puget Sound Bank, Seattle
Rainer Club, Seattle
Safeco Insurance Corporation, Seattle
Saint Martin's Abbey, Lacey, Washington
Santa Barbara Museum of Art, Santa Barbara
Seattle Art Museum
Seattle Arts Commission
Seattle First National Bank, Everett, Washington
Seattle First National Bank
Seattle Public Library
Security Pacific Bank, Seattle
Skagit Valley Courthouse, Mt Vernon, Washington
Spokane Arts Commission, Spokane, Washington
State Capital Museum, Olympia, Washington
Swedish Hospital Medical Center, Seattle
Tacoma Art Museum, Washington
Tacoma Arts Commission, Washington
University of Oregon, Eugene
US Bank, Seattle
Utah Museum of Fine Arts, Salt Lake City
Washington Mutual Savings Bank
Washington State University, Pullman
Whatcom Museum of Art, Bellingham, Washington

Rick **Bartow**

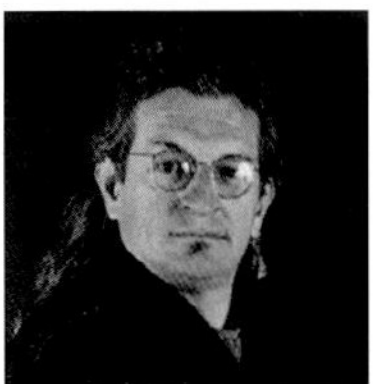
Photograph: David Cohen

1946 Born in Newport, Oregon
Lives in Southbeach, Oregon

Education and Awards

1969 Western Oregon State College, B.A.
1987 Oregon Arts Commission, Fellowship in Visual Arts
1988 Brandwine Visiting Artist Fellowship, Philadelphia
1990 Betty Bowen Special Recognition Award, *PONCHO*, Seattle Art Museum

Solo Exhibitions

1994 *My Eye, Your Eye*, Jamison/Thomas Gallery, Portland
Questions of Belief, Yanagisawa Gallery, Tokyo, Japan
The Oar of The Boat, Peiper-Riegraf Gallery, Frankfurt
Circles and Shadows, Francine Seders Gallery, Seattle
Four Songs To Sing, Gallery of Tribal Art, Vancouver
1993 *Truth Abandoned*, Gallery of Tribal Art, Vancouver
Visiting Artist Series, Clatsop Community College, Astoria, Oregon
Art In the Governor's Office, State Capitol, Salem, Oregon
1992 *Wings and Sweat*, Jamison/Thomas Gallery, Portland
Oregon Spotlight '92, Coos Art Museum, Coos Bay, Oregon
Drawings, Paintings, Masks, Sun Valley Center Gallery, Ketchum, Idaho
1991 *Stories*, Jamison/Thomas Gallery, Portland

1990 *Rick Bartow: Drawings and Dance Masks*, Rutgers Barclay Gallery, Santa Fe, New Mexico
Recent Work, Jamison/Thomas Gallery, Portland
Rick Bartow Drawings, Chase Gallery at City Hall, Spokane, Washington
Rick Bartow Drawings, Fairbanks Gallery at City Hall, Spokane, Washington
1989 Recent Drawings and Sculpture, Jamison/Thomas, New York
Recent Work, Salishan Lodge, Gleneden Beach, Oregon
Drawings, Susan Cummins Gallery, Mill Valley
1988 *Works on Paper*, Jamison/Thomas Gallery, Portland
Jamison/Thomas Gallery, New York
1987 *Man in a Box*, Jamison/Thomas Gallery, Portland
Marianne Partlow Gallery, Olympia, Washington
Jamison/Thomas Gallery, New York
American Indian Contemporary Art Gallery, San Francisco
1986 Jamison/Thomas Gallery, Portland
Sacred Circle Gallery, Seattle
1985 Jamison/Thomas Gallery, Portland
Mask Exhibition, Marianne Partlow Gallery, Olympia, Washington

Selected Public Collections and Commissions

1992 Governor's Arts Awards 1992, Newport, Oregon: chosen to create awards presented to recipients Oregon Corrections Division, print commissioned for Oregon Arts Commission
1991 Washington State Arts Commission, *Who We Are: Autobiographies In Art*
Heard Museum, Phoenix
Metropolitan Arts Commission, Portland
Oregon Health Sciences University, Portland
Portland Art Museum
Saks Fifth Avenue
Washington Country Public Services Building, Hillsboro, Oregon
Washington State Arts Commission

Paul **Berger**

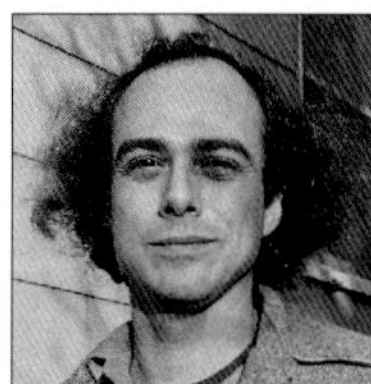

Photograph: Vick Scuri

1948 Born in the Dalles, Oregon
Lives in Seattle

Education and Awards

1970 UCLA, B.A.
1973 SUNY, Buffalo (Visual Studies Workshop), M.F.A.
1979 National Endowment for the Arts, Individual Artist's Fellowship
1986 National Endowment for the Arts, Individual Artist's Fellowship

Selected Solo Exhibitions

1993 Fuel Gallery, Seattle
1990 Seattle Art Museum
1989 USC Altier Gallery, Santa Monica
Cliff Michel Gallery, Seattle
1985 University Art Museum, UCSB, Santa Barbara
1984 California Museum of Photography, UCR, Riverside
1983 BC Space Gallery, Laguna Beach
1982 Light Gallery, New York
1980 Light Gallery, New York
Seattle Art Museum
Blue Sky Gallery, Portland
1979 Tyler School of Art, Temple University, Philadelphia
1977 Light Gallery, New York
1975 Art Institute of Chicago

Public Collections

Art Institute of Chicago
Bibliotheque National, Paris
IMP/George Eastman House
Los Angeles Country Museum of Art
Museum of Fine Art, Houston
San Francisco Museum of Modern Art

Christine **Bourdette**

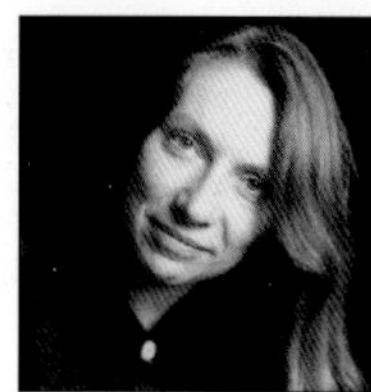

Photograph: Rebekah Johnson

1952 Born in Fresno, California
Lives in Portland

Education

1970–74 Lewis & Clark College, Portland, B.A. in Art

Solo Exhibitions

1989–94 Jamison/Thomas Gallery, Portland
1993 Hoffman Gallery, Oregon School of Arts & Crafts, Portland
1990 Bush Art Center, Salem, Oregon
1981–89 Klein Gallery, Chicago
1988 Wentz Gallery, Portland Art Museum
1987 The Art Gym, Marylhurst College, Portland
Galerie l'Aire du Verseau, Paris
1985 Trisolini Gallery, Ohio University, Athens, Ohio
Kirkland Gallery, Milliken University, Decatur, Illinois
The Art Gym, Marylhurst College, Portland
1984 Alexandria Museum, Alexandria, Louisiana
Traver Sutton Gallery, Seattle
1981 Northwest Artists Workshop, Portland
1980 Portland Art Museum, Oregon
Contemporary Crafts Gallery, Portland
1979 Wentz Gallery, Museum Art School, Portland
1978 Mayer Gallery, Marylhurst College, Portland
1977 Northview Gallery, Portland Community College, Oregon Pence Gallery, Davis, California

Public Collections

Metropolitan Arts Commission (portable collection and public sculpture at Inverness County Jail), Portland
Milliken University, Decatur, Illinois
Portland Art Museum
University of Iowa Art Museum, Iowa City
Washington State Arts Commission, Kettle Falls, Washington
Wustum Museum of Fine Arts, Racine, Wisconsin

Michael **Brophy**

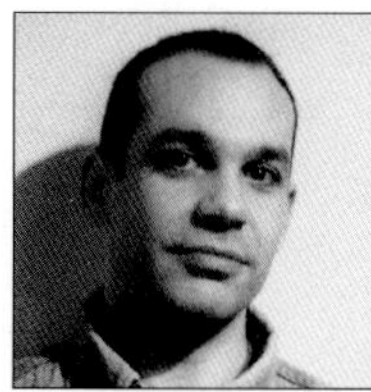

Courtesy of Laura Russo Gallery

1960 Born in Portland
Lives in Portland

Education and Awards

1978–82 University of Oregon
1983–84 Studio Arts Centers International, Florence
1985 Pacific Northwest College of Art, Portland, B.F.A.
Weiner Travel Scholarship, Pacific Northwest College of Art, Portland
1990 Western States Arts Federation, National Endowment for the Arts, Individual Artist's Fellowship
1991 Juror's Award, Oregon Biennial, Portland Art Museum
1980 Exchange Program, University of London, Humanities

Solo Exhibitions

1993 The Laura Russo Gallery, Portland
1992 The Laura Russo Gallery, Portland
1991 The Laura Russo Gallery, Portland
1989 Quartersaw Gallery, Portland
1988 Quartersaw Gallery, Portland
1987 Quartersaw Gallery, Portland

Public Collections

Beaverton Arts Commission, Beaverton City Hall, Beaverton, Oregon
City Center Parking, Oregon Trail Building, Portland
City Center Parking, Postal Building, Portland
Copeland Landye Bennett & Wolf, Portland
Mentor Graphics, Hillsboro, Oregon
Metropolitan Arts Commission, Portland
Microsoft Corporation, Redmond, Washington
Morse & Bratt, Vancouver, Washington
Tonkon, Torp, Galen, Marmaduke & Booth, Portland
USHIO, Newberg, Oregon
Washington State Art in Public Places Program, Seattle Community College, District Offices, Seattle
Washington State Arts Commission, Centennial Elementary School, Graham, Washington

Beliz **Brother**

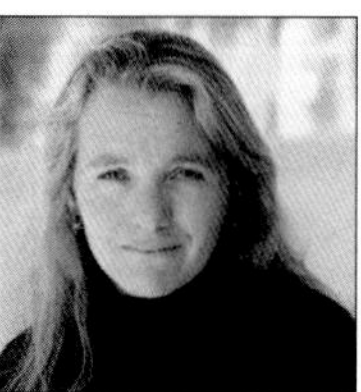

Photograph: Barbara Penoyar

1950 Born in Connecticut
Lives in Seattle

Education and Awards

1968–72 Prescott College, Prescott, Arizona, B.F.A., Apprenticeship with photographer Frederick Sommer
1987 New Langton Arts, NEA/Rockefeller Interdisciplinary Project Grant

Washington State Arts Commission, Project Grant
King County Arts Commission, *Performa '87* Project Grant
1988 Pilchuck Glass Center, John Hauberg Award
1989 Allied Arts Foundation Project Grant
Artist Trust Cap Grant
National Endowment for the Arts, InterArts Grant
1990 Artist Trust Design Fellowship
Art Matters, Inc, Grant
Adolph and Esther Gottlieb Foundation Award
Goodwill Arts Festival Individual Project Commission
NW Institute of Architecture & Urban Studies, Rome Fellowship
1991 Seattle Arts Commission, Northwest Major Works
1993 Western States Arts Federation, National Endowment for the Arts, Sculpture Fellowship
Lila Wallace & Arts International, Artist Fellowship
Artist Trust GAP Grant

Selected Solo Exhibitions and Commissioned Installations

1995 *Prison Sentences: The Prison as Site/The Prison as Subject*, Eastern State Penitentiary, Philadelphia
Documents Northwest, Seattle Art Museum
1994 *Lush Mechanique* (collaboration with choreographer Llory Wilson), On the Boards, Seattle
1993 *Welling*, Fuel Gallery, Seattle
Threshold (invitational exhibition), Bumbershoot Festival, Seattle Center
22 Adagio (sculpture installation in 22 places), Washington DC
1992 *22 Adagio* (sculpture installation at Wall of Sound and series of 22 cello performances), Seattle
Art in Public Places, Seattle Arts Commission, Five Urban Community Centers
Solarium design and artwork for Bailey Boushay AIDS Hospice (in collaboration with Mary Ann Peters), AIDS Housing of Washington, Seattle
1991 *Moving Light*, invitational exhibition, John Michael Kohler Arts Center, Sheboygan, Wisconsin
Public Art Master Plan Team and integrated artwork, Harborview Medical Center, King County Arts Commission, Seattle
Northwest Major Works Commission, Seattle Arts Commission
Interactions, invitational exhibition, Philadelphia Institute of Contemporary Art
Count (solo exhibition), New Langton Arts, San Francisco
Trace (inviational exhibition), The Art Gym, Marylhurst College, Portland
Lunasphere (public sculpture), Pier 61 & 62, Seattle
In Site (solo exhibition), Center on Contemporary Art, Seattle
1990 *Shared Site* (public sculpture), Goodwill Arts Festival, Seattle
1989–90 *This Cordate Carcass* (collaboration with choreographer Llory Wilson, sculpture and light), Sushi Gallery, San Diego; Moming, Chicago; Painted Bride, Philadelphia; Dance Theater Workshop, New York; On the Boards, Seattle
1988 *Homes for Art* (sculpture installation), 911 Contemporary Arts Center, Seattle
1987 *Seven/Uneven*, Performa '87 (collaboration with choreographer Pat Graney, sculpture and site design), Nature Preserve, Maymoor Park, Redmond, WA, King County Arts Commission
1986 *Glance* (sculpture installation), 911 Contemporary Art Center, Seattle
The distance from my heart to my soul, sculpture installation, Henry Art Gallery, University of Washington
1985 *Childrenz Muzeum* (collaboration with choreographer Pat Graney, sculpture and light), Walker Art Center, Minneapolis; Dance Theatre Workshop, New York; On the Boards, Seattle

Cris **Bruch**

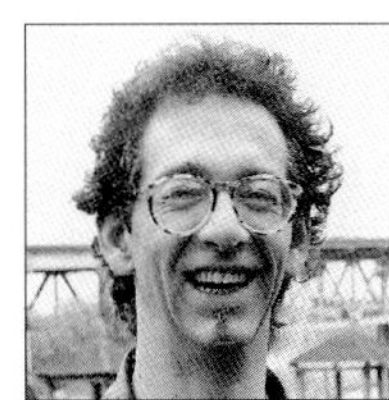

Photograph: Pat DeCaro

1957 Born in Independence, Missouri
Lives in Seattle

Education and Awards

1980 University of Kansas, B.F.A.
1985 University of Wisconsin, Madison, M.A.
1986 University of Wisconsin, Madison, M.F.A.
1990 Betty Bowen Memorial Award

Solo Exhibitions

1993 Fuel Gallery, Seattle
1992 Elizabeth Leach Gallery, Portland
1991 Fuel Gallery, Seattle
1989 Fuller/Elwood Gallery, Seattle
Oregon Art Institute, Portland
1988 Fuller/Elwood Gallery, Seattle
CAGE, Cincinatti

Commissions

1991 *In Public: Seattle 1991*
1989 Northwest Major Works

Public Collections

Seattle Portable Works
Bogle & Gates
Davidson College

George **Chacona**

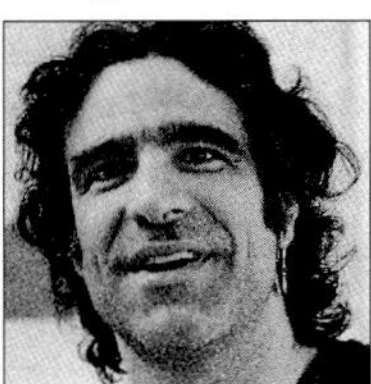

Photograph: Christian Staub

1948 Born in Erie, Pennsylvania
Lives in Seattle

Education and Awards

San Jose State College
1991 Northwest Major Works, Seattle Arts Commission
1989 SeaFirst Faculty Excellence Award, Cornish College of the Arts, Seattle
1989 Art Matters, Inc, New York
1988 Artist Fellowship Award, Washington State Arts Commission
1987 Artist in Residence, Centrum Foundation at Fort Worden, Port Townsend, Washington
1987 Betty Bowen Memorial Award, Seattle Art Museum
1983 911 Contemporary Arts Center, Seattle, Artist Grant

Solo Exhibitions

1994 *Shadow Caste*: A Retrospective, Cheney Cowles Museum, Spokane, Washington
Out of Touch, William Traver Gallery, Seattle
1993 *Detained*, The Art Gym, Marylhurst College, Portland
Detained, Elizabeth Leach Gallery, Portland
1992 *Who Came First*, William Traver Gallery, Seattle
Not for Sale, Elizabeth Leach Gallery, Portland
1991 *Starcrossed*, Elizabeth Leach Gallery, Portland
1990 *Like a Ghost*, Daniel Saxon Gallery, Los Angeles
Event Horizon, William Traver Gallery, Seattle
Something in the Wind, Elizabeth Leach Gallery, Portland
1989 *After Seven Lustres*, William Traver Gallery, Seattle
1988 *Eclipse of Reason*, Seattle Art Museum
1987 *Out of the Blue (The Vain Hope)*, Traver Sutton Gallery, Seattle
1986 *An Air of Lush Decay*, Traver Sutton Gallery, Seattle
The Harmonic Tremor (The Prelude), Traver Sutton Gallery, Seattle
1985 *Hidden Danger*, Pitt International, Vancouver
1984 *A Narrow Escape*, Traver Sutton Gallery, Seattle
1983 *Will You Still Love Me Tomorrow?*, Donnally-Hayes Gallery, Seattle
The Loose End, 911 and/or Gallery, Seattle
1982 *This End Up*, Rosco Louie Gallery, Seattle
1981 *Remains To Be Seen*, Rosco Louie Gallery, Seattle
1980 *Portrait of a Patsy*, Rosco Louie Gallery, Seattle
1979 *Liars in State*, Rosco Louie Gallery, Seattle

Selected Group Exhibitions

1992 *Betty Bowen Legacy*, Security Pacific Gallery, Seattle
Art Discussing Life, University of Idaho, Moscow, Idaho; Paris Gibson Square, Great Falls, Montana
Scared Forms Revisited, Security Pacific Gallery, Seattle
1990 *In Transit*, Metro bus signs, organized by Donald Fels, Seattle
God and Country, Greg Kucera Gallery, Seattle
1989 *Miniatures*, Elizabeth Leach Gallery, Portland
1988 *Betty Bowen Memorial Award 10th Anniversary Exhibition*, Seattle Art Museum
Contemporary: A Visible Presence in the Northwest, Cheney Cowles Museum, Spokane, Washington
Off the Wall: Mixed Media Reliefs, Elizabeth Leach Gallery, Portland
1987 *Northwest '87*, Seattle Art Museum
Source, Davidson Gallery, Seattle
Viewing the Figure/Reflecting on the Self, University of Idaho, Moscow, Idaho
1986 *15th Avenue Studio: Art and Process*, The Henry Gallery, University of Washington, Seattle
1985 *Bumberbiennale*, Bumbershoot Festival, Seattle Center
Neo York, Center on Contemporary Art, Seattle
Seattle Sampler, Pacific Lutheran University, Tacoma, Washington
1984 *Surface, Material, Structure*, Hodges Banks Gallery, Seattle
Seattle, Now, Art Gallery of Greater Victoria, Victoria, British Columbia
Crime and Punishment, Triton Museum of Art, Santa Clara, California
Agit-Prop, Etc, Friction Gallery, Portland

1981 *Greatest Hits*, Rosco Louie Gallery, Portland
Paintings, Drawings, and Prints, Ft Steilacoom Community College, Tacoma, Washington
Color Xerox Annual, Intersection Gallery, San Francisco
1980 *Elvis and Marilyn Invitation*, Rosco Louie Gallery, Seattle

Dale Chihuly

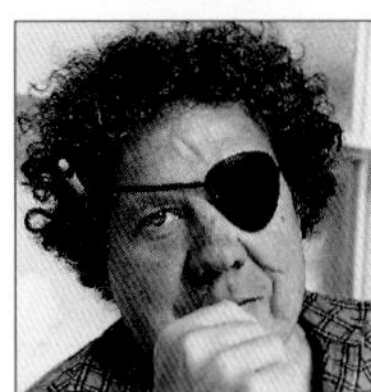

Photograph: Jim Ball

Born in Tacoma, Washington
Lives in Seattle

Education and Awards

1965 University of Washington, Seattle, B.A.
1967 University of Wisconsin, Madison, M.S.
1968 Rhode Island School of Design, Providence, M.F.A.
1968 Fulbright Fellowship to Murano, Italy
1975 National Endowment for the Arts, Individual Artist's Fellowship
1984 American Council for the Arts, New York, Visual Artist's Award
1985 Governor's Art Award, Washington
1986 Honorary Doctorate, Rhode Island School of Design
1988 Honorary Doctorate, California College of Arts and Crafts, Oakland

Solo Exhibitions

1992 Seattle Art Museum
American Craft Museum, New York
1991– Umeleckoprumsylove Museum, Prague, Czechoslovakia
1992 Museum fur Kunst und Gewerbe, Hamburg, Germany
Glasmuseum Ebeltoft, Denmark
1990 Azabu Museum of Arts and Crafts, Tokyo
1989 Museum Boymans-van Bueningen, Rotterdam, The Netherlands
Sao Paulo Biennial, Sao Paulo, Brazil
1988 Dia Art Foundation, Bridgehampton, New York
1987 Musee Matisse, Chateau-Cambresis, France
1986 Musee des Arts Decoratifs, Palais du Louvre, Paris
1984 Bellevue Art Museum, Washington (traveling exhibition to thirteen museums in the United States and Canada)
1981 Lobmeyr Museum, Vienna
1979 Museu de Arte, Sao Paulo, Brazil
1978 Renwick Gallery, Smithsonian Institution, Washington DC
1975 Institute of American Indian Arts, Santa Fe, New Mexico
1971 Museum of Contemparary Crafts (with James Carpenter), New York

Public Collections

Albright-Knox Art Gallery, Buffalo, New York
American Craft Museum, New York
American Embassies, London and Paris
Art Gallery of Greater Victoria, Victoria, British Columbia
Australian National Gallery, Canberra, Australia
Azabu Art and Crafts Museum of Tokyo, Japan
Boston Museum of Fine Arts
Chase Manhattan Bank, New York
Cleveland Art Museum
Columbia Tower Club, Seattle
Contemporary Arts Center of Hawaii
Cooper-Hewitt Museum, Smithsonian Institution National Museum of Design, New York
Corning Museum of Glass, New York
Detroit Institute of Arts
Galerie d'Art Contemporain, Nice, France
Glasmuseum Ebeltoft, Denmark
Glasmuseum Wertheim, Germany
Hokkaido Museum of Modern Art, Hokkaido, Japan
Honolulu Academy of Art
IBM Corporation, New York
Israel Museum, Jerusalem
Johnson Wax Collection, Racine, Wisconsin
Kestner Museum, Hannover, Germany
Kunstindustrimuseum Kopenhagen, Denmark
Kunstmuseum, Dusseldorf, Germany
Lobmeyr Museum, Vienna
Los Angeles County Museum of Art
Metropolitan Museum of Art, New York
Microsoft Corporation, Redmond, Washington
Musee des Arts Decoratifs, Lausanne, Switzerland
Musee des Arts Decoratifs, Palais du Louvre, Paris
Museum Bellerive, Zurich, Switzerland
Museum Boymans-Van Beuningen, Rotterdam, The Netherlands
Museum fur Kunst und Gewerbe, Hamburg, Germany
Museum of Art, Rhode Island School of Design, Providence
Museum of Contemporary Art, Chicago
Museum of Modern Art, New York
National Georgraphic Society, Washington DC
National Museum of American History, Smithsonian Institution, Washington DC
National Museum of Modern Art, Kyoto, Japan
National Museum, Stockholm, Sweden
Philadelphia Museum of Art
Provincial Musee Sterckshof, Antwerpen, Belgium
The Prudential Insurance Company of America, Newark, New Jersey
Queensland Art Gallery, Brisbane, Australia
Renwick Gallery, Smithsonian Institution, Washington DC
San Francisco Museum of Modern Art
Seaman's Bank, New York
Seattle Art Museum
Seattle First National Bank
Suomenlasimuseo, Riihimaki, Finland
Umeleckopromsylove Museum, Prague, Czechoslovakia
US News & World Report, Washington DC
Victoria and Albert Museum, London
Walker Hill Art Center, Seoul, Korea
Whitney Museum of American Art, New York
Yale University Art Gallery, New Haven, Connecticut
Yokohama Museum, Japan

Public Architectural Installations

Chancellor Park, San Diego
Corning Museum of Glass, New York
GTE World Headquarters, Dallas
Hyatt Hotel, Adelaide, Australia
IBM Corporation, New York
Pacific First Centre, Seattle
Rainbow Pavilion, Rockefeller Center, New York
Frank Russell Building, Tacoma, Washington
Seattle Aquarium, Seattle
SS *Oceanic Grace*, Tokyo
Shaare Emeth Synagogue, St Louis
Sheraton Seattle Hotel and Towers, Washington
Tacoma Art Museum, Washington
Tacoma Financial Center, Washington
Yasui Konpira-gu Shinto Shrine, Kyoto, Japan
Tropican Products, Inc, Bradenton, Florida
United States Border Station Blaine, Washington

Judy Cooke

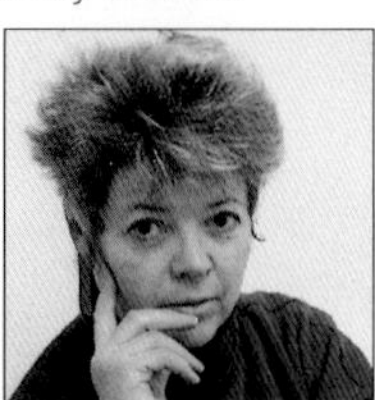

Photograph: David Browne
Courtesy of Elizabeth Leach Gallery

1940 Born in Bay City, Michigan
Lives in Portland

Education and Awards

1963 Diploma with Honors in Printmaking, School of the Museum of Fine Arts, Boston
1965 Tufts University, Medford, Massachusetts, B.F.A.
1970 Reed College, Portland, M.A.T., 1971
1974 Fellowship for Painting, School of the Museum of Fine Arts, Boston
1989 National Endowment for the Arts, Visual Fellowship Grant for Painting
Atlantic Center for the Arts, New Smyrna Beach, Florida (associate to Joan Snyder)
1993 Bonnie Bronson Fellowship Award, Portland
1994 Edvard Munch Residency Award, Oslo, Norway, 1996

Solo Exhibitions

1995 Linda Hodges Gallery, Seattle
Elizabeth Leach Gallery, Portland
1993 Elizabeth Leach Gallery, Portland
1991 Elizabeth Leach Gallery, Portland
1989 Traver Gallery, Seattle
1987 Elizabeth Leach Gallery, Portland
1985 Traver Gallery, Seattle
1983 Blackfish Gallery, Portland
1982 Blackfish Gallery, Portland
1979 Blackfish Gallery, Portland
1978 Foster/White Gallery, Seattle

Selected Group Exhibitions

1994 *Eyes on Public Art*, Seattle Center Pavillion, Seattle
1990 Esther Saks Gallery, Chicago
1988 *De Warande* (traveling exhibition through France and Japan)
1987 *Northwest Art Today*, Seattle Art Museum
1984 San Jose Institute of Contemporary Art
1980 *Northwest Artists: A Review*, Seattle Art Museum

Public Collections

Bank of America, San Francisco
Hewlett Packard, Portland
Itell Corporation, San Francisco
Management Compensation Group NW, Portland
Microsoft Corporation, Redmond, Washington
Orbanco Financial Services Corporation, Portland
Physio-Control Corporation, Seattle
Seattle City Light Portable Works Collection, Seattle
Tonkin Torp and Galen, Attorneys, Portland

Dennis Cunningham

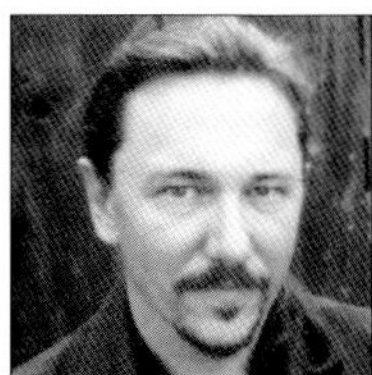

Photograph: Anne Storrs

1949 Born in Medford, Oregon
Lives in Portland

Education and Awards

1975 Museum Art School, Portland, B.F.A.
1988 Western States Arts Federation, National Endowment for the Arts, Fellowship in Printmaking
1991 Award for Design Cooperation, Boston Society of Architects
1992 Oregon Arts Commission, Individual Artist's Fellowship

Solo Exhibitions

1994 *Multiple Images*, Pauling Gallery, Clackamas Community College, Oregon City
1993 *Drawings*, Jamison/Thomas Gallery, Portland
Art In the Governor's Office, State Capitol Building, Salem, Oregon
1991 *Big Fish Eats Little Fish and Other Tales*, Jamison/Thomas Gallery, Portland
1990 Lane Community College, Eugene, Oregon
1989 Jamison/Thomas Gallery, Portland
Northwest Viewpoints, Portland Art Museum
1988 Cabel Center, Catlin Gable School, Portland
1987 Pauling Gallery, Clackamas Community College, Oregon City
1985 Mayer Gallery, Marylhurst College, Portland
Blackfish Gallery, Portland
1984 Oregon State University, Corvallis, Oregon
Empire Gallery, Pendleton, Oregon
1983 Lawson Gallery, San Francisco
Blackfish Gallery, Portland
1982 Eastern Oregon Oregon State College, LaGrande, Oregon
1981 Blackfish Gallery, Portland
1980 Pearl Wright Gallery, Manning, Oregon

Public Collections and Commissions

1977–85 Art in Public Places Projects, Metropolitan Arts Commission, Portland
1986–88 Central Square Modernization Project, Massachusetts Transit Authority
1988–90 Oregon Convention Center Project, Oregon Arts Commission, Portland
Arts on the Line, Central Square Station, Massachusetts
City of Portland Art in Public Places Collection
City of Seattle Portable Works Collection
Colorado Council for the Arts and Humanities, Boulder
Gonzaga University, Spokane, Washington
Holladay Park memorial Hospital, Portland
Kaiser Permanente Collection, Portland
Mt Olive Lutheran Chruch, Forest Grove, Oregon
Mentor Graphics Collection, Portland
Oregon Arts Commission
Oregon Health Sciences Univesity, Portland
Oregon State Arts Commission
Pacific Corporation, Portland
Public Library, City of Lake Oswego, Oregon
St Vincent's Hospital, Portland
Security Pacific Bank, Portland
US National Bank, Portland
The Visual Chronicle of Portland
Washington State Arts Commission
West One Bank, Boise, Idaho

Fernanda D'Agostino

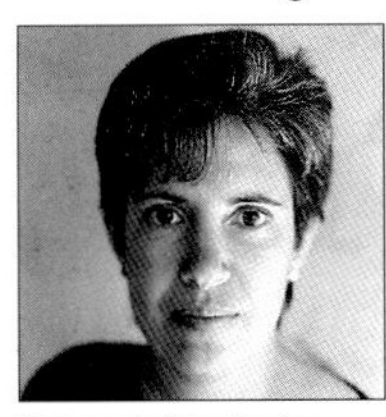

Photograph: Brian Foulkes
Courtesy of the Elizabeth Leach Gallery

1950 Born in Trenton, New Jersey
Lives in Portland

Education and Awards

1968–70 George Washington University
1971–73 Trenton State College, New Jersey, B.S.
1981–84 University of Montana, M.F.A. in ceramics
1984 Montana Arts Council, Individual Artist's Fellowship
1985 Finalist, Fullbright Fellowship
1986 Finalist, Rome Prize Fellowship
1987 Oregon Arts Council, Individual Fellowship
1991 New Genres Grant, Vermont Arts Council
1992 Metropolitan Arts Council, Portland, Project Grant
1993 Viewers' Choice Award, Crosscut, Portland Art Museum

Exhibitions and Performances

1994 *Fate* (with Kristy Edmunds), Elizabeth Leach Gallery, Portland
1993 *Abundance and Scarcity* (outdoor installation), Marylhurst College, Oregon
1992 *Translations*, Elizabeth Leach Gallery, Portland
1991 *Travellers' Rest* (in collaboration with Dennis Kitz: sound), Randolf, Vermont
1989 *Offering*, The Art Gym, Marylhurst College, Portland
Elizabeth Leach Gallery, Portland
1986 *In Bocca Al Lupo* (installation with sound by Dennis Kitz), Yellowstone Art Center, Billings, Montana
1985 *Myth Makers*, Hockaday Center for the Arts, Kalispell, Montana
1984 *La Conoscenza della Nonna* (installation), Gallery of Visual Arts, University of Montana
1983 *Animal Magnetism*, (performance with Sarah Craige), Paris Gibson Square, Great Falls, Montana

Marita Dingus

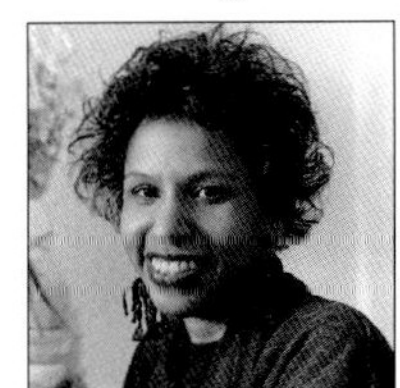

Photograph: Spike Mafford
Courtesy of Francine Seders Gallery

1956 Born in Auburn, Washington
Lives in Seattle

Education and Awards

1977 Temple University Abroad, Rome
1980 New York Visual Art Institute, Summer in Morocco, Tangier, Morocco
Tyler School of Art, Temple University, Philadelphia, B.F.A.
1984 San Jose State University, M.A.
1985 San Jose State University, M.F.A.
1992 National Endowment for the Arts, Travel Grant, National Council for Black Studies, First International Conference, Accra, Ghana (1993)

Selected Solo Exhibitions

1994 *Boundless Spirits*, Francine Seders Gallery, Seattle
Festival Sundiata, Seattle Center; The Newmark, Seattle
1992 Esvelt Gallery, Columbia Basin College, Pasco, Washington
Upstairs Gallery, Francine Seders Gallery, Seattle
1991 Francine Seders Gallery, Seattle
Recent Work by Marita Dingus, Foundation Gallery, Skagit Valley College, Mount Vernon, Washington
1990 Index Gallery, Clark College, Vancouver, Washington
1989 Ankrum Gallery, Los Angeles
1988 Shaiman Contemporary Crafts, Seattle
1987 Shaiman Contemporary Crafts, Seattle
1986 Voodoo Art, Bechtel International Center, Stanford University, Stanford
Shaiman Contemporary Crafts, Seattle
1985 Afro-American Cultural Museum, San Francisco
Masters of Fine Arts Exhibition, San Jose
1984 Bachelors of Fine Arts Exhibition, Philadelphia

Selected Group Exhibitions

1994 *A Matter of Colors III, The African Connection*, Pacific Arts Center, Seattle Center
Artistry From Her Soul, Art Gallery, Seattle Central Community College
Edwin T Pratt Memorial Exhibition, Pratt Fine Arts Center, Seattle
Contemporary African American Artists, The St Paul Companies, St Paul, Minnesota
1993 *Photo Manipulations*, Rental Sales Gallery, Seattle Art Museum
National Council for Black Studies, First International Conference Exhibit, Accra, Ghana
Off Course, Center on Contemporary Art, Seattle
Endowment: Refittings, Museum of History and Industry, Seattle; Italia Restaurant, Seattle
Art Works for AIDS, Seattle Center Pavilion
African American Eclectic, Security Pacific Gallery, Seattle
XX: An Exhibition on the Occasion of the Women's Caucus for Art National Conference, Francine Seders Gallery II, Seattle
1992 *Di Dia De Los Muertos, Day of the Dead*, Rental Sales Gallery, Seattle Art Museum
From Media to Metaphor: Art About AIDS, Center on Contemporary Art, Seattle
The Art to the People Project, traveling in Seattle: Garfield High School, Mount Zion Baptist Church, Rainier Beach High School, Seattle Central Community College
Carnival Arts, Rental Sales Gallery, Seattle Art Museum
Four Points of View, Esvelt Gallery, Columbia Basin College, Pasco, Washington
Edwin T Pratt Memorial Exhibition, Pratt Fine Arts Center, Seattle

1991 *Illuminations*, Museum of History and Industry, Seattle
Come to Your Senses, Bellevue Art Museum, Washington
Symbolic Selections, North Central Washington Museum and Gallery 76 at Wenatchee Valley College, Washington
25th Anniversary Exhibitions: The Later Years 1986–90, Francine Seders Gallery, Seattle
The Artist in the Art: Self-Portraits, Bumbershoot Festival, Seattle Center
Spirit Catchers, Mercer Island Art Gallery, Community Center at Mercer View, Mercer Island, Washington
Collaborators, Tacoma Art Museum, Washington
Seattle Women Artists, Seattle Central Community College Art Gallery, Seattle
A Matter of Colors, Pacific Arts Center, Seattle
1990 *Dreaming the Earth Whole*, Bumbershoot Festival, Seattle Center
Work Using Recycled Materials, Francine Seders Gallery, Seattle
Sculpture, University of Washington Medical Center, Seattle
Four Artists from the Northwest: Selected Works from the Francine Seders Gallery, The Carver Community Cultural Center, San Antonio, Texas
Ancestors Known and Unknown, organized by Coast to Coast, Art In General, New York
From Another Side: Five Artists from the Northwest, Koehler Gallery, Whitworth College, Spokane, Washington
Ancestral Sources, Pacific Lutheran University, Tacoma, Washington
Visual Arts Exhibition, Festival Sundiata, Seattle Center
Art Works for AIDS, Seattle Center Pavilion, Seattle
1989 *Fine Arts Faculty Show*, North Seattle Community College, Seattle
Some Assembly Required, Bumbershoot '89, Seattle Center
Puget Sound Black Artists, Art Gallery, North Seattle Community College, Seattle
Francine Seders Gallery, Seattle
After Africa, Two Seattle Artists—Two Installations, Spokane Arts School, Center for the Visual Arts, Spokane, Washington
Hallie Brown Ford Gallery Invitational, Williametter University, Salem, Oregon
The Masque, The Face of Woman, Charles Allis Art Museum, Milwaukee
Visual Arts Exhibition, Festival Sundiata, Seattle Center
1988 Appalachian State University, Boone, North Carolina
Artists Liaison, Evanston, Illinois
Sommerstown Gallery, Somers, New York
Art Phase I, Chicago
Living to the Rhythm of a Dream, Overeact Gallery, Long Beach
Fifth Alcoa Juried Art Exhibition, Wenatchee, Washington
Dimension '88 National, Levexa, Kansas
Paintings and Sculpture by Candidates for Art Awards, American Academy of Arts and Letters, New York
Atlanta Life Eighth Annual Art Competition, Atlanta, California
Selected Works: In Celebration of Black History Month, Francine Seders Gallery, Seattle
Seattle Urban League Competition, Seattle
Visual Arts Exhibition, Festival Sundiata, Seattle Center
1987 *Spirits in Common*, Western Washington State University, Bellingham, Washington
Northwest '87, Seattle Art Museum
Seventh Northwest International Art Competition, Whatcom Museum of History and Art, Bellingham, Washington
Alonso/Sullivan Gallery, Seattle
Mia Gallery, Seattle
Seattle Urban League Competition, Seattle
1986 *Gift Wrap Competition*, Pacific Art Center, Seattle
Mask Show, Portland School of Arts and Crafts
Furniture and Mask Show, Hundred Waters Gallery, Seattle
Bumbershoot Festival, Seattle Center
The Tallahassee National, University of Florida, Tallahassee
Weird and Witty Constructions, Marylhurst College, Portland
Salute to the Arts, Capitol Hill Arts Festival, Seattle
Visual Arts Exhibition, Festival Sundiata, Seattle Center
Seattle Urban League Competition, Seattle
1985 *The Women's Building Exhibition*, Los Angeles
San Francisco African American Historical and Cultural Society
Grand Oak Gallery, Oakland, California
San Jose State University Faculty Art Exhibition, San Jose
Small Sculpture Exhibition, Triton Museum of Art, Santa Clara, California
Bay Net '85 Art Exhibition, Stanford University
Bay Arts '85, Belmont, California
Sculpture Exhibition, San Jose Institute of Contemporary Art
Bumbershoot Festival, Seattle Center
1984 *San Francisco Art Festival*, San Francisco
San Jose Art League 3 Dimensional Exhibition, San Jose
1982 Seattle Urban League Competition, Seattle
1981 Seattle Urban League Competition, Seattle
1978 *Balboa Circle Exhibition*, Panama City
1977 Student Show, Rome

Installations

1992 *Marita Dingus, Recent Works*, Green River Community College, Auburn, Washington
1991 *Our Bill of Rights* (benefit show), Artist's Products Gallery, Seattle
1990 Sculpture, Franklin High School library, Seattle
1987 Wrapped Seattle Center, Imagination Celebration, Seattle
Wrapped Parking Meters, Capitol Hill Salute to the Arts, Seattle
1985 Wrapped Museum, San Jose Museum of Art

Public Collections

Bailey-Boushay House, Seattle
Junior League of Seattle
Seattle Arts Commission, Portable Works Collection
Washington State Arts Commission

Kristy **Edmunds**

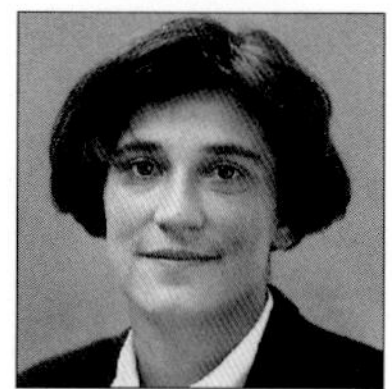

Photograph: Yalcin Erhan

1965 Born in Chelan, Washington
Lives in Portland

Education and Awards

1987 Montana State University, B.S. in Motion Picture Production
1990 Western Washington University, M.A. in Theatre
1991 Metropolitan Arts Commission, Project Grant, Interdisciplinary Arts Category
Metropolitan Arts Commission, collaboration with Helen Lessick, Project Grant, Interdisciplinary Arts Category
1993 Metropolitan Arts Commission/Oregon Arts Commission, Media Art Fellowship

Exhibitions

Butters Gallery
Blackfish Gallery
Elizabeth Leach Gallery

Commissions

1994 Portland International Performance Festival Extended & Summer Programs, Portland State University February (project completion: August 1995)
Lewis & Clark College, Theatre Department Choreography Commission
1991 North Park Blocks Renovation Project, Public Art Commission from the 1% for Art Program, Metropolitan Arts Commission, Portland

Dennis **Evans**

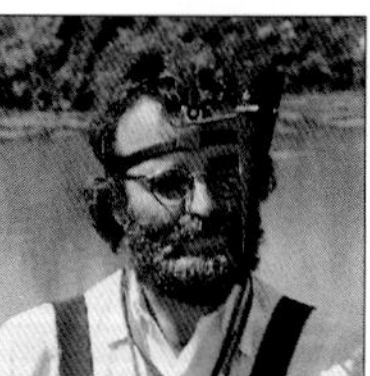

Photograph: Nancy Mee

Born in Moxee, Washington
Lives in Seattle

Education and Awards

1965–69 University of Washington, B.S. in Chemistry
1971–75 University of Washington, B.F.A. in Ceramics
1975–76 University of Washington, M.F.A. in Design
1981 National Endowment for the Arts, Individual Artist's Fellowship

Solo Exhibitions

1993 *The Science of Secrets*, Boise Art Museum, Boise, Idaho
Catagories and The Classics, The Laura Russo Gallery, Portland
1992 *The Critique of Pure Writing*, Linda Farris Gallery, Seattle
1991 *Altered Altars*, Linda Farris Gallery, Seattle
1990 *Liber Mundi Liber Vitae*, Linda Farris Gallery, Seattle
1989 *tHe gardEn foR reMembered deSires*, Linda Farris Gallery, Seattle;

Northwest Point of View Series, Portland Art Museum

1987 *Talking Pictures*, Linda Farris Gallery, Seattle

1985 *Syntax: Sintax*, Linda Farris Gallery, Seattle
Seven Halls of AeDvAeM, Seattle Art Museum

1982 *The Chymical Nuptials Of Soma and Agni or Rather the Allegory of Corny Agrippa and the Slippery Bath*, Linda Farris Gallery, Seattle

1981 *Constructions*, Pacific Lutheran University, Wekel Gallery, Tacoma, Washington,

1980 *Seven Garments and Seven Lies for the Passing of Days*, Linda Farris Gallery, Seattle
(12) Twelve Field Us(e) ages, Whatcom Museum of History and Art, Bellingham, Washington

1978 Braunstein/Quay Gallery, San Fransicso
Eastern Washington University, Gallery of Art, Cheney, Washington
Instruments and Diagrams, Linda Farris Gallery, Seattle

1977 *Soundings*, Linda Farris Gallery, Seattle
The Evergreen State College, Olympia, Washington
Portland State University, White Gallery, Portland

1976 and/or Gallery, Seattle
Musical Instruments of Dennis Evans, Henry Art Gallery, University of Washington, Seattle

Public Collections

Boise Art Museum, Boise, Idaho
The Center for Advanced Studies in the Behavioral Sciences, Stanford University, Palo Alto, California
City of Seattle, Seattle
Eastern Washington University, Cheney, Washington
Henry Art Gallery, University of Washington, Seattle
Metropolitan Museum of Art, New York
Microsoft Corporation, Redmond, Washington
Museum of Modern Art, New York
Pacific Lutheran University, Tacoma, Washington
Patrick J Lannon Foundation, West Palm Beach, Florida
Portland Art Museum
Safeco Insurance Corporation, Seattle
Seattle Art Museum
University of Delaware, Willmington
Whatcom Museum of History and Art, Bellingham, Washington

Claudia **Fitch**

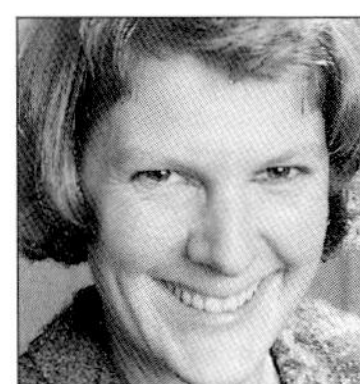

Photograph: Howard Giske

1952 Born in Palo Alto, California
Lives in Seattle

Education

1970–75 University of Washington, Seattle
1974 Yale Summer School of Music and Art
1977–79 Tyler School of Art, Philadelphia

Solo Exhibitions

1993 Cheney-Cowles Museum, Spokane
Fuel Gallery, Seattle

1992 Fuel Gallery, Seattle

1989 Munson Williams Proctor Institute Art Museum, co-sponsored by Sculpture Space, Utica

1986 Franklin Furnace, New York

1984 University of Hawaii, Honolulu
University of Tennessee, Murfeesboro

1982 Storefront for Art and Architecture, New York

1981 Franklin Furnace, New York
Window installation, New Museum of Contemporary Art, New York

1980 Artists' Resource Center, Seattle

1979 Swarthmore College, Swarthmore

Public Collections

Cheney Cowles Museum
Seattle Art Museum
Tacoma Art Museum

Gregory **Grenon**

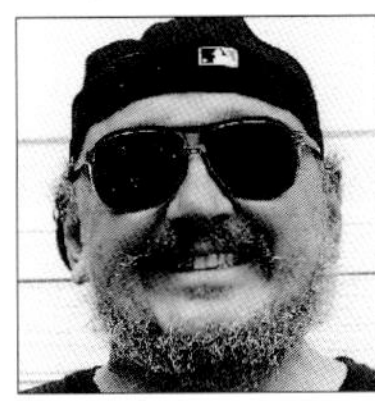

Photograph: Mary Josephson

1948 Born in Detroit
Lives in Portland

Awards

1984–85 Oregon Arts Commission, Individual Fellowship Award

1992 National Endowment for the Arts, Visual Arts Fellowship

Solo Exhibitions

1994 *We Are Not Here To Kill You*, Jamison/Thomas Gallery, Portland
First Lessons In Life, Clark Gallery, Lincoln, MA
Everything Unknown Is Grand, Gasperi Gallery, New Orleans

1993 *The Unidentified Woman*, William Traver Gallery, Seattle
Emotion Precedes Thought, Jamison/Thomas Gallery, Portland

1992 *Deep Dark Motives*, Clark Gallery, Lincoln, MA
The Woman Club, Jamison/Thomas Gallery, Portland
As Far As It Goes, Jamison/Thomas Gallery, New York
About Relationships, William Traver Gallery, Seattle

1991 *Line, Color, Emotion*, Jamison/Thomas Gallery, Portland
Moments, Gasperi Gallery, New Orleans

1990 *It's Against the Rules*, Jamison/Thomas Gallery, New York
Simple Views, Esther Saks Gallery, Chicago
Women on Women in Women, William Traver Gallery, Seattle
Women as a Second Language, Jamison/Thomas Gallery, Portland

1989 *Certain Things*, Jamison/Thomas Gallery, New York

1988 *White Women*, Jamison/Thomas Gallery, Portland
Recent Work, Jamison/Thomas Gallery, New York
Paintings and Screens, Traver Sutton Gallery, Seattle

1987 Jamison/Thomas Gallery, Portland
Jamison/Thomas Gallery, New York

1986 *Traveling Show and Growing Up*, Jamison/Thomas Gallery, Portland

1982-86 The Fountain Gallery of Art, Portland

1983-86 Traver-Sutton Gallery, Seattle

1984 *Documents Northwest: The PONCHO Series*, Seattle Art Museum
Donnally/Hayes Gallery, Seattle

1979 Portland State University, Portland

Selected Collections

Boly/Welch, Portland
Harsh Investment, Portland
Lannan Foundation, Palm Beach
Metropolitan Arts Commission, Portland
Microsoft Corporation, Redmond, Washington
Oregon Arts Commission
Oregon Health Sciences University, Portland
Phias, Schmidt, Westerdahl, Portland
Portland Art Museum
Seattle Arts Commission

Sally **Haley**

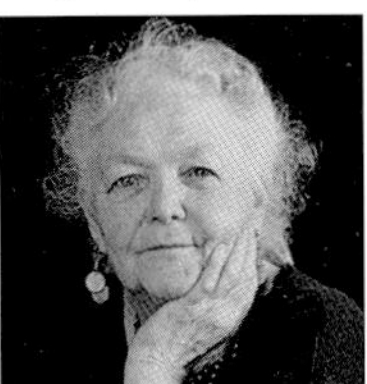

Photograph: Maryanne Caruthers

1908 Born in Bridgeport, Connecticut
Lives in Portland

Education and Awards

1931 Yale University, B.F.A.

1988 Women of Achievement Award for Artistic Excellence, YMCA, Portland

1989 The Oregon Governor's Award for the Arts

Solo Exhibitions

1993 The Laura Russo Gallery, Portland
Marylhurst College (retrospective), Oregon

1990 The Laura Russo Gallery, Portland

1985 Catlin Gabel School (retrospective), Portland
The Fountain Gallery of Art, Portland

1984 AN Bush Gallery, Salem, Oregon
The Fountain Gallery of Art, Portland
Wentz Gallery, Pacific Northwest College of Art, Portland

1981 The Fountain Gallery of Art, Portland

1980 The Fountain Gallery of Art, Portland

1979 Woodside Gallery, Seattle

1977 The Fountain Gallery of Art, Portland

1976 Governor's Office, Oregon State Capitol, Salem, Oregon
Woodside Gallery, Seattle

1975 Maryhill Museum of Fine Arts, Maryhill, Washington
Portland Art Museum (retrospective), Portland

1972 The Fountain Gallery of Art, Portland

1971 Woodside Gallery, Seattle

1965 Marylhurst College, Oregon

1962 The Fountain Gallery of Art, Portland

1960 Portland Art Museum

1942–44 Mattatuck Historical Society, Waterbury, Connecticut

1939–46 Peacock Alley, Bridgeport, Connecticut

1934 Stavoa Gallery, Hartford, Connecticut

Collections

AT & T, New York
Federal Reserve Bank of San Francisco
Kaiser Foundation, Portland

Oregon State University, Corvallis
Pacific First Bank, Portland
Pacific Northwest Bell, Seattle
Portland Art Museum
Portland Civic Auditorium, Oregon
Safeco Insurance Co, Seattle
State of Oregon Capitol Building, Salem
Willamette University, Salem, Oregon

Gaylen **Hansen**

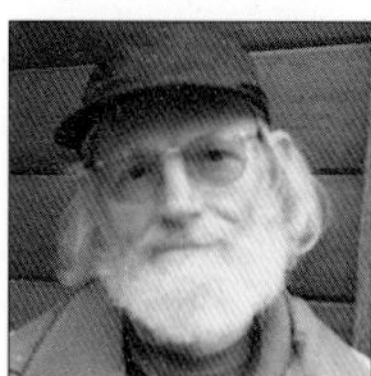

Courtesy of Linda Hodges Gallery

1921 Born in Garland, Utah
Lives in Palouse, Washington

Education and Awards

1940–44 Art Barn School of Fine Arts, Salt Lake City
1953 University of Southern California, Los Angeles, M.F.A.
1984 Sambuca Romana Prize, The New Museum, New York
1989 Governor's Arts Award, Washington State

Selected Solo Exhibitions

1995 Linda Hodges Gallery, Seattle
1994 Koplin Gallery, Los Angeles
1993 Galerie Redmann, Berlin
Linda Hodges Gallery, Seattle
1991 Galerie Redmann, Berlin, Germany
1990 The Arts Club of Chicago, Chicago
Koplin Gallery, Los Angeles
1988 Yellowstone Art Center, Billings, Montana
Linda Hodges Gallery, Seattle
The Whatcom Museum of History and Art, Bellingham, California
1987 Greg Kucera Gallery, Seattle
Galerie Redmann, Berlin
1985–6 *Gaylen Hansen Retrospective*, Seattle Art Museum; Museum of Art, Washington State University, Pullman; Museum of Art, Pennsylvania State University; Portland Center for the Visual Arts; San Jose Museum of Art
1985 Boise Gallery of Art, Boise, Idaho
1983 Monique Knowlton Gallery, New York
1981 Glenbow Museum, Calgary, Alberta, Canada
Monique Knowlton Gallery, New York
1980 Monique Knowlton Gallery, New York
1977 Fine Arts Center, Washington State University, Pullman
1975 Fine Arts Center, Washington State University, Pullman
1972 University of Colorado, Boulder
Fine Arts Center, Washington State University, Pullman
1967 Fine Arts Center, Washington State University, Pullman
1966 University of Idaho, Moscow, Idaho

Selected Group Exhibitions

1994 *Humor*, Frumpkin/Adams Gallery, New York
1993 *Northwest Art/Narrative*, Valley Museum of Northwest Art, La Conner, Washington
Microsoft Collects, Henry Art Gallery, Seattle
1991 *Northwest Tales: Contemporary Narrative Painting*, traveling exhibition, Anchorage Museum of Art, Anchorage, Alaska
1990 *Views & Visions in the Pacific Northwest*, Seattle Art Museum
Northwest by Southwest: Exploring Painted Fictions, Palm Springs Desert Museum, Palm Springs
1989 *Masters of the Inland Northwest*, Cheney Cowles Museum, Spokane, Washington
1987 *The Inland Empire*, The Braunstein/Quay Gallery, Long Beach
1985 *The Second Western Biennial*, Brooklyn Museum, New York
1984 *Painting and Sculpture Today*, Indianapolis Museum of Art
The City as Collector, Seattle Art Museum
1983 *Dogs!* (traveling exhibition), Museum of Contemporary Art, Chicago
38th Corcoran Biennial Exhibition of American Painting/Second Western States Exhibition (traveling exhibition), Corcoran Gallery of Art, Washington DC
Hassam and Speicher Fund Purchase Exhibition, American Academy and Institute of Arts and Letters, New York
1982 *Beast: Animal Imagery in Recent Painting*, Institute for Art and Urban Resources, PS 1, Queens, New York
1981 *Animals in American Art*, Nassau County Museum of Fine Art, Roslyn Harbor, New York
Contemporary Artists, Cleveland Museum of Art
1979 *Sustained Visions*, The New Museum, New York
1976 *In Touch: Nature, Ritual, and Sensuous Art from the Northwest*, Portland Center for the Visual Arts

Selected Public Collections

Boise Art Museum, Boise, Idaho
Chase Manhattan Bank, New York
Cheney Cowles Museum, Spokane, Washington
Cleveland Clinic Foundation
Honolulu Academy of Arts
Microsoft Corporation, Redmond, Washington
Museum of Art, Washington State University, Pullman
Patrick J Lannon Foundation, New York and Palm Beach
Philip Morris Companies, Inc, New York
Seattle Art Museum
Security Pacific Bank, Los Angeles
Walker, Richer Quinn , Seattle
Weyerhauser Corporation, Seattle

Robert **Helm**

1943 Born in Wallace, Idaho
Lives in Pullman, Washington

Education

1967 Washington State University, Pullman, B.A.
1969 Washington State University, Pullman, M.F.A.

Solo Exhibitions

1994 Blaffer Gallery, University of Houston
1991 Edward Thorp Gallery, New York
1987 Edward Thorp Gallery, New York
1984 LA Louver Gallery, Venice, California
Contemporary Arts Museum, Houston
Seattle Art Museum
1982 Galerie Redmann, Berlin
1978 Nicholas Wilder Gallery, Los Angeles
1977 Faith and Charity in Hope Gallery, Hope, Idaho
1976 Nicholas Wilder Gallery, Los Angeles
1974 Museum of Art, Washington State University, Pullman
1970 Nebraska Wesleyan University, Lincoln, Nebraska

Selected Group Exhibitions

1994–95 *Winter Group Exhibition*, Edward Thorp Gallery, New York
1993 *The Idaho Artists*, Moody Gallery, Houston
1992 *Northwest Tales: Contemporary Narrative Painting*, Anchorage Museum of History and Art, Alaska; travelled to University of Alaska Museum; Fairbanks Arts Association, Fairbanks; Alaska State Museum, Juneau
1991 *Gallery Group Exhibition*, L A Louver Gallery, Venice, California
Gallery Group Exhibition, Edward Thorp Gallery, New York
1990 *Selected Paintings, Drawing and Sculpture*, John Berggruen Gallery, San Francisco
Summer, Edward Throp Gallery, New York
With the Grain: Contemporary Panel Painting, Whitney Museum of American Art, Fairfield County, Stamford, Connecticut
Storyline, Edward Thorp Gallery, New York
Northwest by Southwest: Painted Fictions, Palm Springs Desert Museum, Palm Springs
1989 *Masters of the Inland Northwest*, Cheney Cowles Museum, Spokane, Washington
Summer, Edward Thorp Gallery, New York
The Contemporary American Landscape: A Certain Slant of Light, The Dayton Art Institute, Dayton, Ohio
Epiphanies, Edward Thorp Gallery, New York
100 Years of Washington Art, Galerie Redmann, Berlin
1988 *Different Drummers*, Hirshhorn Museum, Washington DC
1987 *The Inland Empire*, Braunstein/Quay Gallery, San Francisco
Group Show of Gallery Artists, Edward Thorp Gallery, New York
1987 Biennial Exhibition, The Whitney Museum of American Art, New York
Woodwork, Martina Hamilton Gallery, New York
1986 *Miracles and Mysteries*, University Art Gallery, California State University, Carson
Gallery Artists, Edward Thorp Gallery, New York
Awards in the Visual Arts Five, Neuberger Museum, Purchase, New York; traveled to Columbus Museum of Art, Columbus, Ohio; Norton Gallery and School of Art, West Palm Beach, Florida; Phoenix Art Museum

Robert **Herdlein**

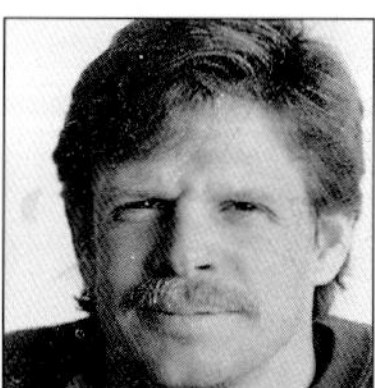

Photograph: Stephen Reip

1953 Born in Hartford, Connecticut
Lives in Kent, Washington

Education

1981 Manchester Community College, Manchester, Connecticut

Solo Exhibitions

1994 *Remember Me*, Jamison/Thomas Gallery, Portland
1993 *The Children's Crusade*, Jamison/Thomas Gallery, Portland

1992 *Rolmarrobji*, Jamison/Thomas Gallery, Portland
Seattle Artists 1991—Robert Herdlein: Great Kids' Art: Part 2, Kindsey Gallery, Seattle University
Davidson Gallery, Seattle
1991 *Ludwig Van Beethoven, Pablo Picasso and Eddie Fisher*, Jamison/Thomas Gallery, Portland
1990 *Assemblages*, Jamison/Thomas Gallery, Portland
1989 Wallingford Center Installation commissioned by 911 Contemporary Arts Center, Seattle
New Works, Henry Art Gallery, University of Washington, Seattle
1988 Cliff Michel Gallery, Seattle

Selected Group Exhibitions

1994 *Stealth*, Seafirst Gallery, Columbia Seafirst Center, Seattle
1992 *Sculpture In the Landscape*, Sept '92–May '93, Marylhurst College, Portland
Sign of the Cross, Jamison/Thomas Gallery, Portland
1991 *Documents Northwest: Seattle IN PUBLIC Artists*, Seattle Arts Museum, Seattle
Big Objects, Tacoma Art Museum, Washington
1990 *Art Works for AIDS*, Seattle Art Pavillion, Seattle Center
Contemporary West Coast Sculpture, Jamison/Thomas Gallery, Portland
Invitational Sculpture Show, University of Washington Medical Center, Seattle
1989 *Objects of Affection*, Fuller-Elwood Gallery, Seattle
Two-Person Show, 911 Contemporary Arts Center, Seattle
1989 Northwest Annual, Center on Contemporary Art, Seattle
1988 Bumbershoot Festival, Seattle Center
Contemporary Seattle Abstraction, Cliff Michel Gallery, Seattle
1985 Public Image Gallery, New York
Nolo Contentre Gallery, New York

Selected Public Collections and Commissions

1991 *Seattle Artists* program, Seattle Arts Commission
In Public: Seattle 1991, Seattle Arts Commission and the Seattle Art Museum
City Light Collection
Microsoft Corporation, Redmond, Washington
Saks Fifth Avenue
Seattle Arts Commission

Malia **Jensen**

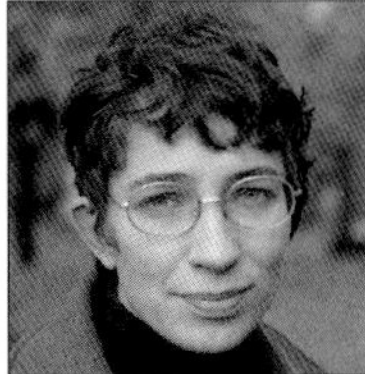

Photograph: Bruce James

1966 Born in Honolulu, HI
Lives in Portland

Education

1989 Pacific Northwest College of Art, Portland, B.F.A.
1984–85 Oregon School of Arts and Crafts

Selected Exhibitions

1994 *Sleepwalking in the Woods*, Butters Gallery, Portland
Art in the Arboretum (installation), Hoyt Arboretum, Portland
Oregon, Common Ground, The Art Gym, Marylhurst College, Portland; ORLO Foundation, Portland
Site-Specific Installation, Metropolitan Arts Commission, Portland Building Lobby, Portland
Open Books (group exhibition), Butters Gallery, Portland
Revised Context (group exhibition), Butters Gallery, Portland
1993 *Crosscut*, Portland Art Museum
Safe Nature, Butters Gallery, Portland
Large Scale, Butters Gallery, Portland
1992 *Inaugural Show*, Butters Gallery, Portland
Retrospective: Anticipations, Butters Gallery, Portland
Charles Parriott/Malia Jensen, Butters Gallery, Portland
Art Futures Auction, Benefit for Pacific Northwest College of Art, Portland
1991 *Detention* (group exhibition), Satyricon, Portland
Portland Art Museum Biennial, Portland
Art Futures Auction, Benefit for Pacific Northwest College of Art, Portland
1990 *New Work, New Talent*, Butters Gallery, Portland
Aftermath, Fuse, Portland
1989 Thesis Exhibition, Portland Art Museum

Illustration

1994 Story by David Duncan, *The Bear Essential*, ORLO
1993 Illustrations for *Mississippi Mud*

Selected Collections

Terry Hopkins, Portland
Henry Hillman, Jr, Portland
Prudence Roberts, Portland
Ann Wall Frank, Portland
Lindley Morton and Karin Oishi, Portland
Marilyn and Tom Deering, Portland
Doug Shafer and Jennifer Mayfied, Portland
Camille and Alex Cook, Western Springs, Illinois
Jan Hartley, New York
David Fox, New York
Ken and Mary Oliver, Surfer's Paradise, Australia

George **Johanson**

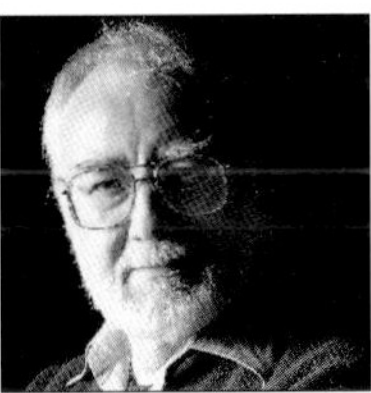

Photograph: Aaron Johanson

1928 Born in Seattle
Lives in Portland

Education and Awards

Pacific Northwest College of Art, Portland
Atelier 17, New York
1970 Art Advocates Grant for printmaking in London
1972 Painting Award, *Artists of Oregon*, Portland Art Museum
1976 Grant for film on printmaking, National Foundation for the Arts
Print Award, *First Editions*, Oregon Arts Commission
1980 Purchase Award, Oregon Printmakers, Mt Hood Community College, Gresham, Oregon
1992 Governor's Award for the Arts

Solo Exhibitions

1992–93 Elizabeth Leach Gallery, Portland
1989–91 Maveety Gallery, Portland
1987–89 Lynn McAllister Gallery, Seattle
Drawings: A 40 Year Retrospective, Museum of Art, University of Oregon, Eugene
1988 *Major Paintings 1972–1987*, Reed College, Portland
Littman Gallery, Portland State University, Portland
1985 Salem Art Association, Salem, Oregon
Wentz Gallery, Pacific Northwest College of Art, Portland
Rentaloft, Seattle Art Museum Pavilion, Seattle
1976–85 The Fountain Gallery of Art, Portland
1982 Oranges & Sardines Gallery, Los Angeles
1977 Governor's Ceremonial Offices Exhibition, Salem, Oregon
1976–77 Traveling show of prints, Washington State Arts Commission, Washington
18 People in 14 Paintings, Portland Art Museum

Selected Collections and Commissions

1992 Three Ceramic Tile Murals, Dixon Aquatic Center, Oregon State University, Corvallis, Oregon
1991 Commissioned painting, *Upstream, Downstream*, for Pacific Development Lobby, Portland
1989 Ceramic Tile Mural, Bremerton High School, Bremerton, Washington
Ceramic Tile Mural, *Northwest Power*, Bonneville Power Administration, Vancouver, Washington
1988 Ceramic Tile Mural, Portland Building, Portland
Chicago Art Institute
Johnson Wax Collection
New York Public Library
Oldham County Collection, Oldham, England
Portland Art Museum
Seattle Art Museum,
Smithsonian Institution, Washington DC National Collection
State of Oregon, Art in Public Places
State of Washington, Art in Public Places
Victoria and Albert Museum, London
Visual Chronicle Collection, Portland

Fay **Jones**

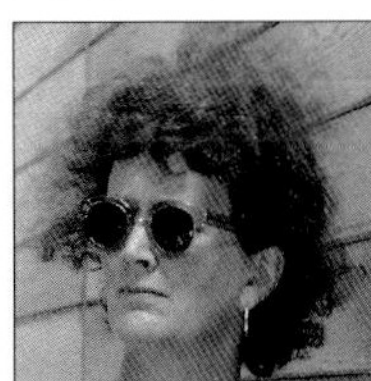

Photograph: Spike Mafford

1936 Born in Boston, MA
Lives in Seattle

Education and Awards

1957 Rhode Island School of Design, Providence, B.F.A.
1983 National Endowment for the Arts, Individual Artist's Fellowship
1989 Two month study grant La Napoule Art Foundation, France
1990 National Endowment for the Arts, Individual Artist's Fellowship

Solo Exhibitions

1993 Francine Seders Gallery, Seattle
1992 The Laura Russo Gallery, Portland
1991 Shoshana Wayne Gallery, Los Angeles
1990 Whatcom Museum, Bellingham, Washington
Francine Seders Gallery, Seattle
1989 Shoshana Wayne Gallery, Los Angeles
Francine Seders Gallery, Seattle

1988 The Laura Russo Gallery, Portland
1987 Francine Seders Gallery, Seattle
Shoshana Wayne Gallery, Los Angeles
1985 *Documents Northwest: Fay Jones*, Seattle Art Museum
Francine Seders Gallery, Seattle
Portland Center for the Visual Arts
1982–83 Francine Seders Gallery, Seattle
1981 Francine Seders Gallery, Seattle
1980 Francine Seders Gallery, Seattle
1978 Francine Seders Gallery, Seattle
1976 Francine Seders Gallery, Seattle
1974 Tacoma Art Museum, Washington
1973 Francine Seders Gallery, Seattle
1970 Francine Seders Gallery, Seattle

Selected Public Collections

Cheney Cowles Memorial Museum, Spokane, Washington
City of Seattle
Microsoft Corporation, Redmond, Washington
Portland Art Museum
Seattle Art Museum
Seattle Opera House
Tacoma Art Museum, Washington
Westlake Station Mural, Metro Transit, Seattle

Mel **Katz**

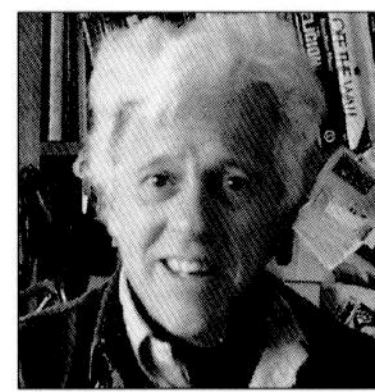

Photograph: Stewart Harvey

1932 Born in Brooklyn, New York
Lives in Portland

Education and Awards

1954–55 Brooklyn Museum Art School, New York
1975 Western States Arts Foundation, Artist's Fellowship
International Print Institute, Santa Cruz, Fellowship
1976 National Endowment For The Arts, Individual Artist's Fellowship

Solo Exhibitions

1993 The Laura Russo Gallery, Portland
1991 The Laura Russo Gallery, Portland
1989 The Laura Russo Gallery, Portland
1988 Portland Art Museum (retrospective), Portland
1987 The Laura Russo Gallery, Portland
Lynn McAllister Gallery, Seattle
1985 The Fountain Gallery of Art, Portland
1983 The Fountain Gallery of Art, Portland
1982 Foundation Gallery, New York
The Fountain Gallery of Art, Portland
Linda Farris Gallery, Seattle
1981 The Fountain Gallery of Art, Portland
Marylhurst College, Portland
1980 The Fountain Gallery of Art, Portland
Linda Farris Gallery, Seattle
1979 The Fountain Gallery of Art, Portland
Museum of Art, Washington State University, Pullman
1978 Linda Farris Gallery, Seattle
Max Hutchinson Gallery, New York
1977 Linda Farris Gallery, Seattle
1976 The Fountain Gallery of Art, Portland
1975 The Fountain Gallery of Art, Portland
Linda Farris Gallery, Seattle
1973 The Fountain Gallery of Art, Portland
1970 The Fountain Gallery of Art, Portland
1968 Bolles Gallery, San Francisco
Portland State University, Portland
1967 The Fountain Gallery of Art, Portland
1966 Gordon Woodside Gallery, San Francisco
1965 Portland Art Museum
1963 Amel Gallery, New York
1961 Amel Gallery, New York

Public Collections

Claremont Resort Hotel, Oakland, California
City of Seattle
Cougar Valley Elementary School, Silverdale, Washington
Good Samaritan Hospital, Portland
Portland Art Museum
Museum of Contemporary Art, Sydney, Australia
Seattle Art Museum

Ken **Kelly**

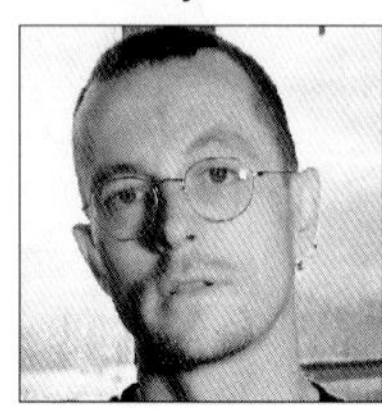

Photograph: Arthur S. Aubry

1955 Born in Magnolia, Arizona
Lives in Seattle

Education and Awards

1973–74 Birmingham-Southern College, Alabama
1974–77 University of Georgia, Athens
1976 Ford Foundation Undergraduate Grant
1977 Ford Foundation Undergraduate Grant
1979–81 University of Arizona, Tucson
1988 Spokane Arts Commission Award, *Northwest Juried Art '88*, Cheney Cowles Museum, Spokane, Washington
Seattle Arts Commission Award, Art in Public Places, *Seattle Artists '88*
1989 Betty Bowen Award, Seattle Art Museum
1992 Grant Recipient, Pollock-Krasner Foundation
Seattle Arts Commission Award, *Seattle Artists 1992*
First Place, Third Annual Juried Art Show and Competition, Kirkland Arts Center
Visiting Artist, Pilchuck School, Stanwood, Washington

Selected Solo Exhibitions

1994 David Beitzel Gallery, New York
Greg Kucera Gallery, Seattle
1993 Littlejohn/Sternau Gallery, New York
Stephen Wirtz Gallery, San Francisco
Mark Moore Gallery, Santa Monica
Pulliam Deffenbaugh Nugent Gallery, Portland
1992 Greg Kucera Gallery, Seattle
1991 Greg Kucera Gallery, Seattle
1989 Henry Art Gallery, University of Washington, Seattle
Cliff Michel Gallery, Seattle
1987 Cliff Michel Gallery, Seattle

Selected Group Exhibitions

1994 Mark Moore Gallery, Santa Monica
Painters, Lisa Sette Gallery, Scottsdale, Arizona
Passion, Linda Farris Gallery, Seattle
1993 *The Art of Microsoft*, Henry Art Gallery, University of Washington, Seattle
Small Works, Lisa Sette Gallery, Scottsdale, Arizona
Littlejohn/Sternau Gallery, New York
Botanic, Sean Elwood Fine Arts, Seattle
1992–93 *The Betty Bowen Legacy: Fourteen Years of Award Winning Art*, Security Pacific Gallery, Seattle
1992 *Recent Acquisitions/New Inventory*, Greg Kucera Gallery, Seattle
Artquake Visual Arts Gallery, Portland
Pulliam Deffenbaugh Nugent Gallery, Portland
1990 Galleria Potatohead, Seattle
1989 *Bumberbiennale: Decade of Abstraction 1979–1989*, Seattle Center
Northwest Annual, Center on Contemporary Art, Seattle
1988 *underexposed seattle*, Spokane Art School, Spokane, Washington
Northwest Juried Art '88, Cheney Cowles Museum, Spokane, Washington
1987 *Inaugural Exhibition*, Cliff Michel Gallery, Seattle
The Hillclimb Show, Pike Place Hillclimb, Seattle
Painting and Sculpture '87, Tacoma Art Museum, Washington
1986 *Northwest Impressions: Works on Paper*, Henry Art Gallery, University of Washington, Seattle
15th Avenue Studio, Henry Art Gallery, University of Washington
1985 *Neo York/Seattle*, Center on Contemporary Art, Seattle
1984 *South of the Border*, Western Front Gallery, Vancouver
1983 *5 Walls/5 Painters*, 911 Contemporary Arts Center, Seattle
1981 *3 From Tucson*, Bisbee Fine Arts Center, Arizona

Selected Collections

Heller, Ehrman, White & McAuliffe, Attorneys, Seattle
Hillis, Clark, Martin & Peterson, Attorneys, Seattle
Microsoft Corporation, Redmond, Washington
Perkins, Coie, Attorneys, Seattle
Portland Art Museum
RAJA Investments, Boise, Idaho
Seattle Art Museum
Seattle City Light, Portable Works Collection
Safeco Insurance, Seattle
University of Washington Medical Center, Seattle

Dianne **Kornberg**

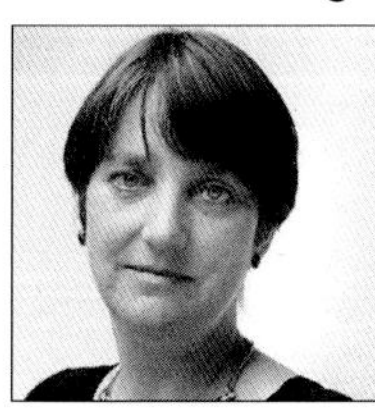

Photograph: Anne Smith

1945 Born in Chicago, Illinois
Lives in Portland

Education

1963–67 University of Washington, B.F.A. in painting
1968–70 Indiana University, M.F.A. in painting

Public Collections

International Center of Photography, New York
Nohra Haime Gallery, New York
Princeton Art Museum, New Jersey
Seattle Art Museum
Portland Art Museum
Costa Rican Museum of Art, San Jose
State of Oregon Public Art Collection

Freg Meyer Charitable Trust, Portland
New Photographics Collection, Ellensburg, Washington
Savage Fine Art, Portland

Solo Exhibitions

1982 Camerawork Gallery, Portland
1984 West Hills Unitarian Fellowship, Portland
1985 Mind's Eye Gallery, Idaho State University, Pocatello, Idaho
Renshaw Gallery, McMinnville, Oregon
1986 Sunspot Gallery, Twin Falls, Idaho
Camerawork Gallery, Portland
1987 SoHo Photo, New York
Dillingham Center for the Performing Arts, Ithaca, New York
Photographic Image Gallery, Portland
1988 E J Bellocq Gallery, Ruston, Louisiana
1989 Creative Art Gallery, St Louis
1993 Mid-Columbia Region Arts Council, Tri-Cities, Washington
Elizabeth Leach Gallery, Portland
1994 Art in the Governor's Office, Salem, Oregon
Nohra Haime Gallery, 41 East 57th, New York
1995 Savage Fine Art, Portland

James Lavadour

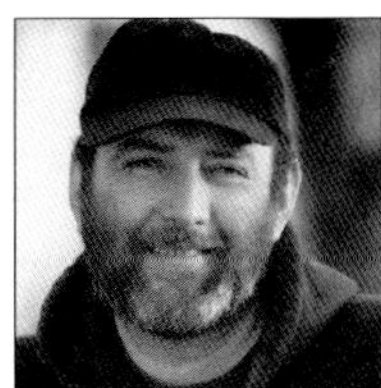

Photograph: Walters Photographers, Oregon

Born in 1951
Lives in Adams, Oregon

Selected Awards

1990 National Printmaking Fellowship, Rutgers Center for Innovative Printmaking, Rutgers University, New Brunswick, New Jersey
1991 Betty Bowe Memorial Recognition Award, Seattle Art Museum, Washington
1994 Oregon Governor's Award for Excellence in the Arts

Selected Exhibitions

1994 *Sacred and Profane*, Jan Baum Gallery, Los Angeles
1993 Greg Kucera Gallery, Seattle
1992 Elizabeth Leach Gallery, Portland
Greg Kucera Gallery, Seattle
Land, Spirit, Power: First Nations at the National Gallery of Canada, National Gallery of Canada, Ottawa, Ontario
Crossing Over/Changing Places: Artists and Collaborators, The Print Club, Philadelphia
1991 Elizabeth Leach Gallery, Portland
Elaine Horwitch Gallery, Seattle
Shared Visions: Native American Sculptors and Painters in the Twentieth Century, Heard Museum, Phoenix
1990 Cliff Michel Gallery, Seattle
Northwest Viewpoints, Portland Art Museum
Northwest by Southwest: Painted Fictions, Palm Springs Desert Museum, Palm Springs
The Undiminished Landscape, Security Pacific Corporation Gallery, San Francisco
Celebrated Selections, Heard Museum, Phoenix
1989 *Crossed Cultures: Five Contemporary Native Northwest Artists*, Seattle Art Museum
1987 *Northwest '87*, Seattle Art Museum
Recent Generations: Native American Art, Heard Museum, Phoenix

Selected Commissions

1989 Northwest Major Works, Seattle Arts Commission
1987 Art in Public Places, Washington State Arts Commission, Olympia

Jacob Lawrence

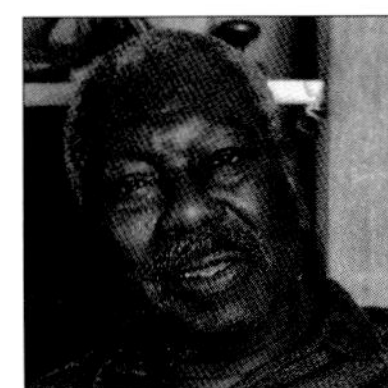

Photograph: Spike Mafford
Courtesy of Francine Seders Gallery

1917 Born in Atlantic City, New Jersey
Lives in Seattle

Education, Awards and Honors

1934–39 Harlem Art Workshop, New York
1938 American Artists School, New York
1940 Julius Rosenwald Fund Fellowship
1941 Julius Rosenwald Fund Fellowship
1942 Julius Rosenwald Fund Fellowship
1970 Springarn Medal (National Association for the Advancement of Colored People)
1978 Nominated Commissioner, National Council of the Arts, by President Carter, confirmed by the US Senate
1983 Elected Member American Academy and Institute of Arts and Letters
1988 NAACP 3rd Annual Great Black Artists Award, New York
1990 National Medal of Arts from President George Bush

Selected Solo Exhibitions

1993–95 *Jacob Lawrence: The Migration Series (1941)*, The Phillips Collection, Washington DC; Milwaukee Art Museum; Portland Art Museum; Birmingham Museum of Art, Alaska; St Louis Art Museum; Museum of Modern Art, New York; High Museum of Art, Atlanta, Georgia; Denver Art Museum; Chicago Historical Society
1992–93 *Jacob Lawrence: An American Master*,Wellington B Gallery in association with Francine Seders Gallery; Diggs Gallery, Winston-Salem State University; Afro-American Cultural Center, Charlotte; St John's Museum of Art, Wilmington; Hickory Museum of Art, Hickory, North Carolina
1992 *Jacob Lawrence: The Early Decades, 1935–1950*, Katonah Museum of Art, Kotanah, New York
1991–94 *Jacob Lawrence, The Frederick Douglass and Harriet Tubman Series of 1938–40*, touring exhibition organized by Hampton University Museum; Memorial Art Gallery of the University of Rochester, New York; Philadelphia Museum of Art; Studio Museum of Harlem, New York; Baltimore Museum of Art; Delaware Art Museum, Wilmington; Art Institute of Chicago; Museum of Fine Arts, Houston; Joslyn Art Museum, Omaha; Los Angeles County Art Museum; M H de Young Memorial Museum, San Francisco; Tacoma Art Museum, Washington
1990 Francine Seders Gallery, Seattle
1989–90 *Jacob Lawrence, Drawings and Prints*, organized by Scripps College of The Claremont Colleges, Claremont, California; traveling show to Africa and Caribbean
1986–87 *Jacob Lawrence, American Painter*, Seattle Art Museum; Oakland Museum, Oakland, California; High Museum of Art, Atlanta, Georgia; Phillips Collection, Washington, DC; Dallas Museum of Art; Brooklyn Museum, New York
1985 Francine Seders Gallery, Seattle
1983 Terry Dintenfass Gallery, New York
1982 Francine Seders Gallery, Seattle
1978–79 Francine Seders Gallery, Seattle
1978 Terry Dintenfass Gallery, New York
1976 Francine Seders Gallery, Seattle
1974/75 *Jacob Lawrence*, Retrospective Show, Whitney Museum of American Art, New York; St Louis Art Museum; Birmingham Museum of Art, Alaska; Seattle Art Museum; Nelson-Atkins Museum of Fine Arts, Kansas City; New Orleans Museum of Art
1973 Terry Dintenfass Gallery, New York
1968 Terry Dintenfass Gallery, New York
1965 Terry Dintenfass Gallery, New York
1963 Terry Dintenfass Gallery, New York
1962 American Society of African Culture's West African Cultural Center, Lagos, Nigeria, and Mbari Artists and Writers Club Cultural Center, Ibadan, Nigeria
1960 *Jacob Lawrence*, Brooklyn Museum, New York; circulated to sixteen United States cities by the American Federation of Arts, New York
1953 Downtown Gallery, New York
1950 Downtown Gallery, New York
1947 Downtown Gallery, New York
1945 Downtown Gallery, New York
1943 Downtown Gallery, New York
1941 Downtown Gallery, New York

Selected Group Exhibitions

1994–95 *New York Realism: Past and Present*, organized by Tampa Museum of Art, traveling exhibition to Japan
1992 *In Good Conscience: The Radical Tradition in 20th Century American Illustration*, Katonah Museum of Art, Katonah, New York; Hood Museum of Art, Dartmouth College, Hanover, New Hampshire; Montgomery Museum of Fine Arts, Alaska
Bridges & Boundaries: African Americans and American Jews, Jewish Museum at the New York Historical Society
1991 *Art of the Forties*, Museum of Modern Art, New York
1990 *Views and Visions in the Pacific Northwest*, Seattle Art Museum
1988 *Diamonds are Forever: Artists and Writers on Baseball*, SITES-New York State Museum, Albany; Salt Lake City; Houston; Baltimore; Chicago; Oakland
1983–84 *The Lane Collection: 20th-Century Paintings in the American Tradition*, Museum of Fine Arts, Boston; San Francisco Museum of Modern Art; Amon Carter Museum, Fort Work, Texas
1981 *Decade of Transition: 1940–1950*, Whitney Museum of American Art, New York
1976–77 *Two Centuries of Black American Art*, Los Angeles County Museum of Art; High Museum of Art, Atlanta, Georgia; Museum of Fine Arts, Dallas; Brooklyn Museum, New York

1971 *The Artist as Adversary*, The Museum of Modern Art, New York
Contemporary Black Artists in America, Whitney Museum of American Art, New York
1951 Sao Paulo Biennial, Sao Paulo, Brazil
1946 *American Paintings*, Tate Gallery, London

Selected Public Collections and Commissioned Murals

1991 *New York in Transit*, Times Square Subway Complex (pending)
Events in the Life of Harold Washington, Harold Washington Library Center, Chicago
1989 *Community*, Joseph P Addabbo Federal Building, Queens, New York
1988 *Time, Space, Energy*, Florida International Airport, Orlando, Florida
1984–85 *Theatre*, Meany Hall, University of Washington, Seattle
1982–84 *Origins*, Armour J Blackburn University Center, Howard University, Washington DC
1979–80 *Exploration*, Armour J Blackburn University Center, Howard University, Washington DC
1978–79 *Games*, Kingdome Stadium, Seattle

Amistad Research Center, Aaron Douglas Collection, New Orleans
Brooklyn Museum, New York
Detroit Institute of Arts, Detroit
Hampton University Museum, Hampton
Hirshhorn Museum and Sculpture Garden, Smithsonian Institution, Washington DC
Metropolitan Museum of Art, New York
Museum of Fine Arts, Boston
Museum of Modern Art, New York
National Collection of Fine Arts, Smithsonian Institution, Washington DC
National Gallery of Art, Washington DC
Philadelphia Museum of Art, Philadelphia,
The Phillips Collection, Washington DC
Seattle Art Museum
Vatican Gallery of Modern Art, Vatican Museum, Rome
Walker Art Center, Minneapolis
Whitney Museum of American Art, New York

Helen Lessick

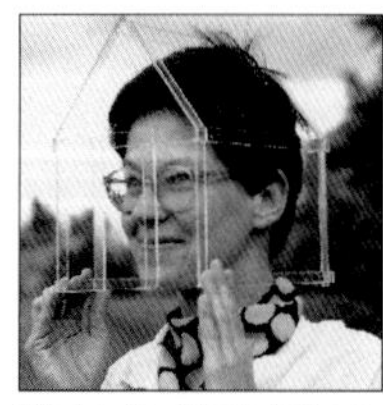

(thinking about) Kepler's Dream, an interdisciplinary performance, 21 & 22 June 1990, Hoyt Arboretum, Portland, Oregon.
Photograph: Brian Foulkes

1954 Born in Abington, Pennsylvania
Lives in Seattle

Education and Awards

1972 Reed College, Portland, B.A. in Studio Art
1982 University of California/Irvine, M.F.A.

Solo Exhibitions and Installations

1995 *The Crowning Glory of Tacoma*, Tacoma Art Museum, Washington
1994 *Homework*, site specific temporary public art installation in a vacant, city-owned, single family residence, sponsored by the Tacoma Arts Commission and Municipal Authority of Tacoma, Washington
1993 *Le Paysage Vivant*, Lycee Agricole du Valentin, Valence, France
Home: House of Memory, site specific temporary public art video installation in a vacant single family home in West Seattle, sponsored by New Langton Arts Interdisciplinary Artists Project Grant
1992 Butters Gallery, Portland
1990 Waterworld, outdoor installation, Bush Barn Park, Salem, Oregon
Art = Anthropology, Butters Gallery, Portland
1989 *Pastel Drawings*, Sierra Nevada Museum of Art, Reno
1988 *Structural Expressionism*, Northwest Artists Workshop, Portland
1986 *House for Spring*, Outside/In installation series, Portland Art Museum
1985 Fine Arts Gallery, Alverno College, Milwaukee
1980 Wentz Gallery, Pacific Northwest College of Art, Portland

Public Collections

Franklin Furnace Archives, New York
Hoyt Arboretum, City of Portland Park Bureau
Museum of Modedrn Art, New York
National Museum of Women in the Arts, Washington DC
New York Public Library
Oregon Health Science Center, Portland
Ruth and Marvin Sackner Archive of Concrete and Visual Poetry, Miami
University of Washington Book Arts Collection, Seattle

Sherry Markovitz

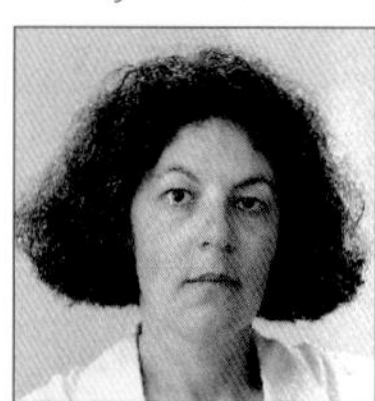

Photograph: Peter Millett

1947 Born in Chicago
Lives in Seattle

Education

1972–75 University of Washington, Seattle, M.F.A. in Printmaking
1965–69 University of Wisconsin, Madison, B.A. in Ceramics and Art Education
1977 Northwest Projects Grant, and/or Gallery, Seattle
1979 Grant for Painting, Washington Honors Program, Washington State Arts Commission
1981 Special Projects Grant, and/or Gallery, Seattle
1990 *Seattle Artists 1990* Grant, Seattle Arts Commission

Solo Exhibitions

1992–93 *ART Currents: Sherry Markovitz*, Mint Museum, Charlotte, North Carolina; Whatcom Museum, Bellingham, Washington
1992 *Life Forms*, Linda Farris Gallery, Seattle
1987 *Documents Northwest*, Seattle Art Museum
1986 Monique Knowlton Gallery, New York
1986 *US Projects*, Artists Space, New York
1983 *Easy Targets*, Linda Farris Gallery, Seattle
1981 *Bucks and Does*, Linda Farris Gallery, Seattle
1979 Linda Farris Galerry, Seattle
Women: Body, Space and Personal Ritual, and/or Gallery, Seattle

Selected Group Exhibitions

1994–95 *Wildlife*, California Center For The Arts, Escondido, California
1994 *Birds and Beasts*, Seattle Art Museum
1993 *The Spirit of the Bead Ornamentation*, Laumeier Sculpture Park, St Louis
The Shell Game: the Button as Craft, Octagon Center for the Arts, Ames, Iowa
Sculptors on Paper, Linda Farris Gallery, Seattle
Washington: Voice in Contemporary Sculpture, Bellevue Art Museum, Washington
1991 *Syncretism*, Alternative Museum, New York
Rodeo in Fact and Fantasy, Philbrook Art Center, Tulsa, Oklahoma
1990 *Views and Visions in the Pacific Northwest*, Seattle Art Museum
New Work, Linda Farris Gallery, Seattle
Structure and Surface: Beads in Contemporary American Art, National Museum of American Art, Smithsonian Institute, Washington DC
1989 *2-D/3-D: Sculptor's Drawings*, Seattle Art Museum
1988 *Contemporary Survey: Visible Presence in the Northwest*, Cheney Cowles Museum, Spokane, Washington
1988 *Structure and Surface: Beads in Contemporary American Art*, John Kohler Arts Center, Sheboygan, Wisconsin
1987 *Aspects of Drawing Part II: Representation*, Public Art Space, Seattle
Northwest Printmakers, Rental Sales Gallery, Seattle Art Museum
Focus: Seattle, San Jose Museum of Art
The Eloquent Object (travelling exhibition), Philbrook Museum of Art, Tulsa, Oklahoma
Standing Ground: Sculpture by American Women, Cincinnati Contemporary Arts Center
The Bead Goes On: Expressions in Contemporary Beadwork, Maude Kearns Art Center, Eugene, Oregon
The Ubiquitous Bead, Bellevue Art Museum, Washington
1986 *Northwest Impressions: Works on Paper*, Henry Art Gallery, University of Washington, Seattle
Western States Biennial, Brooklyn Museum, New York
1985 *American Women in Art: Works on Paper*, Nairobi, Kenya
1984 *Strange*, Henry Art Gallery, University of Washington, Seattle
Seattle Artists, Art Gallery of Greater Victoria, British Columbia
Surface, Material, Structure, Hodges/Banks Gallery, Seattle
1983 *Self-Portraits*, Linda Farris Gallery, Seattle
Bumberbiennial: Art Since 'Century 21' 1963–1983, Seattle Center
The American Artist as Printmaker, 23rd National Print Exhibition, Brooklyn Museum, New York
Group Show, University of Idaho, Moscow, Idaho
Seattle Artists, San Francisco Museum of Art
Pacific Northwest Today, Brentwook Gallery, St Louis
International Art Exposition, Navy Pier, Chicago
1982 *International Art Exposition*, Navy Pier, Chicago
Animal Imagery, Sebastian Moore Gallery, Denver
Urban Vernacular, Henry Art Gallery, University of Washington, Seattle
Curated by Linda Farris, Blackfish Gallery, Portland
Windfall Press Project, Linda Farris Gallery, Seattle
Washington Printmakers, Tacoma Art Museum, Washington
1981 *The Farm Project*, Arlington, Washington
Women Artists From Seattle, Spokane, Washington
Big Paintings, Linda Farris Gallery, Seattle

Portopia '81, King County Arts Commission, Kobe, Japan
Seattle Drawings, Seattle Pacific University
1980 *Contemporary Washington State Artists*, Cranberry Galleries, Ocean Spray Cranberry Inc, Plymouth
1980 *Cornish Faculty*, Institute for Pedagocical Studies, Vladivostok, USSR
Raconteur: A Private View, Henry Art Gallery, University of Washington, Seattle

Selected Collections and Commissions
1975–79 Arts Consultant for Viewlands Substation Project, Seattle Arts Commission 1% for Art Program
American Craft Museum, New York
City Light 1% for Art Collection, Seattle
Junior League, Seattle
Mint Museum, Charlotte, North Carolina
SeaFirst Bank, Seattle
Seattle Art Museum
Sheraton Hotel, Seattle
University Hospital, Seattle

Jeffry Mitchell

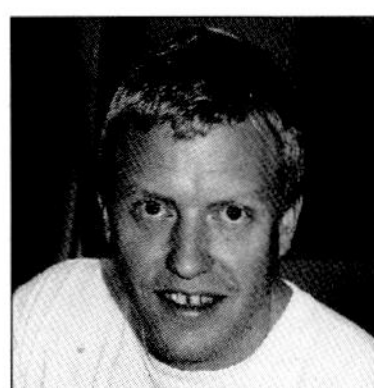
Photograph: Jim Arkatov

1958 Born in Seattle
Lives in Seattle

Education and Awards
1980 Painting, University of Dallas, Irving, B.A.
1988 Tyler School of Art, Temple University, Philadelphia, M.F.A., Printmaking
1989 Residency, Centrum Foundation, Port Townsend, Washington
Seattle Artists 1989, Seattle Arts Commission
Art Matters, Inc, New York, Grant
1992 Pilchuck School, Artist in Residence, Stanwood, Washington

Solo Exhibitions
1994 Rena Bransten Gallery, Seattle
1993 Greg Kucera Gallery, Seattle
1992 WorkSpace Gallery, New Museum of Contemporary Art, New York
Pictures for Boys, Pulliam Deffenbaugh Nugent Gallery, Portland
1991 Greg Kucera Gallery, Seattle
Rena Bransten Gallery, San Francisco
Life, Kittredge Gallery, University of Puget Sound, Tacoma, Washington
1990 Greg Kucera Gallery, Seattle
Documents Northwest, The PONCHO Series, Seattle Art Museum
1989 Greg Kucera Gallery, Seattle
1987 *Lithographs*, Pearl Fox Gallery, Melrose Park
1986 *Opera in Voot*, Virginia Inn, Seattle
1985 *Prints and Drawings*, Watertown, Seattle
1984 *Large Paintings*, Gallery Lover Connection, Nagoya, Japan
Pottery, Maruei Department Store, Nagoya, Japan

Selected Group Exhibitions
1994 Kirkland Arts Center, Kirkland, Washington
Winderkammer, Rena Bransten Gallery, San Francisco
Stealth, SeaFirst Gallery, Seattle
1993 *Time Away: Prints From Centrum's Artist Residency Program*, Tacoma Art Museum, Washington
The Art of Microsoft, Henry Art Gallery, University of Washington, Seattle
Suburban Culture, The Art Gym, Marylhurst College, Portland
1992 *On Paper/Recent Acquisitions*, Tacoma Art Museum, Washington
IN FOregonMATion, Greg Kucera Gallery, Seattle
Paper, Fawbush Gallery, New York
Works on Paper, Parker/Mark Gallery, Los Angeles
1991 *View from the Edge*, Index Gallery, Clark College, Vancouver, Washington
1990 *Artworks for AIDS*, Seattle Center Pavilion
From the Decade, The Print Club, Philadelphia
Watercolor, Watercolor, Watercolor, Bellevue Art Museum
Drawing Power, Western Gallery, Western Washington Univesity, Bellingham
1989 911 Contemporary Arts Window Installation, Seattle
A Rain of Talent: Umbrella Art, Fabric Workshop, Philadelphia; traveled to the American Crafts Museum, New York; Wustum Museum of Fine Art, Racine, Wisconsin; Gallery 400, University of Illinois, Chicago
2-D, 3-D, Seattle Art Museum
Made by Hand, Minneapolis College of Art and Design
1989 Northwest Annual, Center on Contemporary Art, Seattle
1988 *Sum of the Parts*, Greg Kucera Gallery, Seattle
From the Decade, The Print Club, Philadelphia
1987 *Tyler Print Makers*, William and Hobart College, Geneve, New York
Penrose Gallery, Philadelphia
Six From Cornish, Cornish Institute, Seattle
1986 *62nd Annual International Print Competition*, The Print Club, Philadelphia
1985 *A Decade of Prints*, Cornish Institute, Seattle
1984 Gallery R, Seto, Japan
1983 *Foreign Artists Working in Japan*, Gallery R, Seto, Japan

Collections and Commissions
1990 Socrates Sculpture Park (installation), Long Island City
1991 Northwest Major Works, Seattle Arts Commission
Bailey-Boushay House, AIDS Housing of Washington, Seattle
Cheney Cowles Museum, Spokane
Davis, Wright, Tremaine, Attorneys, Seattle
Microsoft Corporation, Redmond, Washington
Neuberger & Berman, New York
Pacific First Federal Savings Bank, Seattle
Safeco Insurance Company, Seattle
Saintsbury Winerym, Napa, California
City Light, Seattle Arts Commission
Surrogate Hostess, Seattle
Tacoma Art Museum, Washington
The Contemporary Museum, Honolulu
University of Washington Medical Center, Seattle

William Moore

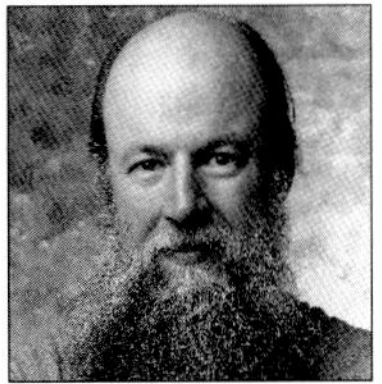
Photograph: Harold Wood

1945 Born in Arlington, Virginia
Lives in Portland

Education and Awards
1967 University of Michigan, Ann Arbor, B.S.
1971 University of Michigan, Ann Arbor, M.F.A.
1982 Oregon Arts Commission, Individual Artist's Fellowship

Solo Exhibitions
1993 The Laura Russo Gallery, Portland
1990 The Laura Russo Gallery, Portland
1985 Blackfish Gallery, Portland
1981 Blackfish Gallery, Portland
1984 Fairbanks Gallery, Oregon State University, Corvallis
1977 Contemporary Crafts Gallery, Portland

Public Collections and Commissions
1994 Creator of individual prizes, Governor's Arts Awards, Oregon Advocates for the Arts
1993 Christmas Ornament for the White House
1993 Washington County Public Services Building, Hillsboro, Oregon
1990 Playground, Ashland, Oregon
1978 Oregon Arts Commission, Eastern Oregon State College, LaGrande
1977 Performing Arts Center, Portland
Clark County Elementery School, Oregon
Couch Park, Portland
Holladay Park Memorial Hospital, Portland
Lake Oswego Library, Oregon
Lipton College, Van Nuys, California
Metropolitan Arts Commission, NE Health Center, Portland
Mt Angel Abbey, Mt Angel, Oregon
National Builders Hardware, Portland
Oregon Arts Commission, Supreme Court Building, Salem
Oregon Commission for the Blind (collaboration with Dennis Cunningham), Portland
Portland Development Commission, Portland
Washington Arts Commission: Carnation & Bellfair, Washington
Wonrick Collection, Burlingame, California

Carl Morris

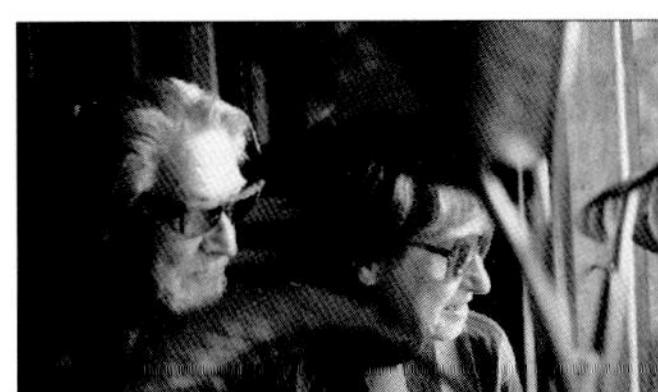
Carl Morris and Hilda Morris, c.1988
Photograph: David Wagoner

1911 Born in Yorba Linda, California
1941– Lived in Portland
1993 Died in Portland

Education and Awards
1931–33 Art Institute of Chicago

1933–34 Kunstgewerbeschule: Werkbund, Vienna
1934–35 Akadamie der Bildenen Kuenste, Vienna
1935–36 Institute for International Education, Paris
1985 Aubrey R Watzek Award, Lewis & Clark College, Portland
1985 Governor's Award for the Arts, Oregon Arts Commission and the Governor's Office
1960–62 Ford Foundation Award: Retrospective Exhibition, circulated nationally by the American Federation of Arts

Solo Exhibitions

1993 Portland Art Museum (retrospective), Portland
Kraushaar Gallery, New York
1992 The Laura Russo Gallery, Portland
1990 The Laura Russo Gallery, Portland
1989 Dennis Ochi Gallery, Boise, Idaho
1988 The Laura Russo Gallery, Portland
Foster/White Gallery, Seattle
1986 The Laura Russo Gallery, Portland
The Fountain Gallery of Art, Portland
Gordon Woodside Gallery, Seattle
1985 The Fountain Gallery of Art, Portland
Triangle Gallery, San Francisco
1984 Kraushaar Gallery, New York
Gordon Woodside Gallery, Seattle
Triangle Gallery, San Francisco
1983 The Fountain Gallery of Art, Portland
1982 The Fountain Gallery of Art, Portland
1981 Kraushaar Gallery, New York
Gordon Woodside Gallery, Seattle
1980 Gordon Woodside Gallery, Seattle
1979 Kraushaar Gallery, New York
The Fountain Gallery of Art, Portland
1978 Gordon Woodside Gallery, Seattle
1977 The Fountain Gallery of Art, Portland
1976 Triangle Gallery, San Francisco
1975 Gordon Woodside Gallery, Seattle
1973 Kraushaar Gallery, New York
Gordon Woodside Gallery, Seattle
Triangle Gallery, San Francisco
1970 Triangle Gallery, San Francisco
1968 Triangle Gallery, San Francisco
1967 Kraushaar Gallery, New York
1966 Gordon Woodside Gallery, Seattle
Triangle Gallery, San Francisco
1965 The Fountain Gallery of Art, Portland
1964 Kraushaar Gallery, New York
1961 Kraushaar Gallery, New York
1960–62 Portland Art Museum (national traveling exhibition sponsored by Ford Foundation)
1958 Kraushaar Gallery, New York
1956 Kraushaar Gallery, New York
1955 Portland Art Museum
1952 Portland Art Museum
1950 Harvey Welch Gallery, Portland
1948 Opportunity Art Gallery, New York
1947 Harvey Welch Gallery, Portland
California Palace of the Legion of Honor, San Francisco
1946 Portland Art Museum
1937 Paul Elder Gallery, San Francisco
1935 Fondation des Etats-Unis, Paris

Public Collections

Albright-Knox Museum of Art, Buffalo, New York
Art Institute of Chicago
Corcoran Gallery of Art, Washington DC
Dayton Art Institute, Ohio
Denver Art Museum
Houston Museum of Fine Arts
Metropolitan Museum of Art, New York
Museo de Arte Moderna, Sao Paulo, Brazil
Museum of Modern Art, New York
National Collection of Art, Joseph Hirshhorn Collection, Washington DC
Oregon Health Sciences University, Portland
Portland Art Museum
Reed College, Kenin Collection, Portland
San Francisco Museum of Art
Seattle Art Museum
Smithsonian Institution, Washington DC
Solomon R Guggenheim Museum, New York
Walker Art Center, Minneapolis

Hilda Morris

1911 Born in New York City
1940– Lived in Portland
1991 Died in Portland

Education and Awards

Art Students League
Cooper Union
School of Art and Architecture, New York
1960 Ford Foundation Grant

Solo Exhibitions

1990 Foster/White Gallery, Seattle
1988 The Laura Russo Gallery, Portland
Ochi Fine Art Gallery, Boise, Idaho
1987 The Krashaar Gallery, New York
Woodside/Braseth Gallery, Seattle
1984 Portland Art Museum
The Fountain Gallery of Art, Portland
1981 Woodside/Braseth Gallery, Seattle
1980 The Fountain Gallery of Art, Portland
Reed College, Portland
1977 Portland Art Museum
1976 Triangle Gallery, San Francisco
Rochester Memorial Art Museum, New York
1975 Woodside/Braseth Gallery, Seattle
1974 Portland Art Museum
The Fountain Gallery of Art, Portland
1972 Woodside/Braseth Gallery, Seattle
Portland Art Museum
Reed College, Portland
1971 The Fountain Gallery of Art, Portland
1970 Tacoma Art Museum, Washington
1969 Reed College, Portland
Albina Art Center, Portland
1968 Woodside/Braseth Gallery, Seattle
1964 The Fountain Gallery of Art , Portland
1963 Salt Lake Art Center
1962 The Fountain Gallery of Art, Portland
1961 The Fountain Gallery of Art, Portland
University of Puget Sound, Tacoma, Washington
1960 Seligman Gallery, Seattle
1958 Barone Gallery, New York
1957 Seligman Gallery, Seattle
1955 Portland Art Museum
Seligman Gallery, Seattle
1947 University of Oregon, Eugene
1946 Portland Art Museum

Collections

Bank of America, Portland and Seattle
California Palace of the Legion of Honor, San Francisco
Chase Manhattan Bank, New York
Dayton Art Museum, Ohio
Memorial Museum of Art, University of Rochester, New York
Mentor Graphics, Portland
Mitsubishi Bank, Portland
Museum of Art, University of Oregon, Eugene
Museum of Munson Williams Proctor Institute, Utica, New York
Oregon School of Arts and Crafts, Portland
Pacific National Building, Tacoma, Washington
Reed College, Portland
Safeco Insurance Corporation, Seattle
San Francisco Museum of Modern Art
Seattle Art Museum
Seattle Opera House
St Martin's Abbey, Lacey, Washington
Standard Plaza, Portland
Tacoma Art Museum, Washington
University of Victoria, British Columbia
Walter P Chrysler Jr Collection, Norfolk, Virginia

William Morris

Photograph: Kim Zumwalt

1957 Born in Carmel, California
Lives in Arlington, Washington

Education and Selected Awards

California State University, Chico, California
Central Washington University, Ellensburg, Washington
1994 National Endowment for the Arts, Individual Artist's Grant

Selected Solo Exhibitions

1994 Dorothy Weiss Gallery, San Francisco
Habatat Gallery, Farmington Hills, Missouri
Friesen Fine Art, Sun Valley, Idaho
Susan Duval Gallery, Aspen, Colorado
1993 Habatat Gallery, Boca Raton, Florida
Betsy Gallery, New York
Laura Russo Gallery, Portland
Maurine Littleton Gallery, Washington DC
1992 Foster/White Gallery, Seattle
Freisen Gallery, Ketchum, Idaho
Lisa Sette Gallery, Scottsdale, Arizona
1992 Foster/White Gallery, Seattle
Friesen Gallery, Sun Valley, Idaho
Lisa Sette Gallery, Scottsdale, Arizona
Betsy Rosenfield Gallery, Navy Pier, Chicago
1991 Maurine Littleton Gallery, Washington DC
Helander Gallery, Palm Beach
Betsy Rosenfield Gallery, Navy Pier, Chicago
Charles Grant Gallery, Ketchum, Idaho
Riley Hawk Gallery, Columbus and Cleveland
1990 Maurine Littleton Gallery, Washington DC
Betsy Rosenfield Gallery, Chicago
Foster/White Gallery, Seattle
Renwick Gallery, Smithsonian Institution, Washington DC

Selected Group Exhibitions

1994 *Collective Brilliance*, Albany Museum of Art, Georgia
Birds and Beasts, Seattle Art Museum
1993 *Glass Installations*, American Craft Museum, New York
Formed by Fire, The Carnegie Museum of Art, Pittsburgh

Selected Public Collections

American Craft Museum, New York

American Glass Museum, Millville, New Jersey
Auckland Museum, New Zealand
Corning Museum of Glass, New York
Hokkaido Museum of Modern Art, Japan
Hunter Museum, Chattanooga
IBM Corporation, Tulsa, Oklahoma
J B Speed Museum, Louisville
Joslyn Museum, Omaha
Metropolitan Museum of Art, New York
Missoula Museum of Art, Montana
Musee des Arts Decoratifs, Paris
Museum der Kunstegewerve, Hamburg, Germany
Museum of Art, Rhode Island School of Design, Providence
Rockefeller Center, New York
Royal College of Art, London
Seattle Art Museum
Shimonosedi Museum, Hokkaido, Japan
Toledo Museum of Art, Toledo
Victoria and Albert Museum, London
Virginia Museum of Fine Arts, Richmond

Ronna **Neuenschwander**

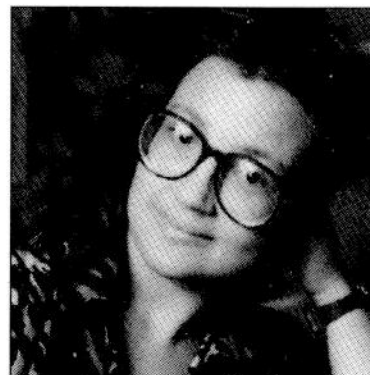
Photograph: David Browne

1954 Born in Hoxie, Kansas
Lives in Portland

Education and Awards
1976 University of Kansas, Lawrence, B.F.A.
1982–83 Oregon Arts Commission Fellowship
1984 Bonnie Bronson Fellowship
1989 Western States Arts Foundation/National Endowment for the Arts Regional Fellowship

Solo Exhibitions
1992 *New Art Forms*, Chicago Navy Pier, represented by Susan Cummins Gallery
1991 *Choosing Camps*, Maveety Gallery, Portland
1990 Susan Cummins Gallery, Mill Valley
1989 Dawson Gallery, Rochester, New York
1988 *Africa Revisited*, Lawrence Gallery, Portland
Wita Gardiner Gallery, San Diego
Susan Cummins Gallery, Portland
1987 Susan Cummins Gallery, Mill Valley
1986 Morgan Gallery, Kansas City
Lawrence Gallery, Portland
1985 *Saharan Shards*, Himovitz/Salomon Gallery, Sacramento
Saharan Shards II, Traver/Sutton Gallery, Seattle
1984 Dawson Gallery, Rochester, New York
Lawrence Gallery, Portland
1981 *The Elephant: Assorted Histories*, Contemporary Crafts Gallery, Portland

Public Commissions
1993–94 North Precinct Police Station: Outdoor Art for the Pedestrian Park (in collaboration with artist Baba Wague Diakite), Portland
1990–91 Washington Park Zoo: Tropical Rain Forest Exhibit Installation (in collaboration with artist Bab Wague Diakite), Portland
1989 My Dinner with the Devil Snake (in collaboration with filmmakers Jim Blashfield and Joan Gratz, and artist Baba Wague Diakite), animated video commissioned by PBS's *Alive From Off Center* program
1980 Mt Scott and Montana Clinics, Kaiser-Permanente Hospitals, Portland

Lucinda **Parker**

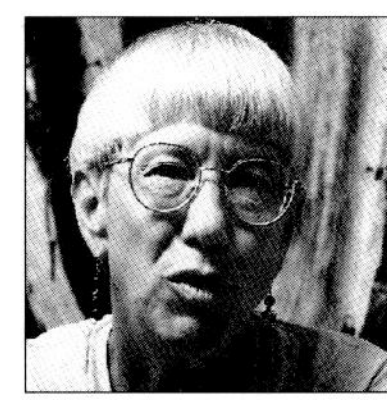
Photograph: Alfred Edelman

1942 Born in Boston
Lives in Portland

Education
1966 Reed College Museum Art School, Portland, combined program, B.A.
1968 Pratt Institute, Brooklyn, M.F.A.

Collections
Bank of America, Portland
Bank of America, Seattle
Bogle and Gates, Portland
Capital Trust Co, Portland
Claremont Resort Hotel, Oakland, California
Coos Art Museum, Coos Bay, Oregon
H J Heinz, Pittsburgh
Harsh Investment Corporation, Portland
Kaiser Foundation, Portland
Microsoft Corporation, Redmond, Washington
Morse & Bratt, Vancouver, Washington
Oregon Arts Commission, Monmouth
Oregon Department of Transportation, Salem
Pacific First Bank, Portland
Portland Art Museum
Safeco Insurance Corporation, Seattle
Seattle Art Museum
State of Oregon Capitol Collection, Salem
State of Oregon Public Art Collections
Western Oregon State College, Monmouth

Solo Exhibitions
1995 Portland Art Museum (retrospective)
1994 Catlin Gabel, Portland
Governor's Ceremonial Office, Salem, Oregon
1993 The Laura Russo Gallery, Portland
1991 The Laura Russo Gallery, Portland
Davidson Gallery, Seattle
1989 The Laura Russo Gallery, Portland
Davidson Gallery, Seattle
1987 The Laura Russo Gallery, Portland
1986 Seattle Art Museum
Linda Hodges Gallery, Seattle
Washington State University, Pullman
1985 The Fountain Gallery of Art, Portland
Hodges/Banks Gallery, Seattle
1984 Brunswick Gallery, Missoula, Montana
Hodges/Banks Gallery, Seattle
1983 The Fountain Gallery of Art, Portland
Suellen Haber Gallery, New York
1982 The Fountain Gallery of Art, Portland
Marylhurst College, Oregon
1981 David Findlay Gallery, New York
1980 The Fountain Gallery of Art, Portland
Foster/White Gallery, Seattle
1979 University of Oregon Art Museum, Eugene
Eastern Oregon State University, LaGrande
1978 The Fountain Gallery of Art, Portland
1977 Foster/White Gallery, Seattle
Reed College Art Gallery, Portland
1975 The Fountain Gallery of Art, Portland
Reed College Art Gallery, Portland
Marylhurst College, Oregon
1974 Wentz Gallery, Museum Art School, Portland
1973 Hoffman Gallery, Arts & Crafts Society, Portland
1972 Marylhurst College, Oregon

Selected Group Exhibitions
1992–93 *Forms of Abstraction*, Portland Art Museum
1990 *View and Visions* (invitational exhibition), Seattle Art Museum
1987 *West Coast Painters*, University of Hawaii, Hilo
1980 *Childe Hassam Fund Purchase Exhibition*, American Academy of Arts and Letters, New York
1978–80 *First Western States Biennial*, exhibition traveled to Denver, Washington DC, Seattle, San Francisco
1977 *35th American Painting Biennial*, Corcoran Gallery, Washington DC

Laura **Ross-Paul**

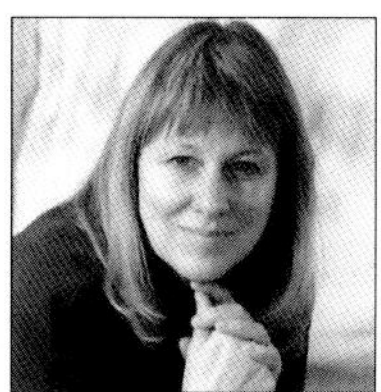
Photograph: Yalcin Erhan

1950 Born in Portland
Lives in Portland

Education
1974 Fort Wright College, Spokane, Washington, B.F.A.
1976 Portland State University, M.F.A.
1978 Portland State University, B.S.
1980 Oregon Arts Commission, Individual Artist's Fellowship
1985 Metropolitan Arts Commission *Visual Chronicles*, for commissioned painting documenting the history of Portland

Collections
Frank Russel Co, Tacoma, Washington
Gordon and Vivian Gilkey Collection, Portland
Health Sciences Moveable Collection Project, Oregon Health Sciences University, Portland
Kaiser Permanente, Portland
Management Compensation Group, Portland
Mentor Graphics, Wilsonville, Oregon
Permanent Collection, Portland State University
Portland Art Museum
State of Oregon, Salem
State of Washington, Olympia
The Visual Chronicles of Portland, Portland

Solo Exhibitions
1994 Elizabeth Leach Gallery, Portland
1993 Francine Seders Gallery, Seattle
1991 Elizabeth Leach Gallery, Portland
1990 *Laura Ross-Paul—A Decade of Painting: 1981–1990*, The Art Gym, Marylhurst College, Portland
Elizabeth Leach Gallery, Portland
1988 Northwest Viewpoints: Laura Ross-Paul/Watercolors, Oregon Art Institute, Portland
1987 Elizabeth Leach Gallery, Portland
1984 The Fountain Gallery of Art, Portland

1982 The Fountain Gallery of Art, Portland
1980 The Fountain Gallery of Art, Portland
1976 The Fountain Gallery of Art, Portland

Selected Group Exhibitions

1993 *Crosscut,* Portland Art Museum
Northwest Tales: Contemporary Narrative Painting, Anchorage Museum of History and Art, Alaska
Brenau College National Invitational Art Exhibition, Leo Castelli, Castelli Galleries, New York, juror of awards; Gainesville, Georgia
1992 *Northwest Tales: Contemporary Narrative Painting,* Anchorage Museum of History and Art, Alaska
1991 *Oregon Biennial,* Oregon Art Institute, Portland
Portraits from the Collection, Portland Art Museum
Tenth Anniversary/Northwest Print Council, Portland Art Museum
1990 *Northwest by Southwest? Painted Fictions* (touring exhibition), Palm Springs Desert Museum, Palm Springs
The Visual Chronicle of Portland; Acquisitions 1985–1989, Oregon Historical Society, Portland
1989 NWPC at the Chicago Center for the Print, Chicago
1987 *Northwest '87,* Seattle Art Museum
Northwest Expressionists, Portland Art Museum
1986 *Color Print USA,* The Museum, Texas Tech University, Lubock, Texas
1985 *Portland Painting Now,* The Art Gym, Marylhurst College, Portland

Glenn **Rudolph**

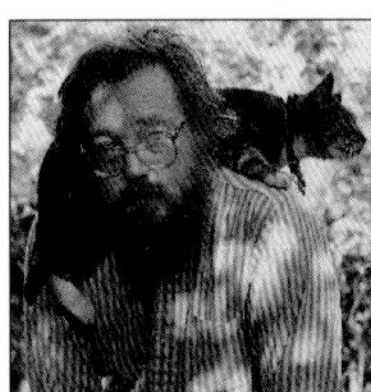

Photograph: Glenn Rudolph

1946 Born in Los Angeles
Lives in Seattle

Education

1968 University of Washington, B.F.A. in Painting

Solo Exhibitions

1993 Elizabeth Leach Gallery, Portland
1990 *Locomotives, Nudes and Animals,* Cliff Michel Gallery, Seattle
The Milwaukee Road, Cliff Michel Gallery, Seattle
1987 Bellevue Art Museum
1986 *Documents Northwest,* Seattle Art Museum
1976 Philips Collection, Washington DC

Collections

Seattle Art Museum
University of Virginia Art Museum
Microsoft Corporation, Redmond, Washington
City of Seattle
State of Washington
University of Washington Library (Northwest Collection)

Michele **Russo**

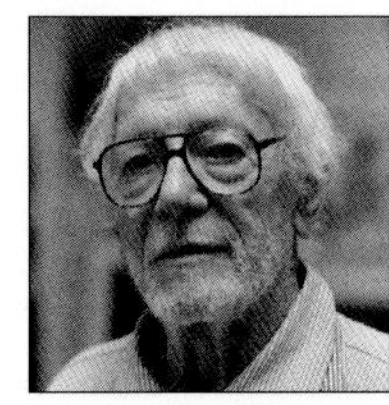

Photograph: Maryanne Caruthers

1909 Born in Waterbury, Connecticut
Lives in Portland

Education and Awards

1934 Yale University, B.F.A.
1937 Fellowship, Colorado Springs Fine Arts Center
1979 Oregon Governor's Award for the Arts
1981 State of Oregon Arts Commission Award
1982 Aubrey R Watzek Award, Lewis & Clark College, Portland
1983 Portland Metropolitan Arts Commission Award

Solo Exhibitions

1994 The Laura Russo Gallery, Portland
1992 The Laura Russo Gallery, Portland
1991 The Laura Russo Gallery, Portland
1990 The Laura Russo Gallery, Portland
1988 Portland Art Museum (retrospective)
The Laura Russo Gallery, Portland
1987 The Laura Russo Gallery, Portland
1986 The Fountain Gallery of Art, Portland
1985 The Fountain Gallery of Art, Portland
Wentz Gallery, Pacific Northwest College of Art, Portland
1984 The Fountain Gallery of Art, Portland
Seattle Art Museum (catalogue)
Marylhurst College (retrospective), Oregon
1983 The Fountain Gallery of Art, Portland
1982 Northlight Editions (lithographs), Portland
The Fountain Gallery of Art, Portland
Fountain Fine Arts, Seattle
1980 The Fountain Gallery of Art, Portland
1978 The Fountain Gallery of Art, Portland
Portland Center for the Visual Arts, Portland
1977 The Fountain Gallery of Art, Portland
1975 The Fountain Gallery of Art, Portland
1971 The Fountain Gallery of Art, Portland
1968 The Fountain Gallery of Art, Portland
1967 Salishan Lodge, Gleneden Beach, Oregon
1966 Portland Art Museum (retrospective)
1965 The Fountain Gallery of Art, Portland
1963 The Fountain Gallery of Art, Portland
Salem Art Association, Bush House, Salem, Oregon
1959 Reed College, Portland
1952 Reed College, Portland
1951 Reed College, Portland

Collections

Bank of America, Seattle
Dayton Art Institute, Dayton, Ohio
Emanuel Hospital, Portland
Federal Reserve Bank, Portland
Gallery Akmak, Berlin
Pacific First Bank, Portland
Pacific Northwest Bell, Portland
Portland Art Museum
Reed College, Portland
Safeco Insurance Corporation, Seattle
Seattle Art Museum
State of Oregon
University of Oregon Art Museum, Eugene

Norie **Sato**

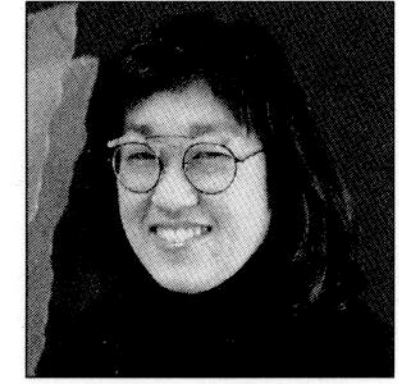

Photograph: Lisa Stone

1949 Born in Sendai, Japan
Lives in Seattle

Education and Awards

1971 University of Michigan, B.F.A.
1974 University of Washington, M.F.A.
1979 National Endowment for the Arts, Individual Artist's Fellowships
1980 National Endowment for the Arts: Art in Public Places Planning Grant for Artists, research involving incorporation of electronic arts in public spaces
1981 National Endowment for the Arts, Individual Artist's Fellowships
1982 Western States Regional Media Arts Fellowship
1983 Betty Bowen Memorial Art Award, Seattle Art Museum
1987 Western States Regional Media Arts Fellowship
1989 Western States Regional Media Arts Fellowship
1989/90 Washington State Arts Commission, Artist Fellowship in video
1994 Artist Trust Fellowship, Media Arts

Selected Solo Exhibitions

1994 *Ghost Movements,* Elizabeth Leach Gallery, Portland
1993 *Transformations and Ghosts,* Linda Farris Gallery, Seattle
1991 *Norie Sato,* Index Gallery, Clark College, Vancouver, Washington
Recent Work, Washington State Capital Museum, Olympia
New Work, Elizabeth Leach Gallery, Portland
1990 *Wings of Transmission,* Linda Farris Gallery, Seattle
1989 *New Work,* Elizabeth Leach Gallery, Portland
1987 *Incidents of Interference,* works on paper and glass, Linda Farris Gallery, Seattle
Incidents of Interference II, works on paper, computer work, etc, Reed College Gallery, Portland
1986 *Memory Zones,* works on paper and glass, Linda Farris Gallery, Seattle
1984 *Virtual Imaging, Documents Northwest: Norie Sato,* installation of works on paper and a video installation, Seattle Art Museum
Phosphor Theater: Interference Display, video installation, Vancouver Art Gallery, British Columbia
1983 *Peripheral Vision,* installation of works on paper and video, Linda Farris Gallery, Seattle
1981 *Image Decay,* exhibition of works on paper and a video installation, Linda Farris Gallery, Seattle
1980 *Video Viewpoints* lecture, Museum of Modern Art, New York

Selected Group Exhibitions

1993 *Washington Voices in Contemporary Sculpture,* Bellevue Art Museum, Washington
1991 *Vanishing Boundaries: Digital Image Making,* Intermedia Arts Gallery, St Paul, Minnesota

1990 *Official Language,* San Francisco Art Institute
1989 *Computers and the Creative Process,* University of Oregon, Visual Arts Resources, Eugene; traveled to various locations
1988 *Home Show,* Santa Barbara Contemporary Arts Forum
1987 *15th Avenue Studio II: The Mechanics of Contemplation,* video installation, Henry Art Gallery, Seattle
1985 *13th Northwest Film/Video Festival,* Award Northwest Film/Study Center, Portland Art Museum
1984 *Video: a Retrospective (Part II, West Coast Focus),* Long Beach Museum of Art, Long Beach
1981 *19 Artists–Emergent Americans,* 2-D work and video, Solomon R Guggenheim Museum, New York
1979 *Projects: Video XXIV* (videotapes), Museum of Modern Art, New York
Lande/Ritchie/Sato (videotapes), Vancoucer Art Gallery, British Columbia; NW Film/Video Center, Portland

Collections and Commissions
1992–97 Portland Westside MAX Light Rail Artist Design Team
1991–92 Seattle Tacoma International Airport Concourse Renovation, Permanent Sculptural installation
1991–93 Dallas Convention Center Expansion, Artist Design Team: Terrazzo floor (70,000 sq feet) and solar pictographs
1990/91 Seattle Arts Commission Art in Public Places Proram, as part of *In Public: Seattle 1991,* temporary installation on waterfront of Seattle
1989 Pacific First Centre, Seattle, site specific sculpture in etched glass, televisions and neon
1988/90 Clark College, Vancouver, Washington, site-directed architectural floor-to-skylight glass work, Washington State Arts Commission 1% for Art Program
Brooklyn Museum, New York
Long Beach Museum, Video Art Archives
Seattle Art Museum
Solomon R Guggenheim Museum, New York
Tacoma Art Museum, Washington

Tad Savinar

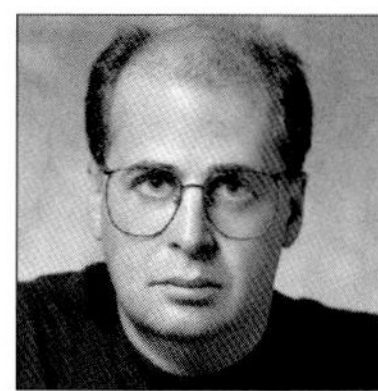

Photograph: PhotoArt, Portlland, Oregon

1950 Born in Portland
Lives in Portland

Education and Awards
1973 Colorado College, B.A. in Fine Arts
1983 Oregon Arts Commission Individual Artist's Fellowship
1984 National Endowment for the Arts, Individual Artist's Fellowship–Sculpture
National Endowment for the Arts, InterArts Project Grant 1984, Portland Metropolitan Arts Commission Project Grant
1986 Metropolitan Arts Commission Project Grant
1987 Metropolitan Arts Commission Project Grant

Solo Exhibitions
1994 Savage Fine Art, Portland
1992 The Fabric Workshop, Philadelphia
Elizabeth Leach Gallery, Portland
1991 Elizabeth Leach Gallery, Portland
1989 Elizabeth Leach Gallery, Portland
1988 Reed College, Portland
Elizabeth Leach Gallery, Portland
1985 Greg Kucera Gallery, Seattle
1983 Los Angeles Institute of Contemporary Art
The Art Gym, Marylhurst College, Portland
Pennsylvania State University, College Station
1982 Artist's Space, New York
1980 Portland Art Museum
1979 Eastern Washington University, Spokane
1978 and/or Gallery, Seattle
John Berggruen Gallery, San Francisco
1977 Blue Sky Photography Gallery, Portland
1976 Northwest Artists Workshop, Portland
Wentz Gallery / Portland Art Museum School, Portland
Polly Freidlander Gallery, Seattle

Collections
American Archive of Theatre on Film
ARATEX Inc
Arlene and Harold Schnitzer Collection
Chase Manhattan Bank
City of Portland
City of Seattle
George Stroemple Collection
Jordan Schnitzer Collection
Mentor Graphics Corp
Museum of Modern Art
Portland Art Museum
Smithsonian Institute
State of Oregon
US Customs Department
University of California Art Museum at Santa Barbara

Buster Simpson

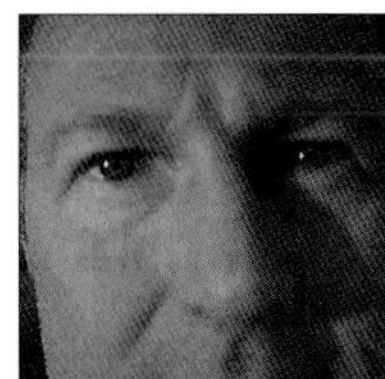

Photograph: Buster Simpson

1942 Born in Saginaw, Michigan
Lives in Seattle

Education and Awards
1963–69 University of Michigan, M.F.A., B.A., Sculpture
1982 National Endowment for the Arts, Individual Artist's Fellowship
1984 Urban Arboretum Project Grant, National Endowment for the Arts, Seattle Arts Commission

Selected Projects/Exhibitions
1994 *Natural Dialogue,* Pratt Manhattan Gallery, New York
Hello Again, FIT Museum, New York
Reuse Refuse, Honolulu Art Academy, Honolulu
Public Introventions, CIA, Boston
1993 *Cistern Drums,* Capp Street Project, San Francisco
1992 *Fragile Ecologies,* Queens Museum, New York
1991 *Effluence of Affluence,* Seattle Art Museum
1991 *Host Analog,* Oregon Convention Center, Portland
1989 *Face Plate,* Installation, Hirshhorn Museum and Sculpture Garden, Washington DC
1988 *Images and Latitude,* Paris
1987 *Art with Community,* PS 1, Long Island
1986–87 *Situation,* MBTA, Boston
1986 *Arts on the Line,* selected artist, MBTA, Boston
1985 *Buffalo Bayou Sculpture Show,* Houston Festival
1985 *From the Crystal Plum,* Portland Center for the Visual Arts
1983 *Outside New York: Seattle,* The New Museum, New York
1983 *90 Pine Show,* Pine Tree Tavern, Seattle (with ongoing installation until demolition, July 1983)
1983 *Oono Home Permanent* (with Steve Paxton), Spaxiozero, Rome
1982 Sound Installation, Institute for Art and Urban Resources, PS 1, New York
1982 *New Music America '81 Festival,* San Francisco
1982 *Two Schools of Fish,* Craft and Folk Art Museum, Los Angeles
1980–81 *West Coast Art for the Vice President's House,* Smithsonian Museum, Washington DC
1980 *When the Tide is Out the Table is Set,* Western Front, Vancouver, British Columbia
Sculpture 1980, Marylhurst Institute College of Art, Baltimore
1979 *Keating/Simpson,* Seattle Art Museum

Selected Commissions and Projects
1993–94 Design team, University of Washington/Tacoma Campus, master plan
1990–93 Anaheim Center Redevelopment Streetscape, Anaheim
1990–91 Alexandria Marsh Gardens, Alexandria, Virginia
1989 Seattle George Monument, Washington State Convention Center, Seattle
1986 Commission for art/urban design for warehouse district, Cleveland
1984 Arts and Industry Program, Kohler Company, Kohler, Wisconsin
1975–78 Artist/Consultant, Seattle City Light Viewlands Hoffman Receiving Substation, Seattle
1978 Artist-in-Residence, ARTPARK, Lewiston, New York

Paul Sutinen

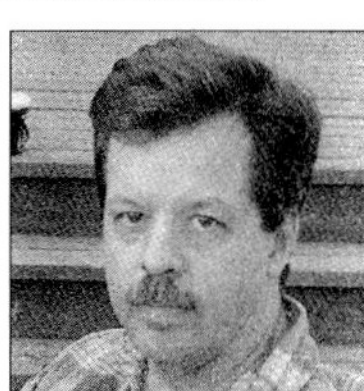

Photograph: Susan Beliveau

1949 Born in Portland
Lives in Portland

Education and Awards
1967–71 Portland State University, B.S. Art, Painting
1979 National Endowment for the Arts, Art Critic's Fellowship

Solo Exhibitions
1994 Nine Gallery, Portland
1993 Nine Gallery, Portland
1992 Elizabeth Leach Gallery, Portland
Nine Gallery, Portland
1991 Nine Gallery, Portland
1990 Elizabeth Leach Gallery, Portland
Nine Gallery, Portland

1988 Nine Gallery, Portland
1987 The Art Gym, Marylhurst College, Portland
1984 Hallie Brown Ford Gallery, Willamette University, Salem, Oregon
1976 Northwest Artists Workshop, Portland
Anne Hughes Gallery, Portland

Public Collections

City of Portland
Oregon Health Sciences University
Portland Community College
Seattle Arts Commission

Mike **Taylor**

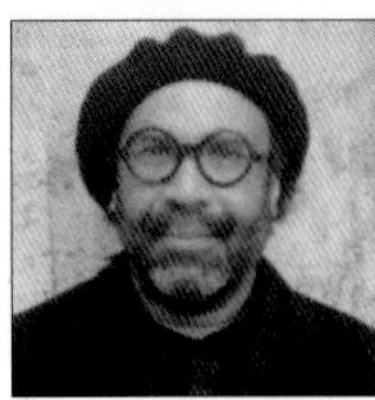

1947 Born in Houston
Lives in Portland

Education

1965–70 University of California, Los Angeles, B.A. in Design, M.A. in Graphic Design, M.F.A. in Graphic Communication

Selected Solo Exhibitions

1993 *Illusions and Transformations*, The Art Gym, Marylhurst College, Portland
1992 Butters Gallery, Portland
1991 Cackamas Community College Gallery, Oregon City
Butters Gallery, Portland
1990 Catlin Gabel School, Portland
1989 Wenatchee Valley College Gallery, Wenatche, Washington
1988 Blackfish Gallery, Portland
1985 Blackfish Gallery, Portland
1983 Renshaw Gallery, Linfield College, McMinnville, Oregon

Selected Group Exhibitions

1993 *3 Sculptors*, Portland Community College, Sylvania, Portland
1992 *Sculpture in the Landscape*, Marylhurst College, Oregon
1992 *Innovations in Sculpture*, Portland Community College
1990 Outdoor Sculpture Invitational, Clackamas Community College, Oregon City
1989 *Special Editions*, Henry Street Gallery, New York
1986 *Five Black Artists*, Portland State University
1984 *New Blood*, Blackfish Gallery, Portland

Collections and Public Commissions

1991 Washington State Arts Commission, mixed media sculpture, *A Kiss Postponed*, for Evergreen High School, Seattle
1989 Washington State Arts Commission, wall sculpture, *Faraway Places*, for Wenatchee Valley College, Washington
Alan Donovan, African Heritage Ltd, Nairobi, Kenya
Micky Wassor, New York
Jeff Butters, Portland
Kally Thurmond, Hope, Idaho
Holland K Millis, Tegucigalpis, Hondouras

Terry **Toedtemeier**

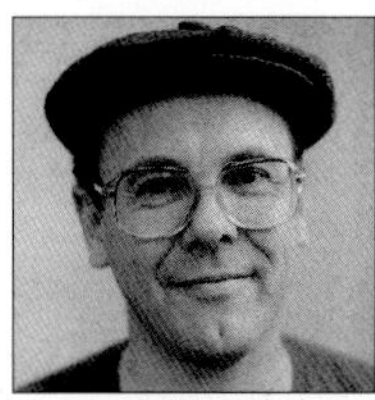

Photograph: Stu Levy

1947 Born in Portland
Lives in Portland

Education and Awards

Oregon State University, Corvallis, B.S., Geology
1979–80 National Endowment for the Arts, grants to research and exhibit the photography of the Columbia River Gorge, 1815–65
1987 Oregon Arts Commission
1990 Oregon Arts Commission, Masters Fellowship

Selected Solo Exhibitions

1992 Governor's Office, Oregon State Capitol, Salem
Mount Hood Community College, Gresham
Elizabeth Leach Gallery, Portland
1991 Wentz Gallery, Pacific Northwest College of Art, Portland
1989 Oregon Health Sciences University, Portland
Maryhill Museum of Art, Maryhill, Washington
1988 Portland School of Art, Portland, Maine
1986 Vollum Art Center, Reed College, Portland
1985 Sheehan Gallery, Whitman College, Walla Walla, Washington
1979 Columbia Gallery of Photography, Columbia, Missouri
The Image Gallery, Copenhagen, Denmark
1978 The Image Center for Photography, Arahus, Denmark
Rice University, Houston
University of California Extension, San Francisco
1977 University of Pennsylvania, University Park
1976 The University of New Mexico, Albuquerque
Blue Sky Gallery, Portland

Selected Group Exhibitions

1992 *Between Home and Heaven: Contemporary American Landscape Photography*, a touring exhibition organized by the National Museum of American Art, Smithsonian Institution, Washington DC
1991 *Barbara Fealy's Gardens*, Marylhurst College, Portland
1990 *Contributing Artist: The Oregon Art Community, 1839–1989*, Oregon Historical Society, Portland
Northwest Photographic Invitational, Kerns Art Center, Eugene, Oregon
Contemporary American Photography in the Soviet Union, invitational exhibition touring Lithuania, Estonia, Ukrania, Moscow and Minsk
1988 Wentz Gallery, Pacific Northwest College of Art, Portland
The Photographic Image Gallery, Portland
Road and Roadside: American Photographs, 1930–1986, San Francisco Museum of Modern Art; Art Institute of Chicago; Illinois State University
1987 *America's Uncommon Places: The Blessings of Liberty*, Museum Gallery of the Summer School, Washington DC
Blue Sky Gallery, Portland
1986 Blue Sky Gallery, Portland
Artist Interprets the Landscape, Blackfish Gallery, Portland
1985 Marylhurst College, Portland
Portland Art Museum
1981–84 *Second Sight, an aesthetic and technical exploration of infrared photography*, Carpenter Center for the Visual Arts, Harvard University, Cambridge
1981 Wentz Gallery, Oregon Art Institute, Portland
1980 *Current Directions in Northwest Photography*, Evergreen State College, Olympia, Washington
Portland Art Museum
1979 *Regional Photography and Printmaking*, Evergreen State College, Olympia, Washington
Henry Gallery, University of Washington, Seattle
1978 *Some Twenty Odd Visions*, Institute of Contemporary Art, Philadelphia
White Gallery, Portland State University
1977 Portland Center for the Visual Arts
Stanford Art Museum
1975 Blue Sky Gallery, Portland

Selected Collections

National Museum of American Art, Washington DC
Portland Art Museum
Seattle Art Museum
Stanford Art Museum
State of Oregon, Public Lands and Geology facilities
Springfield University, Illinois
Joseph Monson Collection, Seattle
Lewis & Clark College, Portland
Washington Arts Commission, Seattle
Stoel, Rives, Boley, Jones and Grey, Attorneys, Portland
Oregon Health Sciences University, Portland

Patti **Warashina**

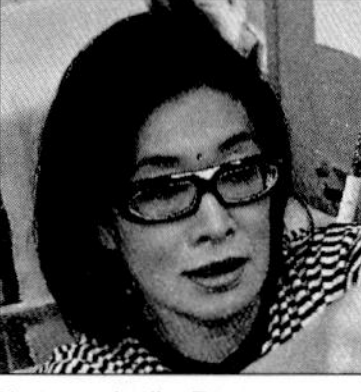

Photograph: Jim Berry

1940 Born in Spokane, Washington
Lives in Seattle

Education

1958–62 University of Washington, Seattle, B.F.A.
1962–64 University of Washington, Seattle, M.F.A. (Studied with Shoji Hamada, Shinsaku Hamada, Rudy Autio, Takashi Nagazato, Robert Sperry, Harold Myers, Ruth Pennington)
1975–76 National Endowment for the Arts, Individual Artist's Fellowship
1978 World Craft Council Travel Grant, Japan-United States Friendship Committee Ford Foundation Grant (Japan, HongKong, Thailand, Singapore, Bali, Philipines)
1980 Govenor's Award of Special Commendation for the Arts, Olympia, Washington
1986–87 National Endowment for the Arts, Individual Artist's Fellowship
1992 Honors Program Award, King County Arts Commission, Seattle
University of Washington Faculty Scholars Award
1994 American Craft Council Award

Solo Exhibitions

1993 Green River Comunity College, Auburn, Washington
Bentley/Tomlinson Gallery, Scottsdale, Arizona

1992 University of Montana Art Gallery, Missoula, Montana
1991 Bellevue Art Museum (retrospective), Bellevue, Washington
Helen Drutt Gallery, New York
North Harris College, Houston
1989 Jane Hartsook Gallery, New York
1984 Foster/White Gallery, Seattle
Morgan Gallery, Kansas City
1983 ASA Gallery; University of New Mexico
Kansas City Art Institute Gallery, Kansas City
1982 Tucson Art Museum, Arizona
1980 Foster/White Gallery, Seattle
Theo Portnoy Gallery, New York
1979 Rochester Art Center, Minnesota
Community Art Gallery, Ellensburg, Washington
Fort George Wright College, Spokane, Washington
1978 University Of Nevada, Las Vegas
1977 Following Sea Gallery, Honolulu
Polly Friedlander Gallery, Seattle
1976 Grossmont College, San Diego
1974 Western Washington State College, Ellensburg, Washington
1972 Northwest Craft Center, Seattle Center
1970 Manolides Gallery, Seattle
Central Washington State College, Ellensburg, Washington
1969 Contemporary Crafts Museum, Portland
Arkansas Art Center, Little Rock
1968 Lantern Gallery, Ann Arbor, Michigan
Left Bank Gallery, Flint, Michigan
1967 Wooster Community Art Center, Danbury, Connecticut
Lantern Gallery, Ann Arbor, Michigan
1966 Wooster Community Art Center, Danbury, Connecticut
1965 Wisconsin State University, Platteville, Wisconsin
1964 Northwest Craft Center, Seattle
1962 Phoenix Art Gallery, Seattle

Public Collections and Commissions

1986 Sculpture, Seattle Opera House, Northwest Special Collections, Seattle Arts Commission 1% for Art Program
1994 Sculpture *Mercurial Miss*, Meydenbauer Convention Center, Bellevue, Washington

American Craft Museum, New York, *Proven Pooder*
Arkansas Art Center, MacArthur Park, Little Rock, *Coupling*
Art Gallery of Western Australia, Perth Cultural Centre, Perth, Western Australia, *Kiss Off*
Bailey-Boushay House, AIDS Hospital, Seattle, *Niche/Prayer Wheel*
Boehn Gallery, Palomar College, San Marcos, California, *Sure Fire Kiln #1*
Canton Art Institute, Canton, Ohio, *Hard as Nails*
Detroit Art Institute, Detroit, Porcelain Sphere
Evergreen State College, Oympia, Washington, *You Captured My Heart; Over the Hill*
Everson Museum of Art, Syracuse, *Caesar's Nightgown*
Henry Art Gallery, Seattle, *Shrine*, jar
Kalamazoo Institute of Art, Michigan, *Canine Campaign*
John Micheal Kohler Art Museum, Sheboygan, Wisconsin, *Car Kiln*
Joe and Emily Lowe Art Museum, Coral Gables, Florida
Memphis Brooks Museum of Art, Memphis, *Wash 'n' Wear*
Meydenbauer Convention Center, Bellevue, Washington, *Mercurial Miss*
National Museum of American Art/Smithsonian Institute, *Convertible Car Kiln*
National Museum of Modern Art, Kyoto, Japan, *American Beauty Rose*
Nelson-Atkins Museum of Art, Kansas City
Palm Beach Comm College, Palm Beach, *Mother Goose*
Sea of Japan Exposition, Kanazawa-shi, Japan, *Loving Cup*
Seattle City Light Collection, *A Procession Automology*
Seattle Kingdome, *Crated Kingdome*
Seattle Opera House, *A Procession, Automology*
Seattle Art Museum, *Tiger Lily*
Tacoma Art Museum, Washington, *Dinnerware Fiesta*
University of Colorado at Boulder (drawing) *Ball Lightning*
University of Puget Sound, Tacoma, Washington, *Rainbow/Mouth Basket*
University of Washington Medical Center, Seattle, *NW Passage*
Wustum Museum of Fine Arts, Racine, Wisconsin, *Crossing the Border*